BETWEEN
TWO
WORLDS

Also by David Callahan

Dangerous Capabilities: Paul Nitze and the Cold War

BETWEEN
TWO
WORLDS

REALISM, IDEALISM, AND
AMERICAN FOREIGN POLICY
AFTER THE COLD WAR

DAVID CALLAHAN

HarperCollins*Publishers*

FIRST EDITION

Designed by George J. McKeon

Library of Congress Cataloging-in-Publication Data

Callahan, David, 1965–
    Between two worlds : realism, idealism, and American foreign policy
after the Cold War / David Callahan. —1st ed.
        p. cm.
    Includes index.
    ISBN 0-06-018213-X
    1. United States—Foreign relations—1989– 2. United States—Foreign
relations—1945–1989.   I. Title.
E840.C33 1994   94-12542
327.73—dc20

94 95 96 97 98 ❖/HC 10 9 8 7 6 5 4 3 2 1

CONTENTS

PREFACE

When I began work on this book in late 1990, Mikhail Gorbachev presided over the Soviet Union, a half-million U.S. troops prepared for war in the Persian Gulf, and foreign tourists were still vacationing in the scenic and peaceful Yugoslav republic of Bosnia-Herzegovina. It is an understatement to say this book has gone through some drastic revisions. At times I would get to the end of a draft only to find that earlier sections of the manuscript had already become outdated. Beyond the pace of world events, the shifting contours of the book can be blamed on my changing view of the Persian Gulf War. Initially this episode lay at the heart of my study because I thought it carried profound implications for the future of world politics and U.S. foreign policy. Over time, however, the Gulf War began to look less significant. Notwithstanding Pentagon efforts to advertise Saddam Hussein as a prototypical villain of the post–Cold War era, I came to see Iraq's invasion of Kuwait as an aberration—a throwback to an era of clear-cut aggression that is fast disappearing.

My interest shifted from the Gulf War to bigger questions about the level of danger that the United States faces in a world without the Soviet threat. The fear of new Iraqs, it is clear, stands as only one element of a broader set of worries that U.S. policymakers now harbor about international affairs. Almost five years after the fall of the Berlin

Wall, annual defense budgets remain at near–Cold War levels and many U.S. troops remain stationed overseas not just because of perceived threats in the Third World, but also because of concerns about a return to past patterns of instability in Europe and East Asia. This book explores the historic roots and present logic of the pessimism guiding post–Cold War U.S. foreign policy. It also offers a critique of that pessimism and an alternative foreign policy vision based upon a more optimistic view of world politics.

Over the past three and a half years I have been helped by many people. Edward Burlingame, my former editor at HarperCollins, shaped this project during its early stages and helped move it away from a limiting focus on the Gulf War. Richard Ullman, my dissertation supervisor at Princeton University, read the book twice, sharing with me his vast knowledge of U.S. foreign policy and assisting me in numerous ways. Other Princeton faculty from whom I received support or inspiration include Fred I. Greenstein, Aaron Friedberg, Michael Doyle, and Richard Falk. My intellectual debt to Michael Klare of Hampshire College is ongoing; both his ideas and his technique have influenced my writing. Earlier drafts of this manuscript were commented upon by Solomon Karmel and William Driscoll. Cynthia Barrett, my editor at HarperCollins, adopted the book at a precarious moment in its life, and her suggestions have made it better. My literary agent Rafe Sagalyn aided the project from its inception. My mother and father, themselves writers, provided above-average parental sympathy at the more difficult moments of this book's journey to publication. Finally, I know that I am lucky to have the friends that I do; their support in recent years has made all the difference.

David Callahan
Princeton, New Jersey
June 1994

INTRODUCTION

Great confusion has surrounded U.S. foreign policy since the end of the Cold War. In Washington, top government officials have stumbled frequently, poorly articulating America's goals abroad and mishandling important crises. Outside of government, experts have waged intensive debate over the goals of post–Cold War foreign policy but have often generated more confusion than clarity. The media, while repeatedly skewering the White House for bad diplomacy and strategy, has done little to advance debate over America's purpose in the world. In turn, the public has been perplexed. Americans are not sure why so many resources still go into staying number one on the world stage when the Soviet Union has disappeared. And they wonder why things so often go wrong in places like Haiti, Somalia, and Bosnia.

Beneath the surface of this turbulence, however, there has prevailed a surprising calm. For some time a consensus among foreign policy elites has existed over the most basic objective of American post–Cold War foreign policy: that the United States must maintain a position of undisputed primacy to ensure global order and a balance of power in crucial areas of the world. The recent debate over foreign policy has been far from fundamental; it has been over means rather than ends. The fierce skirmishes that have occurred on television talk shows and op-ed pages in the wake of one or another overseas debacle should not be mistaken for major battles over the key assumptions guiding foreign policy.

Mainstream experts have argued, for example, about how many U.S. troops are needed in Europe and Asia to head off instability, not whether this danger exists in the first place. They have debated whether NATO should be extended to the states of Eastern Europe, but never doubted that this alliance, along with most other Cold War–era pacts, should be kept alive. They have argued about what, precisely, U.S. vital interests are in the Third World, and they have differed bitterly over the wisdom of military intervention for humanitarian reasons. But there has been near-universal agreement that highly capable U.S. military forces must stand ready to fight major regional wars on short notice in case threats like Iraq emerge. Argument has raged over how best to structure defense spending so that America can rebuild quickly to meet any future global threat and maintain U.S. technological superiority over all challengers, yet more fundamental questions about Pentagon planning in the new era have not been asked. Options for reforming the United Nations have been endlessly dissected, but little serious consideration has been given to proposals for creating a powerful U.N. rapid deployment force, as envisioned under Article 43 of the U.N. Charter. Suggestions have been made for redefining security, transferring resources out of the defense budget to address nontraditional threats like global population growth and environmental degradation, but the sums discussed have been in the millions, not the billions.

The Realist Orthodoxy

American strategy has not been dramatically overhauled in the Cold War's wake because realism remains dominant in the foreign policy establishment. In the realists' view, the end of the Cold War changed the structure of world politics but not its essential nature. That nature is seen as governed by an inescapable reality: no central authority exists to manage the international system. In domestic society there are police, courts, and prisons to deter wrongdoing and keep the peace. The arena of world politics, in contrast, is often called a "self-help" system. Each country must take responsibility for its own security, preparing for the use of military force or living at the mercy of stronger neighbors. The Cold War's end, far from increasing stability, is seen as creating new dangers by replacing stable bipolar rivalry with a less predictable multipolar system in which many strong states compete for position and all states feel less secure.

The prospects for instability in this situation are all the more great, say realists, if the strongest state fails to provide leadership. Its power must serve as the glue that holds a fragile international system together, providing reassurance and punishing transgressors against the established order. The strongest state is now, and will remain to be through the foreseeable future, the United States. If Washington wants global stability, Washington will have to provide it.

This theoretical outlook provides a key rationale for keeping U.S. forces deployed in Europe and Asia after the Cold War. The chief purpose of those forces is now to keep the peace among states with long histories of going to war against one another. America's role in these two regions is to serve as the kind of central authority that does not naturally exist in world affairs. Realist thinking also underpins U.S. policy toward the Third World, where the ancient game of power politics is seen as particularly fierce. In the future, policymakers imagine, well-armed regional powers can be expected to attempt regularly territorial conquest, as Iraq did in 1990, threatening U.S. interests or international order more generally.

Finally, realist logic dictates that the United States should not cut its military establishment too far, even if no major enemies are visible, because world politics can change very quickly in ways hard to fathom now. Friends can turn into foes; hostile alliances may form; new vulnerabilities might emerge. The United States must maintain high levels of research in defense technology, along with an overseas military infrastructure and a well-trained warrior class, in case it must once again field a Cold War–size military machine to contain a global threat similar to Communist Russia or Nazi Germany.

It may be a sacrifice for the United States to maintain a robust global security posture, but realists believe there is little alternative. Collective security arrangements, it is argued, have only limited potential to curb instability and are even less capable of reversing aggression once it occurs. With no other power ready to take over its dominant role, the United States is stuck with the job of policing the international system. Some options exist for lightening the U.S. burden, such as a greater sharing of defense responsibilities with wealthy allies. But, in the end, realism dictates a continuation of American primacy.

The Idealist Challenge

Realism has not gone unquestioned in the post–Cold War era. Government policymakers, while largely embracing realist assumptions, have expressed growing enthusiasm for such classic idealist goals as promoting democracy and strengthening collective security. President Bill Clinton, more so than his predecessor, has advocated policies abroad that reflect the values that Americans champion at home. The priorities of U.S. national security spending still reflect a highly militarized approach to foreign policy, but there is also a new understanding that the United States must address the sources, not just the symptoms, of instability in the world.

Earlier debates in U.S. history between strategies of power politics and high principles have ended with realism easily prevailing. But today's competition between realism and idealism is different. Idealism reached its zenith immediately after World War I, with Woodrow Wilson's crusade for a new world order. But it proved unsuited to a United States with strong isolationist tendencies and unsustainable in an era marked by dictatorship and conquest. Today, a new retreat into isolationism is unlikely, while global trends of democracy and interdependence appear to bolster the optimistic outlook of idealists. During the Cold War, realism's ascendancy was cemented by the specter of Soviet expansionism and the recent memory of German and Japanese aggression. Now, with no global enemy in sight and new hegemonic campaigns almost unimaginable, the pessimistic logic of realism is becoming harder to defend.

Never before have the ideas of realism and idealism competed to shape U.S. foreign policy on a more equal footing. At no prior point in history has the United States been deeply engaged in world affairs yet faced no mortal threat, and never have so many nations shared so much agreement on how people should be governed and how international relations should be managed.

The competition between realism and idealism need not be a

fight to the intellectual death; some blending of the two outlooks in some areas is both possible and desirable. However, in determining the overall thrust of foreign policy, and in directing how America's still-large budget for foreign and military affairs should be spent, realism and idealism dictate very different courses of action. The outcome of the debate between these two approaches will decide much more than, say, whether Washington penalizes China for its human rights abuses. Instead, it will determine the strategies that the United States selects to address global dangers, governing the expenditure of hundreds of billions of dollars over the next decade and dictating how American power is projected abroad.

The word *idealism* is often used as a synonym for naïveté. One dictionary definition of idealism terms it: "behavior or thought based on a conception of things as one thinks they should be." This is not the definition I employ. Instead, I take idealism to mean, as another dictionary put it: "the cherishing or pursuit of high or noble principles, purposes, goals, etc." The distinction here is important. A person (or government) who acts based on how things should be, rather than how things are, is indeed naive. However, one can recognize that things are not as they should be and still be an idealist, striving for noble goals within an imperfect world, making compromises as necessary but never losing sight of long-term aspirations. Idealists can be as practical anybody else.

Idealism does not offer a rigorous paradigm for understanding international relations. Instead, it should be understood as a foreign policy strategy that takes advantage of the global changes that are stressed by liberal analyses of world politics. Liberal theorists argue that the realist approach, with its emphasis on the relentless struggle for survival among nations, is becoming less and less applicable to much of the world. Liberals point to four major trends in contending that the planet is becoming a safer place: the spread of democracy, economic interdependence, the decreasing appeal of wars, and the rise of supranational institutions to regulate world affairs.

The spread of democracy to the former Communist bloc and other areas, while not yet fully consolidated, is creating a growing "zone of peace." Since democracies rarely fight one another, and military force is not an important factor in their relations, this development suggests that power politics will no longer hold sway in some of the regions most vital to the United States. Complementing this trend is growing global economic integration and interdependence. In earlier times large countries could be relatively self-sufficient and go to war without destroying their economies. This is more difficult now that the prosperity of most industrial countries hinges on their participation in the world economy. Less developed countries are often even more dependent on such participation, relying on aid and access to large consumer markets to survive. In today's shrinking world, rogue regimes can be made to pay horrendous economic costs by being frozen out of a global system managed by the industrial democracies.

Complementing the phenomenon of growing interdependence is the decreasing appeal of war. Over the centuries war has become a less and less acceptable means of settling disputes. Perhaps more important, leaders increasingly recognize that war doesn't pay. Not only can it escalate out of control with horrendous results, but in the current era it does not make economic sense to conquer territory.

Finally, liberals point to the growing power of international institutions of all kinds. At a global level, the Cold War's end has breathed new life into the United Nations, reviving hopes that it may yet be able to play a central role in guaranteeing world security. At a regional level, Europe, historically one of the most volatile places on earth, now has overlapping institutions to govern both economic and security matters. In East Asia newly created multilateral institutions are being strengthened. And in the Third World, where cooperation on security matters is more difficult, liberals suggest that the industrial nations can do much to reduce violence and instability by curbing arms transfers and isolating dangerous states.

In the past, idealists such as Woodrow Wilson sought to wish away power politics. Their thinking reflected moral revulsion rather than a defensible judgment that the nature of world politcs had fundamentally changed. Early American idealism was based on hope rather than fact. The new idealism operates from a much stronger foundation. Realism is rejected not because it clashes with American values, but because it is no longer the best compass for navigating in many parts of the world. It offers unduly pessimistic diagnoses that lead to misguided policy prescriptions.

If cooperation is an entrenched norm among the advanced states of

Europe and East Asia, then it follows that American troops are not crucial for preventing new rivalries and instability in these regions, as realist thinking suggests. If territorial conquest, because of its high costs and low returns, has decreasing appeal for national leaders, be they democrats or autocrats, then the United States can worry less than realists counsel about either major new aggressors akin to Hitler or a steady stream of smaller aggressors like Saddam Hussein. And if international institutions have a greater potential than realists give them credit for, then the United States can place more faith in such bodies to maintain stability in key regions and punish aggression when it occurs.

Such shifts in thinking would profoundly change U.S. national security policy. American troops in Europe and Asia, now planned to number 200,000 into the twenty-first century, could be reduced to far lower levels if not withdrawn altogether. The preservation of a military establishment that can be rapidly rebuilt to its Cold War size would be seen as less important. Contingency forces ready to cope with emergencies in areas of the world vital to the United States would be maintained, but preparations for large-scale intervention would take place at a lower level if Iraq's old-style conquest of Kuwait was recognized as an aberration rather than as a portent of things to come.

Movement to an idealist foreign policy begins with the United States escaping from its near-singlehanded management of the international security system, but it does not aim toward a disengagement from world affairs. At the core of an idealist foreign policy should be an active U.S. leadership aimed at consolidating the positive developments that are reshaping the world and countering the negative trends that threaten disorder, especially in the former Communist bloc and the Third World.

This leadership would be reflected in a dramatically different set of national security spending priorities. An idealist foreign policy would ask a basic question: How can increasingly scarce U.S. resources best be used to create long-term global security? The answer, already now apparent, is that military spending does not always "buy" the greatest amount of security in the new era. In many cases military instruments are totally incapable of addressing some of the most serious new causes of instability, from ethnic conflict to population growth to environmental degradation. It makes little sense that the Pentagon now spends far more money to hedge against

resurgent Russian militarism than other U.S. agencies spend to consolidate democracy and market economies in the Communist bloc.
Likewise, the United States has its priorities backward when it lav-
ishes money on military forces designed to quell mounting disorder
in Third World countries while doing almost nothing to address the
causes of that disorder. A realist-based foreign policy is like a domestic
policy that sees more police and prisons as the sole solution to crime.

An idealist foreign policy would center upon far more ambitious
U.S. initiatives for promoting democracy, sustainable development,
and collective security. In this time of fiscal austerity, resources for
such new efforts can only come from one place: the defense budget.
Thus the adoption of an idealist foreign policy cannot be a mere
rhetorical shift or a minor adjustment in how the United States deals
with dictators. It must entail a total overhaul of American national
security priorities.

The approach of this book is relatively simple. The first five chapters
show how the United States arrived at its present juncture in foreign
policy. The purpose here is not to retell the familiar history of American diplomacy or to recapitulate the story of the Cold War's end.
Instead, it is to show how realism became dominant within American
foreign policy and why the realists' case for U.S. primacy outlived the
East-West rivalry. To understand American strategy after the Cold
War it is necessary to study U.S. strategies before containment, for in
large part the case for primacy had already been embraced by foreign
policy elites prior to the emergence of the Soviet threat.

The last three chapters make the case against a foreign policy
based upon realism. I explore in depth the trends that have changed
the nature of international politics, making peaceful cooperation
between states, not armed competition, the norm in ever larger parts
of the world. I also show how many of the much-advertised new
threats to U.S. interests have been greatly exaggerated, and argue that
the United States can get by with a smaller military effort than is now
envisioned. In the concluding chapter I delineate the contours of an
idealist foreign policy, showing how resources that now go into the
defense sector can buy more security if spent in other areas.

1

BECOMING NUMBER ONE

A common understanding of how the United States rose to primacy holds that after World War II, America was the strongest nation in the world but one with little appetite for leadership. It stood ready to manage the world economy but otherwise was inclined toward renewed isolation, eschewing alliance commitments and any permanent overseas military deployments. But with the rise of the Soviet threat the United States was again called to duty, grudgingly manning the ramparts of the free world and patiently waiting for a contained enemy to exhaust itself.

The belief that America became a global power out of exigency, not desire, suggests that the United States can now escape from the geopolitical exertions and military expenditures forced upon it by the Cold War. With the Soviet Union gone, the question goes, shouldn't the United States be able to relinquish the burden of ensuring world security and turn the bulk of its attention to domestic problems?

Perhaps so, and this book will explore that possibility. The construction of the question is simplistic, however, as is the storyline from which it springs. A more accurate understanding of America's rise to primacy holds that the United States was indeed isolationist before World War II, but not as blithely so as is commonly supposed.[1] In fact, American leaders always monitored stability—and its absence—across the oceans. As far back as Jefferson, U.S. leaders worried about the balance of power in Europe, which was seen as critically affecting North American security. They also worried about the balance in Asia and, beginning in the late 1800s, actively sought to prevent any one power from dominating that region.

Following World War II it was not only, or even largely, the Communist threat that propelled Washington to assume a position of international leadership. Instead, by the early 1940s, before the Communist threat was clearly evident, a consensus was emerging among foreign policy elites that the United States had to be permanently engaged in maintaining global stability. It had to become the world's leading power because the international system needed a leader and because nobody else could play that role.

The consensus behind primacy had its roots in the changing American thinking about the nature of world politics. World War II was only the most recent reminder that U.S. security and prosperity were inextricably linked to stability in Europe and Asia and to friendly control of the Atlantic and Pacific oceans. Various American political leaders and strategists had long highlighted these realities, believing isolation to be a chimera. World War II assured that these arguments finally achieved ascendancy among political elites.

A simultaneous and closely related development was the conversion of U.S. foreign policy elites to the tenets of political realism. Realism rejected both idealism and isolationism. It held that the world was a dangerous place in which the struggle for power among nations was unending. America could neither escape involvement in this struggle nor end it by reforming the international system, as Woodrow Wilson had sought to do after World War I. Realists argued that the United States had to remain perpetually vigilant, worrying first and foremost about its survival in the way other nations had for centuries. It could no longer ignore the balance of power in crucial areas of the world as it had in the past, but instead it would have to work relentlessly to assure that the balance never tipped in a threatening direction. American primacy was seen as essential to this task, since the twentieth century had shown that the weight of an outside nation was needed to maintain a balance of power in Europe and Asia.

The Cold War served to amplify and validate these views among

U.S. foreign policy elites; it was not the occasion for inventing them. Today, those who are perplexed by America's failure to quickly shed its international responsibilities have failed to read their history. They mistakenly believe that anticommunism was the principal, if not the sole, rationale for American primacy. They thus imagine that the arguments for U.S. primacy collapsed along with Soviet power. In a further mistake, some charge that attempts to sustain that primacy are rooted in bureaucratic inertia, vested military-industrial interests, and in a plain unwillingness to change old habits and dated thinking.

Now that the Cold War is over, U.S. foreign policy is undergoing substantial modifications. The Clinton Administration has pushed for changes that are somewhat more ambitious than those favored by George Bush and his advisors, but fundamentally the case for American global primacy remains unchallenged in the U.S. foreign policy establishment. To understand why so many insist that the United States must remain number one it is necessary to better understand why the United States became number one in the first place. In large part, this means understanding how concern with stability in Europe and Asia, always present in U.S. foreign policy, finally became its dominant characteristic by the middle of the twentieth century.

IN SEARCH OF STABILITY: THE AMERICAN GEOPOLITICAL TRADITION

During the early days of the republic, primacy in international affairs was not the goal of U.S. foreign policy. Instead, the overriding challenge for the former colonies was mere survival, and in an age dominated by the great powers of Europe, this was no sure thing.

The conventional telling of American history suggests that the young United States maintained a scrupulously isolationist stance, avoiding the reviled world of European power politics. This is only partly true. There were, to be sure, powerful isolationist tendencies in the early republic. "We should separate ourselves as far as possible and as long as possible from all European politics and wars," John Adams said in 1776, expressing the sentiments of many.[2] A resolution adopted in 1783 by the Continental Congress declared: "The true interest of these states requires that they should be as little as possible entangled in the politics and controversies of the European nations."[3]

Washington's famous farewell address, in which he said that "Europe has a set of primary interests, which to us have none, or a very remote relation" and in which he called for an avoidance of "permanent alliances" was the quintessential statement of early U.S. isolationism.[4]

That isolationism, however, was by no means total. America's early statesmen felt a keen sense of vulnerability that resulted in their taking a strong interest in European affairs. What happened in that arena, they saw, could have profound effects on America's security and prosperity.[5]

Jefferson and Europe's Balance of Power

Thomas Jefferson has long been viewed as a pioneer of American idealism in foreign policy and is contrasted often with Alexander Hamilton, who averred that self-interest should be the main compass for U.S. foreign policy. But, in fact, Jefferson had strongly pronounced elements of realism in his world outlook and was attuned to the European world of power politics, for several reasons. First, he was acutely aware of how dramatically Europe's wars could affect American trade with the old world, particularly by turning the Atlantic Ocean into a war zone and imperiling U.S. shipping. Second, he believed that the United States could move advantageously to acquire new territories on the North American continent while the great powers of Europe were preoccupied with warfare.[6] Finally, Jefferson believed that checked and balanced power was a force for peace generally and U.S. security especially. Regarding the warfare between England and France, both of which he viewed as aggressive powers, Jefferson wrote in October 1803: "If they can so far worry one another as to destroy their power of tyrannizing, the one over the earth, the other the waters, the world may perhaps enjoy peace, till they recruit again."[7]

Jefferson shared the fear of many early American statesmen that a single power would come to dominate Europe so totally that it would cast about for new conquests. North America, with its raw materials and growing markets, where both France and England had footholds, would be a tempting target for renewed European adventurism. Therefore, during the Napoleonic Wars, Jefferson hoped that the contestants would exhaust themselves in the fighting, and to the degree that it was possible, he sought to contribute to this end. He was skillful at playing off France and England against each other, generally tilting toward France, which he considered to be less threatening than England because of its lack of naval strength. In Jefferson's mind, wrote Lawrence Kaplan, "France became a counterweight to British influence and an instrument of American survival."[8]

Among his contemporaries, Jefferson had a reputation as a Francophile, but ultimately he was deeply fearful of the possibility of French hegemony in Europe. Writing on January 1, 1814, Jefferson said that "surely none of us wish to see Bonaparte conquer Russia, and lay thus at his feet the whole continent of Europe. This done, England would be but a breakfast. . . . Put all Europe into his hands, and he might spare such a force, to be sent in British ships, as I would as leave not have to encounter."[9]

For all their distaste for European politics, the Founding Fathers nonetheless learned how those politics worked and sought to assure that they produced the best results for the United States.[10] America's early isolationism, far from being wholly divorced from the balance of power in Europe, was in fact predicated on it. As Walter Lippmann observed in the 1940s, the architects of early U.S. foreign policy knew that it was balanced power in the Old World that "made it possible for the weak nations of the New World to isolate themselves, while they were developing, from interference by the Great Powers of Europe."[11]

Early Advocates of American Leadership

During most of the nineteenth century U.S. isolationism was made possible in large part by the stable balance of power that prevailed in Europe following 1815. It was during the decades that followed the end of the Napoleonic war, when no unchecked European hegemons threatened the United States, that the ethos of isolationism became ingrained in the American psyche. "The political system of the United States, is . . . essentially extra-European," John Quincy Adams wrote in 1819. "To stand in firm and cautious independence of all entanglements in the European system has been a cardinal point of their policy under every administration of their government from the peace of 1783, to this day."[12] In the decades following the peace of

1815, diplomatic maneuverings to deal with events in Europe were downplayed and Washington's advice against permanent alliances became a mantra, chanted by one American president after another. Westward expansion and other nation-building projects reinforced an inward-looking U.S. stance.[13]

By the beginning of the twentieth century, with the vast increases in American industrial power, and the new overseas acquisitions gained in the Spanish-American War, the United States was poising to play a central role in world affairs. In the thinking of some influential figures of the time, a new and assertive American leadership was needed to guarantee the stability of the world system generally as British primacy waned and, more specifically, was needed to sustain the balance of power in Europe and Asia as Germany and Japan became increasingly powerful. If England could no longer be number one, America would have to be.

In 1900 Brooks Adams, who would become a top advisor to President Theodore Roosevelt, argued in a book entitled *America's Economic Supremacy* that the United States was destined to take over Britain's role as world leader. Adams believed that the decline in British hegemony after 1870 was producing increasing disorder in the world: "As England has weakened, the old equilibrium has failed. . . . Civilization then seems to have entered upon a fresh epoch of unrest, and the inference is that no condition of permanent tranquility can be reached until a new equipoise should be attained."[14] Adams worried that without a major power to police the system of free trade there was little to stop individual nations from enacting protectionist measures. If the United States wanted a free trade system, and this was an ever more important goal as its economy grew by leaps and bounds, it would have to face up to its emerging status as the world's most powerful nation and guarantee free trade. "The centre of the economic system of civilization is in motion, and until it once more comes to rest, tranquility cannot return. All signs now point to the approaching supremacy of the United States. . . ."[15] Adams suggested that this new responsibility could not be fulfilled without expanded American military power. To fully replace Britain as the world's leading hegemonic power, the United States would need military forces of global reach and an appetite for using those forces.

Roosevelt's Call for Primacy

President Theodore Roosevelt, the first truly internationalist president, shared Adams's outlook. In 1902 Roosevelt told Congress that "the increasing interdependence and complexity of international political and economic relations render it incumbent on all civilized and orderly powers to insist on the proper policing of the world."[16] Roosevelt believed that the United States was one of the powers—if not increasingly the power—with an obligation to keep global order. He was a zealous advocate of a stronger navy, believing that it was an indispensable step toward attaining a position of primacy. In 1905 Roosevelt wrote: "The American people must either build and maintain an adequate navy or else make up their minds definitely to accept a secondary position in international affairs, not merely in political, but in commercial matters. It has often been said that there is no surer way of courting national disaster than to be 'opulent, aggressive, and unarmed.'"[17]

Beyond the general need for American primacy, Roosevelt and others called for a more involved U.S. role in maintaining the balance of power in Europe and Asia. In Europe, the growth of German economic and military strength had become unsettling to some U.S. observers by the first years of the twentieth century. In 1906 Henry Adams, the brother of Brooks, wrote: "We have got to support France against Germany and fortify the Atlantic system beyond attack; for if Germany breaks down England or France, she becomes the center of a military world, and we are lost."[18] In 1910 the celebrated strategist Admiral Alfred T. Mahan published *The Interest of America in International Conditions* in which he argued that the United States shared Great Britain's interest in preserving a balance of power in Europe against Germany.[19] In 1912, as the United Kingdom's decline became more apparent, Roosevelt stressed that if that country could no longer maintain stability in Europe, the United States would have to do so.

"As long as England succeeds in keeping up the balance of power in Europe, not only in principle but in reality, well and good. Should she, however, for some reason or other fail in doing so, the United States would be obliged to step in, at least temporarily, never mind against which country or countries our efforts may have to be

directed. In fact, we ourselves are becoming, owing to our strength
and geopolitical situation, more and more the balance of power of the
whole globe."[20]

While Roosevelt and others argued in the early 1900s that the
day was fast approaching when the United States would have to guarantee the balance of power in Europe, they believed that that day had
already arrived in the Far East.

During the nineteenth century Asian powers were generally not
seen as posing a threat to the United States.[21] But the region did present opportunities, and beginning with the opening of Japan in mid-
century, the United States played an increasingly assertive role in the
scramble for East Asian markets, particularly in the great vacuum of
China, where the United States proclaimed its "open door" policy at
the turn of the century (in essence this policy said that all nations
should be able to trade equally in China). As the U.S. economic stake
in Asia grew, so did its stake in the region remaining stable and open.
The enduring concern of U.S. policymakers was that China would
fall under the control of a single unfriendly power.[22] In *America's Economic Supremacy* Brooks Adams had warned of Russian designs to
build an empire in China, saying that "the United States could hardly
contemplate with equanimity the successful organization of a hostile
industrial system on the shores of the Pacific, based on Chinese labor,
nourished by European capital. . . ."[23] To most observers of the time,
however, Japan was the more likely threat in the region. By the early
twentieth century an industrializing Japan had emerged as the biggest
threat to regional stability and to unfettered U.S. access to East Asian
markets.

In Europe it would not be until World War I that the United
States actively intervened to affect the balance of power. In Asia U.S.
leaders were fully immersed in the game of balance-of-power politics
by 1900. As Bernard Gordon observed, it was widely believed in
Washington that only the United States stood in the way of Japanese
dominance in East Asia.[24] After acquiring the Philippines from Spain
in the Spanish-American War of 1898, the United States sought, in
Nicholas Spykman's words, to maintain its position as an "Asiatic
power." American strategy, wrote Spykman in his 1942 treatise on
U.S. foreign policy, was aimed at "restraining Japan by the individual
or collective action of non-Asiatic powers, or building up local states
as a counterbalance to the dynamic expansion" of Japan.[25]

As president, Theodore Roosevelt had a strong interest in the affairs in Asia, saying in 1905 that "Our future history will be more determined by our position on the Pacific facing China than by our position on the Atlantic facing Europe."[26] Roosevelt's concern for the balance of power in Asia was manifested by his diplomatic intervention to help end the Russo-Japanese War, which began in 1904. Roosevelt and many other Americans had great admiration for Japan, but the president became alarmed after Japan's decisive defeat of Russia. By the time of the Port Arthur surrender, writes Foster Rhea Dulles, Roosevelt "was beginning to foresee the possibility of a too-powerful Japan seriously upsetting the balance of power in the Far East."[27]

Roosevelt's famous decision in 1907 to send America's naval fleet to the Far East and then around the world was motivated in large part by a desire to send a message to Japan. In explaining the decision later, he wrote that he had "become conscious of a very, very slight undertone of veiled truculence in their communications in connection with things that happened on the Pacific slope; and I finally made up my mind that they thought I was afraid of them. . . . it was time for a showdown."[28]

By 1914, nearly three decades before Pearl Harbor, the fear of Japan disrupting the balance of power in the Far East was creating significant tensions in U.S.-Japanese relations. In that year, the *New York Times,* commenting on the state of relations, editorialized: "There is a general belief that it is the policy of Japan to assert and maintain for herself supremacy and control in the Asiatic waters of the Pacific with a view, probably, to the ultimate exclusion of western nations."[29]

The presidency of Theodore Roosevelt, and the work of analysts like the Adams brothers and Admiral Mahan, did much to alert Americans to the perils of instability and unbalanced power overseas. But in the early twentieth century these internationalist views ultimately remained at odds with the dominant view in the United States against taking on a global role, and particularly against getting mired in European affairs.

Considerations about the balance of power in Europe and Asia may have figured in the foreign policy thinking of many U.S. leaders during the republic's first century and half, particularly at certain moments in history, but such concerns were never truly mainstream. The far more widely embraced vision of the U.S. world role revolved around notions of American exceptionalism: that is, the idea that the

United States was different from other nations—more virtuous, independent, generous, democratic, and high-minded in every way. The United States was seen by many as a "city on a hill," a shining example of righteousness that would, as one author put it, lead "people everywhere to yearn for America's blessings and advantages and eventually to adopt American values and institutions."[30] This ideal stood in decided contrast to the entrenched, Old World corruption that many Americans thought was represented by the nations of Europe and their tradition of power politics.

World Wars and the Path to Primacy

It was not until the First World War that the United States first used its power to prevent an unacceptable aggregation of power from forming on the Eurasian landmass. In his well-publicized explanation for U.S. intervention, Walter Lippmann argued that the United States went to war because unrestricted German submarine activity threatened to isolate Britain. If Britain starved and Germany won, the United States would face a major power that dominated Europe and the Atlantic Ocean, a long-feared development that could fatally compromise American security.[31]

Lippmann's emphasis on worries about unbalanced power has not gone unchallenged. Robert Osgood, after an exhaustive critique of the Lippmann thesis, has persuasively argued that Americans "drifted into war, largely oblivious of the practical consequences of momentary impulses, out of an aroused sense of national honor, combined with a missionary zeal to achieve world peace and democracy."[32] Nevertheless, if Lippmann stands guilty of twisting history to advance his personal view, it is also true that the impact of unbalanced power in Europe was widely feared among Woodrow Wilson and his advisors. Osgood acknowledges that at the time of intervention many U.S. leaders and observers had concluded that "America's fundamental interest lay in the continued predominance of the British Navy athwart the vital lines of communication leading into the Atlantic and in the preservation of a European balance of power to prevent an aggressive Germany from gaining a continental hegemony."[33]

This theme was elaborated on by such writers of the time as Roland Usher and H. H. Powers. "The power that acquires control of the Eastern Hemisphere, acquires control of the world," wrote

Powers in 1917. "Is it not plain that the policy of America must be to prevent the domination of the Eastern Hemisphere by any one power?" Citing the growing population and industrial might of major states, Powers warned of the inevitability of hegemonic aspirations in Europe and Asia. He analyzed the danger posed by rising Japanese power and pointed to Russia as the next long-term threat on the Eurasian landmass. "The struggle is with Germany today. It will be with Russia tomorrow," Powers wrote in 1917.[34]

While visions of unchecked power in Europe may not have been decisive in shaping U.S. policy, they did hold influence among President Wilson's advisors. Colonel Edward M. House, one of Wilson's closest foreign policy confidants, was acutely concerned about the dangers that a German victory would pose to the direct physical security of the United States. "It will not do for the United States to let the Allies go down and leave Germany the dominant military factor in the world," House wrote in 1915. "We would certainly be the next object of attack and the Monroe Doctrine would be less indeed than a scrap of paper."[35] However, in coming to advocate U.S. intervention in the war, House was strongly motivated by an idealist desire to help fledging democracies and in fact believed that a purely geopolitical rationale for intervention would never win support from the American public.[36]

In connection with his thesis, Lippmann would argue in the 1940s that the U.S. entry into World War I was often not recognized for what it was—the most concrete affirmation to date that America had a huge stake in a stable and balanced Europe. The reasons Wilson and other officials gave for intervention, Lippmann complained, "were legalistic and moralistic and idealistic reasons, rather than the substantial and vital reason that the security of the United States demanded that no aggressively expanding imperial power, like Germany, should be allowed to gain the mastery of the Atlantic Ocean." Lippmann suggested that it was this failure to place World War I in its proper geopolitical context that allowed U.S. leaders to so blithely ignore ominous trends in Europe between the wars.[37]

Origins of Consensus

If Lippmann exaggerated the geopolitical motivations for U.S. intervention in World War I, he was more correct in his assertion that the

U.S. policymakers of the 1920s and 1930s failed to appreciate adequately the dangers of power imbalances in Europe. The tenets of Wilsonian idealism, along with a general isolationism, were the salient characteristics of official U.S. thinking during these years. By the late 1930s, however, as the tempo of Japanese and German aggression mounted, the seeds of the enduring consensus—a shared belief that the United States must remain permanently engaged abroad to sustain the balance of power in Europe and Asia—were already being planted, as evidenced by signs of a basic shift in U.S. foreign policy attitudes. This shift, along with the growing embrace of realist assumptions that triggered it, will be analyzed in more depth in the next chapter. At this point suffice it to say that discussion of the dangers posed by hegemonic power in Europe and Asia were considerably more explicit in the immediate years leading up to U.S. intervention in World War II than had been the case in World War I.

Roosevelt showed considerably more awareness of these dangers than Wilson ever had. Osgood contends that as president, Roosevelt grasped that "the domination of either Europe or Asia by a hostile and aggressive power would be a disaster for America's hemispheric security. This conception of American security dominated Roosevelt's thinking about foreign policy during the critical years before Pearl Harbor."[38] As early as October 1937, in his "Quarantine" speech, Roosevelt warned that the consequences of Japanese aggression in China could not be seen in purely regional terms. "If those things come to pass in other parts of the world, let no one imagine that America will escape, that America may expect mercy, that this Western Hemisphere will not be attacked and that it will continue tranquilly and peacefully to carry out the ethics and the aims of civilization."[39]

Outside of government a growing number of observers were also warning about the consequences of unchecked territorial aggrandizement.[40] In his 1937 book, *Is America Afraid?*, Livingston Hartley elaborated on the arguments of earlier analysts who maintained that the oceans were no defense for the United States against major shifts in the balance of power abroad. He contended that if either Europe or the Far East was controlled by a single power the task of guaranteeing American security would become unmanageable.

"We look across the Atlantic at a power area far superior to our own and across the Pacific at another power area that is advancing toward superiority. We are in a sense the ham in the world sandwich. . . . If the European or the Far Eastern power areas are ever consolidated, we shall be completely overshadowed by superior military force and the preservation of an American future for our country and our hemisphere will become a hope instead of a certainty."[41]

It was particularly essential, Hartley said, that the naval power of the British Commonwealth remain intact, given the benefits it bestowed on America's security position in both the Atlantic and Pacific.[42] This view reflected the belief, put forth as early as the turn of the century by Brooks Adams and others, that Great Britain's imperial apparatus provided a security framework that ensured both the free flow of commerce on the high seas and continuation of the Monroe Doctrine. In his 1939 book, *Our Maginot Line,* Hartley spelled out the implications of America's stake in balanced power in greater detail, calling for limited U.S. intervention to check German and Japanese expansion.[43]

Another exponent of this view was Edward Meade Earle, of Princeton's Institute for Advanced Study. In a 1941 book, Earle used historical analysis to argue that American security had always hinged on developments across the oceans: "Almost from the beginning it was recognized that our security depended not merely upon relatively geographical remoteness, but equally upon the European balance of power, the maintenance of the British navy, and the existence of a universal concept of international order."[44] Like Lippmann, Earle believed that the central reason for intervention in World War I had been to prevent German mastery over Europe and the Atlantic. And like other authors, he postulated a slow and inevitable chipping away of American security should the Nazis prevail in conquering the continent. These calculations, he said, merited intervention on the side of Great Britain and France.[45]

By the eve of American involvement in World War II the extent of German and Japanese conquests underscored, in far more graphic fashion than had been the case in World War I, the perils that could stem from hegemonic campaigns in Europe and Asia. America's vital interest in sustaining a balance of power abroad, as a matter of ongoing and permanent national policy, was increasingly self-evident. A major military assessment of U.S. security interests, completed a few months before Pearl Harbor, stated unequivocably that America's vital interests included "prevention of the disruption of the British Empire; prevention of the further extension of Japanese territorial dominion; eventual establishment in Europe and Asia of a balance of power which will most nearly ensure political stability in those regions and the future security of the United States."[46]

The U.S. entry into World War II paved the way for the most explicit and sustained discussion yet among foreign policy elites of the need to harness permanently American power to the cause of global stability. By the end of the war there would be few voices in the mainstream foreign policy establishment that disputed this need. Many agreed that the new war was partly, if not largely, a consequence of the failure of the United States after World War I to use its power to ensure an equilibrium in Europe and Asia. This reading of history had an obvious lesson: America could not afford to make such a mistake again; it would have to remain engaged after Germany and Japan were vanquished. Walter Lippmann, by far the most influential foreign policy commentator of the day, hammered relentlessly at this point in his articles and books. "Our primary interest in Europe, as shown during the Napoleonic and the two German wars, is that no European power should emerge which is capable of aggression outside of the European continent," he wrote in 1943.[47] Lippmann called for continued U.S. engagement following the cessation of hostilities and pleaded for a national acceptance of peacetime alliances with other powers.

The Yale scholar Nicholas Spykman elaborated on this theme in an influential 1942 book on U.S. grand strategy. He argued that World War II showed the full potential consequences of unchecked power emerging across the oceans.[48] He made the case, in greater detail than previous commentators, for how the United States could be slowly strangled in its North American redoubt: "If the three landmasses of the Old World can be brought under the control of a few states and so organized that large unbalanced forces are available for pressure across the ocean fronts, the Americas will be politically and strategically encircled." Latin America could easily fall into hostile hands, Spykman wrote, and then it would be simply a matter of time before the United States faced direct and unmanageable threats.

Spykman chastised U.S. leaders for living in a dream world and for not doing enough to promote U.S. security through farsighted diplomacy abroad. "The policy which aims to restrain growing states and is known as the balance of power policy has been part and parcel of the diplomacy of all successful states," he lectured. "If all states were held in check, no state could win a war; and, if no state could win a war, then no state would start a war or threaten war. Equilibrium is balanced power, and balanced power is neutralized power."[49] Spykman observed that equilibrium was neither a gift of the gods nor an inherently stable condition. It had to be carefully and continuously nurtured. If the United States wished to enjoy the fruits of stability in Europe, it had to work actively toward this goal.

Spykman suggested that America's position in Europe was not unlike that of Great Britain's. Historically, Great Britain had often been tempted to retreat from continental affairs, to stay on its island and build up its naval power, but the more intelligent British leaders had been able to recognize the peril in this path. They had sought to use British power to cultivate a balance of power on the continent and hence prevent any aggregation of power that could threaten a cross-channel invasion. "The position of the United States in regard to Europe as whole . . . is identical to the position of Great Britain in regard to the European continent," wrote Spykman. "We have an interest in the European balance as the British have an interest in the continental balance." Indeed, said Spykman, expressing a view that was fast becoming conventional wisdom in some circles, it was Europe's past preoccupation with the balance of power at home that "gave us the opportunity to grow to our present position of power."[50]

Balanced Power and the Emerging Consensus

To the generation of leaders who came of age in the 1930s and 1940s the lessons of history were clear: the United States could not remain, as John Quincy Adams had once suggested, an "extra-European" power. Instead, maintaining U.S. security meant playing a continuous role in the much abhorred game of European power politics. An analysis prepared in the summer of 1944 by the Office of Strategic Services, the forerunner of the CIA, stated this conclusion succinctly: "Our interests require the maintenance of a policy designed to prevent the development of a serious threat to the security of the British

Isles (and of the United States), through the consolidation of a large part of Europe's resources under any one power."[51]

In regard to the Far East, the political and psychological dimensions of the shift in outlook were not dramatic because the United States had accepted, well before World War II, that it was a Pacific power. But in the wake of Japan's bid for hegemony, the need for greater vigilance and a more significant presence in that region appeared obvious to many observers.

The last years of World War II and its immediate aftermath saw much discussion among U.S. foreign policy analysts and military strategists about how to deal with the threat of future hegemonic enterprises. A postwar study by the Council on Foreign Relations noted that a consensus existed that to "protect its own security, the United States would have to make its weight felt in Europe and Asia to prevent the rise of hostile combinations such as the Berlin-Rome-Tokyo Axis."[52] But there was far less agreement on exactly how this should be done. During the war three options were commonly discussed: the United States could impose global order by establishing a Pax Americana; it could try to keep the balance of power tipped in its favor through alliances and power politics; or it could rely on collective security, hoping that an international organization would keep the peace.

The option of a Pax Americana was not popular among most U.S. foreign policy thinkers. Despite enthusiastic talk of an "American century" in some quarters, there was actually little support in planning circles for permanent and far-flung U.S. overseas commitments. The United States was seen as the natural leader in creating a new global order; it was imagined that U.S. economic and military strength would be at the core of that order. But the idea of securing peace through active American domination was never treated as a serious option.

The avenue of alliances and power politics was also frowned upon. American leaders believed that continued cooperation between the major allied powers—especially the U.S., Britain, and Russia—was essential for world peace, yet most were hesitant to turn that cooperation into formal alliances. Soviet postwar aims were unknown, and the idea of a binding diplomatic tie to Moscow was out of the question. An alliance with Britain was more seriously considered. Governor Dewey of New York, for example, publicly championed such a partnership in 1943. Roosevelt himself at times leaned strongly in this direction. Ultimately the proposal did not receive wide support. "Public opinion was definitely cool to the idea," noted the Council on Foreign Relations study. "Americans saw the value of a firm understanding but did not like the idea of 'underwriting the British Empire,' nor of allying permanently with any one of our wartime associates in preference to others and possibly against them."[53]

Collective security was the most widely supported idea for preserving peace after the war. Many Americans believed that America's failure to join the League of Nations had helped precipitate the Second World War, so at the same time they waged war against the Axis powers, U.S. leaders laid the groundwork for a stronger international organization—one in which the United States would be a leading member.

Debate about America's role in the new era raged fiercely at times during the war and immediately afterward. Again, it must be stressed that this debate took place within an overall framework of agreement among foreign policy elites—an agreement in place before the Cold War began—that the United States had to exercise world leadership in some fashion and that a principal purpose of this leadership would to be to ensure stability in Europe and Asia. The death of isolationism was symbolized in a January 1945 speech in which Republican Senator Arthur Vandenberg, a leading isolationist in the prewar period, acknowledged the need for a permanent American engagement in the world.[54]

Though the broad architectural conceptions of how to stabilize the postwar world would be slow in coming, there was never uncertainty about using U.S. power to ensure that neither Germany nor Japan ever terrorized the world again. In 1943 President Roosevelt made this point unequivocally, saying in Ottawa that "peace can come to the world only by the total elimination of German and Japanese war power. Surely by unanimous action in driving out the outlaws and keeping them under heel forever, we can attain a freedom from fear of violence."[55]

Containing Germany and Japan

When discussion of Germany's future began in the U.S. government there was a strong disposition among many officials to see the country permanently divided into two or more states. "A divided Germany would be two steps from aggression, reuniting and rearming, but a united Germany would be but one," commented scholar Gregory Treverton, in describing the thinking of U.S. officials at the time.[56] However, Secretary of State Cordell Hull and other officials opposed Germany's dismemberment, hoping to achieve the same effect through less drastic measures. Hull believed that "in place of partition, every effort be made to promote a federal structure of government in Germany." A loose, decentralized German state would be less dangerous.[57]

Even as dismemberment was ruled out, U.S. officials hatched other harsh plans for dealing with Germany. At a September 1944 meeting between Prime Minister Winston Churchill and President Roosevelt, a statement was issued that in effect called for the permanent hobbling of Germany's economic potential. The statement was based on a plan devised by U.S. Treasury Secretary Henry Morgenthau, and it stated that Germany should be converted into "a country primarily agricultural and pastoral in nature."[58]

This idea was eventually dropped in the face of sustained opposition by Hull and by Secretary of War Henry Stimson. But the fact that it was considered at such high levels is indicative of the kind of sentiments that initially informed American thinking in regard to Germany's postwar treatment. At Potsdam it was agreed to at least "eliminate or to control all German industry that could be used for military production."[59] Even Hull, a moderate on the German issue, showed an intense fear that resurgent German power could one day destabilize Europe. Besides calling for a decentralized German government, Hull suggested that Germany's economy be thoroughly integrated into that of its neighbors, so that the country could never again become a self-sufficient military power. Finally, and most important, Hull believed that "Germany should be kept under military control for twenty-five or fifty years, as necessity might require. . . ."[60] The United States, he believed, would have to take the lead in this policing. The military document that initially governed America's occupation of Germany, JCS 1067, stipulated that the United States should seek to break down dangerous concentrations of economic power.[61]

America's readiness to contain German power was made official in April 1946 when Secretary of State James Byrnes announced that the United States was prepared to occupy Germany for twenty-five years, or even forty years, if other European powers wished. In 1919, after World War I, France had requested that the United States guarantee against future German aggression, yet an inward-looking U.S. had ultimately refused to take responsibility for European security. "The decision to forego strategic commitments abroad reveals that American officials did not consider the nation's vital interests, either strategic or economic, to be at stake in Europe," historian Melvyn Leffler has noted.[62]

In the mid-1940s, U.S. leaders were determined to avoid past mistakes. Roosevelt was hesitant about a postwar security commitment to Europe, saying, in preparation for the Tehran Conference in 1943, that the United States did not expect to keep troops in Europe for more that a year after the war and did not want to be "roped into accepting any European sphere of influence."[63] But he and other officials did believe that an American security guarantee was essential for alleviating European anxieties about Germany and maintaining stability on the continent. Official thinking imagined keeping modest occupation forces in Germany but not having the United States take on a major and permanent military role there. As Gregory Treverton observed, the view in 1946 was that "Europe was to defend itself, so officials thought in both Europe and the United States. America would not abandon Europe as it had after the previous war, but it would return home, its engagement in Europe remaining only that of a backstop and ultimate guarantor of security."[64]

American policy toward East Asia was shaped by slightly different considerations. A significant U.S. military presence was considered both more necessary and more palatable in the Pacific. In Europe, with its long tradition of balanced power, it was possible to imagine the reconstructed nations of France and England, along with the Soviet Union, balancing Germany with backup by an over-the-horizon U.S. security guarantee. There was no similar balance waiting to be reinvented in East Asia. Thus, to ensure against Japan's revival, American strategists imagined a U.S. military presence in East Asia and the Pacific of indefinite duration. It was recognized that the American burden for security in the region would be considerably heavier than it was in Europe. As a 1945 congressional report stated, the maintenance of peace in East Asia and the Pacific was "primarily the responsibility of the United States." Other nations were either "too distant" or did not "have the necessary strength" for this mission. In September 1945 the Navy recommended that the U.S. maintain twenty-seven bases in the Pacific area.[65] Beyond generally securing the region, U.S. forces in Asia would be especially geared toward keeping Japan in a subordinate position. U.S. officials like Hull recommended that a large number of U.S. forces be stationed in Japan itself to ensure compliance with the control system set up to prevent Japanese rearmament. Nobody knew how long this occupation would last, but as with Germany a lengthy stay seemed likely.

A New Military Vigilance

If the chief lesson of World War II was that the United States could not ignore the balance of power in Europe and Asia, a powerful corollary was that America could not neglect its military establishment. Much as it would have to remain perpetually engaged abroad, it would have to remain permanently prepared for war, a necessity that other nations in the arena of world politics had long understood.[66]

In September 1945 the Joint Chiefs of Staff completed the first comprehensive statement of postwar U.S. military policy. The document, never formally approved by the rest of the government, stressed that the United States faced increasing vulnerability in an era of modern long-range weapons. It warned of the unpredictability of world events and called for maintaining a foundation upon which a new military effort could be quickly built. American military forces, the report said, must be "the best trained in the world, and equipped with superior materiel and so disposed strategically that they can be brought to bear at the source of enemy military power, or in other critical areas in time to thwart attack by a potential aggressor. These forces must be supported by an adequate system of bases and machinery for the rapid mobilization of our national resources. Plans and preparations must be kept abreast of developments of new weapons and countermeasures against them and provide for exploitation of our superior mechanical and industrial capabilities."[67]

In addition, the report advocated universal military training for young men, a vigorous effort to collect intelligence, and the stockpiling of critical resources.[68]

To many U.S. planners, one of the most frightening aspects of World War II was the new lethality that advancing tactics and technology conferred upon the age-old tactic of surprise attack. "The 'blitzkrieg' technique is of enormous danger," stated the conclusion of an influential report written by the United States Strategic Bombing Survey in 1946. "A mobilized and well-trained striking force enjoying a certain technical superiority can overwhelm in short order the forces of a country of far greater long-term strength."[69] The devastation wrought by the Japanese at Pearl Harbor involved military technology that had been only barely imagined in the 1920s. Hitler's fast-moving armored columns had made a mockery of French efforts to secure their territory through the static defenses of the Maginot Line. The atomic destruction visited upon Hiroshima and Nagasaki had been made possible by a research and development effort initiated almost from scratch just a few years earlier. The speed with which new threats could arise and do damage to America and its friends seemed to dictate that an intense vigilance would be required in the new era, even if peace appeared secure.

To some planners, prudence in coping with an uncertain world meant more than a foundation for reconstituting a strong military; it meant maintaining an outright position of superiority over other nations. "If the United States is not be forced to hasty and inadequate mobilization every time the threat of aggression arises in the world, it is essential that in the field of military weapons and tactics she be technically not merely abreast of, but actually ahead of any potential aggressor," stated the Bombing Survey report, authored mainly by Paul Nitze.[70] Although written in 1946, when the contours of the bipolar competition were already becoming evident, the report stressed that its proposals were predicated on an optimistic prognosis of international relationships.[71]

It was not the Cold War that demanded a new military vigilance on the part of the United States—it was the basic nature of world politics.

The Cold War: Primacy Affirmed

Whether the Cold War had occurred or not, it is clear that the United States would still have played a much greater global leadership role after World War II than it did after World War I. It would have remained engaged in both Europe and Asia to assure a balance of power, executing a "containment" policy aimed at Germany and Japan. It still would have sought to create and manage a new global trading system. For quite apart from the problem of security, postwar U.S. economic growth was seen as requiring international economic order that could only be guaranteed if the United States took over the position of a declining Britain.

The Cold War had two principal effects: it assured that America's global leadership role was far more militarized and far-reaching than it might otherwise have been, and it served to entrench and sustain the consensus that U.S. engagement was needed to assure balanced power abroad. Barring the Cold War it is not clear how long that consensus would have lasted after World War II.

The rise of Soviet power in the wake of Hitler's defeat added new weight to the arguments of those like Lippmann, Spykman, and Earle that hegemonic expansionism was a natural feature of world affairs, prevented only by an active nurturing of balanced power. Once again there appeared the specter of an aggressive empire dominating the Eurasian landmass. Once again there were warnings, from both within government and without, that the United States could find itself isolated in the Western Hemisphere, facing eventual strangulation and attack. George Kennan, head of the State Department's newly created Policy Planning Staff, stressed the importance of keeping the industrial potential of Western Europe and Japan out of hostile hands. This should be done not through a heavy-handed American hegemony but by revitalizing the strength of nations in those areas. "All and all our policy must be directed at restoring a balance of power in Europe and Asia," Kennan wrote in late 1947.[72] In early 1948 the National Security Council drafted a paper that warned "there are in Europe and Asia areas of great potential power which if added to the existing strength of the Soviet world would enable the latter to become so superior in manpower, resources, and territory that the prospect for the survival of the United States as a free nation would be slight."[73]

This warning echoed concerns that had been evident in U.S. strategic thinking as far back as Jefferson, but U.S. policy was manifestly informed by more recent historical lessons. Discussing NATO in early 1949, Secretary of State Dean Acheson commented, "We have learned our history from two World Wars in less than a century. That experience has taught us that control of Europe by a single aggressive, unfriendly power could constitute an intolerable threat to the national security of the United States. We participated in those two great wars to preserve the integrity and independence of the European half of the Atlantic community in order to preserve the integrity of the American half."[74]

Cold War planners saw containment policy in East Asia as similarly rooted in power realities and historical lessons. As a 1949 NSC document stated: "The domination of Asia by a nation or coalition of nations capable of exploiting the regions for purposes of self-aggrandizement would threaten the security of Asia and of the United States. Recognition of these principles has been implicit in our traditional policies toward Asia: We have consistently favored a system of independent states and opposed aggrandizement of any powers which threatened eventual domination of the region."[75]

The new and pressing need to contain the Soviet Union altered but did not entirely transform the policy of containing the former Axis powers. "Any world balance of power means first and foremost a balance on the Eurasian landmass," wrote Kennan in 1948. "That balance is unthinkable as long as Germany and Japan remain power vacuums." The task ahead was "to bring back the strength and the will of those peoples to a point where they could play their part in the Eurasian balance of power, and yet to a point not so far advanced as to permit them again to threaten the interests of the maritime world of the West."[76] Rearmament of Germany was announced in September 1950, not long after the Korean War began; Japan was encouraged to rebuild its power after 1951.

The transformation of these former outlaw states into Cold War allies was the source of enormous controversy. Those European and Asian nations unfortunate enough to border Germany and Japan were deeply apprehensive about a resurgence of the militaristic monoliths that had menaced them for decades and overrun them only a few years earlier. These worries were insistently transmitted to American policymakers, who themselves harbored considerable, if less acute, concerns about the revival of former enemies. In 1948 Kennan expressed the views of many U.S. planners when he wrote of the necessity of firmly integrating Germany into Europe: "If there is no real European federation and if Germany is restored as a strong and independent country, we must expect another attempt at German domination." He articulated a principle that would be central to the Truman Administration's policy toward Europe when he wrote that "the relationship of Germany to the other countries of western Europe must be so arranged as to provide mechanical and automatic safeguards against any unscrupulous exploitation of Germany's pre-eminence in population and military-industrial potential."[77] This principle would also be embraced by the Eisenhower national security team.[78]

Integrating Germany

The debate in the early 1950s concerning West Germany's rearmament was impassioned and complex.[79] France in particular hoped to keep Germany confined to a subordinate status among the Western nations. "To the French the creation of the German army presents the gravest fears and dangers," wrote Secretary of State Dean Acheson in a 1951 memorandum. "They believe that this would raise the historical dangers of German military aggression; that it might lead to the involvement of Western Europe in a German crusade to recover Eastern Germany and the lost provinces; and that it would certainly involve putting Germany in the position of holding the balance of power. . . . The French, I believe, will not cooperate in a program of German rearmament which does not give what they regard as adequate safeguards."[80]

What might such safeguards look like? First, Paris insisted that Germany's military contribution be made solely through multilateral defense arrangements. There could be no independent German army or German general staff. A variety of options were discussed for achieving this goal,[81] most notably the idea of a European Defense Community (EDC), favored by France, in which German soldiers would be part of a European army that would serve as the security arm of the European Community.[82] The United States believed that adequate safeguards would exist within NATO to prevent a dangerous resurgence of German power in Europe. Nevertheless, both the Truman and Eisenhower administrations gave their backing to the EDC concept.[83] In NSC 160/1, "United States Position with Respect to Germany," dated August 17, 1953, the benefits of this arrangement of containing German power were spelled out. "Integration of Germany in the European Community would channel the immense vitality and resources of the reviving German nation into strengthening Europe without endangering Western Security. An evolving European Community could harmonize the interests of its members and reduce the risk of conflicts, crises, and wars. . . . The European Defense Community applies this concept to defense. It is designed to harmonize three aims: (1) the securing of a German contribution to European defense; (2) the provision of acceptable safeguards against a revival of German militarism; and (3) the cementing of Germany firmly to Europe and the West."[84] In the end, when the EDC treaty failed to win adequate support (ironically, it was rejected by the French National Assembly), it was agreed that Germany would be accepted into NATO and that its military forces could be used only for NATO operations.[85]

France was prepared to accept German inclusion in NATO and the European community more generally on the condition of deepened U.S. involvement in European security matters. A U.S. military planning document, prepared in 1953 when the EDC was still under consideration, explained France's outlook: "The Federal Republic's capability for leadership within a unified Western European community will be feared by France, unless potential German predominance in a united Europe is compensated by closer and more organic ties between Europe and the United States. . . ."[86] Not only would Germany's military be firmly embedded in NATO, but the United States would take responsibility for leading the alliance. In effect, Germany's military would be under U.S. command and could pose no threat to Europe as long as this remained the case.

A rearmed Germany might have produced widespread anxiety in the Europe of the 1950s, but a rearmed Germany divided in half, occupied by large numbers of American troops, integrated into an alliance run by Washington, and pledged to refrain from acquiring nuclear weapons, was something Europe could live with.[87] NATO thus came to serve multiple purposes: its aim, the saying went, was to "keep the Russians out, the Americans in, and the Germans down."

Restraining Japan

Japan's neighbors were reassured in much the same manner. The Japanese constitution, drafted by American occupiers, explicitly forbade any use of force that was not wholly defensive.[88] A close bilateral relationship between Washington and Tokyo would be the chief instrument for managing Japan. The 1951 Security Treaty between the two nations made clear that Japanese military power was to be closely controlled by the United States.[89]

As with Germany, Japan would be prevented from following an autonomous security policy. Also as with Germany it was hoped that this newly rearmed enemy would be a powerful ally against Communist expansion. A 1954 memorandum by the Joint Chiefs of Staff stated: "Basic to the establishment of a non-Communist position of strength in the Far East is the rehabilitation of the Japanese military forces—not along the lines of the ultra-national military attitude of pre–World War II, but along moderate and controlled lines that will enable Japan to exert a stabilizing influence in the Far East." The possibility of a new Japanese threat would remain, but it was seen as manageable. "In addition to restrictions which would be imposed upon Japan by economic and political factors, it is believed that so long as the United States furnishes the principal offensive air and naval elements of the combined military forces in the Far East, adequate safeguards against the recrudescence of Japanese military power as an aggressive force would be provided."[90]

The United States was not able to embed Japan within a regional alliance akin to NATO, though the idea was considered. During discussions in the early 1950s about the creation of security pacts in the Far East various obstacles emerged to the idea of including Japan in any multilateral arrangement. After one discussion in early 1952 John Allison, Assistant Secretary of State for Far Eastern Affairs, commented that though a comprehensive Pacific pact was desirable, it probably would not be very effective without Japan's participation, and was not likely to become a reality because of tensions among Asian nations, particularly between Japan and the nations of Southeast Asia that it had occupied during the war.[91]

The Eisenhower Administration was also interested in a comprehensive Pacific security pact but encountered the same problem. Collective security in the region, stated a 1954 NSC planning document, was hampered by the "deep-seated national antagonism and differing assessments of national interests which divide these countries from each other and severely hamper efforts to combine their collective resources for their own defense and welfare."[92] Some in the administration urged the inclusion of Japan into a limited security arrangement that would also include Taiwan, the Philippines, and South Korea and would have ties to other limited security organizations, such as the ANZUS treaty that bonded Australia, New Zealand, and the United States. Even a pact of only these four countries was deemed unfeasible. As a State Department official wrote in 1954: "Until the Japanese are themselves ready to engage in such a pact, until Japan-Korean relations are placed on a more constuctive foundation, and until the reparations problem is settled between Japan and the Philippines, it is impossible to foresee any real sense of interdependence or to think of a security organization in the area."[93]

The abandonment of plans to seek strong regional security organizations had two important consequences. First, it strengthened the belief in Washington that U.S. power was essential for containing Japan in the postwar era, since no strategy of embedding Japan into an integrated community of nations would work. Second, the pessimism regarding multilateral security organizations in the Far East would take on the status of conventional wisdom among U.S. foreign policy analysts, exerting a powerful influence over U.S. thinking toward the region even into the post–Cold War era.

Beyond Double Containment

By the mid-1950s the United States had fashioned the grand bargain that would underpin the Western coalition for the next thirty-five years—the revival of German and Japanese power would be tolerated, but only if both nations were kept on a short tether by the United States and only if their power was explicitly harnessed to the anti-Communist agenda. Visible American military commitments in Europe and Asia were essential to the bargain.

The double-containment strategy would remain in place for the duration of the Cold War. Over time, fears of a militarist resurgence by either Germany or Japan would decline to the point that they were no longer a topic of frequent discussion within U.S. policy circles or among allied officials.[94] But those fears never disappeared completely. The Cold War rivalry neutralized the German and Japanese problems, and it kept concerns about the aggressive potential of these two powers far below the surface of Western political life. However, it could not blot out historical memory, and as the Cold War ended it became clear that in some European and Asian capitals the prospect of unfettered German and Japanese power was still viewed with considerable wariness. In the United States policymakers and analysts were also wary, but not because they themselves were excessively concerned about resurgent German and Japanese militarism. Few in U.S. policy circles took seriously the prospect of new belligerence on the part of the former Axis powers. Rather, the fear was that any large-scale reduction of U.S. involvement in Europe and Asia following the end of the Cold War that led to a more independent security stance on the part of Germany and Japan would lay the groundwork for new instability as old adversaries again began to eye each other uneasily. Even if it were possible for lingering memories of World War II to be forgotten or suppressed, many worried that instability could arise from the structural imbalance presented by growing Japanese and German power.

The collapse of Soviet power removed the need for one pillar of the double-containment strategy. But the containment of Germany and Japan, and prevention of structural instability more generally, remained a necessary objective in the view of many Americans, Europeans, and Asians. Later chapters will explore efforts by the U.S. foreign policy establishment to maintain U.S. primacy—and thus the second pillar of containment—after the Cold War and show that these efforts have been fundamentally misconceived.

Before getting to this discussion, it is necessary to look more closely at the theoretical conceptions of world politics that have lay behind the development of U.S. foreign policy. Clearly, the historically grounded fears about massed power in Europe and Asia exerted a strong influence on U.S. foreign policy. To fully understand these fears it is crucial to understand a development that paralleled and often fueled their rise: the triumph of realism over idealism within the U.S. foreign policy establishment during the twentieth century.

2

REALISM, IDEALISM, AND AMERICA'S RISE TO PRIMACY

When the Cold War subsided there was widespread hope in the United States that the days of compromising American values abroad in the name of security would be coming to an end. With no global enemy in sight, many hoped idealist goals such as promoting democracy and strengthening collective security would be able to move to the forefront of U.S. foreign policy. Yet during the early 1990s America's post–Cold War foreign policy evolved only slowly in a more idealist direction. Fears regarding a still-dangerous international environment have determined U.S. diplomatic policy and dictated the allocation of national security resources to a far greater degree than efforts to promote an idealist agenda.

This disappointing record must be understood in its proper historical context. For the last two centuries the United States has stood as one of the most idealistic nations in the history of the world, but idealism has rarely been the centerpiece of its foreign policy. Before World War II American weakness and the lack of consensus behind a sustained international engagement meant that the United States did not promote its values and political beliefs abroad in any kind of systematic fashion. During the 1940s the consensus that finally did form behind permanent international engagement grew more out of a sense of insecurity than out of a missionary zeal. This chapter shows how realist assumptions about the dangerous nature of world politics came to be more central to U.S. foreign policy than efforts by America to reshape the world in its image.

A DANGEROUS WORLD: THE RISE OF REALISM IN AMERICAN FOREIGN POLICY

Before World War I the way U.S. foreign policy was conducted was a rather rudimentary business. American leaders were sensitive about the balance of power in Europe and Asia, and at times made modest efforts to manipulate it, such as during the Napoleonic Wars in Europe and the Russo-Japanese War in Asia. But such geopolitical strategizing was never the focus or defining characteristic of early U.S. foreign policy. During the nineteenth century America's inward orientation and lack of significant military forces, along with a general distaste for the power politics of the Old World, kept it from being a major participant in international affairs. Americans did meddle heavily in the matters of other countries, but they did so locally—in the Western Hemisphere where U.S. mastery was undisputed. Even early U.S. involvement in the Far East was not quite like playing in the major leagues, since the region was largely a power vacuum and America's stakes there were relatively small.

Up until the early twentieth century a feel for the nuances of geopolitics simply never became a survival skill for the leaders of a nation protected by thousands of miles of ocean—seas controlled by a relatively benign power, Great Britain. Nor was such sophistication considered, by most Americans, to be something worth striving for. Power politics was considered the dark art of European aristocrats. Americans were not impressed by the fact that calculations of brute strength and amoral approaches to diplomacy had reigned in Europe for hundreds of years, accepted as the only wise basis for foreign policy in a dangerous world. There existed the sense that the United States could do things differently and engage in the world on its own terms, guided by ideals rather than cynicism.

From Hamilton to Lippmann

The realist tradition in American foreign policy is often traced back to Alexander Hamilton. Enlightenment ideals of how a community of nations should behave, so popular among many of his contemporaries, were largely dismissed by Hamilton. Instead, as Paul Varg has written, "Hamilton and the Federalists started their formulations with a recognition of the existing system of international relations and were willing to work within the framework of current practice."[1]

Yet during the nineteenth century the Hamiltonian approach to foreign policy was never widely embraced. It would not be until the first decade of the twentieth century that realist ideas were widely read and discussed. Robert Osgood observed that the timing of this development was unsurprising: "Great shifts were taking place in the relative strength and prestige of nations. Coalitions were forming. Naval rivalry was growing intense. Everywhere the instruments of power were bulging ominously behind the curtain of diplomacy. For the Realist who surveyed the international scene, there was much to confirm the view that the quest for national self-interest and power is the moving force in the world."[2]

Selling this outlook to a nation of isolationists and missionaries was another thing entirely. One of the most energetic proselytizers of realist foreign policy thinking in the early twentieth century was Alfred T. Mahan, a naval officer and strategic thinker whose writing on international affairs and sea power reached a wide audience.[3] Mahan believed in a simple starting point for all realist thinking: "The law of the states, as of man, is self-preservation." From this axiom Mahan sought to legitimize the idea of national interest, which had never been prominent in U.S. foreign policy. He argued that "it is vain to expect governments to act continuously on any other ground than national interest." Mahan referred, with approval, to Germany's single-minded pursuit of its national interest: "That, under the name of Realism, is the frankly avowed policy of German statecraft."[4] He warned that unless the United States adopted such an outlook it would find itself vulnerable in an international system where an "aggressive restlessness" underlay the continuous struggle for survival among great powers.[5]

Like Brooks Adams and other contemporaries, Mahan believed

that America's economic expansion demanded a more assertive geopolitical posture. Growing industry at home meant multiplying trade relationships abroad, and amid recurrent violence and instability in the international system, the United States would have to stand ready to protect its increasingly far-flung commercial interests with military power. In a dangerous world America could not venture abroad unarmed, and a vastly more powerful navy was Mahan's central solution to U.S. vulnerability.[6] Theodore Roosevelt embraced much of Mahan's thinking, and in addition to being the first internationalist president, he is rightly viewed as one of the first realists to occupy the White House.

Another early popularizer of realist foreign policy thinking was Walter Lippmann. As early as 1915, in *The Stakes of Diplomacy*, he put forth the idea that he would preach for decades to come—that world politics must be seen first and foremost as a self-interested struggle for power among nations. "The grand disputes of states are not over the interpretation of recognized law," Lippmann wrote. "The real disputes are matters of policy." In domestic society, fundamental differences of this kind were settled by elections. But this was not an option in a world without central authority. "Between governments no adequate machinery exists by which one policy can be made to supplant another," Lippmann wrote.[7] Military power was thus the final arbiter of political difference, and Lippmann argued firmly that an ample supply of this commodity was essential for the protection of U.S. national interests.

Lippmann initially had measured faith in the power of international institutions to manage the problems of international security. However, this faith did not outlast World War I. As Lippmann saw it, sound geopolitical reasoning may have underpinned Wilson's decision to enter the war, but unfounded idealism characterized his handling of the peace negotiations that followed. Lippmann, who served in the U.S. delegation to the Paris peace conference only to be disillusioned with the results, later provided a stinging summation of what was wrong with the President's view of world politics: "The Wilsonian vision is of a world in which there are no lasting rivalries, where there are no deep conflicts of interest, where no compromises of principle have to be made, where there are no separate spheres of influence, and no alliances. In this world there will be no wars except universal war against criminal governments who rebel against the universal order."[8] Lippmann insisted that he and the rest of humanity lived in a very different world than that which Wilson imagined.

Following his disillusionment with Wilsonian thinking Lippmann would spend the next several decades refining his realist outlook. He believed that the United States committed a devastating blunder when it relied on Wilsonianism to guide its diplomacy in the 1920s and 1930s. Lippmann's most persistent complaint concerning that vision was that it did not appreciate the need to predicate collective security on strong alliances. Instead, in the Wilsonian ideal, alliances were seen as incompatible with a successful League of Nations. "This collective security was to be the remedy and the substitute for alliances," Lippmann later wrote.[9]

In the wake of World War I, with many citing Europe's web of alliances as one reason for the catastrophe that occurred in 1914, the Wilsonian view was understandable. But it was also untenable according to Lippmann, who argued in 1918 and would argue ever afterward that a nucleus of leading states, allied for the defense of their vital interests, was needed to enforce peace through a system of collective security.[10] This view was ignored during the interwar period, and although the United States did not join the League of Nations, substantial diplomatic energies were engaged in implementing the Wilsonian collective security vision, particularly in regard to disarmament. "The net effect," Lippmann wrote in 1943, "was to dissolve the alliance among the victors of the first World War, and to reduce them to almost disastrous impotence on the eve of the second World War."[11]

In the mid to late 1930s, as toothless collective security mechanisms failed and German and Japanese power grew, the realist view of world politics was increasingly embraced by U.S. foreign policy thinkers. In the academic arena scholars began to shift their gaze from the institutions that were supposed to govern international life to the configurations of power that actually did. "Lacking the will to establish, let alone maintain, an effective political organization on a world scale, the vital points of conflict in the world community are, in the last resort, still resolved by power politics," stated a 1940 textbook on international relations.[12] At the policy level there was a growing awareness that America's friends overseas were facing basic threats to their existence and that U.S. survival in a world of hostile hegemonic powers could not be taken for granted.

Realism Triumphant: World War and Its Aftermath

The experience of World War II led to the emergence of realism as the central tenet guiding U.S. foreign policy. Events of the late 1930s and early 1940s seemed to provide compelling evidence of the Darwinian nature of international politics. In a world of Hitlers and Tojos it was hard to have faith in good intentions and in high-minded schemes for collective security. "The international community is without government, without a central authority to preserve law and order, and it does not guarantee the member states either their territorial integrity, their political independence, or their rights under international law," wrote Nicholas Spykman in the conclusion of his magnum opus on U.S. grand strategy. "States exist, therefore, primarily in terms of their own strength or that of their protector states and, if they wish to maintain their independence, they must make the preservation or improvement of their power position the principal objective of foreign policy."[13]

Spykman stressed that this iron law of world politics did not exempt the United States from its jurisdiction. Oceans may have served as a reliable buffer in an earlier, simpler time. But in an era of aircraft carriers and convoys, they could now function as highways for aggressors. "The world has become a single field of forces," Spykman wrote.[14]

Like other states through the centuries the United States now had to contend with the reality of strategic vulnerability, many observers concluded. It could not escape from world politics or the harsh and unending game of national survival that was so central to that politics.

Near the end of World II U.S. diplomats devoted considerable energies to founding the United Nations, but this undertaking did not signal an unequivocal embrace of the Wilsonian vision, as has often been suggested. Instead, President Franklin D. Roosevelt explicitly rejected this vision, saying during the war that "the well-intentioned but ill-fated experiments of former years did not work" and that "nothing could be more futile" than another body like the League of Nations.[15] Roosevelt was initially hesitant about creating a new international organization at all, believing that a great power alliance, with the United States and Britain at its core, might be preferable. When he did throw himself into the task of creating the United Nations, he worked to ensure that concrete power—not rules and ideals by themselves—would be the cornerstone of that body. Thus, at the Tehran conference, for example, Roosevelt proposed that the new organization have a super council at its core made up of the United States, Great Britain, Russia, and China—"powers that would have to police the world for many years to come."[16]

This concept of "four policemen" would eventually manifest itself in the creation of a powerful Security Council in the United Nations comprised of the four leading powers, plus France. The success of the U.N., American leaders understood, would require sustained cooperation among these powers. They accepted the Lippmann view that the only reliable hedge against aggression was a defensive arrangement among a nucleus of powerful, like-minded states. As Henry Stimson, Roosevelt's secretary of war, later said, "However attractive it might be to think in terms of a world organization, the real guarantee of peace could only come from agreement among the major powers."[17] Even Secretary Hull, a disciple of Wilson's, readily acknowledged this hard reality. In a 1944 speech, Hull said that without an enduring partnership between the United States, Great Britain, Russia, and China, "all organizations to preserve peace are creations on paper and the path is wide open again for the rise of a new aggressor."[18]

The United Nations was sold to Congress and the public on idealist rather than realist grounds. In a speech to Congress on March 1, 1945, Roosevelt said that the U.N. would mean "the end of the system of unilateral action, exclusive alliances, and spheres of influence, and balances of power."[19] Cordell Hull had argued the same point in 1943 after laying the groundwork for the U.N. during a trip to Moscow. But these statements may more properly be seen as reflecting a belief held in the Roosevelt Administration that U.S. involvement in global affairs would only be accepted by the public if it were justified on idealist grounds.

Realism Refined

The onset of the Cold War served to enshrine realist thinking among American foreign policy experts. The specter of a hostile Soviet monolith gobbling up Eastern European states appeared to provide further confirmation that brutishness was the natural state of world politics. George Kennan, a career diplomat who became the chief architect of the U.S. containment strategy, was a firm realist. Kennan was deeply apprehensive about the legalistic-moralistic ideals that had dominated American diplomacy in the first half of the twentieth century. These ideals, Kennan believed, had their origins in America's domestic political system, which was highly juridical in nature. Kennan thought it no coincidence that so many U.S. foreign policy officials had come from the legal profession.

Kennan believed that the past failures of American diplomacy lay in misguided efforts to apply values cherished at home to challenges encountered abroad. He saw little hope, as he wrote later, that it was possible to "suppress the chaotic and dangerous aspirations of governments in the international field by the acceptance of some system of legal rules and restraints."[20] There was simply no viable source of international authority that could enforce such a system. As a consequence, all nations that wished to ensure their survival had to rely, ultimately, on their own power and self-interest, Kennan believed. The United States was not exempted from this mandate.

By far the most successful proponent of the realist paradigm during the early postwar period was Hans Morgenthau, a German émigré who was a political scientist at the University of Chicago. In his classic book, *Politics Among Nations*, first published in 1948 and revised often through the ensuing decades, Morgenthau set out the basic principles of realism. Some of his ideas were familiar to anyone who had read Spykman or Lippmann, but Morgenthau elevated realist theorizing to a new plateau of sophistication. He argued that the desire for people to dominate others was part of human nature and that this produced a struggle for power at every level of human organization, from the family up to the realm of international politics. Morgenthau could imagine no way to change this reality: "Even though anthropologists have shown that certain primitive peoples seem to be free from the desire for power, nobody has yet shown how their state of mind and the conditions under which they live can be re-created on a worldwide scale so as to eliminate the struggle for power from the international scene." A glance back at the vast sweep of history provided scant comfort to those seeking to imagine an alternative human reality. "It cannot be denied," Morgenthau wrote, "that through historic time, regardless of social, economic, and political conditions, states have met each other in contests for power." Such would continue to be the case as long as basic human nature remained unchanged, Morgenthau contended.

Almost as certain as this reality were the inevitable efforts to wish it away. "Since the end of the Napoleonic Wars, ever larger groups in the Western world have been persuaded that the struggle for power on the international scene is a temporary phenomenon, a historic accident that is bound to disappear once the peculiar historic conditions that have given rise to it have been eliminated." Nowhere was this delusional tendency stronger than in the United States, where Morgenthau detected an entrenched belief that "nations have a choice between power politics and other kinds of foreign policy not tainted by the desire for power."[21]

Between 1949 and 1951 Morgenthau served as a consultant to the State Department's Policy Planning Staff. This small group of foreign policy experts, directed first by George Kennan and then, beginning in 1950, by Paul Nitze, wielded tremendous influence over the formation of U.S. national security policy. Shifting his attention from the nature of world politics to the contours of American foreign policy, Morgenthau delivered a series of lectures on the subject at the University of Chicago during the spring of 1950. A year later, an enlarged version of these lectures was published as a book entitled *In Defense of the National Interest*. This predictably critical book was the first comprehensive realist critique of American foreign policy.

Morgenthau identified four intellectual errors in U.S. foreign policy: utopianism, sentimentalism, legalism, and neo-isolationism. Utopianism was the failure by U.S. leaders to recognize the immutable law of power politics, an error that was abundantly in evidence at the end of World War II. Morgenthau faulted Roosevelt and his top advisors—unfairly, it can be argued—for failing to recognize that the international struggle for power was a continuum. They did not realize, he wrote, that "the downfall of one ambitious nation calls forth the ambitions of another, and that the business of war does not end with military victory but only with the establishment of a viable distribution of power." All of this naïveté was embodied in the United Nations, Morgenthau charged. His critique of American policy in regard to the U.N. echoed Lippmann's condemnation of Wilsonian idealism. "For the United States the new world organization in the form of the United Nations was a substitute for power politics," Morgenthau complained. "It was supposed to do away with the balance of power, spheres of influence, alliances, the very policies seeking national advantage and aggrandizement."[22]

Morgenthau also saw the United Nations as embodying the misguided legalism of American foreign policy, a flaw closely linked to utopianism. Legalism was only viable in a world in which there was substantial agreement among the major powers, said Morgenthau. He did not entirely ignore evidence that Roosevelt and his aides had recognized the need for great-power cooperation in creating the U.N., but he charged that counting on such cooperation was naive in the extreme. When faced with renegade actions by a Security Council member, the other powers would find legal principles scant consolation in trying to restore law and order. Instead, coercing a major power to accept a settlement would always require threatening war. "Faced with the risks and sacrifices of such a war," Morgenthau wrote, "all nations will be guided in their decisions by what they regard as their national interests rather than by legal abstractions." Thus, in the end, bottom-line considerations of power politics would always prevail.[23]

Morgenthau saw a dangerous sentimentalism underlying the utopian and legalistic thinking in American foreign policy. American leaders and citizens had a basic conviction that national interests were not worthy objectives for a nation to pursue and that only universal moral values could serve as the basis for foreign policy. Lippmann had made the same point in earlier critiques of Wilsonianism. Both men worried that unless the United States was engaged in a righteous crusade, the American people would always be deeply suspicious about overseas involvements. Yet righteous crusades were very risky—they were easy to get into and hard to escape from. In his 1943 book on U.S. foreign policy, Lippmann had said that America's idealistic streak prevented policymakers from thinking clearly about means and ends. Instead, the American tendency was to blindly make commitments based upon lofty principles and to worry about fulfilling those commitments later. Early realists like Mahan and Theodore Roosevelt, who wove a missionary agenda into their worldview, had not been immune from this tendency.

In a thin volume on American diplomacy published in 1951,

Kennan argued forcefully that when legalism and moralism began driving U.S. foreign policy, things could easily go too far. Indignant crusading could replace the cool and calculated pursuit of the national interest. This potential was especially evident in wartime. "A war fought in the name of high moral principle finds no early end short of some form of total domination," Kennan wrote.[24] In a 1952 book, *Isolation and Alliances,* Lippmann hammered this concern home. When morality and legalism drive foreign policy, "all wars are wars to end wars, all wars are crusades which can be concluded only when the peoples have submitted to the only true political religion. There will be peace only when all the peoples hold and observe the same self-evident principles."[25]

Writing about the postwar realists, Joel Rosenthal observed that they struck at the core of American foreign policy as it had heretofore been practiced. The realists "criticized American foreign policy for being too American—too puritanical, too crusading, and too sure of American exceptionalism. They questioned both the missionary zeal of policymakers and the presumption that foreign affairs could be governed by American standards of political morality."[26] An enduring project for the postwar realists was to reduce the role of morality in foreign policy, but these men did not entirely dismiss the importance of moral thinking, as their critics so often charged. They imagined a foreign policy that reflected American values—one that made Americans comfortable and even proud.

Where they drew the line was at proselytizing those values. "Let us, by all means, conduct ourselves at all times in such a way as to satisfy our own ideas of morality," wrote George Kennan in 1954. "But let us not assume that our moral values, based as they are on the specifics of our national tradition and the various religious outlooks represented in our country, necessarily have validity for people everywhere."[27]

The realists demanded fundamental changes in the conduct of foreign policy. American participation in world politics could not be an on-again off-again affair, punctuated by moral crusades and then abrupt withdrawal, all underscored by a naïveté in regard to international realities. Instead, the realists erected a new criterion for a sound foreign policy, one starkly at odds with American tradition: the United States had to effect sustained international engagement predi-

cated on few, if any, lofty principles. The goal of ensuring a balance
of power in Europe and Asia was viewed as a central purpose of this
engagement. Indeed, a chief project of realist thinkers was to provide
a theoretical context in which to place widespread fears of unbalanced power. The real problem that Americans needed to understand, realists argued, was not the occasional rise of predatory mega-
lomaniacs like Hitler and Stalin; it was the permanently competitive
nature of the state system.

If World War II served to assure the ascendancy of the realist
worldview within the U.S. foreign policy establishment, the Cold
War had the effect of cementing it as orthodoxy among policy elites
and scholars.[28] The struggle with communism also conditioned a traditionally idealist and isolationist public to accept that the international system was not as America might like it to be, and that U.S.
leadership was a basic prerequisite for global security. Unlike the
world wars, which had been relatively brief spasms of violence, the
Cold War was an unending tutorial in realism's validity. For over four
decades the centrality of power in world politics would be supremely
self-evident. Year after year the news was filled with stories of armed
competition, proxy war, and successful or attempted conquest. Moreover, with the United Nations reduced to impotence by the East-
West conflict, it was difficult to argue for the notion of world peace
by covenant.

Challenges to Realism

Not until the 1970s would the realist orthodoxy be seriously challenged. That challenge, when it came, was not predicated on a
revived faith in Wilsonian idealism. Rather, a variety of scholars and
analysts pointed to global trends toward interdependence, which they
said undermined the realist picture of a world where independent
states were the all-important actors and where military force was the
main currency of influence. They cited the rising power of multinational corporations and the growth of other powerful nonstate actors
like the Organization of Petroleum Exporting Countries (OPEC)
and the European Community (EC). Most important, they put forth
a picture of a shrinking world where powerful forces of integration
were at work. Advances in communication and transportation were

reducing the distances between peoples, while growing trade was boosting the stake that peoples of different nations had in one another's welfare. All of these ties, moreover, were being increasingly regulated by international agreements and the regimes set up to implement them. As actors on the world scene, states were finding their freedom of action more and more constrained by trends beyond their control.

Joseph Nye and Robert Keohane were among the most influential scholars who challenged realist explanations and analyzed the forces that were reshaping international politics. In their 1977 book, *Power and Interdependence*, they rejected the argument that states were still unchallenged actors on the world stage. At the same time, they found unconvincing claims that the state was becoming irrelevant. The truth, they argued, lay somewhere in between.

Keohane and Nye were hesitant to embrace some of the more optimistic claims about the impact of interdependence. A highly interdependent world would not necessarily be a world of peace and cooperation; conflict could easily occur. However, in relations between states in which there was "complex interdependence," the optimistic claims could be quite accurate. Under complex interdependence, societies are connected by multiple channels: by traditional diplomacy, by economic interaction, by cultural exchanges, by immigration, and so forth. In this situation, said Keohane and Nye, there is no clear hierarchy of issues. Security issues do not, as the realists claimed, overshadow and underlie all else. When conflict arises military force is not used.

Keohane and Nye believed that realism still retained value but contended that much of international politics could no longer be explained through a realist paradigm. The world was becoming increasingly complicated and the Morgenthau view of an unending Darwinian struggle, with military force as the final arbiter, failed to explain much of what was going on.[29] Other writers were much more forceful in dismissing the realist view, arguing that rising interdependence was creating a community of advanced nations in which warfare was all but inconceivable.[30]

A highly integrated and peaceful world had long been a dream of idealists. Now, as history seemed to speed up at the dawn of the information age, this dream—at least among the developed nations—

appeared to be within reach. And it was not contingent on the effective functioning of any kind of world government scheme.

Zbigniew Brzezinski was another prominent advocate of the view that powerful integrative forces were reshaping the world. These forces had the potential to transform global politics, he said, ushering in a situation in which cooperation rather than discord and insecurity would be the norm. Brzezinski warned that the triumph of such forces could not be taken for granted. The traditional state system, with its reliance on power politics, was still very much alive; chaos and conflict were just as likely in the world as integration and harmony. Thus he advocated, in his 1970 book aptly titled *Between Two Ages*, that the U.S. undertake deliberate efforts to accelerate the process of international cooperation among the advanced industrial nations.[31]

Brzezinski saw that this task would require big changes in American foreign policy. Instead of being obsessed with traditional geopolitics, the United States would have to focus on promoting far-ranging ties with its industrial allies. Brzezinski imagined that increasing prosperity in the Western trilateral sphere—made up of East Asia, Western Europe, and North America—would condemn the Soviet Union to irrelevance. He warned that if the United States failed to shift its attention to this new reality, if it remained fixated with Cold War concerns, then it could face decline in a new era dominated by the other advanced nations.

The Trilateral Commission, which Brzezinski helped found and directed, was designed to continue U.S. world leadership, but leadership with the goal of building a new world order based on economic and political cooperation. Military preeminence was to be a secondary concern. Jimmy Carter was a member of the Trilateral Commission, and as a candidate for president he talked often of world order politics and expressed contempt for the realist worldview. "For too long," Carter said in March 1976, "our foreign policy has consisted almost entirely of maneuver and manipulation, based on the assumption that the world is a jungle of competing national antagonisms, where military supremacy and economic muscle are the only things that work and where rival powers are balanced against each other to keep the peace."[32] With Brzezinski serving as Carter's national security advisor, the stage seemed set in the late 1970s for a fundamental shift away from the realist assumptions that had reigned unchallenged through the Cold War. This was not how things worked out.

Realism Reaffirmed

Brzezinski proved to be far less bold and innovative than his earlier writings might have suggested. Once in the White House he became deeply worried about the Cold War competition and about other traditional geopolitical issues. Far from serving as a laboratory for experimenting with trilateralist formulas, Carter's foreign policy establishment became an internecine battleground where hawks and doves clashed in sterile debate. With the Cold War heating up again, the hawks gained the upper hand, and by the end of his administration, Carter was resorting often to the tough language of power politics.

In the scholarly world the realist counterattack was unrelenting during the 1970s. Many writers rejected the claim that recent global changes presaged any real alteration of the nature of international politics. Robert Gilpin, for example, conceded that the rise of the multinational corporation was important. "But in general," he stated, "there is little evidence to substantiate the argument that the multinational corporation as an independent actor has had a significant impact on international politics."[33] Kenneth Waltz rejected claims about interdependence as a glue that would bond the world together. He argued that "interdependence is low and, if anything, on the decrease."[34] In any case, he doubted that interdependence would serve to reduce conflict among nations. In 1979 Waltz published *Theory of International Politics*, a highly influential book that reaffirmed the Morgenthau view that the world was a dangerous place in which each state had to rely, ultimately, on its own power for survival.

Waltz pushed realist thinking beyond the earlier emphasis on human nature and the lust for power, and he refined the arguments of those who stressed that constant insecurity was guaranteed by the structure of world politics. As long as the world was organized into a state system in which individual units competed against one another for power and position, conflict would be inevitable.[35] Like Morgenthau's treatise *Politics Among Nations*, Waltz's book quickly became a standard text in college and graduate courses on international politics.

By the early 1980s the so-called neo-realists, or structural realists, had recaptured much of the ground that realism had lost in the 1970s. The presidency of Ronald Reagan and resurgent Cold War tensions contributed to the realist revival.

In the late 1980s, as the Cold War ended, realism still reigned as the orthodoxy of the U.S. foreign policy establishment. And when the United States began exploring the frontiers of the post–Cold War era, the realist paradigm would serve as the chief compass for U.S. foreign policy officials.

IDEALISM IN U.S. FOREIGN POLICY

Understanding the way in which the realist outlook and concerns about unbalanced power came to shape U.S. foreign policy in the twentieth century is crucially important. Too often in recent debate these influences have been underappreciated, with the consequence that much analysis of post–Cold War foreign policy has been muddled.

But it is important, in highlighting these themes, not to allow them to blot out the entire historical picture. Clearly, idealist thinking has also had a huge impact on the evolution of U.S. foreign policy. In justifying involvement abroad, U.S. leaders have often cited, more prominently and passionately than anything else, the pursuit of idealist goals such as the protection of democracy, reform of the international system, and the thwarting of evil.

A key question that remains unanswered, however, is to what degree idealist rationales have actually shaped foreign policy decisions, as opposed to being employed later, in the wake of essentially realist decisions, to sell overseas involvement to the American public. This question is difficult to answer because through the twentieth century idealist and realist goals have often been indistinguishable. The interventions abroad to back democracies in World War I, World War II, and the Cold War can be seen both as moral crusades to protect free peoples from conquest and as efforts to prevent unbalanced power from arising that could eventually threaten the United States. To some degree one can use historical analysis to cull through the evidence and separate out, in each episode, the manner in which realist and idealist considerations shaped policy. But it is naive to expect definitive answers from this process, given the way that these considerations have often interlocked.

Nonetheless, there can be little doubt about the enduring weakness of idealism in U.S. foreign policy. Before the United States became a world power at the turn of the century, the promotion of America's values and political system was never the main thrust behind foreign policy because the republic lacked both the power resources and inclination for such missionary policies. After the United States became a world power, idealism became a crucial feature of U.S. foreign policy, but never the principal driver of it, except for a few brief moments in history, such as the period immediately following World War I. Idealism was an important factor behind the interventions in the world wars and the Cold War. Yet in the absence of pressing security threats in all three instances, idealist goals probably would not have been enough to motivate large-scale U.S. intervention. In both world wars the United States intervened not when the threat to European democracies first became serious, but when the challenges to its own security interests could no longer be ignored.

This understanding of the historical weakness of idealism in U.S. foreign policy has important implications for analyzing developments of recent years. It sheds light on why the safeguarding of U.S. security continues to be a far higher priority in post–Cold War foreign policy than the pursuit of idealist goals.

Early Idealism

Americans have always had the hope that their values and political system would spread through the world. In the first century of the republic, however, a foreign policy that actively pursued this goal was seen by most American leaders to be neither feasible nor attractive. As diplomatic historian Norman Graebner has argued, "Early democratic idealism did not, in a single instance, determine the fundamental policies of the nation."[36]

On purely practical grounds, limited power projection capabilities made it difficult for the United States to intervene overseas in a significant way on behalf of groups or states that it felt sympathy with. Diplomatically, the United States could and did express its support for fledgling democrats in Europe and elsewhere during the nineteenth century. But militarily there were few if any moves to back up that rhetoric with action.

In terms of population and industrial power the United States had entered the ranks of the great powers by the second half of the nineteenth century.[37] If it had so desired it could have fielded the military power needed to support a missionary foreign policy. But early American leaders did not conceptualize the U.S. idealist mission as an activist one. Instead, the United States would provide moral leadership by example. It would not compromise itself by involvement in Old World power politics. It would resist engagement in anything resembling imperialism. The American mission would be, as the famous phrase put it, to stand as a "city upon a hill." As one historian has explained it, "That mission was to live morally and righteously, and to show the old and corrupt nations of the world that God's work could indeed be done on earth."[38]

Thomas Paine put it another way: the new nation in the new world would be "an asylum for mankind." Benjamin Franklin also used this term,[39] and it was a notion that was very much a continuation of the ideal that had underpinned America before independence, when many who came to the colonies were those fleeing religious and political persecution. Paine himself was gloomy about the future of freedom elsewhere and favored active American efforts to support like-minded democrats abroad. But the majority of the Founding Fathers held a more teleological outlook. Many of them had a strong faith, rooted in enlightenment thinking, that the idea of America would spread because it embodied reason and progress, forces that were destined eventually to triumph in the world. With history on its side, the Founding Fathers felt that a still weak America should not take risks abroad.[40]

Quite apart from the distinctly American reasons for isolationism there existed another enlightenment idea that appears to have underlain early U.S. foreign policy. During the eighteenth century European enlightenment thinkers (the "philosophes") argued energetically against the obsession with foreign affairs. "Their thesis was that the great role which foreign affairs played in the political life of their time was one of the most fundamental evils of the existing political system," wrote historian Felix Gilbert. The philosophes attacked not only the overemphasis on foreign policy, which they saw as a distraction from internal political and cultural challenges, but also attacked the way in which such policy was conducted, seeing it as a nasty form of recreation for amoral and often bloodthirsty aristocrats. They deplored power politics and all the double-dealing and inevitable warfare that accompanied balance-of-power diplomacy.[41]

This thinking was widely embraced by early American leaders who believed that democratic nations were both inherently more attentive to the needs of their citizens and by nature less warlike. "Princes fight for glory, and the blood and the treasure of their subjects is the price they pay," stated an 1803 report by a congressional committee. "In all nations the people bear the burden of war, and in the United States the people rule."[42]

As discussed earlier, the early American distaste for the war system did not induce a complete rejection of all matters related to foreign affairs. Some early leaders like Jefferson and Madison proved quite adept at manipulating the European game of power politics. Yet even as they played that game they looked beyond it, harboring optimism about possible changes in the international system. Early U.S. foreign policy, says Gilbert, "was idealistic and internationalist no less than isolationist." Jefferson, for example, was "convinced that the relations between nations in the future would take forms different from those of the diplomacy of the past."[43] As with their faith in the inexorable spread of democracy, the Founding Fathers believed that the international system would inevitably change as reason came to prevail in the world. Still, they and their immediate successors did not believe the United States should lead crusades, or even cultivate active diplomatic alliances, to speed up this process.

Idealist Imperialism and Realist Idealism

"For nearly a hundred years," observed the historian Charles Beard, "the Government of the United States consistently and insistently maintained that it would not employ the engines of diplomacy and force for the purpose of doing good to other peoples by interfering with their domestic and international quarrels, by imposing on them American systems of economy, politics, and morals."[44] This restraint disappeared at the end of the nineteenth century, when the United

States went to war against Spain. In his special message on the war in April 1898, President McKinley said that liberating Cuba from Spanish rule had to be undertaken in "the name of humanity, in the name of civilization. . . ."[45] Later, in explaining why the United States took control of the Philippines, McKinley said that he could not turn the islands over to some other Western power, nor could the Filipinos be granted independence, since "they were unfit for self-government." Thus, he said, "there was nothing left for us to do but to take them all, and to educate the Filipinos, and uplift and civilize and Christianize them. . . ." Despite the mass deaths of Filipinos at the hands of American occupation troops, McKinley's biographer, Charles S. Olcott, was moved to later write that "William McKinley was the first of our Presidents to answer the call of broad philanthropy toward other less fortunate people."[46]

The Spanish–American War signaled not only the emergence of a strong imperialistic streak in U.S. foreign policy, but it also marked the widespread acceptance of the idea that growing U.S. power must be used to combat evil in the world and act as a civilizing influence. Even those figures of the time who are now considered realist pioneers believed in such a moral obligation. "Nations, like men, have a conscience," wrote the otherwise hard-nosed Mahan. And sometimes that conscience demanded a resort to arms for the control of evil, Mahan said: "To right what is amiss, to convert, to improve, to develop, is of the very essence of the Christian ideal. Hence the recognition that if force is necessary, force must be used for the benefit of the community, of the commonwealth of the world." Theodore Roosevelt echoed these sentiments in his 1906 message to Congress: "It is wicked for a nation to regard only its own interest, and foolish to believe that such is the sole motive that actuates any other nation. . . . A really great nation must often act, and as a matter of fact often does act, toward other nations in a spirit not in the least of mere self-interest, but paying heed chiefly to ethical reasons."[47]

The views of Mahan and Roosevelt are early examples of thinking that would later metamorphose into Cold War internationalism. Its proponents embraced a deeply pessimistic view of world politics and saw military force as the final guarantor of national survival. At the same time, they parted company with pure realists in their commitment to bettering the world through a wise and righteous application of American power—power that they tended to view as nearly limitless in supply.

During the two world wars, and through the Cold War that followed, U.S. actions were primarily shaped by strategic considerations. Much of the moralistic rhetoric that surrounded these struggles was, it seems clear, intended to mobilize a public that tended to be unmoved by the kind of strategic reasoning that foreign policy elites employed among themselves. Still, there can be no doubt that some of this rhetoric also conveyed the genuine sentiments of American leaders. Elihu Root, former secretary of war and state, spoke for many in the foreign policy establishment when he called World War I "a great struggle between the principles of Christian civilization and the principles of pagan cruelty and brute force. . . . "[48]

The barbarism of Nazi Germany and Imperial Japan generated even greater moral indignation among U.S. leaders. In the Cold War, there is no question that American officials found the Soviet system deeply repugnant, as has been amply evidenced by the declassification of top secret government documents written for internal use only.

The Rise and Fall of Wilsonian Idealism

As the United States became increasingly engaged in world politics during the early twentieth century, idealist foreign policy thinkers began to talk more specifically about how America should aim to create a better world. Two ideas would become central to their vision: the promotion of security through the extension of international law and the creation of new international organizations, and active support for democracies abroad on the assumption that such states were more friendly. Idealists also argued that greater economic interdependence among nations would foster peace.

All these ideas guided President Woodrow Wilson in his approach to world affairs, particularly in his diplomacy after World War I. Ultimately, however, Wilson's idealist vision would stand as a centerpiece of American foreign policy for no more than a brief period.

The desire to remake the international system existed as early as Jefferson's time, but it was not until World War I that the United States had both the means and the opportunity to pursue its vision.[49] To be sure, American entry into World War I reflected, in large part, geopolitical calculations. Yet for many, especially Wilson himself, the U.S. aim was more than the suppression of the German menace; America, it was hoped, could use its power after the war to secure a lasting peace based on the rule of law. It is therefore a mistake to dismiss entirely, as Walter Lippmann did in his writings in the 1940s, the idealist motives for U.S. intervention. Wilson was not engaged in a purely cynical exercise when he said in his war speech to Congress in April 1917 that America sought "a universal dominion of right by such a concert of free people as should bring peace and safety to all nations and make the world itself at last free."[50] Nor was he seeking to mislead when, two months after the war's end, he expressed the sentiment that "If the future had nothing for us but a new attempt to keep the world at a right poise by a balance of power, the United States would take no interest." The United States "is not interested merely in the peace of Europe, but in the peace of the world."[51] And of course the most compelling evidence of Wilson's sincerity was his effort to create the League of Nations, a body that he hoped would abolish power politics and replace it with collective security.[52]

The famous Fourteen Points, first articulated by Wilson in January 1918 and the basis for U.S. diplomacy at the Versailles Peace Conference in Paris, stands as the most comprehensive outline of an idealist agenda ever set forward by an American statesman. For decades afterward Wilson's vision would animate foreign policy idealists. Among the points that would have lasting resonance were Wilson's statements that "a general association of nations must be formed under specific covenants for the purpose of affording mutual guarantees of political independence and territorial integrity of great and small states alike" (Point XIV); that international legal covenants must be strengthened and respected (Point VIII); that world peace required that negotiated measures be taken to assure that "national armaments will be reduced to the lowest point consistent with domestic safety" (Point IV); that peace would also be furthered by the "removal of, so far as possible, all economic barriers and the establishment of an equality of trade conditions among all the nations consenting to the peace and associating themselves for its maintenance" (Point III); and that the struggle of minorities for sovereignty should be treated with far greater sympathy if the world of states were to be a just place (Point V).[53]

Even though the League was never ratified by the U.S. Senate, Wilson's crusading spirit continued to guide American foreign policy through the 1920s and 1930s. Those decades are rightly remembered chiefly as a time of isolationism, but it is also true that U.S. diplomats were hard at work creating multilateral arrangements for disarmament and seeking other measures to prevent conflict.[54] Such furtherance of collective security, it was supposed, would institutionalize the force of reason in relations among states. Woodrow Wilson may have died a disappointed man, but Wilsonian idealism would continue to have a powerful influence within the U.S. foreign policy establishment.

During World War II America's foremost intention was, again, to safeguard its security. But as in World War I, a missionary zeal to remake the international system was from the start a prominent feature of U.S. policy. On September 3, 1939, two days after Germany invaded Poland, Roosevelt stated: "It seems to me clear, even at the outbreak of this great war, that the influence of the United States should be consistent in seeking for humanity a final peace which will eliminate, as far as it is possible to do so, the continued use of force between nations."[55] As noted earlier, Roosevelt's secretary of state, Cordell Hull, had been a disciple of Wilson and was a strong believer in Wilsonian principles. In many ways he was an idealistic missionary at heart. On his return from the Moscow Conference of 1943, where the groundwork had been laid for the U.N., Hull told Congress that in the future "there will no longer be the need for spheres of influence, for alliances, for balance of power, or any other of the special arrangements by which, in the unhappy past, the nations strove to safeguard their security or promote their interests."[56] This comment aside, it is now apparent, as argued earlier, that the United Nations was a far more realist enterprise than the League of Nations and that U.S. thinking about the postwar world was less naive than it had been in World War I.[57] The idealist desire to reform the international system was still a powerful force among foreign policy officials in the early 1940s, but these efforts were now informed by realist assumptions about the nature of world politics.

The onset of the Cold War and the triumph of realist ideas in the U.S. foreign policy establishment effectively ended the Wilsonian quest to remake the international system. Hopes for collective security plummeted as an East-West deadlock immobilized the United

Nations.[58] Yet even in the face of these odds the idealist impulse was not wholly extinguished. As late as 1957, for example, U.S. policy-makers in the Eisenhower Administration seriously discussed a new effort to give the U.N. Security Council greater powers to enforce international peace. This move came amid mounting calls from some members of Congress and various independent experts that the United States should take the lead in establishing a permanent U.N. force to help prevent or defuse conflicts around the world. State Department proposals for creating a standing U.N. force were ultimately shot down within the bureaucracy, but the simple fact that they were considered at the height of the Cold War is testament to the staying power of Wilson's vision.[59]

Also significant in this regard is a 1957 proposal by Secretary of State John Foster Dulles, the quintessential Cold Warrior of his time, that the United States continue its quest for collective security by establishing a new large-scale organization that would be separate from the paralyzed United Nations. Exposing a strong Wilsonian streak, Dulles complained in a memo that the "collective security system contemplated by the [U.N.] Charter has never even begun to be established." Any step to remedy this "should meet the crying need for (a) a more developed body of international law; (b) more solid and dependable processes for peaceful settlement of disputes; (c) a more effective and dependable system of international force to deter, and if need be resist, those who would violate agreed principles of law, and (d) the organization of control of armament, particularly nuclear weapons." Dulles proposed that consideration be given to bringing together in a new collective security organization or convention all the states of the free world, effectively creating a parallel United Nations. This plan was never seriously debated. But, again, the mere fact that Dulles proposed it is significant.[60]

The enduring strength of idealism in foreign policy was also evident in America's postwar effort to create a global trade and financial system based on laissez-faire principles. Although national interest was the overriding motivation behind U.S. policy, powerful ideological forces were also at work. Ever since the republic's founding, free trade had been viewed by foreign policy elites as a major element in the enlightenment ideal of a harmonious international society. Trade meant interdependence among nations, which was seen as translating into incentives to be peaceful since it raised the costs of going to war. High levels of trade were also viewed as a key to greater prosperity and economic diversity, which could be important in aiding democracy's growth. Before World War II the United States had lacked the influence and willpower to propagate free trade on a global scale. But after the war U.S. efforts on this score became, along with anticommunism, a central crusade underpinning American internationalism.[61]

Today, the idealist foreign policy agenda is associated foremost with the promotion of democracy. In the past, however, this goal was seldom pursued in an activist manner. The crusades of the first half of the twentieth century to protect the European democracies began, as previously discussed, as emergency measures taken in the face of mounting security threats. They were not the culminations of long-standing pro-democratic activism on the part of the United States. Washington, for example, did not orchestrate an international pressure campaign against Germany when Hitler came to power in 1933 or covertly support his democratic opponents as Nazi repression escalated. In 1939 Assistant Secretary of State Adolph A. Berle spoke for many and expressed a long-standing American distaste for overseas meddling when he commented that "a nation coerced into democracy is not a democratic nation."[62]

The U.N.'s Universal Declaration of Human Rights, drafted mostly by Americans, declared democratic governance to be a basic right to which all humans were entitled. But the U.N. Charter expressly forbade outside interference in the sovereign affairs of U.N. member states. These two documents captured the historic conundrum of American foreign policy: while a more democratic world was deeply desired, spreading democracy at the point of a sword was widely seen as anathema to what America stood for.

Following the defeat of the Axis powers, democratization became a cornerstone of U.S. policy toward its former enemies.[63] American officials believed that open domestic processes could help prevent a return to aggressive foreign policies. In both Japan and Germany efforts at democratization were highly successful,[64] but these experiences were never seized upon by U.S. policymakers to justify the conquest and transformation of other countries.

During the Cold War there would be frequent discussion of

"rolling back" Soviet power from Eastern Europe and bringing democracy to captive peoples. However, such ideas never became the basis for policy because of the high risks they entailed. The United States remained passive even in the face of democratic uprisings initiated by Eastern Europeans themselves, in 1956 and 1968.

In the postwar era the United States crusaded to thwart the Soviet menace and preserve the integrity of the West; in certain parts of the world this effort entailed strengthening democracy through foreign assistance and covert action. But it would be a mistake to view the Cold War as principally a crusade for democracy and human rights, even though these goals were obviously central to America's long-term agenda. Insuring Western security was the overriding goal of U.S. policy; promoting democratic values was a secondary goal that sometimes supported security objectives. When it did not, U.S. Cold War policymakers showed themselves to be quite tolerant of authoritarian regimes, as long as they were anti-Communist. In several instances Washington even actively worked to subvert democracy.

In over two hundred years of conducting foreign policy the United States has never mounted a major crusade for its political ideals as an end in itself. Yet as an idea, missionary politics has always had a powerful hold on the popular imagination and a constituency among portions of the foreign policy establishment. The rising influence of realism in the twentieth century did little to dampen public idealism, but it did severely limit support for an idealist foreign policy among foreign policy elites. Realist arguments that the world was an inescapably dangerous place had begun to discredit the idealistic strain of U.S. foreign policy even before World War II, and by the 1950s, Wilsonian idealism was widely regarded as naive, thanks in part to popular commentators like Walter Lippmann and influential academics like Hans Morgenthau who relentlessly hammered at this theme. Quite apart from the powerful theoretical attacks leveled at idealists, the daily reality of the Cold War prevented serious debate about pursuing an idealist agenda in foreign affairs. Even in the 1970s, when the Cold War slightly eased its grip on the political imagination, realists proved effective in discrediting the idealist view that global integration would lead to a peaceful community of advanced nations and that the traditional geopolitical agenda would become less important in U.S. foreign policy. The renewal of Cold War tensions in the 1980s appeared to confirm the centrality of military power in world affairs.

As the Cold War ended, realism may have stood as the prevailing orthodoxy in the foreign policy establishment and idealism may have been largely discredited, but the stage was set for a more equal competition between them.[65] The peaceful triumph of liberal values in the Communist bloc served to renew idealist arguments that the power of ideas could shape history. At the same time, the concrete consequences of the Cold War's end—more democracies, disappearing divisions within international organizations, greater economic and cultural interdependence among a wider circle of market economies—accelerated trends that idealists had long cited as promoting peace. In determining American foreign policy in a world with no global threat, post–Cold War policymakers have had more leeway to experiment than policymakers of any previous era.

3

PRIMACY REAFFIRMED: STAYING NUMBER ONE AFTER THE COLD WAR

The winding down of the Cold War in the late 1980s caused many Americans to think that an end was in sight to the United States' long duty as global policeman. The rapid implosion of the Soviet bloc held the promise of eliminating the rationale for a majority of America's military forces and much of its overseas involvement. Often repeated claims that the United States was in decline served to reinforce the idea that a far-reaching strategic retrenchment was unavoidable. And even before the term "peace dividend" became widely used in late 1989 there was debate over how the savings from the Cold War's end, imagined to be vast in size, should be used.

But inside the Bush Administration, and in much of the mainstream foreign policy establishment, discussions about how to respond to global changes bore little relation to the public debate.[1] In these circles it was widely recognized that some strategic retrenchment was warranted in response to the Cold War's end. However, the conception of this retrenchment was extremely cautious. The foremost principle at work, as Under Secretary of Defense Paul Wolfowitz suggested in the middle of 1990, was that "In the euphoria of the moment, we must not repeat the mistakes of the past."[2] The main mistakes of the past, in the view of most foreign policy experts, were to ignore the fact that American security at home ultimately hinged on stability abroad; to believe that international order and balanced power across the seas could be maintained without active leadership by the world's leading power; and to deny the fact that the United States was that power. The history of U.S. foreign policy thinking in the twentieth century is largely the story of how U.S. leaders came to accept the burdens of global primacy.

To avoid the mistakes of the past, foreign policy elites called for sobriety amid the celebrations that attended communism's demise. They reminded each other and the public that the need for American leadership was rooted in the laws of world politics, laws that remained in force even as communism collapsed. "For the international system to work, leading powers must lead," stressed Secretary Baker in 1991. "This is the lesson we learned from our own reluctance to play an active role in world affairs in the period between the two world wars."[3] Harvard political scientist Joseph S. Nye, Jr., elaborated on this view: "If the strongest state does not lead, the prospects for instability increase." More specifically, "Without American leadership in providing a stable military balance and geopolitical framework, the processesof economic and social evolution in world politics could be disrupted."[4]

This idea was an article of faith in the Bush Administration. It stood as the unshakable pillar of a national security policy that was often otherwise muddled and undirected.[5] "Winston Churchill used to say that in confusing situations it was always best to resort to first principles," explained Secretary of State James Baker in his first major foreign policy address. "Those principles, I think, begin with the necessity of continued U.S. leadership."[6] Nearly a year later, after the fall of the Berlin Wall, Baker was, if anything, more emphatic about America's indispensable role in the world. "Truly, political freedom, economic growth, and global security are interdependent," he told Congress in February 1990. "And they are all dependent on American leadership, strengthened alliances, and worldwide engagement."[7] If the presence of a hulking Soviet monolith on the Eurasian landmass had once been the principal justification for U.S. primacy, this was hardly a plausible rationale after the events of late 1989 through 1991. But without breaking stride, the administration—and numerous foreign policy experts outside of government—now argued a different line: that U.S. primacy was needed to combat the disorder that was likely to dominate the new post–Cold War era.

Shortly after the collapse of the Berlin Wall, a reporter asked George Bush, "Where is the threat now?" The president had a firm reply: "The enemy is instability, the enemy is uncertainty." National Security Council aide Robert Gates put the matter more concisely in June 1990: "Our central mission is shifting from containment of an enemy to the promotion of stability."[8] By 1991, after the war in the Persian Gulf, this mission stood as the indisputed cornerstone of American postwar national security policy, repeatedly articulated by Bush Administration spokesmen and widely endorsed, albeit with assorted reservations, within the mainstream foreign policy establishment. "Despite the emergence of new power centers, the United States remains the only state with truly global strength, reach, and influence in every dimension," said an official White House statement of U.S. national security strategy released in August 1991. "In the 1990s, as for much of this century, there is no substitute for American leadership."[9]

The Clinton Administration fully embraced this principle as it began charting its foreign policy in 1993. "The American people have called for a new administration, yet there is essential continuity in our foreign policy," President-elect Clinton said, days before taking office.[10] The United States, he and top aides explained during the following months, would not reduce its level of global leadership. Nor would it fundamentally change the nature of that leadership. Overall national security spending for defense, intelligence, and foreign aid would decline only slightly less than the Bush Administration had envisioned. American troops would remain stationed in Europe and East Asia to help maintain stability in those regions, and there would be no abandonment of the American-led alliances of the Cold War era. The United States would continue to be the ultimate guarantor of Western security interests in the Third World.

The Clinton Administration differs from the Bush Administration in its stronger emphasis on using foreign policy to promote democracy and American economic interests. It also has shown more enthusiasm for multilateral approaches to overseas problems, supporting the United Nations in a way the Bush Administration never did and changing policy on issues such as protecting the international environment and curbing global population growth. Yet ultimately it is not these departures that are striking but rather the continuity in foreign policy. Equally striking is the lack of apology for this continuity and the absence of serious criticism among Democratic policy analysts outside of the administration on this score. While the fierce debates in 1993 over Somalia, Bosnia, and Haiti underscore differences about the uses of American power, especially in areas peripheral to U.S. vital interests, a basic consensus exists on the broader aims of foreign policy in the post–Cold War era.

The relative ease with which U.S. foreign policy thinkers have updated the case for American primacy is hardly miraculous. For in significant respects there is nothing new about what Defense Secretary Dick Cheney would come to call the "stability mission," what Baker would eventually dub "collective engagement" and what Clinton's national security advisor Anthony Lake would label a strategy of "enlargement." Instead, the emergent post–Cold War U.S. national security policy embodied the same geopolitical concerns and theoretical ideas that came to shape America's approach to world affairs before the Cold War. Those concerns and ideas were adapted for the new era by the Bush Administration and, so far, have continued to shape the foreign policies of the Clinton Administration.

EUROPE AND ASIA: AGAIN IN SEARCH OF STABILITY

Near the end of World War II, before Soviet power was a clear threat, the task of creating balance in Europe and Asia seemed to hinge on containing Germany and Japan. This goal became subsumed to broader strategic objectives during the Cold War, but it never disappeared. Western analysts recognized, as former National Security Agency head Lt. Gen. William Odom put it, that the "big problems in this century, larger than the Soviet threat, have been the emergence of German and Japanese power."[11] Even as West Germany and Japan became models of democracy and stalwarts of the Western community, their neighbors did not forget what had transpired in earlier times. Nor did U.S. leaders and strategic thinkers forget the instability that came from unbalanced power in Europe and Asia.

None of these concerns mattered as long as the Cold War continued. The anti-Soviet NATO alliance and the strong U.S. military presence in East Asia assured that neither Germany nor Japan would become major independent military powers. Instead, under the umbrella of American power, they could keep their defense establishments small in relative terms and concentrate on economic development. In this way the Cold War made everyone happy. The United States was assured of stability across the oceans; the nations surrounding Japan and Germany could be confident they weren't going to be overrun or intimidated by their traditionally aggressive neighbors; the Germans and Japanese, conflicted by their past abuse of power, did not have to wrestle with the dilemmas or responsibility that would have come with the need to assure their own security; and even the Soviet Union itself could take comfort in the way the United States kept in check two potential military powerhouses on its perimeter.

As the Cold War ended, U.S. leaders and foreign policy thinkers were acutely aware of the stability that was being left behind. "For all of its risks and uncertainties, the Cold War was characterized by a remarkably stable set of relations among the great powers," said Deputy Secretary of State Lawrence Eagleburger in a 1989 speech. "A brief look at the history books will tell us that we cannot say as much about the period leading from the birth of the European nation states up through the outbreak of the Second World War."

In the popular view, the end of the Cold War was seen as leading the world away from a nuclear abyss. At one level, of course, this sense of relief was shared by a foreign policy establishment that had been obsessed for decades with strategic crisis stability. At another level there could be no peace for professional worriers, and Eagleburger voiced the concerns of many when he invoked the discouraging record of history—the dawning multipolar world, concluded Eagleburger, was not "necessarily going to be safer place than the Cold War era from which we are emerging."[12]

American primacy was seen as a key ingredient for stability amid new dangers, but nearly all mainstream analysts agreed that it should be exercised through astute balancing, rather than any kind of Pax Americana. "History so far has shown us only two roads to international stability: domination or equilibrium," commented Henry Kissinger in early 1991. "We do not have the resources for domination, nor is such a course compatible with our values. So we are brought back to a concept maligned in much of America's intellectual history—the balance of power."[13] More specifically, Paul Wolfowitz commented in February 1990 that the "presence of our forces in Europe and Asia will be required to help ensure stability in a time of shifting power balances."[14]

Few foreign policy experts disagreed with the basic thrust of this analysis. During his presidential campaign, Bill Clinton attacked the American "reliance on old balance of power strategies. . . ."[15] But in retrospect this must be seen as little more than campaign rhetoric, because the Clinton Administration has never challenged the view that American power remains essential to maintaining balances of power in key regions of the world.

Reassuring Europe

The chief concerns of U.S. post–Cold War policymakers centered, as always, on Europe. "We must never forget that twice in this century, American blood has been shed over conflicts that began in Europe," President Bush said in one of his first policy addresses about Europe. "We must never forget that to keep the peace in Europe is to keep the peace in America. . . . Though hope is now running high for a more peaceful continent, the history of this century teaches Americans and Europeans to remain prepared."[16] Bush's national security advisor Brent Scowcroft was more blunt: "To our peril, we have learned that when the U.S. does not play a role in Europe, disaster often ensues."[17]

In arguing for continued U.S. engagement in Europe analysts emphasized three principal threats to security on the continent: reemergent German power that could cause uneasiness; the inherent instability that could come from a return to multipolarity; and new threats from the East, including a reversal of reform in the Soviet Union or Russia that could result in a renewed major military threat, and wars between or within former Communist bloc nations. Beyond this, it was widely argued that U.S. forces should be kept in Europe so that they could be deployed to the Middle East more quickly in a crisis and because they provided Washington with leverage over its European allies that could be used in nonmilitary areas. It was widely agreed inside the foreign policy establishment that the way to ensure that all these goals would be met was to keep NATO alive and to maintain intact some of America's military infrastructure in Western Europe.

The German Question Revisited

To many observers twentieth-century European history carried an inescapable lesson: beware of unchecked German power and recognize that power from beyond the continent was needed to provide a check. It was a basic fact, political scientist John Mearsheimer wrote in 1990, that failure by Great Britain and the United States "to balance against Germany before the two world wars made war more likely in each case."[18] With the end of the Cold War the problem of assuring that German power would be balanced once again loomed large in Western thinking about the political and security architecture of Europe, as it had after World War I and World War II.

The challenge was not, as it had been in the past, to find a way to shackle a militaristic Germany. Nearly all experts agreed that Germany had finally learned its lesson and was highly unlikely to be a deliberate menace to European peace. The problem instead, as Michael Mandlebaum put it in 1990, was "fitting this large, dynamic country located in the middle of the continent into a political, military, and economic framework that is comfortable for the other Europeans and, not least, for the Germans themselves. The problem was solved after 1945 by dividing, occupying, and submerging Germany. That solution is now obsolete. A new one must be found."

In the view of most foreign policy experts, inside government and out, at least one new solution was totally out of the question: a united Germany could not be allowed to chart an independent course on security matters. Quite possibly no harm would come from such a course. "The presence of a large, independent, well-armed Germany in the center of Europe, even a Germany with its own nuclear weapons, would not necessarily lead to catastrophe," wrote Mandlebaum. But the prospect of German power producing new tensions could not be ruled out. Although the Germans "have been unimpeachably peaceful and democratic since 1945," Mandlebaum noted, "the recollections of their neighbors reach back before that time. Rightly or wrongly, other Europeans are palpably nervous about the prospect of German unification, because of the painful memories of the past and the uncertainties surrounding the future of a Germany acting as an independent great power."[19]

This was certainly true of the Russians, who had suffered most at the hands of Germany in World War II.[20] During the 1990 U.S.-Soviet negotiations over the unification of Germany, Soviet leaders often invoked history in expressing their unease at the prospect of a united Europe. At a February ninth meeting with Secretary of State James Baker, Gorbachev spoke of his country's deep fear of Germany and of the tens of millions who had died in World War II. He and Soviet Foreign Minister Eduard Shevardnadze, also at the meeting, expressed their concern that a unified Germany would create instability and uncertainty in Europe, and that future German leaders could turn more assertive after unification. Gorbachev warned that any new move toward German nationalism after unification could produce a parallel nationalistic response in the Soviet Union.

Ultimately, a key reason the Soviets were willing to tolerate a unified Germany remaining in NATO was because they accepted the long-standing idea that alliance membership could serve as a pacifier of Germany. This idea was implicit in a rhetorical question Baker posed in the February ninth meeting: "Would you prefer to see a united Germany outside of NATO and with no U.S. forces, perhaps with its own nuclear weapons? Or would you prefer a unified Germany to be tied to NATO, with assurances that NATO's jurisdiction would not shift one inch eastward from its present position?"[21]

In the early 1950s there had been wide agreement in both Europe and the United States that a rearmed Germany would be destabilizing in the absence of deep transatlantic ties, and that U.S. troops in Europe were the most important manifestation of such ties. In the early 1990s many analysts showed an acute awareness of the dual purpose that U.S. troops in Germany had served. As a report on the future of NATO by the Johns Hopkins Foreign Policy Institute stated: "The U.S. presence reassured the French and British, and even the Soviets, that German militarism would be unlikely to reemerge, just as it reassured Germany that it could remain a non-nuclear and peaceful power, despite the nuclear weapons and huge conventional armies arrayed against it."[22]

From this premise it was a small step to argue that a U.S. troop presence would remain a prerequisite to European stability after the Cold War. Another study by the Johns Hopkins Foreign Policy Institute, a "Policy Consensus Report" that was endorsed by a wide range of analysts, ranging from the hawkish former diplomat Paul Nitze to the liberal Congressman Lee Hamilton, stated: "A military withdrawal from Europe would result in a substantial devaluation of U.S. policy influence in Europe and would risk the end of the stability provided, in part, by the U.S. commitment to European security. A leadership vacuum could result. This would place great pressure on the Federal Republic of Germany to assume a leadership role in European security and create corresponding concerns in European countries, West and East."[23] Thus, as former defense secretary Harold Brown argued in May 1992, NATO's "main purpose should be what it has been before: namely, to reassure Europeans that the United States has a commitment to their security and a corresponding influence in their security matters, and that no single country will dominate Europe. That is a code phrase for Germany."[24]

While non-governmental national security analysts talked openly of the problems posed by Germany in the new Europe, officials from the Bush Administration were exceedingly circumspect in discussing this issue. During the negotiations over German unification, national security advisor Brent Scowcroft was asked by UPI reporter Helen Thomas whether NATO's new mission was to "keep the Germans down." Scowcroft denied this, repeating Bush's phrase that "the enemy is unpredictability. The enemy is instability."[25] His answer, of course, begged the question of who or what might cause unpredictability and instability.[26]

Commenting on the U.S. troop presence in Europe, General John Galvin, head of the U.S. European command, gingerly told Congress in 1992: "I do not think it is a stabilizer in the sense that anybody believes, right now, that the Germans are some kind of military danger. That is not the point." But in the same statement, Galvin also mentioned Europe's past "history" and commented that "U.S. forces there provide a kind of glue. In other words, I am not sure at all that with the absence of U.S. forces, NATO would hold together. It might split along historic lines."[27]

Galvin's comment on U.S. forces as "glue" closely reflected the assumption, dating back to the 1950s, that a U.S.-dominated NATO was needed to bind together a historically fractious West, particularly France and Germany. "The presence of U.S. troops in Europe has served not just to defend against the Soviet threat," commented William Odom in 1992. "Those forces have also allowed NATO to serve as a substitute for a European supranational political institution."[28] John Mearsheimer predicted that "without a common Soviet threat and without America as the night watchman, Western European states will begin viewing each other with suspicion, as they did for centuries before the onset of the Cold War."[29] Other analysts suggested that NATO's adhesive faculties had served not just to dampen rivalry between the states in Europe, but also between Europe and the United States.[30]

Structural Instability

With the exception of Lawrence Eagleburger's 1989 speech on the potentially dangerous consequences of multipolarity, U.S. government officials did not tend to expand on their thinking about why the Cold War's end could cause instability in Europe. The subject was nearly impossible to address without pointing a finger at likely troublemakers such as Germany, Russia, or various ethnic groups. Thus, despite constant offhand references, there was limited public talk of any depth by U.S. officials about future European instability. Government analyses seldom were more specific than a DOD statement in January 1992 that "centuries-old fears and competing claims have emerged, rekindling historic antagonisms which again threaten European stability and integration."[31]

But a variety of outside experts, uninhibited by diplomatic niceties, talked freely of the dangers that lurked in the new Europe. Of the many commentators who began spinning pessimistic scenarios, Mearsheimer of the University of Chicago was the most systematic, focusing on why the structure of power in a multipolar Europe was likely to cause instability. Suggesting, as others did, that the United States may soon come to miss the Cold War, Mearsheimer argued that bipolarity "made Europe a simpler place in which only one point of friction—the East-West conflict—had to be managed to avoid war." An equal military balance and nuclear weapons were other elements that guaranteed stability.

As bipolarity disappeared with the end of the Cold War, Mearsheimer suggested that a return to multipolarity in Europe was a nearly certain formula for catastrophe. "The structure of power in Europe would look much like it did between the world wars, and it could well produce similar results."[32] This prognosis was grounded in a rather simple theoretical critique, well articulated by Kenneth Waltz, of how things could go awry in a multipolar system.[33]

In such a system, Waltz said, alignment and alliances tend to be unstable and states must always fear that their allies will become their enemies or that their neighbors will gang up on them. The more states there are, the more unpredictable the situation was apt to become. "Uncertainties about who threatens whom, about who will oppose whom, and about who will gain or lose from the actions of other states accelerate as the number of states increases," Waltz wrote.[34]

Beyond the dangerous structural defects of multipolarity, Mearsheimer and others predicted that the new Europe would have a profoundly unstable political geography that would, as in the unhappy past, pit Germany and Russia against each other. Historically these two nations, the most powerful in Europe, have been in almost perpetual rivalry. That rivalry erupted into warfare twice in the twentieth century and had been a central feature of the the Cold War. With Germany reunited and the Cold War over, it was widely predicted that new tensions between Russia and Germany would arise. Mearsheimer, for example, argued that a struggle in the power vacuum of Eastern Europe was nearly inevitable. The region is directly adjacent to the two countries, he observed, and "has considerable economic and strategic importance; thus trouble in Eastern Europe could offer even greater temptations to these powers than past conflicts in the Third World offered the superpowers."[35] A 1991 study on the future of NATO echoed this conclusion by saying that turmoil in Eastern Europe could push Germany toward a more interventionist foreign policy and compel it to increase its military capabilities. "A shift in Germany toward more assertive policies, in turn, could both encourage greater aggressiveness on the part of the Soviet government, as well as encourage small nations in Eastern Europe to seek protection against possible German domination by developing closer relations with the USSR."[36]

The prospect of trouble in Eastern Europe stood as one of the most dependable features of European politics. During the Cold War long-standing nationalist and ethnic aspirations in Eastern Europe had been repressed by Soviet power. In the new era it was widely expected that they would reemerge.[37]

Given the general problem of structural instability, U.S. forces in Europe were seen by many as crucial for providing psychological comfort. In the new security order, suggested Michael Mandlebaum, all European states would "need to be reassured that they need not fear sudden, disruptive, worrisome changes in the military deployments on the continent. Some military forces would be necessary to avoid the uncertainties that a power vacuum would create, uncertainties that could cause some countries to build up their armed forces simply out of fear that other countries were planning to do so."[38]

Threats from the East

Even as the Soviet bloc collapsed in disarray and U.S. officials conceded that the military threat to Europe once posed by the Warsaw Pact had essentially evaporated, overall U.S. strategic thinking continued to take into account the possibility of new threats from the East. A permanent American military presence was seen as important for balancing the power of Russia, which would remain the largest military power in Europe after the Cold War and could again pose a hegemonic threat to the continent, albeit one of lesser scope than the more powerful Soviet Union's. It was also widely argued that American troops in Europe, along with vigorous U.S. leadership in NATO, could be important in curbing instability in Central and Eastern Europe, either through providing reassurance in general or, more concretely, by backing up new security guarantees extended to young democracies in the region.

Through the early 1990s U.S. officials agreed on two things in regard to the Soviet Union, and then Russia: first, events there were moving in the right direction; second, no guarantee existed that this would continue to be the case. Even optimists conceded that it would take many years before democracy and free markets were consolidated in Russia. Until then many agreed that European security planning must continue to take into account the possibility of a renewed

threat from Russia.[39] For much of the Cold War the United States
had based its defense policies on Soviet capabilities rather than intentions, which were seen as largely unknowable. Elements of this
approach continued to shape policy in the new era. "It is an old saw,
but nonetheless true, that defense planners must focus more on capabilities than intentions," said Under Secretary Wolfowitz in April
1991. "It is not that intentions are entirely unpredictable or that we
can never place any reliance on them. But they are subject to change
in circumstances or political leadership that can take place much
more rapidly than the time it takes to build high-quality forces or
develop advanced technology."[40] In his 1992 testimony before
Congress, General John Galvin, commander of U.S. forces in Europe,
argued that he, for one, could not ignore this potential if he were to
do his job responsibly. Despite the end of communism, said Galvin,
the Russian threat "is still there" because Russia remained "the
strongest military power in Europe."[41] Discussing NATO's future in
1992, JCS chairman Colin Powell suggested that it would be unwise
to allow such might to exist without a counterweight: "We cannot
simply ignore our responsibilities as the leader of this great alliance,
go back, and let a leader in the Kremlin, whoever he may be, look
across the Kremlin wall and see no U.S. forces until he gets to Fort
Dix, New Jersey. That is very destabilizing."[42]

Although there was wide agreement on the need for a continuing
U.S. balancing role against Russia, there emerged no consensus in the
early 1990s on how the United States could harness its presence in
Western Europe to deal with instability in Eastern Europe. There was
intense disagreement, for example, on whether NATO should extend
membership to states in the former Communist bloc.[43] And the failure by the Bush and Clinton administrations to intervene in the crisis
in the former Yugoslavia in 1992 and 1993 underscored the acute
uneasiness that U.S. policymakers felt about any involvement in conflicts in the region.

Nevertheless, policymakers did believe that a deep American
engagement in Europe could be an important factor in stabilizing
Eastern Europe. While there was no consensus on the extension of
NATO membership, Bush officials played a lead role in setting up the
North Atlantic Cooperation Council (NACC) in 1991, a liaison
body to NATO that included the six former members of the Warsaw

Pact.[44] And while there was fierce debate over when and where U.S. troops should be prepared to intervene to save new democracies in the East, there was general agreement that the continued presence of U.S. forces on the continent was reassuring to Eastern European states. As Thomas M. T. Niles, assistant secretary of state for European affairs said in 1991: "Support for the U.S. presence in Europe is remarkably strong in countries of Eastern Europe, where the U.S. role is recognized as a key factor for stability."[45] German analyst Joseph Joffe offered some insight into Eastern European thinking before a congressional committee in October 1991: "The East Europeans, traditionally squeezed between Germany and Russia, want the United States on the inside almost more than anyone else."[46] Leaders of these states explicitly made this point in conversation with U.S. officials.[47]

The NATO Solution

The consensus that the United States must continue to play a balancing role in Europe after the Cold War was complemented by a widespread agreement that NATO was the best vehicle for achieving this goal. In one sense there was nothing surprising about the conviction that NATO should be kept alive indefinitely. The alliance had been founded with the explicit purpose of containing Soviet power, but it had also been seen as a way to assure a U.S. security presence in Europe and to bind Germany into the fold of Western democratic states. The collapse of the Soviet threat, by this analysis, eliminated only one of NATO's missions. NATO may no longer have been needed to "keep the Russians out," but many still believe NATO is useful for keeping the "Americans in and the Germans down."

Indeed, more than simply keeping the United States in Europe, NATO was seen as a chief means for Washington to assert its primacy over European states in the security arena and to gain leverage on a range of other issues. The alliance had always been run by the United States, as symbolized by the fact that the supreme commander of NATO forces in Europe had always been an American general.[48] Without NATO, it was argued, the United States would not only have a harder time keeping troops in Europe, but it would also lose the principal forum in which it led the West on security matters.[49]

This leadership remained important to U.S. leaders because it could be used, theoretically at least, to influence the foreign policies of Western European states in positive ways and to galvanize responses to future international emergencies.[50] In particular, Bush Administration officials harbored hopes that the NATO structure could be more explicitly adapted to handle security challenges beyond Western Europe.[51] As for leverage outside the security realm, arguments were heard that the continuation of NATO, and especially the ongoing deployment of U.S. troops, provided Washington with influence on issues such as trade.[52]

As the Warsaw Pact collapsed in late 1989 and through 1990 numerous commentators suggested that NATO's days were numbered. "It is simply not possible to sustain an alliance such as NATO without an enemy such as the Soviet Union has been," wrote Ronald Steel, expressing a widespread view.[53] Many argued that a new and more comprehensive European security organization should take NATO's place.[54] Such an arrangement, it was commonly imagined, would mean a much smaller role for the United States. After all, in an age of diminished danger from the East, why should a non–European power oversee the security affairs of European nations that were well on the road to economic integration? More bluntly, why should the Europeans allow the Americans to keep bossing them around?

Bush Administration officials never seriously entertained the idea of abolishing NATO in favor of some alternative organization. But they realized that sustaining NATO would be no easy task. "The Cold War alliance structure was fastened together primarily with the glue of anti-communism," acknowledged Baker aide Robert Zoellick in September 1990. "As the perception of that threat recedes, neither the United States nor Europe can take these associations for granted."[55]

Secretary Baker and other U.S. officials devoted enormous energy to keeping NATO alive, fighting what would turn out to be a winning battle. An important part of this effort focused on resisting European moves toward greater independence in the security realm. U.S. officials believed that such moves would run the risk of undermining the all-important transatlantic tie that ensured America's continuing role as a continental balancer. They thus warily eyed plans, announced in December 1991, to boost the profile of the Western

European Union (WEU), the long-dormant defense arm of the EC. And they were unenthusiastic about a French-German plan to establish an independent defense relationship and create a joint military force of roughly thirty thousand troops. "If it is an attempt to fashion a security role for the European community in order to deal with circumstances in which NATO is not involved, I see nothing wrong with it," Scowcroft said of the Franco-German Corps plan in May 1992. "If it is designed to compete with and ultimately supplant NATO at some point, then the U.S. has a problem. . . . Since NATO represents the American voice, it is essential that it be preserved."[56]

The Bush Administration's success in keeping NATO alive was a major diplomatic accomplishment. But it almost certainly would not have been possible in the absence of a consensus in both the United States and Europe that new threats to European stability demanded that America continue to play the role of balancer. It is a testament to the durability of the consensus that at no time in the early 1990s was there anything resembling a fundamental debate, on either side of the Atlantic, over the need for a continuing U.S. troop presence. Even during the war in the former Yugoslavia, when NATO faced harsh questions about its relevance, the broader consensus in favor of U.S. engagement endured and in fact was strengthened by the inability of the Europeans to cope with the problem by themselves. The lesson to many was that if the United States didn't spearhead responses to major continental security challenges, nobody would. "We are looking for the United States to take the lead again," William Van Eckehen, secretary general of the WEU, said in May 1993. "Our European credibility has fallen very low."[57]

The Clinton Administration had no intention of challenging this consensus when it took power. Clinton and his aides share the wariness of Bush officials about the instability that might follow any withdrawal of U.S. forces from Europe.[58] The Pentagon's *Bottom-Up Review*, completed by September 1, 1993, concluded that the permanent size of U.S. forces in Europe should be around 100,000, a number not significantly different than what the Bush Administration had envisioned.[59]

During its first year the Clinton Administration showed no interest in overhauling the security architecture of Europe. Instead, Secretary Christopher heaped familiar praise on NATO for its indispensable role in maintaining the transatlantic bond. "The U.S. commitment to European security will continue to be expressed first and foremost throught NATO," he affirmed in a June 10, 1993, speech to NATO leaders.[60] The Clinton Administration has slightly distinguished its stance on European security issues by giving greater emphasis to ties with the countries of the East through the North Atlantic Cooperation Council (NACC), a stepped-up liaison program called "Partnership for Peace," and by exploring ways that both NACC and NATO can interface with the collective security bodies of the U.N. and CSCE.[61] The Clinton Administration has also given greater backing to the drive for European unity and shown more willingness to countenance European independence on security matters, encouraging the allies to take a greater leadership role in handling problems in their own neighborhood. At the January 1994 NATO summit, for example, U.S. officials backed a plan that would allow NATO assets to be used in European operations that did not involve U.S. troops.[62]

Still, it would be wrong to say that the administration's actions during its first year constituted a fundamental departure from the Bush Administration's approach to European security. Like their predecessors, Clinton officials have sought the best of both worlds: They want new collective security measures that will bring stability to the former Communist bloc but resist anything that might dilute the cohesion of NATO or commit the United States to defending the new democracies. They publicly support more European independence on security matters, but privately worry that too much independence might fray the transatlantic link. They embrace the principle of continued U.S. leadership in the new Europe but, like the Bush team, are wary of any sacrifice that such leadership might entail.

These divided sentiments were on display in regard to Bosnia, where the new administration, like the old, eschewed military involvement. In a February 1993 news conference, Secretary Christopher commented that the "continuing destruction of a new U.N. member state challenges the principle that internationally recognized borders should not be altered by force" and said that "no great power can dismiss the likely consequences of letting a Balkan conflict rage." The conflict in Bosnia, declared Christopher, "tests our willingness and that of our allies to help our institutions of collective security, such as NATO, evolve in ways that meet the demands of this new age."[63]

Despite these pronouncements the Clinton Administration did not intervene militarily during 1993 to stop the fighting in Bosnia, and its intervention in early 1994 was limited to the use of air power. There are numerous reasons for this restraint, including the primacy of the administration's domestic agenda and uncertainty about whether intervention could be effective. But at a fundamental level U.S. inaction in the Balkans, during 1993 as well as 1992, reflected the absence of any consensus in the foreign policy establishment that the United States should play an activist role in guaranteeing security in Europe's eastern areas.

Considered within the long-term trajectory of U.S. foreign policy, the limits on U.S. involvement in European security matters observed by both the Clinton and Bush administrations are readily understandable. The chief rationale for U.S. engagement in Europe during two world wars and the Cold War was to prevent dangerous concentrations of power that could eventually threaten the United States. This fear, along with a desire to prevent tensions between the major powers that could lead to conflict, has continued to guide U.S. policy since the Cold War's end. For all its horror, the war in the former Yugoslavia has not been seen as a prelude to a new continent-wide hegemonic enterprise or as leading to conflict among the major powers. In the future it is likely that American policymakers will continue to resist involvement in European crises or wars that similarly fail to present either of these threats.

Stabilizing Asia

In East Asia, more so even than in Europe, a firm consensus developed among both government officials and mainstream foreign policy analysts that the United States needed to retain its position of primacy. That position is rooted in a tradition that extends back to the beginning of the twentieth century. Years before the first major U.S. intervention in European affairs, American officials had accepted the need to use U.S. power to maintain an equilibrium in East Asia and prevent any one power from dominating the region.

As in Europe, the end of the Cold War did not alter the fundamental U.S. objective of maintaining stability in East Asia. On the contrary, the potential for insecurity and conflict was considered more serious in Asia than in Europe. American officials pointed to several dangers in justifying continued U.S. primacy in the region: the destabilizing impact of Japan charting a more independent security course; the structural instability of a region with little history of multilateral cooperation but growing military capabilities; and the remaining presence in East Asia of several Communist states.

Fears of Japan

The concerns surrounding Japanese power in East Asia very much parallel those regarding Germany in Europe. "Without American ships and planes in the area Japan might well feel the need to increase its own military forces to counterbalance the Soviet Union and China, its two nuclear armed neighbors," predicted Michael Mandlebaum in 1990. "This would spread unease through East and Southeast Asia."[64] Analysts I. M. Destler and Michael Nacht argued the same point. The U.S. security presence in East Asia, they said, effectively safeguarded Japanese security interests in the region and thus "dissuaded the Japanese from acquiring power projection forces of their own." As long as American protection continued, it would quiet those elements in Japanese society who argued that Japan needs to begin building military might and political power "commensurate with its economic might." If the United States withdrew from Asia, a major and destabilizing surge in Japan's regional power would follow, Destler and Nacht predicted.[65]

Japan's neighbors, more so than Germany's, have had difficulty forgetting World War II. And many analysts have argued that Japan's inability to come to grips with its past aggression is the reason. Former Singapore prime minister Lee Kuan Yew has commented that "Unfortunately, unlike the Germans, Japan has not been open and frank about the atrocities and horrors committed in World War II. Because Japan avoids talk about it, the victims suspect and fear that Japan does not think these acts are wrong, and that there is no genuine Japanese change of heart." Lee's comment came in 1993, well after Japan's prime minister Toshiki Kaifu publicly expressed Japan's contrition for World War II for the first time on May 3, 1991, and after Tokyo had made other efforts to confront the legacy of Japanese aggression. Lee concluded that "fear of Japan's remilitarization is more emotional than rational. But this fear is a reality that influences attitudes in many East Asian countries not only toward the remote eventuality of a Japanese invasion but also toward the more likely possibility of Japan assuming a wider security role in the region. Unfortunately, there has been no open discussion among East Asians of their secret doubts, suspicions and fears."[66]

The possibility of tensions between a remilitarized Japan and its immediate neighbors, South Korea and China, was treated with particular concern as the Cold War ended. In both countries substantial resentment lingers of a Japan that rolled over much of northeast Asia in the 1930s, leaving enormous carnage in its wake. Higher levels of Japanese defense preparations as part of a more independent security stance would not be viewed with equanimity in either of these countries, many suggest. As the Singapore defense minister Yeo Ning Hong said in early 1992, "The Chinese and the Koreans, who have not forgotten the past atrocities inflicted on their people, [will be provoked] to build up their respective armed forces to counter and contain Japanese rearmament."[67]

Some analysts have argued that the greatest danger lies in a struggle for regional dominance between Japan and China. As China's economic growth continues, the argument holds, it will come to challenge Japan in all spheres of power and the stage will be set for a dangerous confrontation.[68] "East Asian traditions suggest that China will be unwilling to accept a subordinate role to Japan," suggested Gerald Segal. "China believes that the natural order of international relations in East Asia is for China to dominate. . . . China will expect Japan to accept a subordinate role—not to mention to pay for the evils done to China in the past century."[69] And Japan, in turn, could be expected to respond assertively to a growing economic and military challenge from its huge authoritarian neighbor. In the absence of an American presence in East Asia, many worry that the negative dynamics of this relationship could be drastically amplified.

Besides sparking a military competition in northeast Asia, one that might lead Japan and South Korea to acquire nuclear weapons, it has been further suggested that a U.S. military withdrawal that led to a rise in Japanese power could destabilize southeast Asia. "The feelings of ASEAN [Association of Southeast Asian Nations] members toward Japan are colored by memories of World War II and resentment of domination by other Asians," wrote Japanese international affairs analyst Tatsumi Okabe in 1992.[70] None of these nations would tolerate Japan taking over America's leadership responsibilities. In 1988, for example, Southeast Asian nations reacted negatively to a suggestion by Secretary of the Navy James Webb that Japan patrol sea lanes into the Indian Ocean.[71] As the Cold War ended, Predictions abounded that regional security conditions would deteriorate and that the ASEAN nations would step up their military preparations if Japan were thrust into an Asian leadership role.[72]

To this unsettling picture of possible instability, analysts added another element: the potential for an outright U.S.-Japanese rivalry. In the 1980s relations between the United States and Japan grew increasingly testy amid escalating trade disputes and cultural clashes.[73] But what helped keep these tensions under control, many experts believed, were the strong security ties between the two nations. "The American alliance with Japan represents more than shared military purposes, structures, and operations; it is the political 'glue' that binds the nations together in ways that go well beyond traditional strategic concerns," argued Asia expert and former government official Alan D. Romberg.[74]

If the United States dramatically scaled back its military presence in East Asia in response to the end of the Cold War, its heavily paternalistic alliance with Japan could be expected to wither. The consequences, in the pessimistic view, could be not only Japan's emergence as an independent military power but a deterioration of overall relations between Washington and Tokyo as well. Down the line, the scenario went, Japan and the United States—the two most powerful states in the world—could find themselves in a political-military rivalry fueled by trade tensions and growing nationalism on both sides of the Pacific.[75]

Structural Instability

As in Europe, Bush Administration officials were often vague in describing the exact sources of future instability in Asia, since doing so would mean identifying potential troublemakers by name. But they left little doubt that such instability could span the entire region. In describing the need for a permanent post–Cold War U.S. military presence in Asia, Admiral Charles Larson, commander in chief of the U.S. Pacific Command, commented in early 1992 that there are "territorial disputes and historic animosities between nations, religious, ethnic, and culture groups. Historically, these tensions have served as flashpoints for conflict—some occurring now."[76]

Regional experts explained these various problems in greater detail. The most salient territorial dispute in the area involves the Spratley and Paracel Island chains in the South China Sea, which are said to contain oil deposits and are claimed by several Asian states including China, Taiwan, Malaysia, Vietnam, and the Philippines.[77] Japan and China disagree about the status of the Diaoyutai Islands in the East China Sea. Japan and Russia are at odds over Russian occupation of the Kurile Islands of northern Japan.[78] Thailand, Cambodia, and Vietnam have disputes in the Gulf of Thailand.[79]

The potential for ethnic conflict is smaller in East Asia than in other parts of the world, but it is still significant. As one analyst observed, "Rivalry between Malays and Chinese could complicate Singapore's relations with either Indonesia or Malaysia. The prominent role of overseas Chinese in many Southeast Asian countries, both Communist and non-Communist, has been a significant irritant in those nations' relationships with China. The discrimination encountered by Koreans in Japan could easily become an issue in Toyko's relationship with Seoul."[80]

Finally, Japan's legacy of aggression is not the only basis for animosity in the region. China is also widely feared. For Southeast Asian nations, it is a geographically closer threat than Japan, and one that history suggests can also not be ignored. As Tatsumi Okabe has written: "ASEAN's fear of Southeast Asia being placed within China's sphere of influence stems from a number of factors, including China's continued adherence to socialism, vivid recollections of trouble perpetrated by Chinese-affiliated Communist guerrillas, haunting historic memories of China's dominance, and especially misgivings about the intentions of a country whose population exceeds one billion."[81] China and Vietnam went to war in 1979. China and Taiwan have been in a Cold War for decades. China's military buildup and bid to annex the Spratley and Paracel Islands in the early 1990s has done nothing to quell concerns about Beijing's regional ambitions.

Fears of instability in East Asia have been fed by ominous signs that a new arms race is under way in the region. Between 1985 and 1991 nearly every East Asian country increased its annual defense expenditures in huge leaps.[82] In the early 1990s nations such as Thailand, Singapore, Taiwan, Malaysia, Brunei, and Indonesia began acquiring billions of dollars' worth of new conventional weaponry. Among developing states, countries in East Asia bought 44 percent of all imports of major arms in 1990.[83] Military equipment that could be used to project power, such as naval vessels and transport planes, has featured prominently in these new purchases.[84] China's military buildup has been widely seen as reflecting a shift in military strategy that emphasizes preparations to fight in regional conflicts on its periphery.[85] Among Southeast Asian countries, efforts to build up air and naval forces have signaled a shift away from defense postures that had previously emphasized domestic security.[86]

As the Cold War ended, instability in East Asia was viewed with particular concern because, in contrast to Europe, the region lacks two crucial elements for regulating its own security affairs: a natural balance of power and a tradition of multilateral cooperation.

In Europe the potential exists that Germany's power can be offset by strong neighbors such as Britain, France, and Russia. But power imbalances are a natural feature of East Asia's geopolitical geography.[87] Japan's economic might dwarfs that of its neighbors. China's power is also grossly disproportionate to that of many countries in the region.

Unlike Western Europe, East Asia has never had strong regional organizations. The most significant regional organization, the Association of Southeast Asian Nations (ASEAN), does not include Japan and until recently never moved beyond limited economic cooperation. A new organization founded in 1989, the Asia-Pacific Economic Cooperation (APEC), which encompasses all the ASEAN nations plus the United States, Canada, Japan, South Korea, Australia, and New Zealand, remained weak and ill-defined in the early 1990s.[88] Statecraft in the region is undeveloped because of the historic lack of a core group of near-equal powers.

During the postwar era the glue of security relations in East Asia had not been regional cooperation but assorted bilateral security ties with the United States. Japan, South Korea, Taiwan, and the Philippines all forged formal defense relationships with the United States. The United States also had strong ties to Thailand, Singapore, and Indonesia. As the Cold War ended, Bush Administration officials believed, as had officials since the Truman and Eisenhower administrations, that it was unrealistic to imagine a comprehensive collective security organization in East Asia. As Assistant Secretary of State Richard Solomon said in March 1991, "East Asia is not Europe; it is far more diverse culturally and politically, and the Cold War did not weld the region into two opposing blocs. We see the region's problems addressed more appropriately through existing institutions or ad hoc coalitions of states rather than through a large and unwieldy region–wide collective security forum."[89]

Unrepentant Communists

At the same time that U.S. officials worried about the inherent instability of post–Cold War Asia, they continued to believe that a U.S. presence was required to deal with elements of the Cold War still lingering in that region. East Asia, they emphasized, was home to the most powerful of the remaining Communist states in the world, including Vietnam, China, and North Korea. While neither China nor Vietnam were seen as immediate threats in the 1990s, North Korea was still viewed as a major menace to South Korea.

During the 1970s and 1980s South Korea's economy had grown rapidly, dwarfing that of its Communist neighbor. By 1990 South Korea's GNP was ten times larger than that of North Korea and its population was nearly twice as great. By 1990, moreover, North Korea had been essentially abandoned by its traditional patrons, China and the Soviet Union. Nevertheless, U.S. officials argued that the more than thirty thousand troops stationed in South Korea would be indispensable for its security well into the 1990s. They noted that North Korea had significant numerical advantages in key elements of military equipment and argued further that it had restructured its military forces in the 1980s to make them more mobile and offensive-oriented. They portrayed the North Korean leadership as unpredictable and belligerent. "In the final analysis," commented General Robert W. Riscassi, commander of U.S. forces in Korea, "successful deterrence rests on the counterbalance provided by U.S. forces."[90]

Beyond the conventional imbalance of forces on the peninsula, U.S. officials worried about North Korean efforts to develop nuclear weapons, especially after the Gulf War, when it was discovered that Iraq had been closer to this goal than anyone previously had suspected. "North Korea's nuclear program is our greatest security concern in Northeast Asia," said CIA director Robert Gates in early 1992.[91] A nuclear weapon in the hands of North Korea, it was believed, could have far-reaching destabilizing effects. The prospect of South Korea, or even Japan, developing its own nuclear weapons in response could not be ruled out.

America as Balancer

The likelihood of post–Cold War instability in East Asia, and the lack of indigenous mechanisms for curbing it, underpinned the consensus among U.S. foreign policy experts, both in government and out, that the United States should maintain its Cold War position of primacy in the region. As with Europe, the Bush Administration was less than forthcoming about its geopolitical calculations and generally refused to engage publicly in the kind of pessimistic speculation about East Asia's future that was common among independent experts. An exception to this could be found in the statements of Pentagon leaders, who were willing to speak frankly about their fears of instability in Asia. Under Secretary of Defense Paul Wolfowitz, for example, freely acknowledged that a long-standing purpose of U.S. forces in Asia, quite apart from their Cold War mission, had been to play the role of regional balancer and ensure that "no single power assumed a predominant military posture." In considering the consequences of a U.S. withdrawal from the region, Wolfowitz said in April 1990, "one question we must ask ourselves is, who else could play that balancing role? Who would we want to play that role?" Embedded in the question was an implicit answer: regional hegemony by a resurgent Japan would be unacceptable to both the United States and to Japan's neighbors. Wolfowitz offered this prediction: "A reduced U.S. commitment to the region—whether perceived or real—would create a security vacuum that other countries would be tempted, or might feel compelled, to fill. This could lead to regional arms races and possible military confrontation." A major report that Wolfowitz helped produce on the future of the U.S. security presence in East Asia concluded that substantial reductions could safely be made in U.S. deployments there as the Cold War ended. But it argued that, ultimately, the United States would have to continue indefinitely to serve as the final guarantor of security in the region.[92]

The Clinton Administration has never questioned the argument that U.S. forces should continue to play a balancing role in East Asia. "By virtue of history and geography, the United States is the one major power in Asia not viewed as a threat," Winston Lord said in March 1993 at his confirmation hearing to be assistant secretary of state for East Asian and Pacific affairs. "Virtually every country wants us to maintain our security presence. While balance-of-power considerations have declined in the wake of the Cold War, they remain relevant as Asian-Pacific nations contemplate their fates. Each one harbors apprehensions about one or more of its neighbors. A precipitous American military withdrawal would magnify these concerns. Add the increasing resources available for weapons purchases in the rapidly growing Asian nations, and there is a recipe for escalating arms races and future confrontations that could threaten U.S. interests."[93] The Pentagon's *Bottom-Up Review* concluded that roughly 100,000 troops, the same number of forces as in Europe, should be maintained indefinitely in East Asia.[94]

While largely continuing Bush polices, the Clinton Administration did seek to change U.S. policy toward East Asia in two respects. First, in accord with its greater emphasis on promoting U.S. prosperity through foreign policy, the administration expressed a determination to pay more attention to a region with which the United States now has over 40 percent of its trade; it vowed to better ties with Japan and seek more open markets both there and in other East Asian countries.[95] Second, the administration ended long-standing U.S. opposition to the establishment of a new regional collective security organization. "Asia is not Europe," Lord reminded Congress in March. "We do not envisage a formal CSCE-type structure." But he emphasized that there now existed a historic opportunity for security cooperation in the region that should not be wasted. "For the first time in this century, there are no adversarial fault lines among the great powers in Northeast Asia: the United States, Japan, Russia, and

China. . . . It is time to step up regional discussions on future security issues."[96]

The steps toward collective security taken in 1993 were modest and unfolded within ASEAN's so-called Post-Ministerial Conference (PMC) during July. This forum included seven Asia-Pacific nations in addition to the original six ASEAN states. The July meeting in Singapore, in which Secretary Christopher was a key participant, produced a plan to establish a Regional Security Forum. American officials, quoted anonymously, said they envisioned it as functioning as an Asian CSCE.[97]

The existence of a collective dialogue among so many states of the region, undertaken with U.S. blessing, constituted an important, even historic, development. But U.S. officials stressed that it did not alter basic post–Cold War U.S. strategy toward East Asia. "Some in the United States have been reluctant to enter into a regional security dialogue in Asia," Clinton said in late July. "They fear it would seem a pretext for American withdrawal from the area, but I see this as a way to supplement our alliances and forward military presence, not to supplant them."[98]

In other words, collective security could be helpful in East Asia, as it could be in Europe. But in both regions American military power continued to be seen by U.S. officials as the ultimate guarantor of security.

Blueprint for Primacy: The Defense Planning Guidance

The assumptions that guided America's post–Cold War strategy were brought sharply and publicly into focus in March 1992 when excerpts from a secret five-year Defense Planning Guidance paper were leaked to the press. The document, a preliminary draft prepared by Wolfowitz's office, explicitly spelled out the geopolitical thinking that had long been implied by administration statements. It called, in short, for continued U.S. global primacy after the Cold War.

Drawing on deeply rooted traditions of U.S. foreign policy doctrine, the document said that the United States should seek to prevent the reemergence of a new rival in Europe and Asia by stopping "any hostile power from dominating a region whose resources would, under consolidated control, be sufficient to generate global power."

The chief means to this end would be a robust U.S. hegemony that guaranteed security in critical regions of the world. The United States must "show the leadership necessary to establish and protect a new order that holds the promise of convincing potential competitors that they need not aspire to a greater role or pursue a more aggressive posture to protect their legitimate self-interests."

The document made clear what had been frequently hinted at—that the United States would consider enhanced regional military roles for Germany and Japan to be destabilizing. Overall, U.S. policy toward the advanced industrial nations would be "to discourage them from challenging our leadership or seeking to overturn the established political and economic order."

In Western Europe this approach would mean, as had often been publicly suggested, preserving NATO "as the primary instrument of Western defense and security, as well as the channel for U.S. influence and participation in European security affairs." The document reaffirmed that the United States supported the goal of European integration but said bluntly that Washington must "prevent the emergence of European-only security arrangements, which would undermine NATO."

The recommendation regarding East Asia was also familiar. The United States must maintain its status "as a military power of the first magnitude in the area. This will enable the U.S. to continue to contribute to regional security and stability by acting as a balancing force and prevent emergence of a vacuum or a regional hegemon." Japan and Korea, the document suggested, should be discouraged from stepping up their security role in the region.[99]

The release of the Defense Planning Guidance precipitated a wave of criticism about the administration's overreadiness to act unilaterally in security policy. Top government officials quickly backed away from the document, insisting that it was only a preliminary draft. Within two months a new draft was leaked to the press, which contained a major change of tone. The unilateralist thrust of the original draft was eliminated, as was much of the blunt geopolitical language. Far more emphasis was now placed on international military cooperation.[100]

But despite this overhaul the general thrust of the document was not fundamentally altered. The new document continued to intimate that Germany and Japan could eventually become rivals of the United States by retaining the statement that any nation combining "modern defense, industrial and technical capacity, and a sizable population" would be capable of generating a global threat. However, it played down the outright talk of U.S. hegemony over the industrialized nations, saying instead that a primary U.S. task is to carry "long-standing alliances into the new era" and to continue to "build a democratic security community." The revised language was less muscular, but the message was the same: the United States hoped to maintain the basic security framework of the Cold War—an arrangement, of course, that had been predicated on American primacy.[101]

The argument for America as a lone superpower was also said to have been made in a Pentagon study undertaken in summer 1991, which had concluded that America should seek to retain its status as the world's most powerful state. This study was said to have suggested that one of the principal risks to U.S. security in the post–Cold War era came from the possibility of "Germany and/or Japan disconnecting from multilateral security and economic arrangements and pursuing an independent course."[102]

Defense Secretary Cheney, trying to defuse the controversy surrounding the initial draft of the Defense Planning Guidance, wrote a *New York Times* op-ed article in an effort to explain the administration's position. Cheney scoffed at the charge that the United States intended to "go it alone" in the new era: "Far from being against greater efforts by our allies, we regard such efforts as essential. We have pressed our allies in Europe and Asia to take on a larger share of responsibility."[103]

This point begged the issue, however. As any seasoned observer of alliance politics knew, the United States had always wanted its allies to do more in the security realm. It was greater independence on their part that Washington opposed. And Bush Administration policy statements on the future of security arrangements in Europe and Asia were consistent in hinting at the dangers of such independence.

Cheney did not contest the idea that the United States should remain the ultimate guarantor of its allies' security in the post–Cold War era. Nor did he or any other administration official back away from the goal of preventing the reemergence of new global powers. Cheney, in fact, had alluded to that goal in public a few weeks before the Defense Planning Guidance had been leaked to the press. In selling the 1993 Pentagon budget, in January and February, he had strongly emphasized that the U.S. forward presence was aimed at preventing vacuums from arising in Europe or Asia that new hegemonic powers might be tempted to fill.[104] Not a single member of Congress had openly questioned this logic. On March 22, with the furor of the Defense Planning Guidance still raging, Cheney again illustrated this thinking in testimony to the House Foreign Affairs Committee, referring to the situation in Asia: "If we were to withdraw our forces from the Western Pacific, take everything out of Japan, it would leave a vacuum. I would expect sooner or later somebody may try to fill that vacuum. People not even tempted at this point, or who would not even consider the possibility of building significant forces because we are there, would feel that perhaps for their own purposes they have to build up and others might react."[105] Nobody on the committee challenged this point.

Notably, while the initial Defense Planning Guidance draft was strongly criticized, the revised version, containing many of the same points, was not. Many foreign policy experts outside of government, Democrat and Republican alike, shared Pentagon fears that new independence on the part of allies in Europe and Asia could cause instability.

The flap over the Defense Planning Guidance underscored the intense sensitivity that surrounded the issue of continued U.S. primacy over the industrial nations. While most foreign policy elites in Europe and Asia, as in the United States, supported American post–Cold War primacy on security matters, the issue made for explosive domestic politics. In nations like Japan and Germany, where national pride was increasing along with economic power, the presence of large contingents of U.S. troops—combined with the perception of American paternalism—was seen as objectionable in some quarters. Outright talk by Washington of continued hegemony did not help matters. In the United States the issue was often seen in terms of cost and fairness: Why should U.S. taxpayers foot the bill for a security blanket for wealthy allies who were beating the United States in global economic competition?

The unwillingness of U.S. government leaders to talk frankly about the rationales behind American security policy in Europe and

Asia has complicated the task of building public support for post–Cold War foreign policy. U.S. officials have used idealist rhetoric to sell a global engagement predicated largely on realist assumptions. Walter Lippmann, reflecting on America's entry into World War I, believed that one of Woodrow Wilson's great mistakes had been his failure to explain clearly to Americans the geopolitical calculations that drove U.S. policy. The consequence, said Lippmann, had been the public's failure to understand what was at stake when a new European threat arose in the 1930s. Had Lippmann been alive in the early 1990s he surely would have leveled the same charge, couched in far broader terms, at both the Bush and Clinton administrations.

A NEW TURBULENCE: THIRD WORLD THREATS

American officials have been much more candid when it comes to U.S. policy toward the Third World. Here the specter of instability seems not only more real but it can be invoked at will by American officials without any diplomatic awkwardness, since most potential troublemakers are already on America's enemies list. Even more so than potential instability in Europe and Asia, it was the prospect of trouble in remote regions of the world that the Bush Administration, and later the Clinton Administration, most often cited to justify continued U.S. global primacy. American foreign policy analysts argued that the end of the Cold War could have the effect of making the Third World less stable while not reducing U.S. interests there; that the proliferation of high-tech weapons, including weapons of mass destruction, in the Third World posed new threats to the United States and its allies; and that only the United States had the military power and political will to enforce order in a developing world where traditional territorial aggression would remain a fact of life. After August 1990 the Iraqi invasion of Kuwait was cited as evidence to substantiate all of these arguments.

As the Cold War wound down it was widely hoped that the Third World would become a less violent place. After all, much of the warfare in developing countries through the postwar period had been part of the broader East-West rivalry and had been actively fueled by the superpowers. Predictions abounded in the late 1980s that not only would conflict decline, but that the overall quantity of military hardware transferred to the Third World would drop as Washington and Moscow stopped supplying various client states and insurgent groups. At the same, some suggested that the Third World would become less important to the United States because there would no longer be a need to fear Communist gains in otherwise unimportant regions.[106]

Events at the end of the 1980s gave reason for optimism. As the Cold War concluded, diplomatic settlements were achieved in the blood-soaked nations of Angola, Afghanistan, El Salvador, Nicaragua, and Cambodia. In just a few years the primary postwar goal of U.S. security policy in the Third World—containing or toppling Soviet-backed regimes while assisting friends who took a strong anti-Com munist stance—was rendered irrelevant, as was U.S. planning, much in vogue during the 1980s, to counter any possible thrust of Soviet military power into the Persian Gulf region. Measured against the standards set over four decades, the Third World might reasonably be seen as moving in the direction of greater stability. And it appeared as well that the likelihood of armed U.S. intervention in the Third World was decreasing, since that intervention during the postwar period had almost always been motivated by Cold War concerns.

But Bush Administration officials offered a different assessment. They warned both of the Third World's enduring volatility and of its continued importance to the United States. "A lessening of tension between the Soviet Union and the United States will not in itself lead to the resolution of regional conflicts," argued Under Secretary of State Robert Kimmitt in early 1990. "Indigenous factors—often beyond U.S. or Soviet control—will affect the course of such conflicts. As wealth and power continue to diffuse, and as sophisticated arms become available to irresponsible governments, the potential for regional conflict outside of the U.S.-Soviet rivalry has grown. . . . Instability and regional conflicts will pose an extensive threat to U.S. interests for the foreseeable future."[107]

Some analysts, both in and and out of government, added a further refinement to this train of thought: the end of the Cold War, they said, could actually worsen regional tensions because the super-powers would no longer be imposing political-military restraints on their clients.[108] As Baker aide Robert Zoellick commented in September 1990, the superpowers "maintained a rough capability to

restrain clients, or at least prevent an escalation to the verge of obliter-
ation."[109] The sudden freedom on the part of potential Third World
troublemakers could result in new aggression, officials argued. In particular, they worried that withdrawal by the superpowers from various regions could tempt aspiring local hegemons to fill the resulting
power vacuums. In addition to this, some analysts predicted that a
withdrawal of foreign assistance to suddenly unimportant Cold War
client states could result in increasing internal violence—especially
ethnic conflict—in the Third World as central governments lost their
ability to govern.[110] Others pointed to growing economic, demographic, and environmental pressures in predicting increased disorder
and violence.[111]

Mounting instability mattered to the United States for several reasons, it was argued. First, by 1990, over 35 percent of U.S. exports
were to Third World countries. Second, Western dependence on
Persian Gulf oil was expected to increase in the 1990s and beyond.
Third, a breakdown of order in the Third World could mean an
increase in terrorism, illegal immigration, and drug trafficking.[112]

The proliferation of dangerous weapons, both conventional and
unconventional, was seen as a major factor fueling new instability in
the Third World and as posing direct security threats to the United
States and its allies. In the view of most security experts, Third World
wars of the future could well resemble the First World's wars of the
past. "In the new high-tech era, these may not be 'brush-fire wars'
any longer," said NSC aide Robert Gates in June 1990. "We may
sometimes call them 'low-intensity conflicts,' but they can be pretty
high-intensity if you're in the middle of them."[113] Gates recited a
grim litany to substantiate this point: twenty nations in the world
were capable of producing chemical weapons, and many were developing biological weapons; nuclear proliferation was a continuing
problem, with such states as Iraq in hot pursuit of the bomb; and perhaps most alarming of all, numerous Third World countries either
possessed ballistic missiles or were striving to develop them. By the
year 2000 Gates estimated that fifteen Third World countries might
be capable of producing such missiles. Secretary Baker, speaking in
the spring of 1989, warned that the "spread of these missiles will put
states in volatile regions on hair triggers and will increase their incentives to acquire or deploy chemical or nuclear weapons. Can there be

any doubt that such developments constitute an increasing danger to world peace?"[114] Other officials stressed the growing conventional arsenals of Third World powers, observing that many nations in the Middle East now had larger tank fleets than nations in Europe.[115]

Outside of government, independent experts were also sounding the alarm about the advanced weaponry that was fast becoming available to Third World governments. To many, this development had replaced the U.S.-Soviet arms race as the central security challenge faced by the global community.[116] Some even saw it as more dangerous than the superpower competition, since unstable Third World states could be more likely to employ their frightening arsenals.[117] Iraq, for example, during its war with Iran in the 1980s, became one of the first states to use chemical weapons since World War I.

As in Europe and Asia, the United States could not shirk its responsibility to keep order in the Third World, U.S. experts argued. Indeed, whereas it was conceivable—albeit not wholly desirable in Washington—to have other major industrialized nations play a greater role in policing their own regions, no one could be expected to police the Third World regions. "U.S. forces are the final guarantee of regional stability in many areas vital to the United States," said Kimmitt.[118] Iraq's invasion of Kuwait in August 1990 was cited by Bush Administration officials as a vindication of their predictions of post–Cold War threats arising in the Third World and their argument that U.S. primacy was required to cope with these threats.

The Clinton Administration did not offer a significantly more optimistic picture of the Third World upon taking office. In a September 1993 speech, national security advisor Lake warned of the continuing prevalence of Third World dictators. When these dictators sat atop regional powers like Iran and Iraq, they "may engage in violence and lawlessness that threatens the United States and other democracies. Such reactionary, 'backlash' states are more likely to sponsor terrorism and traffic in weapons of mass destruction and ballistic missile technologies. They are more likely to threaten their own people, foment ethnic rivalries, and threaten their neighbors. . . . We must always maintain the military power necessary to deter, or if necessary defeat, aggression by these regimes."[119]

The *Bottom-Up Review* called for continuing Bush Administration defense policies aimed at preparing for new major regional contingencies. Les Aspin argued, as Bush officials had, that U.S. military power was crucial for sustaining the balance of power in key regions of the developing world where U.S. friends bordered powerful and belligerent regimes. And while he initially talked of abandoning the Bush Administration's pessimistic planning assumption that the Pentagon should be prepared to cope with the two major regional contingencies at one time, the *Bottom-Up Review* ended up embracing it.[120] The Clinton Administration also accepted the view put forth by Bush officials that the United States must be able to handle major challenges in the Third World by itself.[121]

4

REALISM VS. IDEALISM IN POST–COLD WAR FOREIGN POLICY

It would be a distortion of reality to imagine that clear-eyed political beliefs are what usually drive foreign policy. Often policy is instead a product of expediency, muddled compromises or plain neglect. Bureaucracies may stumble forward with poor guidance from above, or guidance that bureaucrats choose to ignore. At all levels, up to the president, paths of least resistance are taken; boats are not rocked; selected powerbrokers are appeased; standard operating procedures are followed. Micromanagement by Congress, or merely the anticipation of such meddling, can water down policies to the point of incoherence. In the area of defense policy, economic factors can in some instances be a far more powerful determinant of what weapons the Pentagon buys and deploys and where it stations troops. The sheer size and complexity of the national security establishment ensures that change within comes slowly, even during revolutionary times.

An appreciation of these facts must inform any effort to explain post–Cold War foreign policy with broad paradigmatic strokes. But it should not discourage such an effort. Beliefs about the nature of world politics can have a profound impact on policy by shaping the assumptions of decision makers and framing the terms of debate. Today, pessimistic realist axioms underpin the consensus that American primacy is crucial for stability in the post–Cold War world. Balance-of-power considerations have guided the thrust of American diplomatic efforts and, perhaps more important, have dictated the allocation of U.S. national security budgetary resources. In contrast, two classic idealist goals, promoting democracy and strengthening collective security, have played a negligible role in shaping post–Cold War foreign policy.

REALISM AFTER THE COLD WAR

Early in the Cold War, Hans Morgenthau complained that since "the end of the Napoleonic Wars, ever larger groups in the Western world have been persuaded that the struggle for power on the international scene is a temporary phenomenon, a historic accident that is bound to disappear once the peculiar historic conditions that have given rise to it have been eliminated."[1] Nowhere was this tendency more prevalent than in the United States, he suggested.

Had Morgenthau lived to witness the end of the Cold War, he surely would have commented on the resilience of the desire to wish away power politics. And again he would have singled out Americans for being particularly fallible in this regard, criticizing the optimism about the future of world politics that sprung up nationwide as communism collapsed. However, Morgenthau would have also found that his charge could not be applied equally to everyone in the United States—that, in fact, Bush Administration officials and like-minded foreign policy thinkers were not at all guilty of wishful thinking about the nature of world politics. "Our world without the Cold War confrontation is a safer world, but it is no Garden of Eden," Bush said in 1991. "This not the end of history. Men and nations still have their propensities for violence and for greed and for deceit."[2] As a consequence, Paul Wolfowitz reminded one audience, it was wrong—the "worst kind of utopianism"—to believe fashionable suggestions "that wars have no winners, or that violence is irrelevant to international politics. . . ."[3] Despite the end of the Cold War, the realist view remained the compass by which much of the U.S. foreign policy establishment navigated in the arena of international affairs and was embraced by Democrats and Republicans alike. As former State Department official Francis Fukuyama observed in 1992: "Realism, whether consciously called by that name, is the dominant framework for understanding international relations, and shapes the thinking of virtually every foreign policy professional today in the United States and much of the rest of the world."[4]

The realist assumptions at the core of U.S. policy were rarely stated explicitly by government officials. Theoretical discourses on the nature of world politics are not the sort of material included in foreign policy addresses, which instead tend to focus more concretely on the architecture of the state system. To the trained eye, however, the centrality of realist axioms to U.S. foreign policy was readily apparent. The conception of the post–Cold War world put forth by the Bush Administration and taken up by the Clinton team was of a world threatened by disorder, power vacuums, and interstate aggression. It was a world where democracy and economic interdependence were spreading rapidly but could not be relied on to keep the peace. The realist orthodoxy survived the Cold War's end precisely because its adherents believed, as Morgenthau had long ago put it, that "states have met each other in contests for power" through history "regardless of social, economic, and political conditions." As long as human nature remained unchanged and the state system remained predominant, these contests would continue.

By this logic, even a seismic global shift like the collapse of communism meant little. In the realist view there was nothing about the Cold War's end that promised to alter the iron laws of power politics. The international system would still be anarchic in nature, lacking a central authority that protected states from one another. Thus each state would continue to face the possibility that other states might use, or threaten to use, force against it. For this reason all states would still have to be perpetually on guard, making national survival their paramount priority. In an anarchic system, they could never fully trust other states, since betrayal, whether it be an enemy reneging on a peace agreement or a friend becoming an enemy due to a change in government, could lead to catastrophe. Nor could states entrust their security to international institutions, realists argued, since there was no guarantee that such bodies would be able to restrain major aggressors, even with the end of the Cold War political division at the United Nations.

While all observers celebrated the triumph of liberal democracy over communism, and many predicted an era of greater peace, realists restated their basic views. States could guarantee their survival by only one of two ways: they could be part of a hegemonic system in which a major power guaranteed their survival and brought stability to their region, or, in the absence of such an option, they would have to fend for themselves, endlessly maneuvering to increase their power in relation to other states through military buildups and balance-of-power politics. To realists, the former arrangement was far superior to the latter. When states were left to their own devices and took "self-help" steps to guarantee their security, they tended to inspire fear in one another. They obsessed about becoming militarily inferior or about being ganged up on by an alliance. Otherwise stable relations could deteriorate amid mounting paranoia and misinterpreted military measures. The final outcome of this so-called security dilemma could be war.[5]

It is difficult to say how completely U.S. officials have embraced realist analyses of world politics. Some Bush officials were obviously more pessimistic about the future nature of world politics than others, while the Clinton foreign policy team has shown itself to be generally more optimistic than their predecessors. Yet as a whole, there is little question that top members of both administrations' national security establishments have accepted the basic realist view that distrust and insecurity are permanent features of the international landscape. More specifically, realist thinking has underpinned several pivotal assumptions of post–Cold War planning, some of which have already been discussed: first, that the collapse of Soviet hegemony would produce a volatile multipolarity in the former Communist bloc in which numerous states, formerly protected by a superpower, suddenly had to secure themselves; second, that a withdrawal of U.S. security guarantees in Western Europe and East Asia was undesirable because it would allow a resuscitation of old rivalries in those regions, even between democracies; third, that new hegemonic powers, both regional and global in scope, could rise to threaten U.S. interests unless the United States took preventive measures; and fourth, that traditional interstate aggression would remain a major, if not common, feature of international relations in the Third World.

The Unstable East

While welcome on one level, the collapse of Soviet control in Eastern Europe and, finally, the demise of the Soviet Union itself, raised intense concerns. Suddenly, in a vast region historically known for its nationalist and ethnic passions, there existed some twenty countries which were not in the fold of a strong hegemony. According to realist thinking, this dawning multipolarity was a formula for escalating regional tensions, even if most of the states were nominally democratic. "History is not over. It has simply been frozen and now is thawing with a vengeance Americans ignore at their peril," CIA director Robert Gates said in December 1991.[6] In a January 1992 review of the former Soviet bloc, Gates elaborated: "Ethnic and territorial disputes in Eastern Europe have risen to the surface and threaten political instability and civil war, despite promising prospects for the development of democratic institutions and market economics."[7]

In a 1990 article on the future of Europe John Mearsheimer stated unequivocably that there "has been no war among the states" in Eastern Europe "during the Cold War because the Soviets have tightly controlled them." Mearsheimer cited the example of Hungary and Romania, between whom there had long been tensions over Romanian treatment of the Hungarian minority in Transylvania. "Were it not for the Soviet presence in Eastern Europe, this conflict would have brought Romania and Hungary to war by now, and it may bring them to war in the future." Mearsheimer observed that there are many possible dyads across which war could occur in the East. And because "the results of local conflicts will be largely determined by the relative success of each party in finding external allies, Eastern European states will have strong incentives to drag the major powers into their local conflicts."[8]

General Galvin, in his March 1992 testimony to Congress, outlined a scenario by which the fragile multipolar system in the East could be swept up by the dynamics of the security dilemma: "Reformist failures in Moscow, Kiev, Minsk, or other emerging democratic states would pose direct threats to neighboring nations.

Historical border disputes could provide the catalyst for reactionary forces to consolidate internal power and externalize domestic problems. Resurgent nationalism could well lead to regional militarization, confrontation, and territorial seizures. . . . Belligerency on the part of any Central/East European country to include Russia poses the greatest threat to regional peace and stability. All of these states harbor territorial claims against Russia and each other. Each historical claim is a potential flashpoint for post-2000 Europe triggered by failure of reforms."[9]

The preliminary 1992 Defense Planning Guidance echoed these concerns, warning that "the U.S. must keep in mind the long history of conflict between the states of Eastern Europe, as well as the potential for conflict between the states of Eastern Europe and those of the former Soviet Union."[10] Few U.S. officials were surprised when relations between Russia and the Ukraine worsened in late 1991 and early 1992; it seemed a portent of things to come.

There were limits to Washington's ability to promote stability in the former Communist bloc in the aftermath of the Cold War. The United States had no tradition of influence in the region nor was there any consensus in the early 1990s about extending Western security commitments eastward. The one card that the United States and its allies could play, economic aid to the former Communist states, was not guaranteed to be decisive in its impact. As U.S. officials saw it, the former Soviet bloc was probably doomed to years of instability.

One didn't have to be a realist to come to this conclusion, of course. A variety of observers agreed that unrelenting economic problems could lead to setbacks for democracy, increases in nationalism, and new insecurities. The distinctiveness of realist thinking toward the East was in the conviction that nationalism would manifest itself in territorial ambitions and belligerency, producing rivalries so intense that economic interdependence, especially with the West, and the mediation of multilateral organizations like the CSCE would have little mitigating effect.

The implications of such worst-case thinking for U.S. policy were threefold and have already been touched on: first, the United States would need to prepare continually for the possibility of a resurgent Russian effort to dominate its neighbors; second, a U.S. troop presence in Europe was needed to provide general reassurance to jittery states in Eastern Europe; and third, any extension of NATO's collective security commitments eastward would be foolhardy since it could embroil the United States in new conflicts. The validity of these concerns will be examined in later chapters.

Ensuring Community in the West

If U.S. officials felt generally powerless to affect stability in the East, they did believe they could take steps to avoid instability in other parts of the world. Underlying Washington's preference for continued U.S. primacy in Western Europe and East Asia was a distinctly realist mindset.

While much of the concern among U.S. policymakers about a new multipolarity in Europe centered on the former Communist bloc, where failed democracies could end up in rivalries with one another and where turmoil could pull Germany and Russia into conflict, there were also fears of tension among members of NATO.

Policy analysts have tended to discuss this possibility by referring to historically grounded suspicions within the West. Realist scholars use theory to explain why these suspicions can be so poisonous even within a democratic group of nations. They argue that in multipolar systems all states, whether democratic or not, whether economically interdependent or not, relate to one another uneasily. States worry about other states in the system joining a coalition against them, or about neighbors with more power becoming unfriendly and harnessing that power to aggressive ends. Realists contend that it is not the internal character of states that determines whether a system is stable but the distribution of power within that system.

By realist logic, relations among Western European nations in the absence of a dominant American security role would be unstable for two reasons: because the natural tendencies among these nations to balance against one another would be inherently less stable than continued hegemony, and because German power would be disproportionately great, making a true equilibrium impossible. In regard to the second point, Kenneth Waltz has bolstered the concerns of policymakers about resurgent German (and Japanese) power with the theoretical claim that basic rules of international politics dictate this outcome: "For a country to choose not to become a great power is a structural anomaly. . . . Sooner or later, usually sooner, the international status of countries has risen in step with their material resources. Countries with great-power economies have become great powers, whether or not reluctantly."[11] Christopher Layne's prediction of Germany's inevitable assertiveness is also grounded in realist theory.[12]

Realist thinkers challenge the notion that the ancient dynamics of power politics can be neutralized by the prevalence of democracy and economic interdependence. The European Community is no fire wall against new rivalries and war, they argue, and suggest that the Western unity that existed during the Cold War was primarily an artificial phenomenon. As John Mearsheimer explained, a "powerful and potentially dangerous Soviet Union forced the Western democracies to band together to meet the common threat. Britain, Germany, and France no longer worried about each other, because all faced a greater menace from the Soviets. This Soviet threat muted concern about relative gains arising from economic cooperation among the EC states by giving each Western democracy a vested interest in seeing its alliance partners grow powerful, since each additional increment of power helped deter the Soviets."[13] Such a partnership, along with the all-important American hegemony in Western Europe, served to mitigate the effects of anarchy and produced forty-five years of peace among Europe's Western democracies.

But take away the common threat and send home the Americans, the realist argument goes, and Europe's democratic states might not be so friendly. As natural economic competitors, they could begin worrying more about gains that made neighbors stronger and these worries could inject new tension into their relations.[14] Also, without a hegemonic power like the United States to guarantee regional security, Western European states would have to take their own defense more seriously. They would again be in an anarchic environment where, ultimately, only their own power could guarantee national survival. The combination of economic strains and a new attention to national defense could well set the stage in Western Europe for insecurity and even war.

The prevalence of liberal democracy did not change things, realists said, taking issue with the view put forth by Francis Fukuyama and others that the triumph of democracy presaged an end to major conflicts between developed countries.[15] Democratic peoples were not more prone to fear the costs of war nor more likely to respect the rights of people in other democratic countries.[16] Mass publics, whether democratic or not, "can become deeply imbued with nationalistic or religious fervor, making them prone to support aggression regardless of costs," Mearsheimer wrote. Harvard political scientist Samuel Huntington added to this point, writing that even among liberal states there could be serious differences. Democratic states of differing ethnic groups, cultural identities, or national experiences could find much to disagree about and misunderstandings could easily become confrontations.[17]

The ever-quickening pace, complexity, and competitiveness of global affairs could serve to work against stable ties between states. "In the emerging world, relations between countries are likely to become more complicated, more volatile, and conceivably more duplicitous than they were during the Cold War. Today's friend is more likely to become tomorrow's enemy and vice versa," Huntington told a congressional committee in fall 1990. "All of this means a world characterized not by the final triumph of democracy but a rather complex, ambiguous jungle-like world of multiple dangers, hidden traps, and unpleasant surprises."[18]

Even if democracy could soften the harsh edges of power politics, realists suggested it would never be a reliable panacea. Mearsheimer wrote that the "possibility always exists that a democracy will revert to an authoritarian state. This threat of backsliding means that one democratic state can never be sure that another democratic state will not change its stripes and turn on it sometime in the future." Thus every liberal state would always have to worry about the military capabilities of even friendly neighbors, since a change of government could lead to those capabilities being used for aggression.[19]

It is not clear to what extent Bush and Clinton administration officials have shared the most extreme fears of realist thinkers about the future of post–Cold War Western Europe. Much official foreign policy rhetoric has actually been at odds with realist assumptions. In a March 1990 speech, for example, Secretary of State Baker argued that "Free peoples cherishing democratic values are unlikely to go to war with one another."[20] Baker also talked often of how economic ties could help promote peace. He was particularly emphatic in suggesting that the best way to avoid new threats from the former Soviet bloc was to bind that region into the global economy. In Baker's worldview, democracy and economic interaction nearly always facilitated political cooperation. President Clinton and his top advisors share this outlook.[21]

In their rhetoric, and through some of their actions, U.S. officials have expressed faith in various measures that realism's critics believe can mitigate insecurity between states. But in practice this faith has proved limited. The U.S. determination to play a major balancing role in Western Europe underscores an intense fear of allowing a truly multipolar environment to develop on the continent. American power, U.S. officials believe, remains the final guarantor of stability. At its core, America's European policy reflects realist assumptions.

East Asia: The Logic of Primacy

The realist outlook has been even more in evidence in U.S. policy toward East Asia, where political and economic underdevelopment make realist predictions of instability appear highly compelling. Critics of realism agree that the prospects for stable peace in a region are reasonably good when democracy is entrenched, when there is a lot of economic interdependence, and when regional organizations are strong. Realists emphasize the importance of states in a region having roughly the same amount of power. In East Asia none of these conditions were fully met as the Cold War ended. Democracy is still young or barely existent in such states as South Korea, Thailand, the Philippines, and Taiwan, while it has not taken root at all in North Korea, China, and Vietnam. For the immediate future, states in East Asia will have to worry about authoritarian neighbors, or about democratic friends who could still backslide into authoritarianism. Economic interdependence in the region is high, but it is often rough edged, with Japan's trade and investments in Southeast Asia, for example, sometimes leaving resentment in its wake and fierce competition characterizing economic relations throughout the entire region. In terms of power, there are major inequities between states in the region. Japan is economically far more powerful than China and South Korea, and all three of these states overshadow all others in the region. Finally, there is no strong tradition of multilateral institutions.

One does not need to be a realist to worry that in light of these factors a U.S. withdrawal from East Asia could produce an unstable situation. But as will be shown later, non-realists can and do disagree about this conclusion—realists do not. And the fact that there has been no serious dissent from the conclusion within the U.S. government is a telling indicator of the predominance of realist thinking among foreign policy elites.

In the relationship between Japan and the United States realists have detected evidence for their view that democracy and economic interdependence do not necessarily ensure good relations, and in particular that concerns about "relative gains" can sour ties between democracies. Joseph Grieco, in an essay on anarchy and cooperation, explained the way realists view the relative gains issue: "States worry that today's friend may be tomorrow's enemy in war, and fear that achievements of joint gains that advantage a friend in the present might produce a more dangerous potential foe in the future. As a result, states must give serious attention to the gains of partners." In an economic relationship the question is not whether both sides are getting rich, but whether one side is getting richer at a faster rate.[22] When a state sees evidence that it is falling behind another state, cooperative ties can deteriorate as the lagging state looks for ways to curtail the elements of the relationship that might be helping its competitor.

In the view of some realists this dynamic was already enveloping U.S.-Japanese relations as the Cold War ended. Solidarity in the face of a common foe was giving way to growing division and distrust, much of it emanating from an economically lagging United States. Samuel Huntington commented that "the United States is obsessed with Japan for the same reasons that previously we were obsessed with the Soviet Union. We see Japan as a major threat to our primacy in a crucial arena of power." Ten years earlier, Huntington said, the Soviet threat was on everyone's mind and public debate focused on comparative statistics of the Soviet and American military arsenals. "Today, the Japanese economic threat is on people's minds, and the concern is not with missile vulnerability but with semiconductor vulnerability. Public discussions focus on comparative Japanese technology exports, savings, investments, patents, research and development, and so forth and so on."[23]

In one well-publicized opinion poll finding, a majority of the

American public said that they would rather see the United States grow at a slower rate and remain economically on a par with Japan than grow at a faster rate and fall behind Japan. Another poll, taken before the Cold War's end, showed Americans feeling that Japanese economic competition was a greater threat than Soviet military power.[24] These anxieties were cited by realists to bolster the point that economic interdependence does not necessarily further peace and harmony. On the contrary, as Kenneth Waltz argued in *Theory of International Politics*, high interdependence could breed friction between two countries that might not be present if they had a lower level of economic contact.[25]

In addition to anxiety over relative gains, good relations among democracies can be hampered by cultural, religious, or ethnic differences, realists observe.[26] This problem, too, could be detected in U.S.-Japanese relations. In the early 1990s relations between the two nations were rocked as public figures in Japan and the United States exchanged insults across the Pacific.[27] The general theme of the derogatory Japanese comments—comments that reflected the opinions of many Japanese—was that Americans were lazy, wasteful, and undisciplined. Americans, in turn, saw the Japanese as overly disciplined, aggressive, and arrogant. For some watchers of Japanese culture, it appeared that increasing economic strength was feeding nationalist pride while doing little to alleviate the natural insularity of Japan. In the United States, on the other hand, it seemed that long-standing American racism toward Asians was being brought to the surface as the nation declined.

Whatever the case, the bad chemistry between the United States and Japan had a direct bearing on the issue of U.S. hegemony in Asia: if the United States military withdrew from Asia, the declining sense of shared fate on security matters between Japan and the U.S. could leave the two countries with decreased shared interests but the same array of conflicts. From there, according to realist logic, tensions between the two nations could easily deteriorate rapidly, even leading to a military competition.

As with Germany, realist theory predicted the inevitable rise of Japan. Waltz suggested in 1993 that Japan could resist the pressures to become a great power for only so long. In the long term its political-military capabilities would eventually be brought into balance with its economic position. The threat of China assuming preeminence in East Asia was likely to accelerate this process.[28] Layne's predictions of rising Japanese power likewise paralleled his views on Germany.[29]

Again, it is not clear to what extent Bush Administration officials reasoned in such starkly realist terms, since they rarely articulated their theoretical assumptions in public. The Defense Planning Guidance of 1992 hinted at the possibility of Japan developing into a rival if U.S. primacy in East Asia were ended, but there is no evidence that this possibility was taken seriously elsewhere in the U.S. government.

Ultimately, the case that America's post–Cold War East Asia policy has been shaped by realist assumptions must remain little more than a compelling deductive argument. Realists have argued that a U.S. withdrawal from the region would create a textbook case of unstable multipolarity and possibly a major deterioration of U.S.-Japanese relations. Most American policymakers, under both Clinton and Bush, manifestly have believed the same thing.

A Darwinian Arena: The Third World

Realist logic also underpins the case for U.S. primacy in the Third World. Here, the logic has been far less controversial in its application. Whereas many contest the view that conflict is inevitable in the industrial world in the absence of superpowers to provide stability, even critics of realism take it for granted that there will continue to be violent contests for power among states in Third World. As Francis Fukuyama wrote in 1992, there would be two worlds for the foreseeable future: the "post-historical" industrial world, in which liberal democracy was triumphant and realist principles were less relevant, and the "historical" Third World, which would "still be riven by a variety of religious, national, and ideological conflicts" and in which "the old rules of power politics continue to apply."[30] Scholars James M. Goldgeiger and Michael McFaul have made the same point: "Structural realism is inadequate to explain the behavior of states in the core but is relevant for understanding regional security systems in the periphery."[31]

The basis for this judgment is the observation that in many Third World regions few of the factors needed for cooperation are present: democracy is often absent or not well established; economic prosper-

ity and trade ties are often shaky or unequal in nature; gross dispari-
ties of power among local actors are commonplace; and regional
organizations tend to be weak. As a consequence of these realities
many have argued that the brutal game of power politics will continue in the Third World, and that traditional interstate warfare will
remain a fact of life there. Stephen David has predicted that some
Third World leaders will continue to make war both because they
rationally conclude that war is in their interests—whether to gain territory or to distract an oppressed citizenry—and because there exist,
in many cases, domestic conditions that allow them to pursue aggressive policies. In the Third World, as in Europe earlier in the twentieth
century, David writes, militarism and nationalism remain powerful
forces. And, argues David, the absence of democratic checks in Third
World countries means that it is easier for Third World leaders to ini-
tiate and sustain belligerent policies—and survive politically, as Saddam Hussein has, if those policies result in catastrophe.

The proliferation of advanced weaponry can serve to aggravate
instability in the Third World. Arms buildups by rogue states may
rightly be seen by neighbors as threatening developments that demand
countermeasures. But even new arms purchases by moderate or democratic states may increase tensions in a region. Under the dynamics of
the security dilemma, legitimate searches for security on the part of
friendly neighbors can inadvertently produce arms races and even war
among them. As realists like to say, the question is not "Why do wars
happen?" but rather "Why don't wars happen more often?"

One does not have to be a realist to take a pessimistic view of
security matters in the Third World. But what distinguishes the realist
analysis of the Third World from other approaches, which will be
explored later, is the heavy emphasis on interstate conflict and
regional hegemony. Firm in their conviction that the state is the all-
important actor in world affairs, realist thinkers suggest that the
dynamics of international relations in the Third World closely parallel
those in the developed world. This view presents many problems and
will be critiqued in later chapters. Here let it be simply pointed out
that Bush and Clinton administration officials, in their repeated
warnings of new territorial aggression, were plainly in the realist
camp on this issue.

Since the Cold War's end the public debate over U.S. interests in the Third World has often been characterized by intense controversy and confusion. Yet ultimately it has been a debate waged within the margins of a basic consensus. Mainstream analysts have argued about what precisely the U.S. national interests are in the Third World, and how those interests should be defended. But there has been little dissent from the view that American power remains the ultimate guarantor of Western interests in critical areas of the Third World, such as the Persian Gulf, and that U.S. forces must stand ready to intervene in such areas on a massive scale, unilaterally if need be.

IDEALISM AFTER THE COLD WAR

If the powerful influence of realist assumptions in post–Cold War foreign policy is clear, so too is the negligible role that idealist goals have played in shaping strategy and diplomacy in the new era, despite widespread hopes that the Cold War's end would make possible a more high-minded approach to world affairs. Idealism has not been entirely absent from U.S. foreign policy in recent years. On the contrary, it has been a more visible and important component of America's global role than at any time before, save for a brief period after World War I. The United States is giving more help to fledgling democrats abroad than at any time in its history; it is showing genuine enthusiasm for the United Nations after decades of dismissing that institution; and in 1992 it dispatched troops to Somalia in an unprecedented large-scale humanitarian intervention.

These developments are noteworthy, but they do not signal the emergence of idealism as a principal driver of U.S. foreign policy. In particular, neither the promotion of democracy nor a commitment to collective security, two classic pillars of the idealist agenda, have been central to the formulation of post–Cold War foreign policy. Neither has been so elevated on the list of policy priorities as to alter fundamentally either the way the United States divides up its national security budget or the manner in which it conducts diplomacy around the world.[32]

Promoting Democracy

As the Cold War ended the Bush Administration insisted loudly and often that the penultimate purpose of American foreign policy was to build a more democratic world. There is no doubt that the president and his advisors believed in this mission. And outside of government, few foreign policy professionals argued with the idea that U.S. actions abroad should help strengthen and expand the community of democratic states. Since taking office the Clinton Administration has made the promotion of democracy an even more salient goal in its public statements on foreign policy.

But as through much of the twentieth century, there has been a major chasm between U.S. rhetoric and policy when it comes to promoting democracy. This chasm reflects a lack of consensus about whether such a goal can be a practical centerpiece of foreign policy.

For much of U.S. history America's weakness and isolationist tendencies militated against any kind of global crusade to promote democracy. Another restraining factor was the widespread belief that America should lead in this realm through example rather than activism, standing as a "city on a hill" and resisting the temptation to meddle in the affairs of other states. Although American officials recognized early in the twentieth century that democracies were less threatening to U.S. interests, a desire to make the world more democratic was never powerful enough to be an independent driver of foreign policy. When the United States did finally become active abroad it was guided largely by geopolitical considerations. It intervened in both world wars not when the threat to European democracies first became apparent, but when the security dangers to the United States at last became inescapable.

During the Cold War U.S. officials were never engaged, per se, in a crusade to promote democracy. Instead, the priority of U.S. policymakers was to consolidate the anti-Communist bloc and prevent major war with the Soviet Union. Ideally, the members of the anti-Communist bloc would be democratic, and in Western Europe, building democracy and consolidating the bloc were seen as basically the same goal. But overall, democracy was never a prerequisite for good ties with Washington during the Cold War. The United States was even willing to subvert democratic governments to install more reliable anti-Communists. As for the goal of preventing war, this effectively ruled out any vigorous efforts to promote democracy in Eastern Europe.

Idealists in Principle

With the Cold War's end the idea of predicating foreign policy on the active promotion of democracy was seriously debated for the first time in U.S. history. With no global enemy in sight many believed there was no longer a justification for subordinating democratic principles to geopolitical imperatives. Indeed, it was widely agreed that democracy's spread and consolidation had itself become a top geopolitical imperative. Many believed also that the best, and perhaps only, way to sustain public support for U.S. engagement abroad after the Cold War was to center that engagement on idealist objectives.

Secretary Baker showed considerable sympathy for this line of reasoning. In one of his first foreign policy addresses, Baker called for a reassessment of the realpolitik tradition in U.S. foreign policy. "The idea that American moral values and engaged foreign policy are somehow in contradiction, I think, is clearly incorrect. . . . Realism today means not the exclusion of values but their inclusion as the guiding light of our policy." Baker also emphasized that such an approach was needed to maintain public support for foreign policy. "A democratic society will not long support a policy which is at variance with its beliefs."[33]

Baker's comments, however, were not echoed frequently by other administration officials, and through 1989 the promotion of democracy was by no means a conceptual centerpiece of U.S. strategy. It was a goal ritualistically invoked in nearly all foreign policy addresses, but the administration never laid out a comprehensive plan for achieving it or committed substantial resources to that end.

The events of late 1989 moved the promotion of democracy to the forefront of U.S. foreign policy thinking, both inside government and out. Many worried that the window of democratic opportunity that had opened in Eastern Europe, and was fast opening in the Soviet Union, could easily be shut as old traditions of authoritarian rule in the region reemerged. In his first statement to Congress after the fall of the Berlin Wall, in February 1990, Secretary Baker said that America's preeminent foreign policy challenge "is consolidating democracy."[34] In a March 30 speech Baker said that the promotion of democracy would be the new organizing principle of U.S. foreign policy. "Beyond containment lies democracy," he declared.[35]

But the Bush Administration would remain halfhearted in its pro-democratic position. In his March speech Baker made clear that he was not entirely rejecting the tradition of realpolitik. Instead he argued that the "old arguments of idealism vs. realism must be replaced by idealism plus realism." A policy abroad that violated U.S. values was unacceptable, but so was a policy based on moral exhortation that ignored U.S. interests. Baker suggested there was no reason that morality and the national interest could not be pursued simultaneously.

Unfortunately, policymakers constantly face choices of the kind Baker said could be avoided. In the Bush Administration, when such choices arose, there was a distinct preference for realpolitik options— that is, realism minus idealism. When it came to China, for example, the administration was far more interested in maintaining good ties with Beijing than in supporting the democracy movement.[36] In regard to the Soviet Union, the administration appeared to favor the stability and familiarity of Gorbachev over the insurgent democrat Boris Yeltsin. In the Middle East, the administration worked in 1989 and 1990 to cultivate closer ties with Saddam Hussein's Iraq, even though a policy of sanctions would have been more appropriate, given the dictator's well-known inhumanity to the Kurds.[37] After the Gulf War, the Bush Administration made little effort to push its Arab allies toward more democratic policies. And overall, the Bush Administration was never known for its strong commitment to human rights.

When it perceived the geopolitical stakes as high, the Bush Administration was willing to put American values on the back burner to further its conception of the national interest. When the stakes were low the administration was ready to be pro-democratic. It was one thing to aid democrats who opposed the government in strategically vital China, quite another to support democracy through international sanctions in a backwater like Haiti. What "realism plus idealism" apparently meant was that the United States could pursue an inconsistent foreign policy.

The Bush Administration's unwillingness to move the promotion of democracy to the forefront of U.S. foreign policy was most evident in its failure to commit substantial resources to this goal. As with any institution, the priorities of the United States government must be judged in large part by where it spends its money. Two months after the Bush Administration left the White House, policy analyst Larry Diamond testified to Congress that direct U.S. spending to promote democracy amounted to only $400 million annually.[38] This figure did not include economic assistance to Eastern Europe and the former Soviet Union, which together accounted for over a billion dollars in aid spending in fiscal year 1993.[39] Yet even when those figures were made part of the overall total, the money spent on promoting and consolidating democracy remained a small percentage of the 1993 foreign aid budget.

Bipartisan Crusaders

Among many foreign policy thinkers outside of government, both liberal and conservative, there was strong support for making the promotion of democracy the central mission of U.S. foreign policy. Former Kennedy aide Theodore Sorenson argued that promoting democracy is "consistent not merely with the moral impulse traditionally underlying American foreign policy but our long-term national security requirements as well." Sorenson rehearsed the familiar arguments that a democratic world "would be a far safer and friendlier world for the United States," and that a foreign policy predicated on spreading democracy would have the greatest chance of sustaining public support.[40] These points would be widely repeated by liberal commentators during the early 1990s.

On the conservative side of the political spectrum, the case for exporting democracy was made most energetically by Joshua Muravchik. Muravchik explored the reservations that many U.S. leaders had long had about promoting democracy. He contested the argument—articulated decades earlier by Kennan, Lippmann, and Morgenthau—that a championing of democracy could lead to endless crusades abroad. The American people, he said, were not so easily made warlike. He also took aim at the belief that the United States should not try to foist its system of governance on other nations. "The reason it is wrong to impose something on others, presumably, is because it violates their will," Muravchik wrote. "But, absent democracy, how can their will be known?" It was only when human beings were governed with their consent that their will could be known. In Muravchik's view there was nothing wrong with even the forcible imposition of democracy, although that should always be a last resort.[41]

Despite bipartisan support for centering American foreign policy on the promotion of democracy, the idea could not galvanize a consensus among U.S. foreign policy elites during the early post–Cold War period. At the practical level, experts could not agree on concrete measures for promoting democracy. "There are limits to what any official U.S. agency can do to support democracy abroad," acknowledged conservative democracy proponent Larry Diamond. "Many countries remain deeply anxious about U.S. intervention. That suspicion limits what U.S. government agencies can do to assist private institutions. In addition, any activity that might affect the outcome of electoral competition, such as technical assistance to political parties, is inappropriate for a U.S. government agency."

The situation could be particularly sticky in countries with authoritarian rule. To aid democracy in such circumstances meant giving money to organizations seeking to bring down the existing regime. "That is not a suitable task for a U.S. government agency," wrote Diamond.[42] Truly promoting democracy, many worried, would mean (again) getting the United States into the business of subverting sovereign governments. This was an unsavory enterprise, even if the ends were laudable.[43]

Proponents of democracy-based foreign policy recognized this problem, and as a consequence, the proposals of writers like Diamond, Sorenson, and Muravchik were quite modest. In practice, their supposedly bold agenda for redirecting U.S. foreign policy entailed little more than tinkering with foreign aid programs and giving more funding to organizations like the National Endowment for Democracy and to the propaganda organs of the United States government.

A New Crusade?

During his election campaign Bill Clinton criticized President Bush for seeming to "prefer a foreign policy that embraces stability at the expense of freedom, a foreign policy built more on personal relationships with foreign leaders than on consideration of how those leaders acquired and maintained their power."[44] Clinton pledged to restore values to U.S. foreign policy and to make the promotion of democracy a central goal of actions abroad. Clinton officials reiterated this goal in their first year in office whenever discussing the broad objectives of foreign policy and promised new resources to support democracy.

"The promotion of democracy is the frontline of global security," Secretary of State Warren Christopher said in a June 1993 speech. "A world of democracies would be a safer world." Consolidating democracy in Eastern Europe and the former Soviet Union, Christopher declared, "is the strategic challenge of our time."[45] In a speech earlier in the year, President Clinton made the same point, saying that assuring democracy's success in the East was "the greatest security challenge of our generation. . . ."[46]

At the State Department responsibility for democracy and human rights issues has been centralized by a new Under Secretary for Global Affairs, a post filled by former Senator Timothy Wirth. This office took the lead in doing something the Bush Administration had neglected: producing an interagency agreement on how the United States should go about promoting democracy. Wirth's deputy, Jessica Matthews, supervised a task force that included representatives from numerous government agencies. The project, she said in summer 1993, "is an attempt to turn a policy into a program, to define in detail the thrust and the means and priorities of one of the pillars of the President's foreign policy."[47]

At the Defense Department Les Aspin moved quickly to define the promotion of democracy as one of the four main goals of U.S. national security policy, along with reducing nuclear dangers, preparing for regional contingencies, and aiding U.S. economic well-being. Aspin established a new assistant secretary position to deal with the issue and mentioned democracy frequently in his statements. "When democracy falters in key nations, it can have a major impact on America's national security policies and our military needs," Aspin said in one his first budget presentations to Congress.[48] "More dictatorships, more defense spending," he commented on other occasion.[49]

With major pronouncements on the new centrality of promoting democracy, a major shake-up of national security budgetary priorities might be expected. But this has not occurred. The Clinton Administration did push through Congress a $2.5 billion foreign aid package for the former Soviet Union in the 1994 budget, a substantial increase over the previous fiscal year.[50] That request probably represented the upper limits of what was politically feasible in Congress. However, viewed more broadly, spending on this level is hardly commensurate with what the Clinton administration has defined as the high stakes of reform in the East. The $2.5 billion for the fifteen countries of the former Soviet Union is only slightly larger than the $2.1 billion given to Egypt in the same budget package and is less than the $3 billion allocated for Israel. Clinton surely believes that consolidating democracy in Russia is the greatest security challenge of our time, but his fiscal year 1994 budget requested not much more for this goal than it did for research and development for a single new Air Force weapons program, the F-22 fighter jet.[51] Moreover, Russian aid spending was dwarfed by expenditures for the ongoing modernization and maintainence of U.S. nuclear weapons programs.

There are, of course, numerous obstacles that stand in the way of making bold and rapid shifts in the way that national security resources are allocated. The analysis here does not mean to imply that the Clinton Administration is happy with how the budgetary pie is currently sliced or that it doesn't genuinely want democratization to be its main foreign policy priority. The point is simply that it is a misrepresentation of reality to say that a goal is a top governmental priority when little money, in comparative terms, is spent on achieving that goal. There remains a massive chasm between declaratory policy and actual policy.

Collective Security

The end of the Cold War produced widespread hopes that the long-standing idealist goal of safeguarding world peace through collective security was finally within reach. At the United Nations there was a new atmosphere of cooperation within the Security Council, a body that had been paralyzed by East-West deadlock for forty years. In regard to Europe there was talk of building a strong, continent-wide collective security organization that would supplant the two alliances of the Cold War. Even in East Asia some analysts saw the opportunity for an inclusive collective security organization.

Despite these hopes the Bush Administration showed little interest in pursuing bold new collective security efforts, while in the foreign policy community more generally, no consensus developed that collective security could significantly alter the dynamics of world politics in the post–Cold War era. Both the ambivalence of policymakers and the divisions among expert opinion have endured since Clinton took office.

The substantive arguments surrounding collective security will be examined in a later chapter. Here the interest is only in the attitudes of policymakers toward collective security, as manifested in their diplomatic actions and in the allocation of budgetary resources.

The New World Order

When President Bush took office, the first foreign guest he met with in the White House was U.N. Secretary General Javier Perez de Cuellar. This move was intended to send a signal that the Bush Administration viewed the United Nations more positively than had the Reagan Administration.[52] With the Soviets becoming more cooperative in the Security Council in 1989 and 1990, and with Third World radicalism in the General Assembly also declining, the attitude of U.S. policymakers toward the U.N. continued to grow less hostile, as did that of the American public. "We have seen in recent years a spirit of pragmatism and depoliticization replace the atmosphere of sterile rhetoric and confrontation in the U.N.'s preeminent forums, the General Assembly and the Security Council," noted John Bolton, assistant secretary of state for international organization affairs, in May 1990. The Bush Administration publicly committed itself to a new effort at bolstering the U.N.'s effectiveness and increasing U.S. cooperativeness with the institution. "We must reestablish America's reputation as a credible and responsible player at the United Nations," Bolton said in calling for an accelerated effort at paying off U.S. debts to the U.N.[53] President Bush was reported to have personally involved himself in demanding that his administration move more rapidly to eliminate these debts, which had ballooned during the 1980s.

But the Bush Administration also made it clear that its faith in the U.N. was limited. "This is not the Dukakis Administration," said Bolton. "We don't automatically assume the U.N. system should be the first place to go to handle all our foreign policy problems."[54] There was never any discussion within the administration of using the U.N. to resolve the situation in Panama in 1989, and the invasion in December of that year indicated contempt for international law and the ideals embodied in the U.N. Charter.[55] The Bush Administration also showed itself to be lukewarm about Soviet proposals, dating back to 1988, for rejunevating the Security Council's enforcement machinery, particuarly the Military Staff Committee.[56] (On paper, the MSC, composed of top military officers from each of the five permanent members, is supposed to have responsibility for managing U.N. military operations.)[57]

The crisis and war in the Persian Gulf exemplified U.S. ambivalence about the U.N.'s role in the new era. Not long after Iraq invaded Kuwait, President Bush declared in a September 1990 speech to Congress that "we are now in sight of a United Nations that performs as envisioned by its founders." The end of the Cold War, suggested Bush, had unlocked the potential of an institution that has stood essentially moribund from its earliest days: "No longer can a dictator count on East-West confrontation to stymie concerted U.N. action against aggression." The New World Order, as initially defined by the president in this speech, was an exceedingly idealist vision. Bush talked of the possibility of a lasting peace in language reminiscent of Wilson. "A hundred generations have searched for this elusive path to peace, while a thousand wars raged across the span of human endeavor. Today that new world is struggling to be born. A world quite different from the one we've known. A world where the rule of law supplants the rule of the jungle. A world in which nations recognize the shared responsibility for freedom and justice. A world where the strong respect the rights of the weak."[58]

Despite this rhetoric it is clear that the Bush Administration never truly embraced an idealist outlook toward world politics. To begin with, it did not view the Gulf War as an opportunity to rehabilitate the U.N.'s peacemaking capacity, and saw the U.N. as playing only a supporting role in the whole episode.[59] The Security Council did not take the lead in opposing Iraq; Washington did. Bush didn't even mention the U.N. in his original announcement, on August 8, that the United States was deploying troops to Saudi Arabia.[60] And the Security Council's Military Staff Committee did not run the war in the Gulf; the Pentagon did, in consultation with a few leading allies.[61] The whole Gulf expedition, as U.S. officials repeatedly stressed, hinged on U.S. resolve and activism.[62]

After the Gulf War ended President Bush would say, "The coalition effort established a model for the collective settlement of disputes." But this model was hardly an idealist one in which nations would contribute equally to the task of righting wrongs. Instead, Bush saw the model as revolving around United States power. "Among the nations of the world, only the United States of America has both the moral standing and the means to back it up," he said in January 1991. "We are the only nation on this earth that could assemble the forces of peace."[63] Bush also backed away from his hopeful assessment of the changing nature of world politics, saying in April 1991 that "the Cold War's end didn't deliver us into an era of perpetual peace. As old threats recede, new threats emerge. The quest for the new world order is, in part, a challenge to keep the dangers of disorder at bay."[64]

Following the Gulf War there were widespread calls for a new commitment to implementing Article 43 of the U.N. Charter, which gives the Security Council an ability to deploy forces under its command to counter aggression.[65] "The coalition-building process that proved successful in the Gulf War does not constitute an adequate paradigm for all interventions the U.N. may deem necessary," observed Senator Joseph Biden in 1992. "Future crises may require greater speed, and we should strive to create circumstances that do not impose upon the United States the onus either to act unilaterally or to galvanize a U.N. action in which we supply the preponderance of military power. . . . The time has come: the United States, in conjunction with other key nations, should now designate forces under Article 43 of the United Nations Charter."[66]

The Bush Administration remained uninterested in this idea. At a special January 1992 summit of leaders of the Security Council Bush hailed the "sacred principles enshrined in the U.N. Charter," and he embraced an initiative that instructed U.N. Secretary General Boutros Boutros-Ghali to find new ways to put those principles into practice.[67] But when the secretary general's report was being drafted in spring 1992, Assistant Secretary Bolton sent a letter to the U.N. opposing the idea of giving the Security Council a standing force or activating the long dormant Military Staff Committee. When Ghali's report, *An Agenda for Peace,* was published later in the year the United States showed no interest in following up on the portions that dealt with implementing Article 43.

In another testament to its ambivalence about reviving the United Nations after the Cold War the Bush Administration moved slowly to pay off the U.S. arrears to the organization, still over $500 million in 1992, and of which $100 million was owed for peacekeeping operations.[68] Again, if the allocation of resources provides any insight into policy priorities, it is illuminating to consider that the Bush Administration requested nearly four times more money for the B-2 bomber program in 1993 than it did for contributions to fifty-one international organizations, including the United Nations.[69]

The Bush Administration's attitude toward new regional organizations in Europe and East Asia is also evidence of its overall ambivalence, or even antipathy, toward collective security. As already discussed, U.S. officials opposed the creation of a new, more comprehensive collective security organization in Europe, favoring instead the continuation of a U.S.-dominated NATO. In East Asia it believed that a new region-wide organization would be both undesirable and probably unworkable. Finally, the Bush Administration made no effort to apply collective security mechanisms to the task of ensuring stability in the Middle East after the Gulf War.

Clinton and Collective Security

The Clinton Administration entered office pledging a new commitment to collective security generally and the United Nations specifically. "We cannot let every crisis around the globe become a choice between inaction or American intervention," Warren Christopher said at his nomination hearings in January 1993. "It will be our administration's policy to encourage other nations and the institutions of collective security, especially the U.N., to do more of the world's work to deter aggression, relieve suffering, and to keep the peace."[70]

Clinton's choice for U.N. ambassador, Madeline Albright, moved vigorously after taking office and, in language seldom heard during the Bush years, made the case for a greater reliance on collective security, saying it had never been given a fair chance in the past. The League of Nations set up after World War I had been fatally flawed, while the Cold War prevented the United Nations from being fully effective. (Although Albright did note as reassuring the fact that peacekeeping actually worked well, even in the Cold War.)[71] In the new era, she argued, U.S. foreign policy was necessarily heading in the direction of multilateralism, a trend the United States had to adapt to, especially in the realm of preventive diplomacy. "We are going to have to open our minds to broader strategies in multilateral forums. We need to project our leadership where it counts long before a smoldering dispute has a chance to flare into the crisis of the week."[72]

Albright attacked critics of U.N. peacekeeping performance as unfair. The potential for fraud and mismanagement existed in the U.N. as it did in any large organization, she said. The real problem plaguing U.N. activities was not corruption but "the sheer improvisational character of the system. This produces major gaps in institutional capacity on one hand and inefficiencies on the other. In fact, the small peacekeeping staff at U.N. headquarters is superlative, and steps are now being taken to increase its size and effectiveness."[73]

On the presidential campaign trail, Clinton had embraced in principle the need for the U.N. to create a rapid deployment force. Albright referred to this commitment during her nomination hearings,[74] and in May 1993, commented that there "is much work to be done in creating a U.N. military capability to engage in combat operations."[75] Yet Albright laid out no plans the Clinton administration had for doing this work, and during Clinton's first year in office, no significant steps were taken toward making a U.N. rapid deployment force a reality. During his first speech before the U.N. General Assembly in late September 1993, Clinton called for bolstering U.N. peacekeeping capabilities but said nothing about peacemaking or the creation of a rapid deployment force.[76] Similarly, while Albright highlighted in May "the need to establish a much sounder basis for financing and budgeting peacekeeping operations, " the administration had announced no major effort to push toward this goal during its first year in office.[77]

The year 1993, instead of being a watershed for a U.N. revival, proved to be a time of mounting questions among U.S. policy analysts about forging new security ties with the United Nations. There were persistent tensions between U.S. officials and Secretary General

Ghali, while the disastrous turn that America's involvement in Somalia took in fall 1993 was widely, if wrongly, blamed on U.N. incompetence. In regard to Bosnia, the United States refused to accept proposals that would place U.S. troops in a peacekeeping role under U.N. command and Clinton officials expressed a variety of broader doubts about participating in that or future U.N. operations.[78] On Capitol Hill, lawmakers like Senator Bob Dole argued that the United States should never, as a rule, place its forces under direct U.N. command.[79] By January 1994 the Administration had completed a Presidential Review Directive, PRD-13, which placed strict guidelines on when U.S. forces could be used in U.N. operations.[80]

Among outside experts there continued to be no consensus over the role that the United Nations should play in U.S. national security policy. A special panel appointed by President Bush in 1991 to study this issue was divided when it finished its work in September 1993. While most of the members envisioned a new and ambitious post–Cold War role for the U.N., other members, led by former U.N. ambassador Jeane Kirkpatrick, thought such a role was unworkable. The dissenters attacked "the conventional wisdom that the post–Cold War world is ready for a revitalized United Nations." They argued that there was a "dangerous incoherence in the United Nations collective security operations" and said that the United States had to be ready to defend its interests alone.[81] These arguments are hardly unique. And even among those who do agree that the United Nations should play a major role in the post–Cold War world, there is often disagreement about the details.

The Clinton Administration's views about the potential for regional collective security organizations largely parallels those of the Bush Administration. Clinton officials do not believe that NATO should be replaced with a new, more comprehensive collective security organization, and they doubt that European stability can be guaranteed by any institution in which the United States does not play a leading role. In East Asia the administration departed from Bush policies when it announced support for a regional collective security organization. But Clinton officials have also stressed that they do not see such an organization as negating the need for a continued U.S. balancing role in the region or as reducing the centrality of the bilateral security agreements that now tie the United States to various East Asian nations.

THE PRESTIGE IMPERATIVE

For the leading state in the international system staying number one requires a never-ending effort. Even when dominance seems secure new threats can lurk just over the horizon. As the post–Cold War era began, American foreign policy officials showed a keen understanding of the challenge the United States faced in retaining primacy.

In his acclaimed 1981 book, *War and Change in World Politics,* Robert Gilpin drew on centuries of history to describe the predicament of a leading power in generic terms. The legitimacy of a great power's leadership rested on three factors, said Gilpin. "First, it is based on its victory in the last hegemonic war and its demonstrated ability to enforce its will on other states; treaties that define the international status quo and provide the constitution of the established order have authority in that they reflect this reality. Second, the rule of the dominant power is frequently accepted because it provides certain public goods, such as a beneficial economic order or international security. Third, the position of the dominant power may be supported by ideological, religious, or other values common to a set of states."[82]

Each of these factors was understood by U.S. leaders in the early 1990s. American officials knew that the U.S. economic hegemony of the early postwar era was gone; America's great power status of the future could never be what it had been in past. But they also believed that the enduring centrality of security issues assured a basic constancy to how power was exercised in world affairs. Thus, as Gilpin's historical analysis would have predicted, U.S. officials have been deeply committed to maintaining the international security order established after the American victory in World War II; they have been determined to continue to provide "public goods," most notably a security guarantee in Europe, Asia, and parts of the Third World—especially the Persian Gulf. And they view American values as an important, if not always central, element of the U.S. world position.

American policymakers have also understood another factor that

Gilpin stressed in his analysis of how great powers rule: the immense importance of prestige. "Prestige is the reputation for power, and military power in particular," Gilpin wrote. "Whereas power refers to the economic, military, and related capabilities of a state, prestige refers primarily to the perceptions of other states with respect to a state's capacities and its ability and willingness to exercise power. In the language of contemporary strategy theory, prestige involves the credibility of a state's power and its willingness to deter or compel other states in order to achieve its objectives." Prestige is critically important because if a state's strength is recognized it can achieve its aims without having to resort to coercion or force.[83]

During the Cold War U.S. leaders were obsessed with prestige. In National Security Council memorandum number 68 (NSC-68), a pivotal Cold War planning document drafted in 1950, the struggle with communism was portrayed as highly symbolic. NSC-68 suggested that almost no conflict on the planet was unimportant, that the psychology of world politics dictated that any setbacks to the West or its Third World allies would lead to demoralization elsewhere, triggering further defeats. Only the United States could give the world moral and political direction, the document argued; only it could choreograph global stability and security. If the United States were lax in this effort, or if were perceived as lax because it allowed minor challenges to go unanswered, the resultant loss of U.S. credibility could lead to Communist gains worldwide.[84]

It was this logic, in large part, that led to the American commitment in Vietnam. The importance of Vietnam, U.S. leaders emphasized so often, lay not in its material assets or its strategic location. Rather, Vietnam was a testing ground of U.S. willingness to protect its friends against aggression. If the United States failed that test, the logic went, the damage to its credibility could be irreparable.

The end of the Cold War lowered the stakes of U.S. foreign policy; a loss for the United States no longer risked becoming a gain for its sworn enemy. Still, despite the demise of zero sum global politics, foreign policy officials in Washington have remained deeply concerned with prestige. They believe that both the amorphous foe of instability and the more real enemies represented by rogue states can find encouragement in U.S. weakness.

In regard to the developed world, U.S. officials have repeatedly stated their concerns that any hint that the United States lacked the will to guarantee the balance of power in Europe and Asia could trigger escalating tensions and regional arms races. In the Third World and the former Communist bloc, disorder is viewed as an ever present corrosive. For the United States to ignore it in even obscure regions is risky, since it can spread to other, more important areas. Unopposed aggression on one continent might encourage aggression on other continents, and a U.S. failure to defend its minor interests in the Third World might call into question its readiness to defend its major interests.

As long as the United States had some vital interests in the Third World, this adapted Cold War logic suggested, it would have to worry about its credibility in all of the Third World. More generally, as long as the United States viewed itself as the ultimate protector of the international system it would have to worry not just about threats that directly affected the United States but also about those that jeopardized the integrity of the system as a whole. It would want all potential transgressors against world order to believe that American power may be deployed against them. Maintaining a high level of credibility would thus be nearly as important in the new era as it had been in the old.

In the 1970s and 1980s Democratic and Republican foreign policy analysts often disagreed bitterly about when force should be used.[85] But as the Cold War ended this division faded away. Mainstream analysts in both parties increasingly believed that the world would be a more dangerous place if the United States was hesitant about using miltiary force. Concerns about prestige figured prominently in debates over the use of force in Panama, the Persian Gulf, Bosnia, and Somalia.

The December 1989 invasion of Panama, America's first post–Cold War operation, attracted very little criticism.[86] There seemed to be a recognition among foreign policy elites that, given new U.S. pledges to curb renegade regimes and ensure international stability, the disobedience of Panamanian dictator Manuel Noriega was far more than a minor annoyance; it was a challenge to U.S. credibility at a transitional moment in world politics.[87] If America couldn't maintain order in its own hemisphere, who would take it seriously in the more ambitious role of global stabilizer? "We have to put a shingle outside our door saying 'Superpower Lives Here,' no matter what the Soviets do, even if they evacuate from Eastern Europe," Colin Powell reportedly said before the invasion.[88]

Prestige arguments were cited frequently during the Gulf War. The Bush Administration's concept of a New World Order, as articulated within a month of Iraq's invasion of Kuwait, implied that respect for international rules and norms largely hinged on American willingness to use its power to thwart and punish Saddam Hussein. A separate and narrower argument held that the United States would lose the trust of its allies in the Middle East if it did not act decisively, especially after avowing for over four decades that it was committed to the defense of Saudi Arabia and the Gulf region.[89]

Once the United States had fully deployed its forces to the Gulf, and talk turned to the war option, prestige arguments gained increasing salience. Reversing Saddam's aggression may not have been a vital interest of the United States on August 2, argued former defense secretary James Schlesinger in November 1990 testimony to Congress, but the "investment of American prestige, the investment of the prestige of the President of the United States now makes it vital for Iraq to withdraw from Kuwait."[90] Henry Kissinger issued a broader warning : "The perception of American failure would shake international stability."[91]

As the crisis headed toward war, the theme of punishing Saddam as a lesson to other would-be aggressors increasingly entered into the debate over whether sanctions should be given more time to work and whether more flexibility should be shown in negotiations with Iraq. "To reward aggression anywhere is to encourage it everywhere," said former Pentagon official Richard Perle. "That is why there can be no political solution to the crisis . . . no negotiated compromise in which Saddam Hussein, even if he is forced from Kuwait, is allowed to keep the military power he has used to destroy a sovereign state and to threaten the destruction of others."[92] The Bush Administration's hard-line posture on the issues of sanctions and negotiations reflected, it seemed, a determination to make an example out of Iraq.[93] The administration appeared intent on decisively destroying Iraq's power, humiliating Saddam, and proving that those who broke the rules of the new order would not be able to escape severe punishment by the United States.[94] In the wake of the Gulf triumph, U.S.

officials suggested that other regional powers would think twice before engaging in aggression.[95]

Prestige considerations have been the subject of intense debate in regard to Bosnia and Somalia, interpreted in different ways by different observers, but weighing on the minds of U.S. policymakers. In Bosnia the issue of prestige was invoked by both supporters and opponents of U.S. intervention. In 1992 European expert Jeonne Walker voiced the concerns of many when she told a congressional committee that U.S. inaction in the face of Serbian aggression was "signaling to every other potential aggressor throughout Europe and beyond that he can literally get away with murder so long as his victim does not have oil." If the U.S. didn't do anything, warned Walker, "we are saying we really do not want a role in the military aspects of post–Cold War Europe's security."[96]

Bush and Clinton officials by no means dismissed these arguments in 1992 and 1993. Stephen Hadley, assistant secretary of defense for international security policy, commented in August 1992 that the United States had an interest in "ensuring that other states are deterred from following Serbia's approach to resolving ethnic and nationalistic disputes." The former Communist bloc offered many examples of unresolved disputes which one side might tempted to resolve by aggression, said Hadley. "It is therefore important that nations understand that there is a real price to be paid for pursuing territorial expansion by force."[97]

Secretary Christopher, in a February 1993 news conference, made some of these same points. "The world's response to the violence in the former Yugoslavia is an early and crucial test of how it will address the concerns of ethnic and religious minorities in the post–Cold War world," Christopher said. "Bold tyrants and fearful minorities are watching to see whether 'ethnic cleansing' is a policy that the world will tolerate. . . . Our answer must be a resounding no."[98] Christopher did not say that Bosnia was specifically a test of American resolve; he portrayed it as a collective challenge. Yet this language did not obscure the fact that as the undisputed leader of the international security system, and NATO in particular, the United States was being tested far more than any other single country by the situation in Bosnia. To many critics, American prestige during the Bosnia episode was hurt most when the administration was seen as failing to lead decisively NATO allies in the spring of 1993. The administration was widely lambasted for consulting with the allies and trying to persuade them to back harsher action against the Serbs, rather than simply laying down Western policy and making the allies fall into line.[99]

Prestige considerations also weighed heavily against intervention in Bosnia. American officials, particularly military officers, worried as much about unsuccessful U.S. military action as they did about unopposed Serbian aggression. Some invoked the lessons of Vietnam and Lebanon in counseling against intervention. "We have learned to insist on clearly stated objectives for the use of military forces, objectives that are realistically attainable, with a clear understanding of who the enemy is and what constitutes success," said Hadley. "These considerations suggest that we should be very reluctant to go beyond the commitment of military power already made by the President to the Bosnia crisis."[100]

There are many reasons why the United States did not intervene in the former Yugoslavia in 1992 and 1993. High among them was a fear of the damage that a failed intervention could do to American prestige worldwide.

That same fear underpinned the Clinton Administration's resistance to withdrawing U.S. forces from Somalia in the wake of a devastating attack on Americans forces there in early October 1993. In an October seventh speech from the Oval Office, Clinton said the United States could not cut and run in the face of challenges by an aggressive warlord, as many in Congress were suggesting. "Our own credibility with friends and allies would be severely damaged."[101] Instead, the administration dispatched new U.S. troops to Somalia while vowing eventual withdrawal.

Even an episode as minor as the U.S. failure to deploy a few hundred troops to Haiti in October 1993 was cast in terms of prestige, not by the administration this time but by many of its critics. The specter of rampaging thugs in Port-au-Prince preventing a landing by U.S. forces, whose mission was to aid the transition to democracy, was viewed as devastating for American credibility elsewhere. Former Secretary of Defense Dick Cheney expressed a widely held sentiment when he commented in late October: "If you're in North Korea today and you're told by the President of the United States that developing a nuclear weapon is unacceptable, and then you watch the perfomance in Haiti, you have to wonder whether or not you have to pay any attention to what he says."[102]

During the Cold War, the world of American diplomats and strategists was sharply defined by the dangers of the international environment. There was the danger of core Western allies being subverted or intimidated, of strategic Third World countries falling under Soviet control, of piecemeal Communist aggression on nearly every continent, and of course there was the danger of nuclear war. These dangers, often exaggerated, justified a foreign policy containing many elements that were disagreeable to the American public, and sometimes to policymakers themselves. There was little sense during the Cold War that the United States had an opportunity to reshape the international environment in an idealist manner, navigating abroad by the values it embraced at home.

The Cold War's end seemed to make such an enlightened global engagement possible for the first time in American history. Unlike the nineteenth century, the United States had the resources and status of a great power as the twentieth century moved toward a close. Unlike the 1920s and 1930s, its elites had the wherewithal and foresight to know that American well-being was best assured by active involvement in world affairs. And unlike the Cold War, the United States confronted no major threat that demanded moral compromise and policies of expediency.

But as has been argued in this chapter, the dominant characteristic of post–Cold War foreign policy has been a sense of danger rather than an appreciation of opportunities. Realists, not idealists, have been the architects of policy. Ensuring a balance of power in Europe and Asia, and preparing for new aggression in the Third World, have largely dictated how national resources are spent and explain much U.S. diplomacy. The idealist goals of promoting democracy and strengthening collective security may be more important now than at any time in U.S. history, but they are still not the principal drivers of America's global engagement. The continued importance of prestige in official thinking stands as further evidence that despite the Cold War's end many crucial elements in U.S. foreign policy remain unchanged.

5

ARMED FOR PRIMACY

Of all the expectations raised by the Cold War's end, none generated more immediate and widespread anticipation than the prospect of a hefty "peace dividend." In the popular imagination, the disintegration of the Soviet bloc eliminated the need for much of America's military establishment. For forty years the Pentagon had justified nearly every dollar it spent by pointing to the threat posed by the Soviet Union and its client states in Eastern Europe and the Third World. The sudden disappearance of these enemies presumably meant that a rapid reduction of defense spending could begin, freeing up hundreds of billions of dollars in the decade of the 1990s. To many the question was not whether there would be a peace dividend, but how it should be spent. This, in fact, was a topic of fierce debate in the first year after the Berlin Wall came down.

But the debate proved premature. The Cold War's end would not be generating an avalanche of public monies as the Pentagon wound down its global operations. Instead, by the middle of 1990 the Bush Administration had determined that the collapse of the Soviet threat merited only a 25 percent reduction in the size of U.S. military forces through 1997. Defense spending would decline by less than 20 percent.[1] In announcing the new policy in August 1990, President Bush called for a "policy of peacetime engagement every bit as constant and committed to the defense of our interests and ideals in today's world as in the time of conflict and Cold War." As it had in the Cold War, Bush said, the United States "must possess forces able to respond to threats in whatever corner of the globe they may occur."[2]

In 1992, after the Soviet Union's collapse, the administration agreed to additional cuts, and Secretary of Defense Cheney reminded Americans that he was supervising "one of the most drastic changes in U.S. military posture in history."[3] But the administration's long-range plans continued to be ambitious. As Senator Edward Kennedy noted to Cheney during a congressional hearing, defense spending in the late 1990s would be the same in constant dollars as it had been in the 1970s: "In 1997, at the end of the President's 5-year defense plan, 8 years after the fall of the Berlin Wall, 6 years after the breakup of the Soviet Union, we would still be spending as much on defense as during the Cold War."[4]

The sense of disbelief and outrage implicit in Kennedy's comment was not shared by all Democrats. President Clinton, upon taking office, did not propose any fundamental shake-up of U.S. defense policy or sweeping new cuts. Instead, because Clinton officials shared much of the Bush Administration's geopolitical outlook, they also embraced its military planning assumptions, with only a few modifications.

The Bush Administration had explicitly predicated its defense planning on the broad principle that the United States should retain a position of global primacy. In May 1991, JCS Chairman Colin Powell commented, "You've got to step aside from the context we've been using for the past forty years, that you base [military planning] against a specific threat. We no longer have the luxury of having a threat to plan for. What we plan for is that we're a superpower. We are the major player on the world stage with responsibilities [and] interests around the world."[5] The so-called Base Force that the Bush Administration outlined was portrayed, as Powell put it, as the "bottom line" for assuring American primacy.[6] It would keep 1.6 million Americans in uniform indefinitely and U.S. forces deployed around the world in much the same configuration as they had been during the Cold War, although at lower levels. In early 1992, with the tempo of defense cuts increasing, Powell warned that even cutting down to the Base Force plan might be too drastic. America's armed forces, he told Congress, "are reaching the point where, if capability is further reduced, our nation will have to alter its position of leadership in the world and redefine its objectives and policies."[7]

Beyond the general idea of leadership, two assumptions were key to Bush defense policy: first, that continued forward deployments of U.S. forces were needed to guarantee stability in Europe and East Asia; and second, that the United States would have to stand ready to deal with new Iraq-style aggression in the Third World. "If we fail to maintain the necessary level of military power, we are likely to find that a hostile power fills the vacuum," Cheney said in regard to Europe and Asia in early 1992. "We would do better in the future if our clear will and capabilities precludes arms races or aggression in regions critical to our interests before a threat is posed."[8] At the regional level, Cheney and other defense officials emphasized after the Gulf War that the United States had to be ready again to deploy massive forces to the Third World to thwart aggression by a regional power. They stressed that that next time the United States might not have the advantage provided by the military bases and hospitality of Saudi Arabia.

When he took office, Clinton's defense secretary, Les Aspin, announced that Pentagon planning would henceforth be based more on specific threats and less on ill-defined fears of uncertainty. He vowed that he and his planners would construct a post–Cold War defense policy from the "bottom up."[9] But when Aspin finally issued the results of the *Bottom-Up Review* on September 1, 1993, it contained few significant changes from Bush policy.[10] It confirmed what had been clear for months—that the Clinton Administration largely embraced the Bush Administration's key geopolitical assumptions, opposing both significant new troop reductions in Europe and Asia that might leave behind power vacuums, and any diminution of U.S. interventionary capabilities. The administration also accepted a variety of supporting ideas, including plans for fighting two regional wars at once, the case for keeping twelve aircraft carriers, and continued major spending on the research and development of new high-technology weapons.

Finally, the new defense policy illustrated that Clinton officials, like their predecessors, remained deeply skeptical about relying on multilateral cooperation to protect vital U.S. security interests. The Clinton Administration expressed a greater determination to increase such cooperation and a new commitment to having the U.N. play a greater role in assuring world order. But it also felt, particularly in regard to regional threats, that the United States had to have the military capabilities to handle new aggression by itself.[11]

Overall, the Clinton Administration's policy on this issue paralleled that of the Bush Administration, which had been explained in the final draft of the 1992 Defense Planning Guidance: "While the United States cannot become the world's policeman and assume responsibility for solving every international problem, neither can we allow our critical interests to depend solely on international mechanisms that can be blocked by countries whose interests are very different than our own. Where our allies' interests are directly affected, we must expect them to take an appropriate share of the responsibility, and in some cases play the leading role; but we must maintain the capabilities for addressing selectively those security problems that threaten our own interests."[12]

Collective security and multilateral cooperation were nice ideas, but the fate of the republic could not depend on them, Bush and Clinton officials agreed. In the end, as realist dogma held, the international system was a self-help system. And military power was the preeminent self-help mechanism.

In planning for a military establishment that reflected post–Cold War geopolitical assumptions and would sustain a position of overwhelming primacy, Pentagon officials have been guided by four broad ideas: forward presence, reconstitution, crisis response, and preventive medicine. The forward presence of U.S. troops around the world has been driven more by political concerns than military needs, and though this chapter will touch on this issue, the chief focus here is more on the three other ideas. The United States, Pentagon officials have argued, must keep the ability to rebuild, or reconstitute, Cold War–level forces to meet a new global threat. It has to be ever ready to meet any major security crisis that might arise in the world, or two such crises at the same time. And it has to work relentlessly to head off threats before they arise through such mechanisms as military aid.

RECONSTITUTION: A FOUNDATION OF POWER

Like their political counterparts, post–Cold War military leaders have been adept at using history to explain and justify their policies. While the lessons they draw from the past range from the general to the specific, the theme is consistently a cautionary one.

As Pentagon leaders see it, the record of U.S. military planning is a sorry tale, and as the post–Cold War era began they never missed an opportunity to retell it. "Retrenchment after major conflict is a historic pattern for the United States—one that stretches back to the Revolutionary War," commented Army Chief of Staff Gordon R. Sullivan in early 1992. Because of a lack of readiness after the Revolutionary War, said Sullivan, the "White House was burned" in the War of 1812.[13] After the Civil War, U.S. troops were demobilized so totally that they could barely handle the Indian Wars a few years later. During the twentieth century the consequences of overzealous demobilization and disengagement had been catastrophic. "It is widely recognized that our precipitous withdrawal from the world during the 1920s and 1930s contributed to the causes of World War II," commented Powell.[14] Had America remained engaged in Europe after World War I there would have been no power vacuum for Hitler to fill, Pentagon leaders suggested.

After World War II the U.S. erred again. "It only took us five years, five short years, to go from having the strongest military establishment in the world with no challengers to having a force that was barely able to hang on to the Korean Peninsula against the attack of a fourth-rate country," said Under Secretary of Defense Paul Wolfowitz. "We lost three thousand American casualties in the first week of Korea alone. That kind of short-sightedness not only brings wars, it means much bigger American losses when the wars happen."[15] Wolfowitz and other Pentagon officials also cited the drawdown after Vietnam as a further example of past mistakes. Poorly planned cuts had produced a "hollow army"; that is, a military force of substantial size but of low readiness and quality.[16]

Three Lessons of History

The history of twentieth-century military planning has yielded a few inviolate lessons, Pentagon leaders believe. These lessons were forcefully articulated during the Bush years as defense officials sought to stem calls for deeper military spending cuts. They have been largely observed since Clinton's election.

Limited Retrenchment

Lesson number one is that the United States should not abandon forward military positions overseas when threats wane because such withdrawals will be regretted later. The ending of the Cold War presented a huge temptation for retrenchment—never had America seemed safer. No country matched U.S. military capabilities. There were no alliances in existence that were hostile to U.S. interests. No region in the world critical to U.S. interests was under anti-Western domination. America's friends were as numerous as they were prosperous and strong. "The events of the last three years have provided America with strategic depth in which to defend our national interests that we have lacked for decades," commented Cheney in 1992. "We have gained so much strategic depth that the threats to our security are now relatively distant, so much so that they are hard to define with precision."

But this safety could not be taken for granted. The United States had to actively consolidate its position, not abandon it. "Today, we face again a fundamental choice," Cheney warned. "We can make the investments required to maintain the strategic depth that we have won—a much smaller investment than we made to secure it. Or we can fail to secure these advantages, and eventually the threats will not be remote, they will not be vague, and we will not have the alliances and capabilities to deal with them."[17]

Keeping intact the basic framework of America's global postwar military apparatus was among the most important investments.[18] U.S. forces in Europe and Asia can be substantially reduced, defense officials have conceded, but they should never be withdrawn altogether. Beyond promoting stability by heading off regional competitions, these forces are seen as constituting a vital foundation. Should a new global threat emerge, the United States could use this foundation to rapidly return to a Cold War–like military posture.[19] But if there were no foundation, if all the U.S. bases in Europe and Asia were closed down, U.S. officials worry that it would be much harder for the United States to return—not just physically, but also politically and psychologically. If potential challengers recognized these hurdles, they might be more willing to assert their power. As Cheney warned in 1992, the future may come "to depend on others' perceptions of our will and capability to reconstitute forces. . . . Maintaining the U.S.

presence around the world, and maintaining the capacity to respond in a crisis will be absolutely crucial in heading off future crises and dissuading future aggressors from challenging our vital interests."[20]

Most immediately, Pentagon officials believe that the United States must remain prepared for a resurgence of Russian militarism at least through the end of the 1990s. They acknowledge that the near-term threat from Russia is very low. In the judgment of Lt. Gen. James Clapper, head of the Defense Intelligence Agency, speaking in early 1992, the former Soviet Union possessed "no capability to directly threaten the the U.S. and NATO with large-scale military operations." But Clapper expressed widespread concerns when he pointed out that Russia would remain "the single largest military power on the European continent" and that its defense industrial base would continue to give it a "viable capability to produce sophisticated weapons."[21] These facts keep U.S. military planners thinking of Russia as a potential threat even as the United States and its allies have begun providing major economic assistance to it and the other states of the former Soviet Union.

In the year following the August 1991 coup attempt in Moscow, Pentagon officials played up the possibility of a "Weimar Russia." "The history of Weimar Germany exemplifies the dangers ahead for the new emerging democracies," commented America's top military commander in Europe in 1992. "A Weimar Russia poses the greatest threat to stability during the 1990s."[22] Upon taking office, Les Aspin accepted that the potential for Russian backsliding should shape U.S. policy. "Number one, Russia could continue on a course toward democracy and a market economy with a reformer like President Yeltsin," he said in March 1993. "Number two, it could go in an ultranationalistic, hostile, and authoritarian form of government. Number three, there could be a breakdown in authority, and nobody would be in charge."[23] In presenting the results of the *Bottom-Up Review,* Aspin said that Russia could someday present "not just a challenge in manpower and in tanks, but a challenge in new technology and capability."[24] These views were echoed by Aspin's successor, William J. Perry. In justifying a $264 billion defense budget for 1995, Perry said that the United States needed hedges to protect itself against the possibility of a resurgent Russia. "It is possible that Russia will emerge from her turbulence as an authoritarian, militaristic, imperialistic nation, hostile to the West," Perry said in a March 1994 speech. "In such a situation, we could indeed see a renewal of some new version of the old Cold War."[25]

In Weimar Germany, it took more than a decade for democracy to fail. Likewise, American officials believe that the uncertainty surrounding Russia's political future might well continue into the twenty-first century. In early 1992 Pentagon documents were leaked to the press that described hypothetical crisis scenarios to guide U.S. force planning through the rest of the decade. By far the most serious of these envisioned "an expansionist authoritarian government" assuming power in Moscow and then attacking Lithuania.[26]

According to some analysts of Russian military doctrine, such a scenario was well within the realm of imagination. James Sherr, a British expert on Russia, argued in late 1992 that Russia's military was becoming ever more autonomous and that its strategy now stressed the possibility of using force in the former Soviet republics to protect ethnic Russians. Sherr suggested that the potential for Western rearmament would serve to deter Russian military leaders with excessive ambitions, but commented that "the Russian military establishment shows little sign of being reconciled to the post–Cold War status quo that Westerners widely celebrate."[27] In Congress, lawmakers voiced concern in 1993 about evidence of a new Russian military doctrine that allowed for the use of troops beyond Russia's borders and that abandoned Russia's long-standing pledge not to use nuclear weapons first.[28] The gains of Russian nationalist politicians in late 1993 elections and the arrest of a high-level Russian spy in the CIA in early 1994 was seen as further evidence that Moscow still could not be trusted.

The possibility of a sudden turnaround in the East was only one of the surprises that U.S. policymakers worried about as they devised long-term defense plans in the early 1990s. In the wake of Iraq's invasion of Kuwait, defense officials stressed a theme that applied both to the developed and developing world: unpredictability. In his March 1992 testimony to Congress, Cheney observed that the U.S. government had failed to predict Pearl Harbor, the invasion of South Korea, early Soviet development of nuclear weapons, the collapse of communism, and the invasion of Kuwait. "The history of the twentieth century is replete with instances of major, unanticipated strategic shifts over 5-, 10-, or 20-year time frames," Cheney said. More recent events showed the "difficulty of predicting, with precision even over short periods of time, those kinds of crises that require significant military efforts."

Given this history, American military planners would be imprudent not to plan far ahead. Cheney noted that it took nine years to build a nuclear-power aircraft carrier, thirteen years to bring a new aircraft on line, and twenty-five years to train an officer who can command an armored division in combat. "We cannot base our future security on a shaky record of prediction," he concluded.[29] Aspin's *Bottom-Up Review* echoed this point in arguing for a substantial force structure: "It is difficult to predict precisely what threats we will confront ten to twenty years from now. In this dynamic and unpredictable post–Cold War world we must maintain military capabilities that are flexible and sufficient to cope with unforeseen threats."[30]

Technological Superiority and Industrial Capability

Lesson two of twentieth-century history, U.S. planners believed, was that the United States should not lag behind in the realm of military technology or lose the specialized industrial base needed to generate major weapons systems. "Time and again, we have seen technology revolutionize the battlefield," President Bush said in his August 1990 defense speech. "The nature of national defense demands that we plan now for threats on the distant horizon."[31]

For Pentagon officials the horizon was not even so distant. They believed, as did most other analysts, that the world of the 1990s was in the midst of a rapid military-technological revolution. This revolution encompassed such areas as stand-off precision weaponry—that is, guided missiles that could be launched from beyond the range of air defenses and hit their targets with near-certainty; stealth technology that would allow aircraft to evade radar and attack with total surprise; sophisticated sensors that could track objects both in the air and also on the ground from hundreds of miles away; and space-based military systems that continually transformed the realm of intelligence and communications. "The exploitation of these new technologies promises to change the nature of warfare significantly, as did the earlier advent of tanks, airplanes, and aircraft carriers," Cheney told Congress in January 1992.[32]

To Americans who watched the high-tech wizardry of the Persian Gulf War on their television screens, it may have seemed like the United States was already utilizing state-of-the-art military technology. But this was not the case. Most of the technology used in Desert Storm was developed in the 1970s and deployed in weapons systems in the 1980s. What this meant, said the Pentagon, was that the U.S. military forces of the early 1990s were already at risk of obsolescence. And this problem would get worse. As Admiral David Jeremiah, vice chairman of the JCS, commented, "The rate of technological innovation is accelerating every day, especially in information and data processing systems." The United States had to continually introduce new technology into its military, said Jeremiah, "so that our forces will not have to fight with systems that are technologically inferior to those of some future adversary." The United States also had to make sure it could produce cutting-edge technology itself, and Pentagon officials stressed the dangers of increasing U.S. dependence on imported defense technology.[33]

Pentagon thinking about military technology in the post–Cold War era offered another glimpse of the Bush Administration's realist assumptions at work. With the collapse of the Soviet Union's military-industrial complex and its desperate economic problems, it was highly unlikely that any future resurgent Russia could challenge America's military technological lead. But Japan and Germany were capable of posing such a threat. The Pentagon's vague talk of high-tech future adversaries seemed, at times, to reflect the intimations of the original Defense Planning Guidance draft of early 1992 that current allies could become future enemies. In a 1991 Pentagon assessment of military trends, the Soviet Union was shown to be lagging in nearly every category of critical military technologies while concern was expressed about how Japan was pulling ahead in a number of areas.[34] Presumably, a Japanese lead in defense technology would be of little worry if the interruption of U.S.-Japan security cooperation in the future was considered unimaginable. Likewise, U.S. dependence on military technology made in Western Europe and East Asia would not be seen as such a big problem if one had total faith that allies in those regions would remain allies.

Pentagon officials surely did not spend much of their time worrying about a future U.S.-Japan military rivalry as the Cold War ended. But the possibility seemed to be an implicit part of their long-term strategic outlook. The threat that allies could someday cut back defense technology imports was considered more likely. "Our future dependence on foreign sources could give these governments undesirable political leverage that might be used in a manner detrimental to U.S. national interests," warned Admiral Jeremiah in early 1991.[35]

In the realist view there is no such thing as a totally reliable friend. It was naive to believe otherwise. In the high stakes game of national survival, played out in a world without a central authority, realists argue that states are well advised to be as self-sufficient as possible in the realm of military security.[36] Pentagon planners obviously do not embrace or articulate realist logic in its purest form. However, the issue of defense technology once again shows the strong influence of that logic within the U.S. government.

A prime example of how the Pentagon's emphasis on high technology transcended the Cold War has been its continuation of the F-22 fighter program, originally known as the Advanced Tactical Fighter (ATF). Despite the end of the Cold War, the Pentagon announced in 1991 that it would continue ahead with the F-22, a warplane designed as a follow-on to the F-15.[37] Its post–Cold War case for the plane was built around Pentagon arguments that a continued large U.S. military establishment would be needed to fight Third World challengers and cope with any new global military threat that might arise. "We must maintain technological superiority in an environment that is changing," said Air Force official John J. Welch. Just because threats were currently unclear, it did not mean that the United States should cancel weapons systems that "our grandchildren will probably operate."[38] Air Force Secretary Donald Rice and other Pentagon officials warned that the Soviet Union was bound to field new fighter planes. But they also warned that France and other European nations were in the process of developing highly advanced fighters. In early 1992, pointing to both threats, Assistant Secretary Welch commented that that the "F-22 will dominate the Flanker/Fulcrum generation fighter and any of the forecasted CIS follow-on-fighters— as well as all aircraft under development throughout the world."[39] Yet given the collapse of the Soviet military industrial complex by 1992, it was only really the Western allies who had the potential to challenge U.S. fighter plane superiority.[40] Again, Pentagon officials never openly suggested that current allies could become enemies; the idea that U.S. and French fighter pilots might one day meet in combat was surely seen as farfetched, to say the least. However, apparently the idea was not so farfetched as to be dismissed from the imagination entirely. As Pentagon officials so often stressed in the early 1990s, national intentions could change and threats could arise faster than the United States could field new technology from scratch. From this logic it was a small step to argue that even close allies should not be allowed to pull far ahead in military technology.

To prepare for the worst, the United States needed more than laboratory research and development of advanced military technology, defense planners believed. It also needed a residual capacity to produce major weapons systems on a large scale. But given post–Cold War budget cuts that permanently ended the production of numerous weapons systems, analysts worried that key elements of the defense industrial base would be lost. As the Pentagon's 1991 Joint Military Net Assessment warned: "In the future, the number of major contractors for shipbuilding, nuclear power propulsion units, and combat vehicles may shrink to unacceptably low levels." Important military subcontractors could also disappear at an alarming rate, threatening the U.S. "ability to field state-of-the-art weapon systems on a timely basis."[41]

The Pentagon estimated that by the late 1990s it would take two to four years to restart from scratch closed production lines for major weapons systems. Such lead time was considered adequate given the long warning the West would have of any resurgence of Russian militarism. Moreover, Pentagon leaders pledged to make special arrangements for continued production in the case of weapons systems that were especially unique.[42] The decision to keep building Seawolf submarines after the Cold War illustrated this approach. By nearly all accounts the Seawolf was an archetypal Cold War artifact. Its original mission was to counter the Soviet submarine threat, specifically tracking Soviet nuclear missile-carrying subs. Like the F-22 fighter, the Seawolf represented cutting-edge military technology, and at almost $2 billion a sub it did not come cheap. With the end of the Cold War most analysts agreed that the Seawolf was no longer essential to U.S.

security. But in confirming in September 1993 plans to build a third Seawolf submarine, Secretary Aspin argued for his decision on industrial grounds. "We are concerned about whether there are some critical technologies that will be lost," he said in referring to the long gap in submarine production that would arise if a third Seawolf were not built.[43] The sincerity of this statement is impossible to assess in light of the political and economic factors that militated in favor of Seawolf production. However, it should be noted that Aspin had expressed concern about the nuclear propulsion industrial base before becoming defense secretary.[44]

To Pentagon leaders, the areas of military technology and the defense industrial base underscored the huge risks involved in winding down the Cold War defense establishment. History taught that big spending cuts could not be made quickly or cavalierly, and the Pentagon's inclination was to err on the side of prudence, even if the costs of doing so were enormous.

Keeping the Warrior Class

Lesson three of history, military planners believed, was that the United States should not lose its warrior class and the values it embodied. "Warriors win wars," summed up Cheney in 1992.[45] Throughout history, the argument went, nations that lost wars were often those that had begun neglecting or even denigrating their professional soldiers. In a world governed by power every society needed trained killers. Democracies were often uncomfortable with this fact and could be counted on to seek periodically to banish martial values, particularly after unpopular wars.[46]

At no time in American history was the public mood more antimilitary than in the 1970s. For many American military leaders of the 1980s and 1990s, the Vietnam War and its aftermath was remembered as a time of deep personal pain and profound national failure. A main source of the pain was society's denigration of military professionals. The national failure, in the military's view, was the appalling manner in which U.S. armed forces had turned into a "hollow army" in the 1970s, poorly equipped and trained for battle. In the opinion of Pentagon leaders like Colin Powell, the "Vietnam Syndrome" meant not only a crippling hesitancy to use military force abroad but also described the overall lack of appreciation for America's career warriors. Reinstilling such appreciation and safeguarding it through the future was a shared, deeply felt goal for the Vietnam generation of U.S. military leaders.

With the end of the Cold War emergency, military leaders had two concerns: that warriors might be seen as less important in the hopeful new era and that overzealous cutbacks could demoralize U.S. personnel and reduce U.S. readiness. They worried, in short, that America's traditional ambivalence about a large standing military would resurface as the wartime posture vis-à-vis the Soviet Union ended.

Pentagon officials countered this threat by emphasizing that America's warrior class, like its defense industrial base, had to be nurtured and protected. "While certain material stocks can go into deep reserve, the same is not true of perishable warfare skills, or of highly trained personnel whose abilities are the foundation of U.S. combat capabilities," observed the commandant of the Marine Corps in 1991.[47] The sophisticated U.S. war machine depended on specialists of every kind, many of whom required a decade or more of service to master the technology with which they worked. To Pentagon leaders their knowledge was a national treasure, which, if lost, could be gone for good. "It takes a long time to build a force of the quality that we have today, unmatched in the nation's history," Colin Powell commented in March 1992. But he added that the "force can be broken overnight" and "if you break the force, we may not be able to fix it in time, the next time it is needed."[48]

To avert a catastrophe of this kind Powell and other Pentagon leaders stressed that the post–Cold War drawdown could not move too quickly. "All of this build-down effort takes time," Powell said in early 1992. "These actions cannot be precipitous, they cannot be rushed. They must be carefully executed. As we downsize and restructure, we must not move so fast that we break this magnificent military we have painstakingly created over the past decade."[49] Already, reducing to the Base Force of 1.6 million by 1996 meant releasing roughly 100,000 people from service every year. Layoffs of this scope, in any organization, tended to produce widespread disruption and unhappiness. To cut deeper and faster would be extremely unwise, Pentagon leaders argued.

As for the forces who did remain, the nation could not be stinting in providing rewarding career opportunities for its professional soldiers and training them as well as possible. During the dark days of the 1970s, budget cutbacks had impacted on such areas as training time, weapons maintenance, and pay raises. The "hollow army" resulted from an emphasis on quantity over quality. "The services sought to retain force structure, retain numbers of airplanes, retain numbers of tanks, retain numbers of ships, in the wishful hope that over time the ammunition and the spares and the support would catch up," a top Air Force general remarked in late 1991. "They protected force structure at the expense of a robust capability to support it."[50]

Powell was relentless in hammering home the mistakes of the past drawdowns. "We've either broken the force, crippled it, or destroyed it every time we've done this in the last seventy or eighty years," he said in late 1991. "We won't let that happen again."[51]

Shortly after taking office, in February 1993, President Clinton put this point into the form of a solemn pledge: "The men and women who serve under the American Flag will be the best trained, best equipped, best prepared fighting force in the world, so long as I am President."[52]

During the early 1990s many observers found it hard to fathom why the Pentagon still needed to spend so much money in an era in which the Soviet threat no longer existed. But the Pentagon's view of history provides insight into this riddle. In the past, abandoning overseas positions had been a mistake; thus many Cold War deployments would have to be continued at a substantial cost. In the past, allowing weapons technology to become dated and the defense industry to lag had been regretted; thus the United States would have to stay ahead of even hypothetical technological threats and build weapons just so it did not lose the capability to do so. And finally, in the past the warrior class had been cavalierly cut back and neglected by an America tired of militarism; thus the country should pay handsomely to avoid making this error again, keeping its people in uniform well equipped and well trained.

Together all these basic requirements added up to a tremendous effort. Even without preparing for near-term threats in the Third World the Pentagon and many other analysts believed that a sizable military was required as a foundation from which to reconstitute a force capable of taking on a new global enemy.

The Pentagon's outlook found widespread support within the foreign policy establishement. In early 1990, not long after the fall of the Berlin Wall, Colin Powell warned ominously that "Some people are poised to make decisions calling for the precipitous dismantlement of the very strength that brought the prospects for peace," adding that in the 1990s "we will engage in a great struggle to determine whether we will repeat the failures of the past and cause dismantlement or, having learned our lessons, continue to maintain the needed strength to avoid putting America at risk."[53]

As it turned out, this struggle never occurred. By March 1992 Powell believed that a consensus had emerged on defense issues: "In my view, despite all of the noise of this debate, there is a surprising degree of unanimity to the direction we should be moving in."[54] Most mainstream experts agreed with the Pentagon's basic reading of history; they agreed on the enduring importance of military power in world politics and on the need to maintain a foundation of power. Few advocated gouging the defense budget. For example, an alternative defense plan outlined by Congressman Les Aspin in early 1992 received much attention for the significant cuts it proposed. Yet Aspin's plan was hardly radical. His base force would be 1.4 million troops instead of 1.6 million and his proposed defense spending through 1997 would be roughly $1.3 trillion as opposed to the administration's $1.4 trillion.[55]

CRISIS RESPONSE: SAFEGUARDING ORDER

During the Cold War, U.S. strategy toward the Third World had sought to contain communism or other radical movements, keep markets open, and retain access to natural resources. Military power had always been a key element in this strategy. The end of the Cold War did not drastically alter U.S. security aims in the Third World. There was no need to contain communism any longer, but radicalism remained a threat, defense planners believed. Radical regimes could seek to limit Western influence in the Third World and disrupt the status quo. As for markets and raw materials, access to these was a perennial strategic goal of the United States. In fact, as the twenty-first century approached, markets in the Third World were becoming

more, not less, important to U.S. economic well-being, and oil from
the Persian Gulf region was expected to account for a steadily growing share of U.S. oil imports.[56] The proliferation of ballistic missiles
and weapons of mass destruction also raised the specter, however dim
and distant, that the United States could one day face an apocalyptic
threat from Third World nations much akin to the one it faced from
the Soviet Union and China.

New Enemies

Long before the Cold War ended, U.S. national security analysts had
begun to make the case that threats could emerge from the Third
World that were quite independent of the U.S.-Soviet competition.
During the early and mid-1970s, such events as the India-Pakistan
war, the Arab-Israeli War, the Arab oil embargo, and the outbreak of
terrorism were profoundly alarming to U.S. analysts. They raised the
prospect of mounting instability in the Third World, which had little
to do with the Cold War. During this same time, developing nations
began making growing demands for greater political power and a
larger share of the global economic pie. The rising assertiveness of
Third World states in the United Nations underscored this trend, as
did the proposals they put forth for a New International Economic
Order.

In a 1977 report entitled "Military Implications of a Possible
World Order Crisis in the 1980s," RAND analyst Guy Pauker wrote:
"There is a non-negligible chance that mankind is entering a period
of increased social instability and faces the possibility of a breakdown
of global order as a result of the sharpening confrontation between
the Third World and the industrial democracies." Behind this development was the fact that "the gap between rich and poor countries is
so wide that no solution satisfactory to both sides is likely to emerge"
in the foreseeable future. Pauker predicted explosions in the Third
World "comparable to the peasant rebellions that in past centuries
engulfed large parts of Europe and Asia." The United States, he said,
will be "expected to use its military force to prevent the total collapse
of the world order or, at least, to protect specific interests of American citizens." In a 1974 article, General Maxwell Taylor, a prime
architect of U.S. counterinsurgency doctrine under President

Kennedy, put this point in less subtle terms: "As the leading affluent 'have' power, we may expect to have to fight for our national valuables against the envious 'have-nots.'"[57] In its sentiments, this comment echoed George Kennan's 1948 prognosis that a great global clash would inevitably occur as the poorer countries, representing the vast majority of the human race, challenged the West's right to control most of the world's wealth.

Some analysts of the 1970s compared the new security anxieties of Western elites to the fears felt by South African whites, and they used the term "global apartheid" to describe the emerging world situation. Like the white minority in South Africa, Western elites—also a small minority in global terms, and mostly white as well—sat atop a system that was economically inequitable and racially polarized. The global apartheid system was one in which, as Gernot Kohler wrote, integration of those in the West and those in the rest of the world "is made extremely difficult by barriers of complexion, economic position, political boundaries, and other factors." It was a system also in which "economic development of the two groups is interdependent," and in which "the affluent white minority possesses a disproportionately large share of world society's political, economic, and military power."[58]

Of course, the global apartheid analogy stretched only so far. Western elites did not subscribe to a fascist ideology and were committed to the political and economic development of Third World states. They knew that their own economies would do better if the Third World became richer, and that global security would grow as democracy spread. The applause that greeted the success of such countries as Taiwan, South Korea, and Singapore underscored this fact.

Nevertheless, the essential thrust of the global apartheid analogy had a powerful explanatory logic: the world was and would remain a grossly unequal place; Westerners knew that their wealth was both coveted and resented, and some of them saw military power as the most reliable means to assure that the aggrieved majority would not violently overturn the status quo.

The events of the late 1970s bolstered American concerns about disorder that was disconnected to the Cold War. The Islamic mobs in Iran and the revolutionaries in Nicaragua demonstrated the potential of the aggrieved majority. It was a majority that could oust American-backed governments, nationalize U.S. corporate holdings abroad, and cut off raw material flows that the United States depended on. It could take American citizens hostage or blow up American airliners. And once radical segments of this majority achieved success in one place, they could incite other aggrieved people. Mounting chaos could be the consequence.

In early 1980 the Defense Department, for the first time, cited disorder in the Third World unrelated to communism as a new threat that the United States would have to counter. "Political, economic and social grievances exist on a worldwide basis and provide fertile soil for sabotage, subversion, terror, and civil war," warned Secretary of Defense Harold Brown. Such grievances were fueled by a continuing failure to "provide for the basic needs of people and narrow the explosive disparity between weath and hunger." New tensions in the world were arising from "differences about the proper world distribution of income and natural resources." The international economic disorder stemming from increased global turbulence, said Brown, "could almost equal in severity the military threat from the Soviet Union."[59]

Brown and other strategic thinkers believed that U.S. armed forces must stand ready to deal with an array of threats quite different from traditional Cold War challenges. In the vital Persian Gulf region, for example, U.S. planners of the 1970s were primarily concerned about a Soviet threat to Western oil supplies. But there had also been talk since the Arab oil embargo of how the United States might have to respond some day to indigenous threats in the Gulf. In May 1975 Defense Secretary James Schlesinger commented that "we might not be entirely passive to the imposition of another embargo. I'm not going to indicate any prospective reaction other than to point out that there are economic, political, and conceivably military measures in response."[60] Independent analysts were less circumspect in their speculation, suggesting that the United States should use force to occupy Saudi Arabia and Kuwait if radical governments there cut off oil exports.[61]

The new concern about threats in the Third World produced, in 1977, a Pentagon concept called the Rapid Deployment Force (RDF). The purpose of the RDF was to enhance the U.S. ability to respond rapidly to crises in distant parts of the globe, and particularly the Middle East. With the revolution in Iran and the invasion of Afghanistan, bolstering the RDF became a major focus of Pentagon defense planning efforts. In 1983 the Reagan Administration institutionalized this planning by creating the Central Command, an interservice command that would be responsible for planning and executing any U.S. military intervention in the Middle East.[62]

Arming Against Disorder

During the Reagan years, U.S. national security policy in the Third World reflected the administration's single-minded anticommunism. However, as the Cold War waned and peace came to some East-West battlegrounds in Africa, Asia, and Latin America, U.S. planners shifted their focus. In the view of many analysts, both in and out of government, a world order crisis of dangerous new dimensions was brewing. And the Third World was the cauldron. A number of disturbing trends have been cited to substantiate this judgment by U.S. officials, including the alarming growth in world population, declining agricultural productivity, environmental degradation, and increasing poverty and urbanization in the Third World.[63]

By the late 1980s and early 1990s many U.S. officials worried that the world had already entered a period of increasing violence and that there was little prospect of change for the better. "Without a countervailing trend to point to, it appears that internal conflict and critical socioeconomic problems in the Third World will continue, at least at their present levels," commented a top Pentagon official in 1991. "It is probable that these dilemmas will expand in coming decades, with population and environmental degradation adding new pressures on weak economies and unstable political systems. As a consequence, it is certain that the impact of these geopolitical circumstances upon our national interests will compel the United States to engage directly or indirectly in some of these struggles."[64]

Pentagon officials saw an ominous link between the trends toward mounting chaos and weapons proliferation. More nations and groups with more reasons to fight were acquiring more deadly weapons. As mentioned earlier, there was in addition widespread concern that the end of the Cold War would create power vacuums in the Third World and remove some of the restraints that the superpowers had previously imposed on potential regional hegemons. General Carl Stiner remarked in March 1991, in outlining Third World threats: "In every region of the world, one or more states has the potential to attempt to establish regional hegemony."[65]

Even before the Cold War ended, elements within the defense establishment were already discussing ways to deal with the new world order crisis. In 1988 a blue ribbon panel, the Commission on Integrated Long-Term Strategy, released a well-publicized study on the future of U.S. defense policy. Among its conclusions was that America's defense establishment should give more attention to growing threats in the Third World, since this was where the United States was most likely to fight its next war. "Differences between the military capabilities of the Northern and Southern Hemispheres are steadily diminishing," stated one of the commission's spin-off studies. "By the first decade of the next century, we must anticipate a world in which groups hostile to the United States—governments and non-government political or criminal organizations—will have access to both weapons of devastating power and reliable means to deliver them."[66]

Paul Wolfowitz, Cheney's chief policy advisor, entered office with a deep appreciation for this outlook. "While the threat of a major conflict in Central Europe may be declining, the risk of the United States finding itself involved in conflict in the Third World is probably increasing," Wolfowitz commented during his nomination process. "Disturbingly, the lethality of weapons in those areas is increasing significantly to include ballistic missile technologies and chemical capabilities."[67] In late 1989 Wolfowitz suggested that the United States could face powerful foes in the Third World. "Potential adversaries in the Third World are no longer trivial military problems, if indeed they ever were," said Wolfowitz in a speech a few days after the Berlin Wall came down. "Grenada is not the kind of conflict we are likely to see often, nor is it the challenge against which we should measure our requirements." Instead, Wolfowitz envisioned the United States being challenged by major Third World nations, many of which had substantial armed forces. "The Iraqi army's tank fleet, for instance, is comparable in size to that of the West German Bundeswehr," Wolfowitz pointed out.

During the Cold War U.S. officials had justified a vigilant military posture in the Third World by saying that only the United States had the power to thwart Communist expansionism there. In the early 1990s this argument was adapted to a new era. Wolfowitz and others suggested that only the United States could keep order in an increasingly dangerous world. "We will remain the ultimate guarantors of order in many parts of the world," Wolfowitz said.[68]

Pentagon officials cite simple military arithemtic to prove this point. While all Western nations are threatened by events in distant parts of the Third World, the United States is the one nation that can, for example, impose a naval blockade on an aggressive Third World power. "To put it in perspective for you, in the West, the next navy of any size has fewer than one hundred ships," said Chief of Naval Operations Admiral Frank B. Kelso II, in 1991. Such a force is inadequate both to blockade and carry out other tasks.[69] The United States is also the only Western nation that can send major land forces to the Third World on short notice. Only the United States has the cargo ships and planes to carry large numbers of tanks, armored vehicles, and attack helicopters thousands of miles.

Both France and Great Britain have some power projection capabilities and a history of using them in recent times. Great Britain successfully retook the Falkland Islands from Argentina in 1983, proving that it could wage war against a substantial Third World nation some 8,000 miles away. France's Foreign Legion has also frequently shown itself to be a capable interventionary force.

However, as the Cold War ended, Pentagon officials emphasized that the day was fast fading when a small Western task force could handle Third World disturbances. In 1990 there were some half-dozen Third World nations that had tank fleets larger than any Western European country. Many Third World nations have substantial air forces and air defenses. Quite a few have submarines. Even small Third World nations are often armed with powerful precision-guided munitions. (The devastating French Exocet missile used by Argentina against the British fleet during the Falklands War underscored the threat such weapons can pose.) The spread of chemical weapons further bolsters the resources that Third World nations have to counter Western intervention.

In addition to the limitations of French and British interventionary capabilities, there is the problem of Germany and Japan. Neither of these leading industrial nations, both with a huge stake in the free flow of goods and raw materials, are interventionary powers, and both have constitutional limits on the use of military force abroad.

In short, U.S. officials believed that if the United States forfeited its ability to police the Third World, nobody else could take its place and that the industrial world would be essentially helpless in the face of threats to economic stability and resource availability. Therefore the military network that the United States had built in the Third World during the Cold War, along with the U.S. forces designed to fight in the Third World, still had a vital mission in the new era. Indeed, because the gravity of Third World threats was seen as increasing, the capability of U.S. interventionary forces would likewise have to be boosted. This could be done, it was argued, by reorienting the first-class forces designed to fight the Soviet Union to regional missions.

By coincidence, President Bush's speech officially announcing the new regional defense strategy was scheduled for August 2, 1990, the day Iraq invaded Kuwait. Perhaps no speech in presidential history has ever been more easily adapted to an unforeseen event. In addition to announcing the 25 percent force reductions and spelling out the rationale for keeping forces in Europe and Asia, Bush talked of how Third World challenges would now be the chief focus of U.S. military planning: "Notwithstanding the alteration in the Soviet threat, the world remains a dangerous place with serious threats to important U.S. interests wholly unrelated to the earlier patterns of the U.S.-Soviet relationship."[70] The invasion of Kuwait, Bush said, illustrated this point. The United States had to stand ready for unexpected emergencies on various points of the compass. It needed powerful standing forces that could be deployed without delay. It had to be ready to fight and win distant wars against a variety of possible foes.

Preparing for Intervention

When they took office in early 1993, Les Aspin and his defense team did not alter the regional strategy constructed during the Bush years. This strategy is based on a number of planning assumptions.

Two-War Scenario

During the Cold War U.S. defense planners had assumed that U.S. forces might have to fight more than one foe at a time. The fear was that the Soviet Union and its allies might coordinate simultaneous attacks on U.S. interests. A Soviet thrust in central Europe could be accompanied by a new attack by the North Koreans. Or aggression by the Soviet Union in Southwest Asia could ignite a conflict in Europe. Also feared was the prospect that bad geopolitical luck might require the U.S. to deal with two unrelated contingencies at the same time.

This planning assumption was carried over into the new era. The Pentagon assumed that if two things could go wrong at once, they would. As Colin Powell said in early 1992, "The most dangerous situation is you get tied down in one spot with no capability to do anything anywhere else and others see that and say, 'We have been waiting for just such a situation, where the United States cannot respond to what we may do.'"[71] For this reason, past policy would remain unchanged: "We must be able to project power to Europe, the Middle East, and Asia rapidly and in sufficient strength to defeat any aggressor," Powell said in 1992. "At the same time, we must retain sufficient force to deter or deal with another crisis happening elsewhere in the world."[72] Pentagon documents drafted in 1991 and 1992 directed the services to plan for simultaneous warfare in the Persian Gulf and Korea, as an illustrative scenario of the demands that could be placed on U.S. forces.

When Aspin took over the Pentagon he briefly toyed with the idea of abandoning the two-war strategy, arguing that air power could be used to hold one regional aggressor at bay while the United States defeated the other. But this strategy, known as "win-hold-win," was ultimately rejected amid fierce internal criticism.[73] And when the *Bottom-Up Review* was unveiled in September 1993 it reaffirmed the "win-win" strategy, saying the U.S. had to be able to defeat North Korea and Iraq simultaneously. "Well, is it really likely they would happen at the same time?" Powell asked at a Pentagon briefing. "Probably not. But while we are committed to one of these, it would be irresponsible, in our judgment, and unwise in our judgment, not to have sufficient capabilities to deal with the second, thereby perhaps encouraging the very conflict we do not want to happen."[74]

The two-war requirement had a major impact on U.S. force structure planning and the defense budget. Les Aspin said in March 1993, when his *Bottom-Up Review* was getting underway, that judgments about how many wars to prepare for is what "really shapes and sizes the defense budget."[75] Properly preparing for two wars would require twelve aircraft carriers (the same number deployed in 1980), twelve Army divisions, and twenty-four Air Force wings. The "win-hold-win" strategy would require ten carriers, ten divisions, and twenty air wings. If the United States only planned to fight one war at a time, while having enough troops left over for peacekeeping or humanitarian operations similar to the Somalia intervention, it would be need eight carriers, eight Army divisions, and sixteen air wings.[76]

Rapid Response

During the Cold War, U.S. war planning had a static quality. The same major threats existed for decades and planners could spend entire careers pondering how the U.S. would respond to a Soviet armored attack into West Germany or a new North Korean lunge for Seoul. This predictability would not exist in the post–Cold War era, Pentagon officials insisted. "We can still plausibly identify some specific threats—North Korea, a weakened Iraq, perhaps even a hostile Iran," commented Powell. "But the real threat is the unknown, the uncertain. In a very real sense, the primary threat to our security is being unprepared to handle a crisis or war that no one expected or predicted." The suddenness of the Gulf crisis had illustrated this point. " Paul Wolfowitz said after the war, "It should be clear from history, particularly from recent history, that regional threats can arise and embroil us in conflicts with very short warning."[77]

In the face of such uncertainty Pentagon leaders believed that the United States had no choice but to maintain substantial standing armed forces, always ready for battle at a moment's notice, which could be adapted to a wide range of situations. As Secretary of the Army Gordon Sullivan commented in early 1992, "Army forces will not be structured for combat in a specific theater, but rather will train to a more generic set of battle tasks and be tailored at the appropriate time to the requirements of the particular region in which they are to be employed."[78] Sullivan noted that during the Cold War half of the

U.S. Army had been deployed overseas near likely hot spots. In the future, the majority of the Army would be based in the United States. This meant that the Pentagon would have to increase its investment in strategic lift—that is, cargo planes and ships that could quickly move U.S. soldiers and their equipment to battlefields anywhere in the world. Such an investment would not come cheap. In fiscal year 1993 the Pentagon requested $2.9 billion for the C-17 transport aircraft alone.[79]

For the Navy, the requirement of rapid response is another consideration that has shaped force structure. Ships take a long time to move around the world and crews cannot be kept at sea for unduly long periods of time. If the United States wants quickly to have naval forces at the scene of a crisis, those ships cannot be too far away. Aircraft carriers based in the Indian Ocean are not ideally positioned to handle a crisis in the Caribbean, and vice versa. Since the Pentagon wants to be prepared for crises in nearly every part of the world, it sees the need for permanently stationing naval forces in much the same positions they had occupied during the Cold War. This assumption, along with the two-war requirement, explains the conclusion by the *Bottom-Up Review* that the United States has to keep eleven carriers on active duty, along with one additional training carrier.[80]

Heavy Ground Forces

Among national security analysts it was briefly popular in the 1970s and 1980s to argue that U.S. interventionary forces should be light and mobile. The original Rapid Deployment Force was conceived along these lines. Airborne troops and amphibious forces were key elements of the early RDF. The invasions of Grenada and Panama were the kind of operations for which such forces were designed.

Anxiety about growing Third World military power helped to undermine confidence in light interventionary forces. To fight nations with large tank forces, the United States has to be ready to deploy its own armored forces in the Third World, U.S. officials came to believe. This means not only developing strategic lift capable of moving the heaviest of equipment in vast quantities, but also keeping U.S. forces well trained in modern maneuver warfare. An enduring feature of the Cold War was the military's relentless preparation for a great land battle with the Red Army. The evaporation of that enemy from Central Europe brought such preparations to an end. But now the Pentagon sees itself facing a more challenging task: to keep armored forces based largely in the United States ever ready for combat on some distant and unfamiliar battleground. The desert of the Saudi peninsula proved to be ideal terrain for U.S. forces. However, Pentagon officials emphasize that a future combat expedition could be vastly more daunting. As Powell said in 1992, "No armed force has ever been given a more incompetent or accommodating enemy. We cannot count on that in the future. We also had months to get ready. Next time I doubt we would have months to get ready."[81]

Following the spectacular display of U.S. air power in the Gulf War, some analysts argued that it may be possible to win future wars with only a minimum of ground combat. These claims were reminiscent of those made after World War II, and as was the case then, they were fiercely contested by the U.S. Army. "While the circumstances of warfare have changed considerably in terms of weapons system advances and capabilities . . . the essential nature of warfare has not changed," said Army Chief of Staff Gordon Sullivan in May 1993. "Units are still required to close with the enemy to get within direct fire range, engage the enemy, and either destroy him or force him to move off of contested terrain. War takes place where people live and people live on the ground. It is there that all the effects of our great military establishment are directed, to seize and control territory and make the enemy amenable to our will."[82]

Naval Dominance

During the Cold War the justification for a big Navy was always said to be the Soviet threat; only the Soviet Union had the ability to jeopardize U.S. control of the seas. With the end of the Cold War the Soviet Union disappeared as a threat to U.S. naval superiority. Russia even lost control of one of its major ports when the Ukraine became independent and took over the vital Black Sea naval facilities.

As the 1990s began the world's seas were friendlier to the United States than at any time in its history. But this did not mean that the United States should become lax about its Navy, Pentagon officials believed. "We are the world's leading naval power today," said Cheney in June 1990. "There is no reason in the world why we should give that up."[83] Under the Bush Administration's original Base Force plan, the Navy would be reduced from about 560 ships in 1990 to 450 by 1996—about the number of ships deployed in 1980. The *Bottom-Up Review* envisioned deeper cuts through 1999, but not below 346 ships.[84]

To many outside observers, the need for a still vast Navy in the post–Cold War era was unfathomable. How was it that America's chief naval adversary had collapsed, yet the United States still needed to maintain such an overwhelming command of the seas?

Naval planners had a ready answer. Given the requirements of planning for simultaneous crises and ensuring quick reaction to regional emergencies, they argued that reductions to 450 ships and below would push the limits of prudence. "With a smaller Navy force structure, we will find it increasingly difficult to maintain the wide balance of capabilities required to counter sudden, unexpected geopolitical challenges and newly emergent threats," warned Admiral Kelso in 1991.[85] "To influence the outcome of a crisis, we need to be there when it starts," he commented a year later. "If our forces arrive late, we may ultimately have to deploy much larger forces, which could increase costs in lives, dollars, and resources." Kelso noted that it took forty days for naval forces to get to the Persian Gulf from either coast of the United States.[86] In the case of extended crises, moreover, a smaller force would make it more difficult for the Navy to adequately rotate personnel and ships.

Navy planners emphasized two other points. First, in an era of increasing uncertainty the United States could not depend as much on overseas bases. The Communist threat had been the glue that had held together the U.S. global military network. With that threat gone some nations might no longer feel the need to compromise their national sovereignty and allow U.S. military bases on their soil. The 1992 decision by the Philippines to expel the U.S. military was an example of this. As bases became less reliable the importance of naval power would increase. After the Gulf War Pentagon officials argued that in a future crisis the United States might not have the luxury of operating from bases in an allied country. In fact, there might not be any friendly countries at all in the combat theater. The United States thus needed a vast amphibious capability for "forced entry." It also needed substantial tactical air power based on carriers.

The second point made by Pentagon planners was that naval

threats from Third World foes could not be entirely dismissed. With many Third World nations now possessing guided anti-ship missiles, destroyers, submarines, mines, and advanced attack aircraft, the Navy had to be ready for real combat during regional contingencies. Submarines, for example, were traditionally thought of as a First World weapons system. Many observers assumed that anti-submarine warfare would be among the areas most deeply cut after the Cold War. But naval officials demurred. They argued that Third World submarine threats would not be negligible in the new era and that the United States would thus have to retain much of its ASW capability. "Although Third World submarines don't pose a threat to overall national security, they do represent a significant capability to delay our power projection in regional conflicts," said a top Navy official in 1991. "Unprotected commercial and military resupply shipping in the region of conflict are vulnerable to torpedo, mine, and missile attack."[87] Even the most powerful Third World nations deployed very few submarines: In 1991, North Korea had twenty-two, Libya had six, and Cuba had three. But the Navy pointed out that the export of attack submarines from the industrial world to developing nations was continuing and that history showed that even a modest submarine force could do enormous damage.[88]

High Technology

Through the Cold War the Pentagon justified its expensive emphasis on state-of-the-art military technology by arguing that the United States needed to overcome a numerical inferiority in weapons vis-à-vis the Soviet Union. It argued further that relentless R&D was needed so that the Soviets did not qualitatively pull even with the United States. In the early 1990s both these arguments were adapted for the new era. Beyond citing the potential for revived or new adversaries in the industrial world to field equal or better arms, military planners have suggested that serious high-tech threats may come from Third World nations. They have also said that U.S. high technology is needed to offset numerically superior threats in the Third World.

Again, the F-22 is illustrative of Pentagon thinking. In addition to justifying the warplane by citing the uncertain nature of world politics and the possible emergence of a new global threat, the Air Force has argued that the F-22 is needed to handle future Third World adversaries. "As weapons production becomes global, increasingly lethal weapons are available to smaller powers and regional states," warned a top Air Force general, Richard Hawley. "Third World battlefields will be in many ways as demanding as those we could expect in central Europe."[89] The big threat, as Air Force officials see it, is not that developing nations will produce jets that could rival the F-15 or F-16, America's top-of-the-line fighters. Rather, Pentagon planners worry that Western allies like France, Britain, or Germany could produce new aircraft that would be as good, or even better, than the current generation of U.S. fighters. These planes might then be sold to Third World nations and used against the United States in regional conflicts. The F-22 would safeguard U.S. air superiority in the face of such developments, allowing U.S. forces to prevail "anywhere any time against any threat," as Air Force Secretary Rice told Congress in February 1992.[90]

Pentagon leaders cite the Persian Gulf war to buttress their case for a continued emphasis on cutting-edge military technology. "Future adversaries may have ready access to advanced technologies and systems from the world arms market," warned Secretary of Defense Dick Cheney in January 1992. Iraq, for example, had deployed an arsenal filled with advanced French and Soviet military hardware. "The war showed that we must work to maintain the tremendous advantages that accrue from being a generation ahead in weapons technology."[91] Aspin's *Bottom-Up Review* embraced this outlook.[92]

Building the F-22 would help maintain this advantage in the realm of aerial combat, both as a hedge against Third World nations fielding top-of-the-line imported fighters or against Third World nations with hordes of less advanced fighters. In a September 1991 report the Air Force argued that offsetting large numbers of Third World enemy aircraft with "smaller numbers of even more sophisticated and stealthy F-22's is not merely desirable, but mandatory, if America is to retain its air superiority edge in the potential combat environments of the future."[93]

At times, Cheney and his successor would put the point in less absolute terms. An overwhelming technological edge was not actually a necessity as it had been in the Cold War. Rather, it was a desirable asset that could help win wars more quickly and reduce U.S. losses. As Cheney said: "We cannot afford to trade American lives with tyrants and aggressors who do not care about their own people, and we can afford to make them fight on our terms. This requires a continuing emphasis on technological superiority."[94] Pilots flying the F-22, the argument went, were less likely to be shot down in a future war than those flying the F-15.

Cheney added one other point to the case for why America's new regional strategy required technological superiority: to cope with proliferation threats. In a world of unforeseen perils, the United States "may require advanced systems to deal with the proliferation of weapons of mass destruction, either to destroy them before they are used, to defend against them, or to win decisively to discourage others from contemplating their use." Weapons like the F-22 and cruise missiles might be needed to attack heavily defended nuclear or chemical weapons installations, while tactical antiballistic missile systems like the Patriot would be needed to defend U.S. forces in the field from unconventional attack. As for pulverizing renegade proliferators, this is one of the new conventional missions that the Pentagon has devised for the B-2 Stealth bomber, a plane previously envisioned solely as a nuclear attack system. Before the Cold War ended the Pentagon had planned for seventy-five B-2s. In 1992 the Pentagon decided that twenty B-2s would be adequate.[95] As the Air Force explained it, the B-2's great asset was that it could strike with the same stealth as the F-117—a tactical bomber celebrated for its critical Gulf War missions—yet drop far larger quantities of bombs. "With the B-2, any potential target is at risk within hours, not days," said Air Force Chief of Staff Merrill McPeak in May 1993. "The B-2 will be able to penetrate the most dense enemy air defenses and deliver tremendous payloads against high-value targets."[96] The *Bottom-Up Review* endorsed this vision.[97]

A final realm of technological endeavor that the Pentagon has justified in terms of its new regional strategy is continued development of anti-missile systems. The proliferation of ballistic missiles in the Third World (along with the possibility of accidental missile launches from the unstable former Soviet Union) underscores the need for such work, Pentagon officials argue. The *Bottom-Up Review* called for focusing more of the U.S. anti-missile work on development of robust theater missile defenses to protect American interventionary forces.[98]

On a more ambitious level, Pentagon officials have imagined that American technology can provide a new kind of security umbrella to liberal friends. "We need to deploy missile defenses not only to protect ourselves but also to have the ability to extend protection to all nations that are part of the broader community of democratic values," said Cheney in 1992. "Like 'extended deterrence' provided by our nuclear forces, defenses can contribute to a regime of 'extended protection' for friends and allies."[99]

Such a regime was not publicly discussed by Aspin in 1993.[100] But this idea is consistent with the broader vision of a post–Cold War U.S. security hegemony, which the Clinton Administration has embraced. In the future, if the anti-missile regime concept goes forward, not only would U.S. power projection forces serve as the final guarantor of Western security interests in the Third World, but U.S. missile defenses would offer salvation to the industrial world in the face of rogue states or sub-national groups armed with ballistic missiles. In this way American protection would remain nearly as important to the democratic world in the new era as it had been in the Cold War.

Battlefields of the Future

Despite their relentless warnings about a "still dangerous world," Pentagon officials have often been vague about exactly where new threats might come from. To be sure, they have pointed repeatedly to such foes as North Korea or a revived Iraq. But they have also stressed that nothing can be predicted or taken for granted and that the United States must be prepared to go anywhere and fight nearly anyone. "The potential conflicts we face are many and varied, presenting different challenges in terms of quality of opposition, climate, terrain, distance, infrastructure, and host support," Paul Wolfowitz said after the Gulf War.[101]

Under Cheney, the Pentagon eschewed threat-based planning on the grounds that the international environment was too uncertain for such traditional methods. Under Aspin, an initial promise to use

threat-based planning soon gave way to renewed talk of general instability. In presenting the results of the *Bottom-Up Review,* Aspin and
Powell stressed that scenarios for North Korean aggression and a
renewed Iraqi threat were only illustrative, and that future U.S. intervention might in fact be provoked by other threats. "History suggests
that we most often deter the conflicts that we plan for and actually
fight the ones we do not anticipate," the review stated. Yet instead of
identifying plausible regional threats besides Iraq and North Korea, the
review broadly outlined the military power that some potential aggressors would likely have.[102] In talking about threats in the Middle East
besides Iraq, Powell implied that the United States might have to fight
a variety of powers: "There is such instability in this region of the
world. There are a number of nations that are arming themselves.
There are a number of nations who might not have interests that are
favorable toward our friends in the region and toward our interests."[103]

As will be discussed further in chapter 7, there is a considerable
contradiction in Pentagon thinking. On the one hand, military officials have repeated again and again the lesson they learned from Vietnam and from Lebanon in 1983: that the United States should never
commit forces to combat unless U.S. vital interests are clearly threatened and U.S. military objectives are unambiguous and achievable.
On the other hand, Pentagon statements in the early 1990s about
where U.S. combat forces might go in the Third World have tended
to be open-ended, suggesting that less rigorous standards might guide
future interventions. Part of the problem faced by U.S. military planners is the nature of the U.S. stake in the Third World. In principle,
stability in the Third World as a whole is seen as a vital interest of the
United States, especially given the widespread belief that unopposed
aggression in an unimportant region may encourage belligerency by
despots in more critical areas. In practice, there are only a few concrete places where U.S. military leaders would ever countenance a
large-scale commitment of ground combat forces. Whether deliber-
ately or not, U.S. officials have been nurturing a chasm between
declaratory policy and actual policy.

ARMS, AID, AND INFLUENCE

When the Third World was a battleground between East and West,
national security officials talked incessantly of creeping Soviet influ-

ence in it. For years the chief message of U.S. officials proposing new security assistance or arms sales to the Third World was always the same: if we don't establish a presence, the Soviets or their surrogates might. In 1988 this logic helped justify U.S. arms sales to 93 countries, U.S. military training for 98 foreign armies, and outright military aid to 31 countries.[104]

With the Cold War over, most Americans might have supposed that the great effort to romance developing nations with U.S. military equipment and know-how would taper off.[105] But this has not been the case. Instead, Pentagon leaders contend that the basic reasons for this effort transcend the Cold War.

Keeping Friends

In an era in which regional disorder is seen as a perpetual threat, as grave in some cases as the threat of Communist gains had once been, U.S. officials believe that strong Third World friends are essential and that the United States cannot afford to sever the ties it forged during the Cold War years. While trade and diplomacy can do much toward keeping these ties alive, arms sales and military aid are viewed by both U.S. officials and Third World elites as the most concrete manifestation of U.S. friendship.[106] For example, the royal leadership of Saudi Arabia hinted often in the early 1990s, as it had in the 1980s, that it considered Saudi access to America's most advanced arms to be a test of U.S. reliability as an ally. Bush administration officials, like their Reagan-era predecessors, warned often that congressional resistance to new Saudi arms sales could damage the Washington-Riyadh relationship.[107]

The availability of advanced arms is also a litmus test in U.S.-Israeli relations, and to a lesser extent in U.S. ties with an assortment of other nations. The end of the Cold War has not stopped Third World friends from asking the simple question, How dependable is Washington if it won't provide us with its top-of-the-line weapons?

Military aid also raises a credibility issue. American officials have worried that reductions of military assistance to Third World friends may suggest U.S. indifference to both their specific security needs and to overall stability in their region. Aid to Turkey, for example, had originally been part of a Cold War strategy of containing Soviet power. But since the collapse of Soviet power and the Gulf War such aid has been justified on the revised grounds that Turkey is a dependable ally in a volatile region, and that Turkish military power is a force for stability in the Middle East and in the southern regions of the former Soviet Union. A similar argument is used in regard to Egypt, which has consistently been hailed as an example of moderation in a region prone to extremism.[108] American officials have believed that it would be folly to alienate the governments of Turkey and Egypt by reducing the mammoth military aid programs to those countries. They point to cooperation from Ankara and Cairo during the Persian Gulf crisis to substantiate the argument that nurturing friends in the Middle East (and elsewhere) is as important as ever. "The reality is that, for the foreseeable future, assuring stability—and enabling our friends to protect themselves—will require that we continue to provide arms and related services and training when and where appropriate," said Under Secretary of State Reginald Bartholomew in 1991.[109]

Perhaps the most tangible legacy of Cold War security ties that the United States wants to preserve is access to overseas bases. Military aid can further this objective as well, especially in the Middle East. "Security assistance leads directly to access, and without access afforded by our friends we cannot project U.S. military forces into the area and stay there for any length of time," commented General Norman Schwarzkopf, head of the U.S. Central Command, in early 1990.[110] A program of security assistance and arms sales may also ultimately facilitate large-scale U.S. intervention, officials argue. "It places U.S. weapons and support systems on the ground in countries where the U.S. may deploy and operate," said Schwarzkopf's successor, General Joseph P. Hoar, in discussing the Middle East in 1992. "Within those countries, security assistance programs have created indigenous infrastructures capable of supporting U.S. forces upon arrival."[111] Nowhere was this more true than in Saudi Arabia, where years of U.S. arms sales, base building, and technical assistance made it possible for U.S. forces during the Gulf War to operate with exceptional ease.

Strengthening Friends

In a world of potentially more numerous threats, yet fewer U.S. defense resources, arms sales and military aid are seen as a way to bolster the local policing powers of U.S. friends. "These programs enable us to strengthen friends and allies so that they can play a larger role in promoting regional stability, defending themselves against aggression, and participating in peacekeeping activities," said Under Secretary of State Lynn Davis in May 1993.[112] In effect, the United States is getting Third World nations to take on security responsibilities that it cannot afford, U.S. officials suggest. "To equal the military effect of friends and allies who are 'on the scene,' we would have to spend much more on U.S. force structure, mobility, and logistics," commented one U.S. official, tallying up the material benefits of having well-armed proxies.[113]

American planners believe that pro-U.S. governments can help hold the line against renegade regimes and aspiring local hegemons, sustaining balances of power in key regions. In the Middle East, for instance, Egyptian military power is seen as helping to contain neighboring extremist governments in Libya and Sudan. Israeli military forces regularly swing into action to strike at anti-Western terrorists in Lebanon, and Saudi Arabia's military power, along with that of the other Gulf states, allows it to better defend Persian Gulf oil supplies and offset the power of Iran and Iraq.

The idea that local proxies can be armed to defend U.S. interests first became a central part of U.S. national security policy during the Nixon administration, when the debacle in Vietnam forced a partial retreat from regional commitments. The fall of the Shah of Iran and the misbehavior of various proxies served at times to call into question the wisdom of the so-called "Nixon Doctrine."[114] But fundamentally it remained attractive to Washington officials, and became ever more so once the defense budget began to decline in the late 1980s.

Influencing Friends

American officials often argue that arms sales and security assistance can provide some measure of leverage over the political and military policies of recipient nations. Indeed, Under Secretary Davis has commented that "the importance of a security assistance program should not be judged by the level of funding, but by the degree of leverage we gain. . . ."[115] In the military realm, leverage is seen as useful for

steering governments toward more responsible and pro-Western policies, including adherence to non-proliferation treaties.[116] Even more
direct leverage may derive from the dependence of key elements of a
country's military establishment upon the United States. Sophisticated arms such as fighter planes cannot be maintained long without
a steady stream of spare parts and technical assistance from the nation
that supplied them.[117] In some cases, this dependence can give the
United States virtual veto power over how a client state employs its
high-tech arsenal. Iran is cited as an example. When the Shah fell and
the new Islamic government pursued policies that Washington found
threatening, the United States cut off the supply of spare parts for
Iran's U.S.-made arms, including its fleet of F-14 fighters, which were
never fully combat ready again.

U.S. officials also value security ties with Third World nations
because such ties offer reliable access to political-military elites. During the Cold War such access was prized as an avenue for preaching
anticommunism. In the new era American officials argue that U.S.
military aid can help consolidate democracy, both through military
training programs that instruct Third World officers in the proper role
of the military in a democratic society, and by making U.S.-supplied
Third World military forces hesitant to overthrow democratic governments for fear of losing U.S. aid.[118]

Defending Friends

During the Cold War the United States helped shore up a wide array
of governments in the face of nationalist and Communist revolts. The
largest recipients of security assistance were often those nations combating rural insurgencies or other forms of antigovernment activity.
According to a study by the Congressional Research Service, the
United States was involved in some forty-five instances of low-intensity conflict between 1945 and 1990.[119]

In the view of many U.S. officials the demise of communism as a
messianic ideology will not mean an end to low-intensity threats. On
the contrary, such threats—and the U.S. role in countering them—
are seen as possibly increasing amid a growing world order crisis.
Much of this violence is likely to be ignored by the United States.
However, U.S. officials believe that some future intrastate turmoil will

carry regional or global perils and hence demand a U.S response. Evidence of this trend was already apparent by 1991, Army Chief of Staff Carl E. Vuono has said. Third World disorder, "especially when coupled with the possibilities for international terrorism and narco-trafficking, are demanding an expanded role for military forces in peacetime operations aimed at assisting the threatened countries to enhance their domestic stability and democratic development."[120]

In the Cold War U.S. officials believed it was wiser and cheaper to support beleaguered friendly governments than to contain or fight hostile ones that might replace them. This attitude has endured in the new era, but also important to U.S. thinking, as Vuono suggested, is the idea that it is far better to keep central governments strong than to deal with the rogue groups that could flourish amid anarchy. A single no-man's-land like Lebanon can provide haven for multiple terrorist groups, while an emasculated government like Colombia's can prove powerless to stop the exportation of illegal drugs.

Ironically, the spread of democracy in the Third World may well mean more U.S. involvement in low-intensity conflicts there. Aid to democratic governments in trouble provokes none of the moral unease on the part of U.S. citizens and legislators that surrounds support of authoritarian regimes. Quite the opposite—popular outcry about attacks on democrats abroad can bring pressure on the White House to take action to help them survive in power or restore them to power. (This happened after the democratic government of Haiti was overthrown in a military coup in 1991.)

The preceding exploration of U.S. post–Cold War defense policy has taken Pentagon statements at face value and assumed that defense planners are genuinely concerned about the range of threats they have outlined in recent years. There is, of course, ample room for more cynical explanations of how defense policy has evolved. Like bureaucrats everywhere, Pentagon officials can be counted on to fight hard for the biggest possible share of the pie and to seek the perpetuation of their institution's status and strength. One obvious tactic in this enterprise is to emphasize a highly pessimistic view of global trends and to make frightening predictions about the consequences of cutbacks in defense spending. The Pentagon has always been skilled at such scare tactics.

However, while bureaucratic self-preservation must be considered in any analysis of defense policy, past or present, it is hard to accept it as the principal motive behind post–Cold War military planning. The pessimistic picture of world politics painted by Pentagon leaders has not been markedly different from that painted by other U.S. officials and outside experts. Nor has the Pentagon been alone in emphasizing the need for highly capable U.S. military forces after the Cold War. The U.S. defense policy of the early 1990s is thus best seen as flowing from geopolitical assumptions that are widely accepted within the foreign policy establishment. If one accepts that a new global threat might someday emerge, that U.S. troop withdrawals could create instability in Europe and Asia, that well-armed regional powers will inevitably challenge Western interests, and that U.S. Third World friends are likely to face serious internal and external security challenges in a deteriorating world, then there are few grounds for arguing with Pentagon leaders about the military establishment they have planned for the new era. If one accepts, also, the premise that no other nation has the power or wherewithal to provide leadership on security matters, yet that such leadership is indispensable to global order, then the case for U.S. military primacy becomes even stronger.

Many mainstream critics of recent years have quibbled with defense policy in the margins, suggesting ways, for example, to cut an extra $100–$200 billion dollars out of the military budget over a period of five years. But these critics have not, for the most part, contested the premises upon which U.S. defense plans are based. Instead they have largely accepted those premises and argued, as Les Aspin did in 1992 when he was a congressional critic of the Pentagon, that U.S. primacy could be sustained at a lower cost.

Any serious challenge to U.S. defense policy must be part of a broader critique of the geopolitical and theoretical assumptions that drive America's post–Cold War foreign policy. Must the United States continue to worry about a new global threat emerging in the future? Are the industrial areas of Europe and East Asia so inherently unstable that the presence of U.S. forces is needed to assure order? Is it likely that new Third World challengers will threaten U.S. vital interests, perhaps even in two regions at once? More generally, has the nature of world politics significantly changed in recent years or is the realist outlook still as valid as ever?

It is these questions that I will now take up.

6

A SAFER WORLD: INTERNATIONAL RELATIONS AFTER THE COLD WAR

Since the end of the Cold War, a central task for American national security planners has been to assess the level of danger that now exists in the international environment. Under both the Bush and Clinton administrations, that level has been seen as quite high, and realist assumptions largely account for this verdict. Realism outlived the Cold War because it holds that the struggle for power is an inescapable feature of world politics, unallayed by even such a momentous event as the collapse of communism. Far from being discarded, realist thinking has served as the compass for many foreign policy experts in the unfamiliar terrain of the post–Cold War world.

As long as realist axioms shape policy, the United States government will never feel it can escape from its obligation to serve as an active balancer and sheriff in much of the world. It will never have either the sense of flexibility or the resources needed to vigorously pursue an idealist foreign policy agenda. There will inevitably be further retrenching of the U.S. global position, especially if a domestically oriented Democrat remains in the White House, but the scope of that retrenching will be limited as long as U.S. foreign policy elites embrace the idea that the United States must lead or face the prospect of growing disorder.

As a navigational aid for foreign policy thinkers in the new era, realism suffers from a number of problems. First, by purporting to offer a general theory of international affairs, realism exaggerates the degree that world politics is susceptible to social scientific analysis. Realists confidently offer predictions about the nature of the post–Cold War world that are derived from a theoretical paradigm that cannot be tested because of the limited supply of relevant historical cases. Second, the realist paradigm itself no longer describes reality in much of the industrial world and in some parts of the developing world. Realism portrays the world as a predatory place, where war is a permanent possibility and every state must make security its top priority. Through much of history, this outlook was the soundest approach to interstate relations, and earlier generations of U.S. leaders erred when they failed to fully appreciate this reality.

Obviously, there has not sprung into existence a global government that can now offer a security umbrella to all states. But states in the developed world—and increasingly in the developing world as well—have become far less war prone, and this trend is likely to accelerate with the end of the Cold War. Four major developments in world politics account for this change: the spread of democracies, which tend to not make war on one another; a growing recognition that military aggression no longer pays; increasing economic interdependence between states; and the rising power of supranational institutions to regulate global affairs.

Among international relations scholars, debate has been intense about these trends, with realism coming under greater attack than at any time since the 1970s.[1] For the most part, however, this attack has been highly segmented, with liberal critics of realism highlighting the transformative power of one trend or the other, rather than discussing them together and showing how they reinforce each other.[2] Realism's critics have also done a poor job of explaining how the Cold War's end may strengthen their case. And, in a concession that holds major ramifications for U.S. security policy, liberals have been too ready to accept that realism remains as applicable as ever to the Third World.

Among foreign policy leaders there is widespread agreement on the importance of the trends that are promoting peace. But this new confidence in the liberal view of world politics remains too weak to unseat the realist assumptions that still drive U.S. foreign policy. American foreign policy will not change fundamentally until officials believe that the forces promoting cooperation among nations are now considerably more powerful than those generating conflict. This belief would lead to the recognition that instability and new conflict between states may be phantom threats in the industrial world and highly exaggerated ones in large parts of the Third World. American primacy, in turn, would be seen as less indispensable to the cause of world order.

THE POOR SCIENCE OF REALISM

The realist claim to an iron law of world politics rests on two assumptions, it will be recalled. The first, popularized by Hans Morgenthau, is that human beings are innately distrustful of one another and naturally compete for power and position, readily employing deceit and violence when it furthers their aims. Because world politics, like all politics, is a reflection of human behavior, it will always be a rough business. In domestic politics, central authority in the form of government can keep humans from devouring one another by imposing laws and sanctions to enforce those laws. But no such authority exists in international politics. Thus states must protect themselves by acquiring arms and showing a willingness to use them. Realists acknowledge that various measures such as arms control agreements and alliances can mitigate the severity of this anarchical world but say that fundamentally the international security environment will remain a dangerous place as long as human nature remains unchanged.[3] Nobody claims that the Cold War's end has altered human nature.

The second realist assumption, contributed by the so-called neo-realist or structural realist thinkers like Kenneth Waltz and Robert Gilpin, is that the structure of world politics inevitably breeds conflict. Waltz argues that in a state system made up of separate units there will be unavoidable friction as the distribution of power fluctuates and states maneuver to enhance their security.[4] This is especially true in a multipolar system, where states have to worry about shifting alliances and multiple potential enemies. War by accident or miscalculation in such circumstances is an ever present possibility. Waltz contends that bipolar systems are inherently more stable because confrontation took place along a single familiar axis.[5] Thus the structure of world politics is seen by Waltz and his disciples to have become more perilous with the Cold War's end.[6]

Gilpin's structural realism focuses on the long cycles of history. He states that "the nature of international relations has not changed fundamentally over the millennia." Through the ages, world politics had been shaped by the rise and fall of hegemonic powers. Rivalry and conflict inevitably occur when a declining great power—and all great powers eventually do decline—can no longer maintain its position. Disputing Waltz's contention that war is usually the product of miscalculation, Gilpin suggests instead that "it is the perceived certainty of gain that most frequently causes nations to go to war. . . ." Challengers of a weakened hegemon seek to change the system in a way that will be profitable to them. They use war to advance their interests by nibbling—making war against small states previously protected by the hegemon—or by overthrowing the hegemon altogether and imposing their own hegemon.[7]

Despite their differences, Waltz and Gilpin agree on a fundamental idea: by looking at the structure and distribution of power in the international system, one could accurately predict whether world politics would be stable or not. They also agree on a further point: world politics was more stable when the leading state sustained its position of leadership.

Pessimistic Predictions

In predicting the future of world politics, Gilpin did not suggest that the decline of American hegemony would inevitably produce new conflict. Seeming to contradict his claim that world politics has not changed since the days of ancient Greece, he saw hope that more peaceful processes of international change would become the norm.[8] However, Christopher Layne has built on Gilpin's analysis to predict the inevitable rise of new powers and destabilizing challenges to America's fading hegemony. "As Germany and Japan become great powers, the quality of their relations with the United States will be profoundly altered," Layne wrote. "Relations will become significantly more competitive, greater power security rivalries and even war will be likely, and cooperation will correspondingly become more difficult."[9]

Waltz and his disciples have been even more insistent in applying realism to the new era. John Mearsheimer's grim forecast of future instability in Europe is based in large part on the Waltzian claim that multipolar systems are inherently unstable. The same analysis has been applied to East Asia, where multipolarity and imbalanced power seem to loom in the future. As earlier chapters showed, U.S. foreign policy elites largely accepted this theoretical outlook in the early 1990s, believing that Europe and Asia might spiral toward disorder if the United States withdrew its security guarantee from those regions. They also believed more broadly that activism on the part of the leading power, now the United States, is required to keep order in the Third World.

Before assessing the relevance of the realist paradigm to today's world, it is worth asking a more basic question: Can any theoretical paradigm be a reliable basis for predicting the future of world politics?

Untestable Claims

International relations does not lend itself to good social science. Joseph S. Nye, Jr. has observed: "History provides a poor substitute for a laboratory."[10] It is often far from clear that events in one era can profitably be compared to events in another. Does the behavior of nations in the nineteenth century, before telephones and televisions were invented, tell us anything about how nations might behave in the 1990s? Perhaps so, but it is hard to make reliable comparisons given all the variables that cloud any analysis. Because theorists of world politics do not have a large body of roughly similar case studies to draw from, in which they can carefully control for variables, their theories can never be rigorous.

For example, it is difficult for today's theorists to argue persuasively that multipolar systems are inherently unstable. In the past, multipolar systems in Europe always contained nondemocratic and militaristic states. They were not home to formal collective security arrangements, and they existed before the invention of instant communications and satellite technology that could monitor the military activities of nations from space. Such multipolar systems of the past may be able to yield some insights into the stability of a multipolar system made up of democracies that are party to collective security agreements and informed about one another's military establishments. Certainly they are worth studying with an eye to the future. As scholars Thomas J. Christensen and Jack Snyder point out, thought needs to be given to studying ways to mitigate the unstable effects of multipolarity as the world becomes more multipolar.

Yet such study is likely to yield only limited insights, not hard evidence that can serve as the basis for reliable predictions. Using the cases of Europe in 1914 and 1939, for example, Christensen and Snyder are constrained in their ability to offer analysis that is truly analogous to Europe in the future. They acknowledge in the conclusion of their exhaustive analysis that "We make no claim to be able to foretell the balancing dynamics of the coming decades."[11]

Christopher Layne's argument about why new powers will inevitably rise to challenge America's post–Cold War hegemony also illustrates the limitations of using international relations to predict the future. Layne draws on historical evidence from the periods 1660–1714 and 1860–1914 in contending that unipolar moments, such as the one that now exists, are bound to cause a geopolitical backlash in which new great powers arise. He claims that this evidence supports the theoretical claim that even a benevolent hegemon like the United States will face distrust and challenge.[12]

The problems with this argument are many. Neither the case of French hegemony in the seventeenth century or British hegemony in the nineteenth century are easily relevant to that of American hegemony in the late twentieth century. France under Louis XIV was an absolute monarchy whose growing power posed a major security threat to other European states; the United States is a democracy whose military power is not seen as threatening the security of its long-time Western allies. Indeed, both Germany and Japan have shown a distinct preference in the post–Cold War era for continuing to let the United States manage the international security system while they concentrate on economic growth and trade.[13]

Great Britain in the late nineteenth century was a hegemonic power at a time when all of Europe was scrambling for position in the colonization of Africa and Asia. The period was also one of rapid growth in industrial power, with the United States, Germany, and Japan beginning to flex their new muscles for a variety of reasons, only one of which was a desire to balance against Great Britain. Today, there are no rivalries for colonies; Germany and Japan are far more mature and stable nations, in which many of the causes of militarism have declined markedly; and the shifts in economic power are occurring within a web of multilateral ties and common understandings that would have been unimaginable to national leaders in the nineteenth century.

The point is not that Layne's prediction should be dismissed out of hand, or that the theoretical arguments behind it are nonsensical. His basic claim is a familiar one and will be evaluated in this chapter and the next. Here the argument is simply that his historical evidence is not relevant enough to provide reliable insights. Layne, like those theorists who warn about the inherent instability of multipolarity, does not have the kind of empirical foundation that social scientists require to build strong arguments. Three cases over a three-hundred-year period is not an ideal database, to say the least.

Unpredictable Leaders

Even the existence of more cases might not solve the problem of prediction. History changes course unpredictably. "Politics has the nasty habit of not always behaving as even the most plausible and rigorous theories suggest it should," commented Robert Jervis, a pioneer in international relations theory.[14] The reason for this, in large part, is that world politics can be affected by a relatively small number of people, whose actions are hard to forecast. When social scientists study, say, the behavior of welfare recipients or the voting patterns of legislators, they can draw general conclusions based on a large pool of subjects who are all in essentially the same situation. For the most part, these conclusions will not be invalidated by the actions of a few wild cards.

Realists err in applying the assumption of sameness to states. They suggest that the domestic politics of particular states are of negligible importance in thinking about world politics because the dynamics of the state system, with its inescapable security pressures, ensure that all states will behave in more or less the same fashion. But this notion is weak. Domestic factors are of pivotal importance in international politics.[15] Quite apart from the impact that the nature of political systems can have on the conduct of foreign policy, the characteristics of national leaders can be crucial. History has amply demonstrated that the rise or fall of individual leaders can drastically alter the direction of a country's foreign policy. How states use their power resources in the international arena is often determined by those who lead the states. A leader with a personal desire to foster peace is less likely to engage in aggressive behavior than a ruthless, egotistical leader who romanticizes war and dreams of conquest. More broadly, foreign policy can be decisively impacted by the ideology and priorities leaders bring to office, the strength of their political base, their perceived need to prove themselves in the international arena, the type of advisory structure they set up, and even the views that their spouse happens to hold.[16] In the Middle East, the assassination of Saddam Hussein in July 1990 and his replacement with a moderate military leader might have resulted in no invasion of Kuwait and no Gulf War. Had North Korea's Kim Il Sung been a slightly more moderate or cautious leader in 1950 he might not have launched an invasion of South Korea and the whole course of the Cold War could have been dramatically different. Likewise, the personality and political outlook of Kim Il Sung's successor will have a huge impact on whether that country pursues more moderate policies in the future, including unification with South Korea.

The classic example of how individuals can shape history is Adolf Hitler. World War II did not stem inexorably from a set of predictable behavior patterns or structural flaws in the international system, although these played some role. Instead, the megalomaniacal personality of Adolf Hitler was all-important to the way events unfolded in Europe in the 1930s and early 1940s. Had Hitler been assassinated in 1932, history probably would have taken a very different course.

Events can also have a large impact on history. International affairs during the 1980s may well have been different if equipment failure had not occurred during the April 1980 attempt to rescue the U.S. hostages in Iran. A successful mission might have secured Carter's reelection and in turn this could have led to a much more moderate U.S. foreign policy than was pursued under Reagan. Economic depressions, earthquakes, plagues, technological breakthroughs, the discovery of oil, and environmental disasters are other kinds of events that can lead to unpredictable shifts in foreign policy and relations between states.

As soon as one accepts the evidence that individual leaders and unforeseen events have often shaped the outcome of world politics, theories of international relations begin to look less reliable as tools for predicting the future.

Learning from History

Another characteristic of the real world that confounds theory is the ability of diplomats and strategists to learn from past mistakes and take actions to avoid them in the future.[17] This occurred in the United States during the 1940s when a return to isolationism was rejected and U.S. participation in the U.N. was accepted. In postwar Germany and Japan, the intense aversion to militarism reflects widespread fears that history could somehow repeat itself. In the future, European leaders within a new multipolar system are likely to bear in mind the miscalculations that led to World War I. They can be expected not only to set up arrangements that engender confidence and dampen uncertainty but also to exhibit acute caution in international crises.

The degree of historically informed behavior by and among European leaders will be crucial in determining levels of stability in a future multipolar system, but realist theory offers no tools for predicting the extent to which such behavior will take place. Thus it cannot forecast levels of stability under a new European multipolarity—a shortcoming that is evident in Layne's argument. The likelihood of a new political-military assertiveness on the part of either Germany or Japan hinges on the willingness of leaders and citizens in those countries to put aside deep-seated misgivings about great-power ambitions that spring from historical experience. But realist theory provides little insight into whether this might happen.

"The most important defect of realism," Francis Fukuyama has commented, "is that it ignores historical change and treats international relations as if it were a timelessly self-identical sphere, independent of all the social, political, and economic evolutionary trends going on around it."[18] Realism of such a purist nature is not widely embraced within the U.S. foreign policy establishment, but there is a strong sense that the historical progress toward greater cooperation among states can be easily reversed, with the world sliding back into an earlier, far less stable era. In early 1992, David Abshire crystallized the fears of a return to the past held by many mainstream analysts when he wrote that the "principal long-range threat is on a grand scale; that the Atlantic and Pacific democratic allies will develop conflicts among themselves and, in effect, return to a situation similar to that of the eighteenth and nineteenth centuries."[19]

American primacy will be seen as the answer to this threat as long as U.S. thinkers fail to appreciate fully the trends that have transformed the nature of international politics.

THE DEMOCRATIC ZONE OF PEACE

By far the most important trend reshaping world politics is the spread of democracy. In the early days of the Republic, American policymakers recognized that countries with liberal governments were more likely to be friendly to the United States. As other democratic nations came into being, their leaders also tended to feel more comfortable trusting fellow liberal governments. The belief that autocratically ruled countries were a greater threat to peace was graphically borne out in the twentieth century. In World War I, World War II, and the Cold War, liberal European nations allied with one another and with the United States to thwart nondemocratic enemies. These alliances were more than arrangements of mutual convenience; they were underpinned by a strong sense of shared political values and goals.

Kant Revisited and the End of History

The political scientist Michael Doyle was one of the first writers to argue empirically that democracies do not fight one another. In a survey of two hundred years of interstate conflict, Doyle set out to prove the idea first put forth in the eighteenth-century writings of Immanuel Kant that the spread of liberal governance would create an ever widening "zone of peace." Doyle concluded that "even though liberal states have become involved in numerous wars with nonliberal states, constitutionally secure states have yet to engage in war with each other." He suggested that this was more than a fluke of history; there is, he argued, "a significant predisposition against warfare between liberal states." Even threats of war among such states are considered illegitimate. "A liberal zone of peace, a pacific union, has been maintained and has expanded despite numerous particular conflicts of economic and strategic interests."[20] Since the publication of Doyle's work, scholars have conducted an extensive examination of democratic peacefulness.[21] In a 1989 assessment of the causes of war, Jack Levy wrote that democracies not going to war with one another is "as close as anything we have to an empirical law in international relations."[22]

By the logic of this argument, the end of the Cold War carries the potential to change fundamentally the nature of world politics, not just its structure. With the spread of liberal government to Eastern Europe and the former Soviet Union in the early 1990s, the developed world reached the point—contingent, of course, on the survival of democracy in the East—where the specter of war between its members was finally disappearing.

This idea lies at the core of Francis Fukuyama's essay on the "end of history." Fukuyama defined the end of history as mankind's "ideological evolution and the universalization of Western liberal democracy as the final form of human government."[23] Like Doyle, whose work he drew on, Fukuyama rejected the realist contention that the internal character of a state had no impact on how it behaved in the international system.[24] A chief consequence of the triumph of liberal democracy in the First World would be a lasting peace among those nations, who would now have little of importance to fight over. Fukuyama imagined that as history ended, the world would become a rather unexciting place. He acknowledged, however, that history was still very much under way in the Third World.[25]

Unconvinced Realists

Some realists dismiss the claims of liberal optimists like Doyle and Fukuyama. The possibility of war between democracies is central to Christopher Layne's vision of the future.[26] And John Mearsheimer has written that "mass publics, whether democratic or not, can become deeply imbued with nationalistic or religious fervor making them prone to support aggression, regardless of costs."[27] Even countries that share similar political systems may find themselves divided by historical resentment, deep cultural chasms, and fierce economic competition, realists observe. Japan and the United States are both democracies, but they are different in many other ways. Nationalism and prejudice have shown an ability to take root on both sides of the Pacific. Samuel Huntington emphasizes that the central fault line in world politics in the future will be clashes between civilizations—that is, between peoples who are Islamic, Western, Hindu, Slav, Confucian, and so forth. The passions that drive such clashes will be more powerful than the potential for democracy to mitigate them. "What ultimately counts for people is not political ideology or economic interest. Faith and family, blood and belief, are what people identify with and what they will fight and die for."[28]

The list of democratic nations that harbor long-standing suspicions of one another has been considerably lengthened with the spread of democracy in the former Communist bloc and is sure to grow longer if liberal governance continues to spread in the world. In the future, the power of democracy to ensure peace among states is likely to be tested as it never has been before: in regions where the fires of nationalism burn the hottest, where territorial claims simmer, and where prosperity is elusive. In East Asia, for example, the democracies of South Korea and Japan are hardly natural friends. Many South Koreans bitterly resent the discrimination faced by the Korean community in Japan. They also have not forgotten their country's brutal treatment at Japan's hands during World War II. The Japanese, in turn, view Korea as a potential political, military, and economic competitor in East Asia.

While pointing to the tests that lie ahead, some realists question claims about the past, arguing that the thesis of democratic peacefulness has never actually been proven, as Doyle and others claim. Kenneth Waltz has written that the American-British War of 1812 was "fought by the only two democratic states that existed, and conflict and bitterness between them persisted through the century and beyond." He also notes that the American Civil War was fought between two democracies and argues that Germany was a pluralistic democracy at the time of World War I.[29] Huntington observes that few democracies were geographically contiguous before World War II, thus it is hardly a surprise that they did not go to war, since war most often occurs between states that border one another. After World War II, most of the world's democracies banded together under American hegemony in the face of the Communist threat. These unique circumstances also made war between democracies highly unlikely.[30] The much-cited friendship between France and Germany that followed the democratization of Germany, realists say, may well not have happened without a common enemy for them to unite against.

With the Cold War over, American hegemony fading, and many democratic states with old grudges now living side by side, realists suggest that there is no guarantee that war between democracies will not occur.

The claims and counterclaims surrounding the alleged peacefulness of democracies can neither be substantiated nor refuted on empirical grounds, a debate that once again illustrates the scanty knowledge base upon which theorists of international affairs are forced to rely. Nonetheless, the idea that democracies are peaceful toward one another appears logically sustainable.

Democratic Checks on War

To begin with, as Doyle reminds us, the cornerstone of liberalism is that all people have a right to govern themselves. On an international level, liberalism suggests that "states have the right to be free from foreign intervention," Doyle writes. "Since morally autonomous citizens hold rights to liberty, the states that democratically represent them have the right to exercise political independence. Mutual respect for these rights then becomes the touchstone of international liberal theory." In other words, a democratic state would not forcefully impose its rule on another democratic state since such a move would run counter to its basic principles. As political scientist Stephen Van Evera has succinctly observed, "the ideologies of democracies do not incorporate a claim to rule other democracies, so they have no ideological motives for expansion against one another."[31] This means that even the weakest neighbors of a democratic state can rest assured that they will not be gobbled up during some future campaign of aggrandizement.

Democratic elites who do decide, in a breach of their basic principles, to make war against another democracy, will be hard pressed to sell such a war to their citizenry. They cannot claim to be fighting to free an oppressed people, since the populace of a democratic state are already free. Generally, democratic leaders must ask elected legislators for approval to wage a war. If public opposition is intense, legislators may reject the idea. This process can serve as a check against an ill-considered or unjust war. It is hard to imagine, for example, that a democratic Iraqi parliament, after a genuine public debate, would have sanctioned unprovoked aggression against Kuwait. Indeed, in a democracy it seems unlikely that Saddam would have survived politically after his ruinous attack on Iran in 1980. Democratic checks might also have prevented Argentina's disastrous 1982 invasion of the Falkland Islands, or made possible a negotiated settlement before war occurred with Great Britain.

While it is true that democratic mass publics can be whipped into a war frenzy and become supportive of aggression, this is less likely when democracy functions effectively. Any mass public that has experienced war before will know that it is usually the average citizens of a country who suffer the most during military conflicts. In Iraq the poor and middle class have been far more affected by the Gulf War and international embargo than the elites who support Saddam. In a future democratic Iraq, how many non-amnesiac citizens would be likely to support another foreign adventure that might have the consequence of again depriving them of basic necessities for years on end? Probably not a great many, unless the war is seen as just and unavoidable.

The democratic process can neutralize much of the power of propaganda. As Van Evera observes, "War-causing national misperceptions—militarist myths, hyper-nationalist myths, or elite arguments for 'social imperial' wars, for example—should be dampened by norms of free speech, which permit the development of evaluative institutions that can challenge errant ideas." These institutions will never be perfect, of course, and misguided policies will often be approved by them. But this "danger is smallest in societies that permit free debate, as all democracies must to some degree."[32]

Nations of Laws, Governments to Be Trusted

Democracy also contributes to a nation's peacefulness by making it more likely to respect treaty obligations and defer to international legal authority. A nation's treaties with other nations constitute the law of the land. To abrogate them, a democratic leader must win the approval of the legislative body that initially ratified the treaty. Because of the procedural roadblocks that stop democracies from discarding treaties, nations that have signed nonaggression pacts or arms control agreements with democracies need not worry constantly about sudden betrayal. They can therefore afford to be much less vigilant militarily toward other democracies. Such a stance itself produces stability, since military buildups can produce competition and distrust even among nations that have no major grievances toward one another.

Making a pact with an authoritarian regime is a very different and far more risky proposition. A dictator can violate an arms control treaty without being denounced by opposition leaders or exposed by the press. (Although he may well be caught in the act by foreign intelligence agencies.) The neighbor of a dictator must always be on guard, no matter what agreements may exist on paper. Saudi Arabia, for example, probably rightly surmises that its 1989 nonaggression pact with Iraq is not considered a sacred document by Saddam Hussein.

In the realist worldview, nations can never entirely trust one another because of the ever present possibility that one of them will defect from cooperative arrangements and become an aggressor. With physical survival at stake, realists say that no nation can ever gamble all its chips on such arrangements.

Democratic government is no ironclad solution to this problem, but it does dramatically improve the odds of betting on cooperation. There is probably not a leader in the world who would be as comfortable in an important security pact with a dictatorship as with a democracy. If such considerations of trustworthiness are a key factor in stability, then it follows that the internal characteristics of states do determine how stable an international system will be. An international system made up of open democracies will be more stable than one with with many nondemocratic members.

Beyond respecting treaties, democratic states are more likely to play a constructive role in supranational institutions. Democracies, it is true, may be just as prickly about national sovereignty as dictatorships. But as societies that champion the rule of law in domestic affairs, democratic states are more likely to honor the idea of international law. When disputes arise with other nations, they will be more likely to pursue their goals through peaceful negotiations.

The Backsliding Argument

In addition to doubting the innate peacefulness of democracies, realists question the permanence of such systems, saying that it is always possible that a democracy will revert to authoritarianism. "This threat of backsliding means that one democratic state can never be sure that another democratic state will not change its stripes and turn on it sometime in the future," John Mearsheimer has argued. By this logic the post–Cold War world will not be a stable zone of peace but rather a more familiar anarchical environment where liberal states worry about militarily and economically falling behind friendy democracies that may turn into belligerent authoritarian regimes.[33]

While this claim appears stretched in regard to Western Europe and Japan, non-realists recognize it is as a valid possibility in newer democracies in the former Communist bloc and East Asia. The specter of a "Weimar Russia" is particularly disturbing, since a new authoritarian regime in Russia would have considerable power resources at its disposal. Even the failure of democracy in the smaller states of Eastern Europe is often cited as a major risk, since this could trigger insecurity throughout the region, and new wars between those states might draw in Russia and the powers of Western Europe. In East Asia, the failure of democracy in a unified Korea could cause major anxieties through the entire region, especially if that nation pursued nuclear arms.

The backsliding threat will exist in the First World for some time to come, and it will never disappear entirely. However, other developments in world politics suggests that non-democratic countries might not be as threatening to the liberal community as they once were, and that backsliders will face strong pressures to avoid aggressive policies and return to the democratic fold.

TIES THAT BIND: INTERDEPENDENCE AND PEACE

The issue of economic interdependence has long been one of the most hotly contested points in debates over world politics. Liberals have argued for at least two centuries that trade links between states would make them less warlike toward one another. A world bound together by the common quest for prosperity, liberals have imagined, would be a place of greater understanding and declining conflict. During the 1970s, as the economies of Western Europe and Japan boomed, and as transnational corporations became more powerful and visible, interdependence theory became very popular. A mounting sense of global economic integration called into question the realist view of world politics. Even Henry Kissinger acknowledged in 1975 that "the traditional agenda of international affairs—the balance among major powers, the security of nations—no longer defines our perils or our possibilities. . . . Now we are entering a new era. Old international patterns are crumbling; old slogans are uninstructive; old solutions are unavailing. The world has become interdependent in economics, in communications, in human aspirations."[34]

Realist thinkers mounted a successful counterattack against the liberal optimism of the 1970s. In the academic realm, scholars like Waltz dismissed the idea that interdependence secured peace and restated the belief that military force would always be the most important arbiter of world politics. In the political world, a renewal of Cold War tensions and the ascendancy of a hard-line president ensured that realist premises continued to shape U.S. policies.

The Liberal Revival

Despite these setbacks, liberal analysts of world politics did not abandon their ideas in the 1980s. Instead, they deepened their thinking, showing in new works how agreements and organizations set up to facilitate interdependence were institutionalizing cooperation among nations in a manner that had not characterized previous eras of history.[35] In the 1970s, realists had countered the idea that interdependence could secure peace by observing that trade often created friction between states and that economic ties among European nations were extensive on the eve of World War I. In the 1980s liberals refined their answer to this point: it was not simple levels of interdependence that determined whether cooperation occurred, but the existence of institutions and regimes that regulated ties between nations.[36] In the period before World War I there were few institutions; after World War II there were many. "International cooperation among the advanced industrialized countries since the end of World War II has probably been more extensive than international cooperation among major states during any period of comparable length in history," wrote Robert Keohane in his 1984 study of the world political economy. "International systems containing institutions that generate a great deal of high-quality information and make it available on a reasonably even basis to the major actors are likely to experience more cooperation than systems that do not contain such institutions, even if fundamental state interests and the distribution of power are the same in each system."[37]

In a more traditional approach to this issue, Richard Rosecrance argued in a 1986 book that interdependence was growing in the late twentieth century as trade, communications, and transportation brought nations into greater contact than ever before. The mutual profitability of these links was a powerful incentive for states to pursue peaceful foreign policies, while the stunning success on the part of trading states like Japan set an example that other nations could not ignore. Rosecrance argued that the trading states had little thought of giving up commerce for policies of conquest and that these states represented the wave of the future. "It is not the American model that Japan will ultimately follow. Rather it is the Japanese model that America may ultimately follow."[38]

The world view of interdependence theorists differs from that of realists in a number of respects. Realism suggests that the state is the dominant actor in international affairs; interdependence theory points out that there are now a variety of transnational actors, from multinational corporations to international organizations, which increasingly shape world politics. Developed states are linked by multiple channels, both private and public, official and informal, on a variety of levels. State leaders can no longer interact with one another like chess players who have total control over all their pieces.[39]

Realism argues that military force serves as a final arbiter of relations between states; interdependence theory suggests that once states no longer fear one another, as industrial democracies generally do not, military force recedes into the background of their relationship. Negotiations among friendly states on such vital issues as trade are not going to be affected by who has greater military forces.

Linked to this point is the different way in which realists and interdependence theorists view hierarchy among issues in world politics. Realism holds that the high politics of security affairs will usually dominate the international agenda, since physical survival is the foremost goal of states. But as physical survival is increasingly taken for granted, and the quest for prosperity moves to the forefront of policy, interdependence theory suggests that there will be no clear or consistent hierarchy of issues in world affairs. As Henry Kissinger said in 1975: "The problems of energy, resources, environment, population, the uses of space and the seas, now rank with questions of military security, ideology, and territorial rivalry, which have traditionally made up the diplomatic agenda."[40]

Today, the long-standing foci of power politics are even less dominant on the international agenda than they were when Kissinger made his comment. With the Cold War over, with global economic competition intensifying, and with new pressures being exerted on the globe's environment and natural resource supply, security issues are moving ever farther from the center stage of world politics. In the 1970s and 1980s, the most important international meetings were thought to be superpower summits. Now economic conferences among industrial leaders are clearly the most important meetings. At these meetings the agenda is broader than ever before, with environmental issues increasingly becoming the subject of impassioned discussion and negotiation.

Among U.S. foreign policy thinkers, managing the relationship with the Soviet Union was long seen as the highest priority of U.S. diplomacy. Strategic military issues were central to that relationship. Now there is a growing recognition that America's single most important bilateral relationship is with Japan. Economic issues are at the center of this relationship.

As a tool for describing the current state of international affairs, especially in the developed world, interdependence theory, far more so than in the 1970s, offers a better insight into what guides the behavior of states than does realism. It is also more compelling as a tool for predicting what world politics will look like in the years to come.

Cooperation or Defection?

The optimistic claims of interdependence theorists remain unpersuasive in the new era. A central claim of realism is that states will often have incentives to defect from cooperative arrangements with one another. Because no central authority can prevent such defections, states can never fully rely on cooperation to safeguard their security. They must accept the fact that they live in a self-help system and behave accordingly.

Because states worry so much about their security, they will often see economic issues through this prism, realists say. In the liberal worldview all states should celebrate one another's economic growth, since prosperity in one state usually aids prosperity in another, leading to absolute gains for everybody. Cooperation can further this process, but in the real world, say realists, an insecure state that finds itself outstripped by a trading partner might begin to worry that the partner will someday harness its greater wealth and position to an aggressive agenda.[41] Cooperation can suddenly become a less appealing prospect as states worry more about relative gains, asking not "Will both of us gain?" but instead "Who will gain more?"[42] States may also worry about becoming overly dependent on a particular trading partner for markets or resources, opening themselves up to economic blackmail. Realists argue that these fears serve as a brake on the economic cooperation of states and limits the peace dividend that liberal analysts suggest will come from such cooperation.[43] Waltz argues that even when there are limits on the likely future use of military force, concern "over relative gains continues to be the natural preoccupation of states."[44]

Another problem with interdependence in the realist view is that it can actually increase friction between states. When two states have little to do with each other, the thinking goes, they will likely find little to squabble about. Yet when they are economically intertwined, the possibilities for conflict are great. Huntington invokes this logic in predicting the clash of civilizations: "The interactions between peoples of different civilizations are increasing; these interactions intensify civilization consciousness and awareness of differences between civilizations and commonalities within civilizations."[45] The results can be disastrous: "Wars occur most frequently between societies with high levels of interaction," Huntington writes.[46] Many observers have suggested that ties between the United States and Japan would be less tense if the two countries were only minor trading partners, and some have predicted that relations are likely to improve as Japan begins to shift more attention to markets other than the United States.

As with their critique of the peacefulness of democracies, realists contend that far-reaching economic cooperation within the West during the Cold War era says nothing about the future, since American hegemony and the common Soviet threat was the principal reason for Western solidarity.[47]

Taken together, realist skepticism about the the impact of interdependence serves as a valuable counterweight to knee-jerk liberal optimism. But it does not refute the idea that interdependence of the kind seen today is likely to increase the prospects of peace.

Those prospects hinge on several developments. First, there exists today a liberal international economic order of a breadth and resilience unimaginable in the years before World War II. Belonging to this order—traceable to the 1944 Bretton Woods agreement and represented by such institutions as the General Agreement on Tariffs and Trade, the International Monetary Fund, and the World Bank— is regarded as vitally important by all leaders in the industrial world and many in the developing world. No major state can remain prosperous for long if it is estranged from the global economy. Yet aggressive behavior by a state carries the risk of such estrangement. By raising the costs of defection from cooperation, the liberal economic order makes such defections less likely than they were in earlier times.

Because states today need not be so worried about their neighbors defecting from cooperative arrangements, they need also not be obsessed with relative gains. A neighbor's increased wealth, they can assume, will not be used someday to build an aggressive war machine. As Robert Jervis has pointed out, "Fear of dependence and concern about relative gains are less when states expect to remain at peace with each other."[48] This expectation is entrenched in much of the democratic world.

Given the success of economic liberalism in the last fifty years, and the spread of democracy, realist comparisons between the interdependence of today and that of the early 1900s are not valid. Before World War I, a British observer touring Germany commented that "every one of these new factory chimneys is a gun pointed at England."[49] Today, no mainstream British analyst would make such a comment, because none imagines Great Britain going to war with Germany in the foreseeable future. Nor is the well-known American obsession with relative gains vis-à-vis Japan due to a real fear of future war with Japan.

Beyond moderating the behavior of its core members, the liberal economic order exerts a powerful pull on would-be members. For years to come, the former states of the Communist bloc will be trial members in this order. If they pursue peaceful democratic development they may eventually be granted the privileges of full membership, with all the opportunities for prosperity that such a status entails. But if they revert to authoritarianism or pursue aggression against one another, ostracism and isolation are likely to follow. Egregious offenders against the established order may incur severe penalties such as economic sanctions.

No Escape: A Single-System World

Once, as recently as the 1930s, states were on average larger in size, often possessed colonies, and in many cases could achieve relative economic self-sufficiency, reducing interdependence with other states if the need arose.[50] There were also few institutional mechanisms for economically penalizing rogue states. Then, following the rise and extension of communism, there existed two separate economic systems. Not only could a hostile Soviet Union and its Eastern European allies exist outside the liberal economic order, or so they thought, but they could also offer aid and trade to anti-Western states in the Third World. Under such circumstances, interdependence could never achieve its full potential for making world politics more peaceful.

Beyond altering the nature of world politics by increasing the number of democracies (and the number of states overall), the Cold War's end has resulted in a single-system world economy. It is a system managed by the leaders of the advanced industrial democracies who annually gather to pledge their allegiance to shared political and economic norms. All states must either join it or risk impoverishment. And good standing in the system is becoming ever more dependent on non-predatory behavior. Indeed, as South Africa's white leadership found out long ago, and as Haiti's military leaders discovered in the early 1990s, even internal violations of democratic norms can be grounds for isolation from the system.[51]

Advances in communications and information technology have served to accelerate trends toward a single-system world. Clichés about a "shrinking world" actually convey much insight into the changing face of human affairs. Fiber optic cables, satellite dishes, fax machines, modems, and other technology make it easier for people to communicate across oceans and continents. Tourism, business travel, and international student exchanges increasingly expose people to other countries. Media exports from the United States, mainly television and films, are omnipresent in much of the world. Signs abound that something approaching a global mass media culture may be coming into existence.[52] Isolation and provincialism, and the xenophobia these conditions can often breed, is becoming a less natural state of existence for people in both the advanced and developing world.

Finally, but not insignificantly, mounting environmental degradation on a global scale has created a new type of interdependence. More so than ever before, the human species is becoming aware of its shared fate on a planet where resources are not inexhaustible. Many Americans, for example, now understand that the destruction of rain forests in Brazil or the increased use of fossil fuels in China can contribute to global warming and eventually have an impact on their lives.

Growing environmental interdependence is not guaranteed to promote peace, and it could have the opposite effect in some cases. As environmental and resources problems mount, flash points for conflict will proliferate, both between North and South and within the Third World. It is also becoming clear, however, that the scope and seriousness of these problems has the potential to engender greater cooperation in international affairs. In the years to come the advanced countries and many developing countries may respond to the peril of environmental decline with far-reaching new multilateral arrangements. It may be overly optimistic to predict, as Lester Brown has, that "the battle to save the planet will replace the battle over ideology as the organizing theme of a new world order," and that in the future, environmental alliances to deal with specific transnational threats will become more commonplace and numerous than the military alliances of the postwar era.[53] But the example of the June 1992 Earth Summit in Rio de Janeiro shows how the environmental threat has already resulted in unprecedented efforts at multilateral cooperation between North and South.[54]

THE DECREASING APPEALS OF WAR

Since the end of World War II, while there has been an uneasy peace in the First World, over twenty million people have died in some sixty interstate conflicts or internationalized civil wars in the developing world.[55] Today, most foreign policy thinkers still see war as a central feature of international affairs. With the end of the Cold War, many are concerned as well that war could become more frequent, both because of the demise of stable bipolarity and because of decreasing fears about nuclear escalation. In regard to Europe and East Asia, American policymakers worry that wars could be the end result of the instability and regional tensions that might follow a U.S. withdrawal. In the Third World, U.S. foreign policy thinkers believe that traditional interstate aggression will continue to be a fact of life, and that war among poorer nations will become ever more violent given the proliferation of advanced weaponry. The Persian Gulf War seemed graphically to confirm this fear.

The realist view is that nothing can remove the specter of war from world politics. Without a central global authority to guarantee the peace, states will always fear for their physical security, and as long as this is the case, they will always be forced to prepare for war.[56] A stable hegemony imposed by the leading state or adroit power balancing among states can make war rare, but it can never banish the possibility altogether, say realists. If the majority of states was to agree that war was idiotic and sharply cut their preparations for war, realist theory suggests that these states would be sitting ducks for an aggressor. When the costs of making war decline it becomes a more attractive proposition. As Germany and Japan showed in World War II, it only takes one aggressive state in a given region, or one wolf in a flock of sheep, to make that region a war system once again.

In arguing for the permanence of war in human affairs, realists appear to have the weight of history on their side. But this appearance may be illusory. Quite apart from the peaceful predisposition of democratic states, there are grounds for believing that war has become both an unpopular and impractical tool of state policy among industrial nations. (The attractiveness of war is also declining in the Third World, as will be discussed later in this chapter.)

Deliberate war has long had two great appeals. It was seen, first, as a romantic undertaking where heros were born and wrongs were righted. War helped forge the character of its participants, it was thought, and could cleanse nations of creeping weakness or malaise. Perhaps more important, war was seen as profitable. A state that went to war could increase its wealth through the acquisition of new resources and markets.

Today, these appeals of war have largely evaporated in the First World, both because of evolving societal norms and changes in economics.

An Unfashionable Undertaking

John Mueller has suggested that war has steadily become less and less socially acceptable over the last few hundred years.[57] Mueller compares war to slavery. Before the late 1700s few people expressed any opposition to the institution of slavery, which had flourished since the beginning of civilization, much like war. Yet within a century, slavery came to be recognized as a repulsive and backward practice. Much the same fate befell dueling. For centuries men had settled their personal disputes through ritualized individual combat, often to death. Yet by the dawn of the twentieth century, dueling had vanished from most societies, not because of the laws passed against it, but because it came to be seen as uncouth.

War could disappear in much the same manner as slavery and dueling, Mueller suggests. Before the eighteenth century war never had to be justified on moral grounds. It was not considered either unusual or unacceptable. On the contrary, it was seen as an attractive path to glory and was the main hobby of leadership elites in most pre-industrial societies.

By the eighteenth century attitudes had begun to change. Enlightenment thinkers viewed the game of power politics and war to be a distraction from the vital work of reordering domestic society. They imagined that, in a world ruled by rationality and high ideals, states would not resort to armed combat to settle their differences or amuse their aristocracies. The Napoleonic Wars of 1803 to 1815 galvanized the first organized activism against warfare, and antiwar societies were founded in New York and London.

For Americans, much of the romance of war disappeared on the blood-soaked battlefields of the Civil War. For Europeans, it was World War I that brought home the horror of war. That war showed that a failure to keep the peace could result in a catastrophe beyond imagination. The lesson of World War I was that war could easily escape the control of human beings. In the past, European statesmen engaged in power politics could make ample use of implied threats of military action. Now such threats became riskier to carry out, since limited action could lead to escalating violence and once again start up a continental doomsday machine. The mass slaughter of trench warfare also undercut the age-old association between valor and combat. Before World I, a growing peace movement had condemned war as repulsive and stupid. By 1918 there were few who could contest this claim.

As Mueller tells the story, most people had gotten the message about war's futility by 1918. Yet due to Adolf Hitler's single-minded aggressiveness and Japan's adherence to dated, romantic notions of war, it was not until 1945 that two of the world's most consistently belligerent states got this message as well. In Mueller's analysis, the absence of war in the developed world after 1945 has not been due to the presence of nuclear weapons or the stabilizing affect of bipolarity, but to the collective recognition that war is insanity. Fearing escalation to general war, and knowing the horror of such war, the developed countries have sought to resolve their disputes peacefully. Nuclear weapons reinforced this inclination, but they did not account for its existence. The Soviet Union, for example, would hardly have taken a casual view of risking a new major conventional warfare after World War II, having suffered twenty million dead in its fight with Germany.

The growing aversion to war was not total. States such as the Soviet Union, France, and the United States showed themselves quite willing to go to war against minor foes during the postwar period. However, such lopsided wars on the periphery of the international system do not detract from Mueller's basic argument, an argument that strikes at the core of realist thinking. If it is true that major powers are unlikely to use military force against one another because of the dangers of catastrophic escalation, then the realist view that war is always possible seems less persuasive. War becomes not a feasible option, coolly considered by players of power politics, but a nightmare to be avoided at almost any cost.

Of course, history is replete with leaders who have not thought in entirely rational ways. Hitler did not. Saddam Hussein did not. Quite possibly a new leader of a major power might come along some day who was likewise unbalanced. Realists are not the only analysts who point to the enduring power of nationalism as an irrational force in world politics. Only minor threats have been posed by the dreams of Slobodan Milosevic of an enlarged and ethnically pure Serbia, or president Assad's vision of a "Greater Syria." But a Russian nationalist leader with a similarly chauvinist agenda could pose an immediate threat to the fourteen countries of the former Soviet Union.

Irrational leaders are not the only potential war makers of the future, say realists. Should most states optimistically reduce their levels of military preparedness, a perfectly rational leader might reach the conclusion that aggression could be undertaken without risking a major conflagration. The same conclusion could be reached because of advances in military technology that promise quick victory and low levels of destruction.

Does Conquest Pay?

Yet making war easier does not necessarily make it more attractive. For most of history the nature of human society made war a profitable undertaking. In the pre-industrial era, invading armies could capture land and people. The land could be farmed and timbered and mined, yielding a steady stream of material benefits for the occupying country. The people could be forced to run these operations or, as was often the case in antiquity, they could be turned into slaves. From a military standpoint, the occupation of territory could increase a state's security by providing buffer zones against aggression.

During earlier industrial times the benefits of occupying territory remained considerable. Nazi Germany was apparently able to harness French industry to its own uses, thereby increasing its wealth and war potential.[58] When the Soviet Union conquered the eastern half of Germany, it disassembled German industrial equipment and shipped it back to the homeland, where it became part of the Soviet economy.

Peter Liberman has recently argued that conquest still pays, citing examples from the World War II era.[59] He suggests that because modernization makes states wealthier, conquest is in fact more attractive now than in past centuries. Modernization has also strengthened the ability of conquerors to control occupied territories by centralizing populations in urban areas and giving rise to more sophisticated repressive machinery.

Like so many other claims made by theorists of war and peace, Liberman's argument is based on dated cases. He devotes enormous energy to analyzing Germany's occupation of Europe, but this case is of dubious relevance to the present for economic reasons, discussed below. Even on its own terms, the case is problematic. The Nazis were unusually skilled industrialists and uniquely ruthless occupiers; future conquerors of other lands may not have these characteristics. Germany's occupation of its Western European neighbors lasted only a few years; their ability to have maintained control and efficiency

over many years is unknown. Finally, while Liberman shows that
Nazi occupation costs were low compared to the profits from captured industry,[60] at no point does he analyze the broader economic
equation of Hitler's strategy. Occupation costs came on top of the
1930s' costs of building up a large military force that could engage in
successful aggression. It is not clear from Liberman's analysis that
Germany gained more from its occupation of its neighbors than it
would have gained if it had eschewed a military buildup and put its
energies into reviving its civilian economy and trading with the rest
of Europe.

In the absence of additional cases, particularly ones that are
directly relevant to current conditions, the debate over whether conquest pays must be decided on its intrinsic merits. The changed
nature of economics has altered the calculus of military aggression
since World War II, and especially since the nineteenth century.
Quite apart from the growing costs of war associated with disrupting
interdependent relationships and being ostracized from the global
economy, war is less attractive because physical control of resources
has become less important and the wealth of complex post-industrial
societies have become more difficult for conquerors to extract.[61]

As Japan and other trading states have demonstrated, wealth in the
developed world is ever less dependent upon being rich in natural
resources. This fact, coupled with the growing costs of fielding military forces, makes resource grabs highly unlikely in the developed
world.[62] For example, in a world with ample food surpluses, available
at a reasonable price to any nation, there is little need to occupy territory for its agricultural potential. Raising and sustaining armies is far
more expensive than buying food.

Oil remains a potential target of conquest. Had Iraq been able to
retain and sell Kuwait's vast oil supplies, the costs of its invasion would
have been recouped many, many times over. But as the Gulf conflict
showed, oil is of little use to a nation if it can't be sold on the open
market, and those who obtain oil through conquest are uniquely vulnerable to economic sanctions. (It is possible to imagine oil supplies
being coveted for domestic uses, but as with food, it is probably
cheaper to buy oil on the open market than to raise armies to invade
and occupy foreign oil fields.) While other resources such as plat-
inum, chromium, and manganese are vital to the industrial world,

and exist in only a few countries, there is little likelihood that these countries will voluntarily impoverish themselves by not selling these resources to the rest of the world.

Foreign populations are no longer a prize worth pursuing, either. In earlier times, occupying another country was not a terribly difficult business. When most people were tied to the land and were ruled autocratically anyway, it was easy both to suppress their dissent and to profit from their labor. But this task has become more difficult with the rise of more complicated economies and the spread of democratic ideas. Democratic societies may be hard to occupy because they are made up of socially mobilized people with an appetite for freedom. Over the long term, keeping such populations in check can be an expensive and burdensome proposition. Even countries with no strong democratic tradition are likely to be difficult to suppress in an age of modern communications, which facilitates outside support of dissidents and the diffusion of information.

The impact of more complicated economics is of greater importance. With much basic manufacturing now done in the Third World, the wealth of First World countries is increasingly generated by technological innovation and by service sector institutions. Industry that does remain, automobile manufacturing for example, often depends on subcontractors located in other countries. The capture of Michigan auto plants by Canada would do it little good unless Canada could somehow also occupy the factories in Mexico, Brazil, and Japan that produce large numbers of the parts that go into American cars today. Even capturing certain U.S. defense plants would not be of long-term benefit, since key electronic components for weapons often come from overseas. The interdependence of European defense industries is even more pronounced.[63]

The days are over when foreign masters could keep heavy industry running and thus milk most of a state's wealth-producing and war-making potential. Richard Rosecrance has argued that the Soviet threat to Western Europe was exaggerated, since the Soviets would have gained little wealth from occupying that advanced region.[64] Rosecrance and others have also made the point that the rising cost of weaponry is making the preparation for war harder to afford. In today's world, a state prospers far more from trading with a developed neighbor than from occupying their territory, and it faces relentless pressure to spend more money on civilian investment, lest it lose out in commercial competition. If overall increases in power is the end, militarism is not logically the means.

The Future of War and U.S. Policy

John Mueller draws the conclusion that such is the futility of war that most First World leaders no longer ponder it as a real option. Over time, Mueller imagines that leaders of developed countries will so consistently dismiss the war option as irrational that their "reasoned war-avoidance" will become habitual. The idea of war will become "subrationally unthinkable" in the developed world because it no longer percolates into the consciousness of decision makers.[65]

Realists are probably right when they respond to this point by observing that it takes only one leader in a state system who thinks war is possible in order for all neighboring leaders to suddenly think so as well. But this fact does not discredit arguments about the growing obsolescence of war, which is a phenomenon best seen as operating in conjunction with other trends. Not only has the conquest of territory declined in attractiveness in an information age, but the disruption of trade links has reduced the profitability of war, as it has the possibility of sanctions being imposed by supranational institutions, which are now stronger than ever. These costs can only serve to strengthen the existing predisposition against war among democratic states. Democratic states can also breathe easier about the prospect of backsliding by neighbors, since rational authoritarian leaders may be inclined to avoid war.

Growing checks on the warring impulses of states have important ramifications for U.S. policy. The fear of tensions leading to war in Europe and East Asia in the wake of an American withdrawal may be exaggerated. If the use of force is decreasingly viewed as a realistic option by leaders of advanced states, new rivalries in Europe and Asia may never get to the point of becoming significantly militarized, even if the antagonists are well armed.

The unprofitability of conquest also reduces the chances of another traditional hegemonic power arising. For centuries, hegemonic enterprises have been one of the principal threats to stable state systems, and post–Cold War U.S. security policy treats this as an enduring problem in international relations. In the current age, however, such enterprises no longer make much sense. It is true that non-material considerations like ethnic or nationalist passions or the desire for a greater defensive buffer could be at the root of aggressive designs by a future power.[66] But incentives of this nature would be likely to produce limited agendas, such as the much feared Russian effort to take back portions of the former Soviet Union.[67] They are not akin to the kind of imperial thinking that, for example, fueled Japan's conquest of the Pacific Rim during World War II.

Some preparation for meeting the threat of an ambitious new global enemy is clearly warranted. But exaggerating the likelihood of future hegemonic enterprises, as U.S. defense planners have done, can lead to a large-scale waste of resources. A better approach may be to rely more heavily on collective security measures that can detect the emergence of potential aggressor states and take early action to contain their power.

THE RISE OF SUPRANATIONALISM

To the most utopian of twentieth-century idealists, the solution to global problems was once thought to be world government. Only a powerful international authority could guarantee peace between nations and justice within them, the logic went. Today, this dream is widely recognized to be a chimera; anything akin to world government will probably never be workable because states are unwilling to make major compromises in their sovereignty. Serious policy analysts do not discuss the concept.

Far more realistic is the prospect of strong international institutions that can promote cooperation between states. By establishing rules of behavior and mechanisms to enforce them through set penalties, international institutions can make world politics more predictable. They can allay the distrust between states, and, in the best of circumstances, they may have the potential to guarantee the security of states, making the world, or at least certain regions of it, far less of a self-help system in which each state must constantly worry about its physical survival.

Powerful international institutions are more feasible today than at any time in human history. The triumph of liberal democracy, the growing web of interdependence, and the decreasing appeal of war are all trends that facilitate cooperation between states. But such cooperation will not flourish automatically. International institutions must be nurtured by leaders who deeply believe in their potential to reorder global politics.

Foreign policy elites in the United States support international institutions today more than ever before, but they do not trust them to safeguard world order. Underlying this distrust is an entrenched pessimism that derives both from the disappointing history of international institutions in the area of security and from the theoretical view that the potential for states to cooperate on security matters is inherently limited. As long as this outlook predominates in U.S. policy circles, international institutions will never achieve their potential to relieve the United States of much of its burden for managing global security affairs.

The G-7 and Beyond

Until the late 1960s and early 1970s it was widely thought that the international economic order established at the end of World War II could not be sustained in the absence of American hegemony—that the supervision of a single preeminent state was needed to assure enduring cooperation. This turned out to be a false worry. The end of American economic hegemony in the 1970s introduced new discord into the system, but it did not lead to chaos. "Hegemonic stability has not been needed," observed Richard Rosecrance in 1986.[68] Robert Keohane argued the same point, showing that international regimes can be both created and sustained without the leadership of a hegemon.[69] This view reflects the long-standing liberal assertion that cooperation between states, once instituted and shown to be mutually beneficial, will take on a momentum of its own. Existing regimes will not only be maintained and strengthened, but states will work together to extend cooperation to new areas.

The order that governs international economic cooperation has already begun to extend its reach and take on certain attributes of a supranational authority. The group of seven industrial powers (the United States, France, Great Britain, Germany, Japan, Italy, and Canada), or G-7, is turning into what one observer has called a "global directorate."[70] Originally designed to promote economic consultation through regular summit meetings, the G-7 forum is now used to chart global policy on a wide range of issues.[71] Increasingly, the G-7 powers have shown a willingness to use the economic system they dominate to influence both the internal and external behavior of states. With an expanded mandate to promote human rights and preventive diplomacy, the G-7 has positioned itself for a stepped-up effort to institutionalize the norms of democracy and market economies.

The notion that world affairs over the next few decades will be governed by the G-7 powers, in an arrangement similar to the concert of great powers that managed European affairs in the nineteenth century, is extremely plausible.[72] The more difficult question is how major transgressors against this order will be handled. It is one thing for the leading powers to establish rules for the new order, quite another to enforce them. Economic incentives and penalties may not always work, since some states will occasionally place other goals above the pursuit of prosperity. Military action may at times be necessary to rescue victims of aggression.

This is the acid test of supranationalism. If international institutions cannot provide at least some guarantee of security, the world will remain a self-help system in the final analysis. Even with the spread of democracy and the myriad disincentives of war, many states will continue to worry about their security and take unilateral measures to enhance it. Without collective mechanisms that create predictability and offer reassurance in the security arena, the widespread pursuit of such unilateral measures has the potential to produce instability among even well-meaning communities of democratic states.[73] In the absence of a reliable collective mechanism for deterring and reversing aggression, the United States will continue to feel an obligation, as the world's strongest power, to remain the chief guarantor of peace in many regions of the world.

International organizations and regimes have yet to show that they can guarantee the peace in the face of major challenges. The concept of collective security has not been vindicated to the point where most states are ready to trust their survival to such arrangements. Making collective security work is perhaps the single greatest challenge of American foreign policy.

Collective Security: Promise and Problems

The idea of a collective security organization is that all members commit themselves to opposing aggression, either from within their own ranks or from outside the organization. This setup has several advantages over leaving states to their own informal devices, such as forging ad hoc alliances and other balance-of-power mechanisms.[74] First, it is a more reliable deterrent to aggression. Any state pondering aggression against a member of a collective security organization knows that it will incur the wrath of all the other members. Aggression thus becomes a less appealing proposition, much as assaulting a person in a street gang is more risky than picking on a loner. Of course, there is no guarantee that states in a collective security organization will come to the rescue of a beleaguered member. But the chances are higher that aggression will be opposed than if no such organization existed. As Charles and Clifford Kupchan explain: "Under anarchy, only those states directly threatened by the aggressor and states with vital interests in the threatened areas will band together to resist aggression. Under collective security, because states have clear interests in protecting an international order that they see as beneficial to their individual security, they will contribute to the coalition even if they have no vital interests at stake in the actual theater of aggression."[75]

A second advantage of collective security is that it makes dangerous rivalries less likely to begin with. By bringing officials into constant contact with one another at conferences and meetings and promoting an ongoing dialogue on security issues, collective security enterprises can foment understanding and reduce suspicion. Over the long run, interaction of this kind can deepen trust and lead to further cooperation.

Such enterprises can also lower uncertainty by establishing clear rules and limits governing military activities and force levels. States thus know exactly what other states are allowed to do militarily. Relying on intelligence capabilities that are more sophisticated today than ever before, they can monitor the military behavior of others and rest assured that no unpleasant security surprises lurk over the horizon. As long as rules and limits are being followed, their military needs will be predictable over time. A violation of rules can serve as an early signal of potential danger.

Despite a new U.S. emphasis on multilateral cooperation after the Cold War, particularly by the Clinton Administration, U.S. foreign policy elites continue to have a deep distrust of collective security. They are willing to use collective security mechanisms to reduce armaments levels and to increase confidence. But U.S. officials do not believe, for the most part, that collective security mechanisms can be relied upon to thwart aggression and keep the peace.

The reasons for this distrust are numerous. Skeptics note that states may avoid making firm commitments to a collective security organization for fear of being dragged into wars. For the Security Council to have real military power, states would have to make available contingents of troops, under binding legal agreement, to its command. Many states would balk at this prospect, worrying that its troops would be used in faraway wars that may involve high principles but do not affect the state's vital interests.

Yet if a commitment to provide troops is not binding, there is no guarantee that states will honor their obligation. In such a circumstance, collective security via the Security Council would be unreliable. An unimportant African state, for example, would have no confidence that the Security Council would come galloping to its rescue in the face of external aggression. Instead, it would have to rely, as realists insist that all states must, on its own military might for protection.

According to this critique, the Cold War was only a minor reason why the Security Council was largely powerless for so many decades. The bigger problem that affects collective security is an enduring one: selfish states cannot be trusted to help out one another in a jam for the sake of principle. Even when states are ready to fight for principle, they might be unable to agree on when to do so. One state's noncooperation, assuming it has some kind of veto, can stop an entire organization from responding to aggression. And if a deep conflict of interest emerges in a collective security organization, it may become paralyzed for long periods of time, as happened to the Security Council in the Cold War. The U.S.-Soviet conflict was exceptionally intense, but differences between major states are not unique per se.

Even minor differences in the future, between China and the industrial democracies, for example, could again produce a moribund Security Council.

A final problem to which skeptics point is the concern states have about relative gains. Even states bound together by a collective security arrangement will not stop worrying about how strong their neighbors are, realists argue. These states will always fear that their partnerships may some day turn into antagonisms. As a consequence, they may avoid situations that prevent them from taking all the measures they desire for protecting themselves. As Joseph Grieco writes, "The fundamental goal of states in any relationship is to prevent others from achieving advances in their relative capabilities." A state will "decline to join, will leave, or sharply limit its commitment to a cooperative arrangement if it believes that partners are achieving, or are likely to achieve, relatively greater gains."[76]

Skeptics of collective security make important points.[77] But none of these arguments destroy the case that collective security can work. The realists' dismissal of collective security is based on unduly pessimistic assumptions about how states will behave in today's changed global environment. Also, realist criticisms are far more valid in regard to "ideal" collective security—that is, collective security arrangements involving all states and covering the entire globe—than they are in regard to more limited or regional forms of collective security, which have a greater likelihood of working.

Collective Security After the Cold War

Responsible advocates of collective security have always recognized that certain conditions must be met before cooperative arrangements can safeguard international security. For the first time in world history, such conditions are now in place in the developed world.

First, all major powers must be vulnerable. No state can have so much power, or be so self-sufficient, that it can defeat any opposing coalition or withstand collective sanctions. Such a condition now exists. Militarily, there is no colossus in the industrial world that could prevail over the rest of the industrial states. And, as already argued here, all states are now economically vulnerable as a consequence of the highly integrated world economy. Such is the vulnerability of most states to being isolated from the international economy that the prospect of non-military penalties alone is likely to deter most rational leaders from aggression.

A second condition for collective security, which also now exists, is that all major powers must be in basic agreement on what constitutes a desirable international order. A single obstructionist power can make a collective security organization unworkable. Today, with the collapse of the Soviet Union, no such power exists in Europe. China's continued authoritarianism raises questions about the workability of the Security Council, or any regional security organization in Asia. However, China did go along with actions against Iraq in 1990, and against Libya and Serbia in 1992 and 1993. Despite its form of government, China is not now a revisionist power intent on disrupting the status quo. Its clear desire for a larger role in the global economy suggests that it might become, over time, a reliable collective security partner. (I will return to the issue of China in the next chapter.)

Finally, the success of collective security depends on a strong and widely shared commitment to strengthening the bonds of international community.[78] This condition is perhaps the most important of all, because unless a core group of powerful states are willing to work relentlessly to further cooperation and, in extreme cases, send troops into combat to protect principles, not just vital interests, collective security will founder.

Determining whether this condition now exists or will exist in the future is no easy task, but prospects on this score do seem encouraging. In today's highly interdependent world, where a growing number of states share the same political values, and where the potential for instability is seen as considerable, there is already a keen vigilance in regard to challenges to the established order. More and more states accept the idea that violations of the rules are a threat to everybody. The alarmed response to Iraq's invasion of Kuwait underscored this point. Even if Kuwait had not possessed oil, the clear-cut and unprovoked nature of Iraq's aggression would have generated a worldwide outcry. And even if the United States had not taken a leadership role in reversing that aggression, Iraq probably still would have found itself locked out of the international economy through sanctions, unable to benefit from the spoils of its conquest. The initial failure of the international community to move beyond economic sanctions during the war in Bosnia was a disappointing and costly mistake. At times the behavior of the West was tantamount to appeasement. But the Bosnia tragedy should not necessarily be viewed as a representative failure of collective security. The circumstances of the conflict in Bosnia in 1992 and 1993 were exceptionally difficult. Nearly every major European power has powerful historic reasons for being wary of intervention in the Balkans; the terrain in Bosnia made any limited use of force a dubious proposition; and the conflict was very much a civil war as well as a case of external aggression, with a ferocity fueled by centuries of ethnic hatred that made outsiders skeptical of their potential influence. Collective security is most likely to work in cases of unambiguous interstate aggression, but this condition was not met in the Bosnia war, which at times more closely resembled the civil war in Lebanon than, for example, the invasions of South Korea or Kuwait. In any case, NATO's ultimatum in February 1994 to the Serb gunners around Sarajevo did constitute an effective—if appallingly belated—collective security action.

Serbia's light punishment for international aggression should not obscure the fact that rogue states today are losing the sources of support they benefited from during the Cold War, making collective action against them more feasible. Just a few years ago, renegade regimes could often find sustenance in the arms of the Soviet Union or China. Today there are fewer sources of support for such states, and bandwagoning against international transgressors is becoming more common. Iraq, a former Soviet client state, found itself almost completely isolated following its 1990 aggression; North Korea, once bolstered militarily by China and the Soviet Union, would not be able to count on outside arms supplies if it again invaded South Korea; Libya, another erstwhile Soviet client state, received no significant international support when confronted with U.N. demands that it turn over suspects in the 1988 bombing of Pan Am flight 103; sanctions against Serbia, while not effective in stopping its aggression, have been widely observed.

The ability of leaders to learn from history may influence the likelihood that states will honor collective security arrangements and stand up to aggression. Twentieth-century history shows that faraway aggression, especially that undertaken by a powerful country with the potential for further violence, cannot be dismissed by any state. Democracies in particular are likely to feel a sense of shared common fate. Historically, free people have been aghast at the specter of aggression against other free people. The spread of democracy is thus likely to strengthen collective security arrangements.

Ideal collective security operates on the principle of all against one. But collective security can also succeed under more realistic conditions of most against one. A core group of states that can be counted on is more important to the success of a collective security system than universal participation. Indeed, it has been argued that collective security systems run by a handful of major powers, or "concert," are likely to be most effective.[79]

It is true that many states will hesitate to make new collective security commitments for fear of being dragged into distant wars that do not directly concern them. But it is also true that much of the development of new collective security mechanisms over the next decade will take place at the regional level. Because states are more likely to both make and honor commitments to deal with aggression in their own neighborhoods, such mechanisms have a higher chance of working than arrangements at the global level. The establishment of new regional mechanisms, moreover, means that in some parts of the world there will exist a two-tiered collective security system, with the U.N. serving as a backup to, or working in concert with, local groupings. The next chapter shows why successful collective security arrangements are more possible than ever in regions that are of vital interest to the United States.

Realists are right that collective security itself cannnot end distrust between states. But democratization and interdependence does produce greater trust, and collective security can help institutionalize this trust in the realm of security affairs. Realists are mistaken to believe that states will fail to join collective security arrangements, or drop out of them, because of their fear of partners gaining more from such arrangements than they do. The properly designed collective security arrangement is non–zero sum in nature. It does not confer advantages on some states at a cost to others, although it may let stand preexisting advantages. Instead of abandoning collective security, a state whose neighbor is becoming rapidly more powerful than it is economically has every incentive to pursue such arrangements. Collective security regimes can often be the best hope for containing the military power of economically dynamic states.

If the United States is to decrease markedly its security responsibilities abroad, it must have confidence that arrangements other than primacy can assure stability in crucial parts of the world. With the Cold War over, collective security institutions and regimes have the potential for unprecedented effectiveness in this respect. A central component of an idealist foreign policy agenda would be to place more faith in collective security and nurture it with the explicit goal of allowing transitions away from dependence on U.S. security guarantees.

WAR AND PEACE IN THE THIRD WORLD

Because the realist view of international relations no longer explains how advanced nations relate to one another, there are strong grounds for reassessing the pessimistic assumptions that guide U.S. policy toward Europe and East Asia. But what about the Third World, where direct challenges to U.S. interests are considered most likely in the future? To what degree are the trends that are reshaping the developed world also at work in developing regions?

American foreign policy elites harbor tremendous pessimism about the Third World. Even critics of realism like Fukuyama acknowledge that although it may be an outdated policy compass in the developed world, realism is still very applicable in the Third World. Iraq's invasion of Kuwait seemed to be graphic confirmation that the ancient game of power politics is still the norm outside of the developed regions. The prevalence in many parts of the Third World of authoritarian governments, along with high levels of militarism and nationalism, is seen as further evidence of this point. A principal aim of current U.S. national security policy is to prepare for large-scale military intervention against Third World aggressors engaged in territorial conquest. Another aim is to safeguard American interests in the Third World by strengthening and defending friends, many of whom were also key allies in the Cold War.

Generalizing about the Third World is risky, since there are vast differences between regions. The Third World is not governed by a single international security system but rather by many unique regional systems.[80] Analyses of trends in one region are not necessarily applicable to other regions, and both policymakers and scholars stand guilty of being careless or cavalier in their discussion of Third World security issues.

Beyond this, there are two major flaws in the realist vision underlying U.S. strategy. First, it can be dangerous to apply international relations theory to the Third World. Second, there is evidence that the same trends that promote peace in the developed world are also at work in the Third World. Pessimistic analysts like Stephen David tend to either ignore or underestimate the importance of these trends.

Weak States, Internal Threats

A basic premise of realist theory is that cohesive states are the principal actors in world politics and that all states behave in a similar fashion; they worry constantly about their survival in the face of present or potential external threats. This picture, however, cannot be simplistically applied to the Third World, where weak states are common and internal threats are often of far greater concern to national leaders.[81] "It may not be an exaggeration to claim that outside of Latin America only a minority of Third World countries are socially integrated and able to govern effectively over a unified and disciplined citizenship," writes K. J. Holsti.[82] In many states, there is no single nation of people. Instead, as Brian Job notes, there are often a "variety of communal groups contending for their own securities and for supremacy over their competitors."[83] As a result, many Third World regimes lack legitimacy and popular support, since they seldom represent all groups equally. The state apparatus is often unable to govern the country.[84] Not surprisingly, the chief concern of many Third World leaders are not external threats that jeopardize national survival but internal threats that challenge their personal political survival. Realist thinking, with its emphasis on the structure of the state system and its neglect of domestic politics, offers little insight into how such governments behave. Nor can it explain the dynamics of much of the violence in the Third World, which is internal in nature and lacks the features of regular warfare.

In the last two decades, there has been no shortage of traditional interstate rivalries and conflicts in the Third World, but theories

widely used in the developed world are not always useful for analyzing these. As Stephen David has shown in his work on why Third
World states make and break alliances, traditional balance-of-power
theories do not explain the security motivations of Third World leaders. Such leaders often place their own interests above those of their
states, and it is the all-consuming desire to neutralize internal threats
that drives alignment behavior.[85] Similarly, Western students of world
politics have always been consumed with the problem of hegemony.
The story of European history, in large measure, is of one power after
another seeking hegemony. Realism imagines a world where many
states have an appetite for campaigns of conquest, or could suddenly
develop one.

But this does not necessarily describe reality in the Third World.
Holsti argues that one can find few traditions or ideologies of hegemony in the developing world. "Theorists of international relations
have taken some patterns of the eighteenth- to twentieth-century
European powers out of their historical and ideological contexts and
given them a generic content. If the Hapsburgs, French, Prussians,
Russians, and British all expanded through conquest and predation,
then it is assumed that all powers, regardless of location, history, culture, and the like, must similarly expand. But for the most part, the
pattern is not repeating itself."[86] Often cited potential hegemonies in
the Third World—states like Brazil, India, and Nigeria—have remained
precisely that: potential, not actual, hegemons that have failed to
spread their rule by conquering weaker neighbors. Saddam's Iraq,
Khomeini's Iran, and Assad's Syria are all states that have expressed or
pursued hegemonic intentions in recent years. But they do not prove
that hegemonism is destined to be a salient aspect of future Third
World politics. Pentagon officials talk in sweeping terms about well-
armed aspiring hegemons in the Third World, but they have never
backed up their warnings with a plausible list of any length.

The question of whether interstate aggression in the Third World
will be a common occurrence in the future, and whether it will
threaten the vital interests of the United States, has enormous ramifications for U.S. national security policy. The next chapter will take
up the latter part of this question in some detail. Here I will assess in a
more general fashion whether new Iraqi-style invasions can be
expected.

Forces for Peace, Makers of War

Pentagon predictions of new interstate conflict are shared by some scholars who present detailed arguments for why Third World leaders are far more war-prone than leaders of developed countries. Stephen David, for example, has argued that war is often in the interests of Third World leaders, that the absence of democracy in many Third World countries means there are fewer constraints on the initiation of war, that conquest still pays in developing regions, and that hypernationalism and militarism are often strong forces in developing societies. David gives no indication that these conditions will change anytime soon. On the contrary, he argues that the end of the Cold War and growing environmental and economic stresses serve to increase the likelihood of conflict among Third World states.[87]

This argument is unduly pessimistic. While the trends fostering peace in the developed world remain far less strong among poorer countries, they have been accelerating in recent years. These trends will do little to address growing internal violence, which is unlikely to trigger large-scale U.S. intervention in any case, especially after the searing experience in Somalia. Rather, their main promise is to make major territorial conquest less common in the future and generally to reduce tensions among states in the Third World.

Democracy and Liberalization

Over the past decade, democracy has made major gains in the Third World. In 1979 twelve out of nineteen Latin American countries had authoritarian governments. In 1990 every country but Cuba had elected its president, although a number of these remained only nominally democratic.[88] In Africa long-cynical observers have been stunned by the scope of recent liberalization. As of late 1991, according to one observer, nearly three-fourths of the forty-seven countries south of the Sahara, most notably South Africa, were in the process of political liberalization.[89] In Asia democracy has made inroads in South Korea, Taiwan, Thailand, and the Philippines. According to analyses that link economic prosperity with democratization, there is good reason to think that advances will continue in those countries during the 1990s, with liberalization also spreading to Malaysia and Singapore.[90]

David's blanket dismissal of democracy in the Third World simply does not describe reality. Recent trends should produce more peace between Third World states that are democratic and a greater number of leaders in the Third World who face domestic constraints on their ability to wage war.[91] Today, for example, the entire continent of South America can be accurately described as a democratic "zone of peace" with no dangerous interstate rivalries present. In Southeast Asia the spread of democracy is likely to more than offset the destabilizing effect of rising weapons acquisitions.

It is impossible to assess the long-term strength of democracy in the Third World. Over the last two decades democratic governments have been regularly overthrown in Latin America, Africa, and Asia. Many democratic governments in the Third World are extremely fragile and face the ever present possibility of a return to authoritarian rule. As demographic and environmental pressures mount in years to come, violent reverses could become common. A glimpse of what lies ahead may have been provided by events in Peru in 1992, where a beleaguered elected leader ended democratic processes. Similar occurrences could be seen in important states such as India and the Philippines.

But if the prospects of democracy in various Third World regions are unclear in the short term, history suggests they are clearer over the long term. As Samuel Huntington has shown, every wave of democratization in the twentieth century has been followed by a backlash, yet over time the number of democracies has steadily grown.[92] Even in those cases where major backsliding occurs, the effects on regional security may not be calamitous. In the future, democratic states that revert to authoritarian rule may be likely do so, as in the case of Peru, because of a deteriorating internal situation. The governments of such states will have their hands full dealing with security problems at home and will probably not be a threat to their neighbors. Future backsliders may also be expected to seek a quick return to democracy, so as to avoid extended penalties in the area of aid and trade.

Interdependence

In the developed world interdependence between advanced nations can promote peace by linking societies at a variety of levels, fostering communication and cooperation, and intertwining neighbors to the point where the eruption of war becomes intolerable if not unthinkable. In a few developing regions, particularly Southeast Asia, interdependence of this nature is growing. But this is not true of most of the Third World, where states do not have the same high levels of interaction with one another.

Instead, most of the econonomic interdependence of developing states is with developed states. It is vertical rather than horizontal, North-South rather than South-South. Within this context Third World states in fact have higher levels of interdependence than developed states.[93] With fragile economies often dependent on a few exports or large levels of aid and credit, they are highly vulnerable to disruptions of trade and capital flows; new protectionist measures in the North or stricter lending requirements can mean economic devastation in parts of the South.

There are many lamentable consequences of this situation, most notably volatile relations between North and South.[94] But one benefit of high levels of vertical interdependence is that Third World states are extremely vulnerable to sanctions imposed by the advanced nations, making them easy to penalize for transgressions against international law. At a minimum, disobedient states can be denied bilateral aid and loans from the World Bank or IMF, as well as losing favored trading status in the lucrative markets of the North and their arms supplies. At a maximum, they can be completely isolated from the world economy through U.N.-imposed embargos. The end of the Cold War makes it easier to impose economic punishments since rogue regimes cannot turn to the Communist bloc for sustenance or play the superpowers off against one another to retain aid. Most of these punishments, moreover, can be imposed solely by agreement on the part of the most advanced democracies, without the requirement of a consensus within the U.N. Security Council.

The Decreasing Appeal of War

War is becoming less attractive in the Third World. One reason, as in the developed world, is the declining value of territory. Even though much of the Third World remains dependent on agriculture, there is little incentive to seize territory for its agricultural potential, since food can now be purchased on the international market. Oil and strategic minerals can be a lucrative prize for aggressors, but as Iraq's experience showed us, seizing a valuable resource is not of much use if a state cannot sell it on the world market.

Territory can be coveted for other reasons, such as its religious significance or its strategic position. Also, on continents with arbitrary colonial borders, ethnic groups who rule one state may wish to extend their rule to brethen just over the border in another state. However, as K. J. Holsti notes, there have been remarkably few militarized border disputes between states in the Third World. "Control of territory," he writes, "is declining in importance as a major object of competitive claims and military action."[95]

The recent pursuit of territorial ambitions in the Third World does not present an encouraging record for new would-be aggressors: Iraq suffered terrible consequences as a result of its aggression against Iran in 1980 and Kuwait in 1990; Argentina was defeated and humiliated following its invasion of the Falklands; Israel was traumatized by a long occupation of Lebanon following its 1982 invasion; Vietnam voluntarily sought an exit from Cambodia in the late 1980s; Libya ultimately encountered failure in Chad. While there is no hard evidence to back up the claim that new interstate aggression will be commonplace in the years ahead, there are numerous reasons why Third World leaders increasingly may think twice before embarking on such adventures. Aggression can be particularly unprofitable if it results in a confrontation with a Western power, a lesson that Argentina learned nearly a full decade before Iraq. A leader can gamble that nobody in the developed world really cares about the country he is planning to conquer, but the odds of this gamble have become less favorable amid signs of a revived U.N. Security Council.

If interstate tensions are not high in the Third World, and territorial ambitions are limited, why are governments there buying so many arms? Is the flow of ever more deadly weaponry to the Third World a sign that new wars lie ahead, as U.S. officials so often suggest?

Not necessarily. It is difficult to establish a link between the acquisition of advanced arms by Third World states and the likelihood of interstate conflict. States that buy lots of weapons are usually not planning aggression, and arms races by themselves cannot be shown to cause wars. Moreover, as Keith Krause writes, "The characterization of the entire Third World as rapidly acquiring vast military arsenals is less accurate as one moves the focus into sharper detail." Within each region, the two or three states with the largest arsenals always account for the bulk of arms imports to that region. Globally, a handful of states in the Middle East and Southeast Asia are buying most of the arms sold to the Third World. These facts, says Krause, are "not consistent with a simple picture of the progressive militarization of the Third World."[96]

American policymakers and many scholars point with particular concern to the spread of weapons of mass destruction and ballistic missiles in predicting a more dangerous Third World in the future.[97] Yet there is little evidence that these developments will either raise the likelihood of interstate conflict or embolden dictators to attempt new territorial conquests.[98] As possession of chemical and biological weapons becomes more widespread, for example, the advantages they confer on an aggressor may increasingly be canceled out. The proliferation of nuclear weapons on a large scale in the Third World would be a more worrisome development, but there is no certainty of this happening. Estimates of nuclear proliferation have often turned out to be exaggerated over recent decades, and it is far from clear, as David contends, that in the future the Third World may contain "many small nuclear powers, most of which face many adversaries."[99]

Numerous risks and costs are associated with the acquisition of nuclear weapons,[100] and most Third World countries are not likely to view this goal as either desirable or affordable. Moreover, Third World states seeking to acquire nuclear weapons face increasing resistance by the international community. The United States and other advanced nations are stepping up nonproliferation efforts, and new progress in this area appears likely as the 1995 conference to extend the Non-Proliferation Treaty approaches.

In some regions of the world the dangers associated with nuclear proliferation have actually diminished in recent years. In 1993 South Africa announced that it would become the first nation in history to relinquish its nuclear weapons. Iraq's far advanced effort to build nuclear weapons was ended by U.S. air strikes during the Gulf War and the U.N. dismantling program that followed. Brazil and Argentina, once thought to be likely candidates for a nuclear competition, have renewed pledges to forsake nuclear weapons.

Supranationalism

International institutions and regimes are making the Third World more peaceful in a number of ways. As already discussed, the advent of a single-system world means that the institutions governing economic behavior can be more easily harnessed to the task of modifying political-military behavior. As alternatives to market systems have become less common in the Third World, institutions such as the IMF and World Bank have become involved with states that previously had not been deeply enmeshed in the global economy. These institutions, and the developed states that control them, have greater leverage than ever over an increasing number of Third World states.

Although regional collective security organizations in the Third World do not have the same potential as in the developed world,[101] the revival of the United Nations does have the potential to enhance Third World security. The end of the Cold War reduces chances that U.N. action against rogue regimes will be blocked by a Security Council veto. The U.N.'s actions against Iraq and Libya in the early 1990s, two former Soviet client states, would have been unlikely just a few years ago. With Russia becoming more dependent on Western aid, and China seeking to keep ties to the West friendly for economic reasons, the U.N. Security Council has increasingly become a tool of the Western powers, a fact that has not been lost on Third World leaders.[102]

It remains premature to speculate about which of the many recent proposals for bolstering the U.N.'s conflict management capabilities will be implemented in the 1990s, but some improvement of these capabilities can be expected and could have a number of positive effects in the Third World.[103] First, enhancing the preventive diplomacy powers of the U.N. may be able to forestall or deter interstate conflict. Using his mandate to investigate and mediate any international dispute, a more activist Secretary General can intervene in tense situations to head off aggression and seek to broker political solutions. One suggestion is for the Secretary General to have a far stronger team of deputies who would focus on various regions. A more substantial proposed tool for early intervention, which was heavily emphasized by the 1992 *Agenda for Peace* report, is a greater use of preventive peacekeepers that can be deployed along threatened borders to deter aggressors.[104] Proposals for giving the U.N. its own intelligence capabilities, or ready access to the intelligence gathered

by member states, would allow the Secretary General to better monitor trouble stops.[105] Had better preventive diplomacy mechanisms
been in place during Iraq's buildup along Kuwait's border in July
1990, these might have allowed a better informed and better
equipped Secretary General to signal to Saddam Hussein that his
invasion would be met by U.N. resistance.

As for combating or reversing aggression, the Security Council cur-
rently has no military force on permament call, but this may change.[106]
The *Agenda for Peace* report called for U.N. member states to make available up to one thousand troops each on twenty-four hours notice for
future peacekeeping operations authorized by the Security Council.
The report stated that the option of using military force, called for under
Article 43 of the Charter, "is essential to the credibility of the United
Nations as a guarantor of international security." The existence of troops
on call "could serve, in itself, as a means of deterring breaches of the
peace since a potential aggressor would know that the Council had at its
disposal a means of response."[107]

There are many problems with implementing Article 43, as previously discussed, yet one thing about this debate seems clear: there is
a far greater chance of enhancing the U.N.'s potential to deal with
minor aggressors than with larger powers. As James Woolsey has suggested, a U.N.-commanded force would be inappropriate for dealing
with a major regional contingency such as the Gulf War, but earmarking tens of thousands of troops for rapid transfer to U.N. command could make possible effective action against smaller powers. In
addition, Woolsey predicted that even a standing U.N. force of just
several thousand battle-hardened professional troops could have
impact on the thinking of minor aggressors. "The prospect of facing
an integrated, capable, ready-reaction force of this sort would have,
shall we say, the right sort of bracing effect on Serbian ethnic
cleansers or Somali food-stealers."[108]

7

RECONSIDERING AMERICAN PRIMACY

During the Cold War, the need for American leadership in world politics was self-evident. Fierce debates raged about the exact gravity of the Soviet threat to Europe, the nature of U.S. interests in the Third World, and the best policy on nuclear weapons. But few ever questioned the basic axiom that a potent United States was needed to offset the power of the Soviet Union.

Today, though the world has changed, many of the core assumptions of U.S. foreign policy have not, and a strong consensus endures that America must maintain a position of primacy in world affairs. The arguments behind this conviction have become at once more complex and more controversial with the Cold War's end. They are complex because many of the threats of the future are not readily perceived by the naked eye and instead are understood only through theoretical prisms. They are controversial because they dictate that idealist foreign policy goals again be pushed aside in the face of more pressing security concerns.

Except for the brief periods of triumphalism that attended the collapse of communism in Eastern Europe and America's military victory in the Persian Gulf, post–Cold War foreign policy has been characterized more by resignation than euphoria. To be sure, there are those who have championed American primacy in a unipolar world, and some of these voices clearly have a material and professional interest in sustaining a vigorous national security state. But more typical has been the sense that there is no escape from the responsibilities of leadership: no escape from guaranteeing the balance of power in Europe and Asia; no escape from maintaining a foundation upon which to rebuild a war machine that can contain a new hegemonic threat; no escape from deterring new aggressors in the Third World who practice old-style territorial aggression. For Bill Clinton, a president whose passion is focused at home, America's role as a global sentinel of security has been a source of neither personal pleasure nor political advantage. For his foreign policy team, many of whom are personally committed to promoting idealist goals abroad, there can be no relishing the tenacious centrality of security matters within U.S. foreign policy.

Is there an escape from a strategy that entails the United States serving permanently as an active balancer and occasional sheriff in world affairs? Can the acute sense of danger that now undergirds foreign policy be allayed, allowing the United States not to abandon its position of international leadership, but to reconceptualize it along more idealist lines?

By highlighting weaknesses of the realist view of world politics, the last chapter began to construct an affirmative answer to these questions. When one takes a more optimistic view of global trends, it becomes possible to imagine changes in American foreign policy more fundamental than have yet taken place. If trends in the developed world point to increasing cooperation, not new conflict, then Europe and East Asia are far more stable than U.S. policy assumes. American security guarantees in those regions, while reassuring, can be viewed as less indispensable. If the checks to interstate aggression in the Third World are also growing, then it may be wrong to view Iraq's 1990 invasion as a portent of things to come. Pentagon preparations to fight two major regional contingencies at once can be seen as overly cautious.

THE NEW EUROPEAN ORDER

The American preoccupation with Europe is understandable. That continent has been the scene of chronic violence and confrontation for hundreds of years. Because a new major war in Europe would almost certainly involve the United States, the stakes of U.S. policy there are exceptionally high.

American foreign policy analysts view the future of Europe with a mixture of hope and fear. John Mearsheimer's psuedo-scientific prediction of inevitable European instability is a caricature of academic realism, not a glimpse into mainstream thinking. Most other analysts, including those who shaped Bush Administration policy, recognize that democracy, economic integration, and collective security could well produce a stable multipolar Europe that bears little resemblance to the war-torn continent of the past.

This faith, however, remains too weak to drive American policy, and it is widely agreed that U.S. management of European security affairs must continue, as manifested by the perpetuation of NATO and the continued deployment of large numbers of U.S. troops on European soil. This view stems from several fears: first, that without the United States serving as an active balancer, Europe could return to past patterns of instability. Mearsheimer's argument carries such worries to implausible extremes, but most mainstream foreign policy experts fear this scenario to some degree. American forces in Europe are seen as particularly useful for dampening anxieties surrounding German power and for reassuring the new democracies of Eastern Europe. Second, U.S. planners see the need for keeping a military infrastructure in Europe that can be rapidly expanded should a new global threat, such as resurgent Russian militarism, arise on the Eurasian landmass. American officials have said that the presence of U.S. forces can serve as a deterrent to aspiring hegemons and sustain a hard-won position of strategic depth. Finally, it is argued that American primacy in European security affairs sustains a transatlantic tie that could become perilously weak after the Cold War, and that primacy assures continued leverage on other issues, such as trade and security operations outside of Europe. Forward deployed troops in Europe are also viewed as advantageous because they are closer to potential trouble spots in the Middle East.

Each of these arguments is a questionable basis for policy. A return to old patterns of instability is unlikely in Western Europe; growing German power probably will not take a form that its neighbors find unsettling; U.S. security guarantees should not, and probably will not, be extended to Eastern Europe; and resurgent Russian militarism is a low probability with a limited potential to damage U.S. interests in any case. As for bolstering transatlantic ties and U.S. leverage over Europe, it is hard to pinpoint how these dividends flow from keeping U.S. troops in Europe. Lastly, the advantages of forward deployment are not significant enough to be a determining factor in U.S. policy.

Liberal Europe

More so than any other place in the world, Europe's politics are being transformed by the positive trends described in the last chapter. Pessimistic analysts like to compare the emerging Europe with the Europe of pre-1914 in predicting instability, but the parallels are nonexistent. Today, nearly every state in Europe is a democracy; eighty years ago autocratic governments ruled in Germany, Russia, and lesser Eastern European states. Even democratic states like Great Britain were far less open and liberal than they are now. (Women, for example, did not have the vote.) If it is true that democracies rarely fight each other, a democratic Europe has a better chance of being a peaceful Europe.

Eighty years ago, war was still seen as a viable means for increasing national wealth. This is not the case today. Arguments about the decreasing appeal of territorial conquest are particularly applicable to Europe.[1]

Perhaps most important, the economic picture is now totally different than it was before World War I. In the early 1900s close economic interdependence existed between European states, but distrust was high and there were no strong institutions to orchestrate that interdependence. Today, the European Community, along with security institutions such as NATO, stand as powerful instruments for managing ties in Europe to ensure that anxieties in the economic arena, particularly the fear of other states growing wealthier and then harnessing that wealth to belligerent ends, does not feed political-military conflict.[2] American policymakers have acknowledged the positive impact of this development. As Under Secretary of State Robert Zoellick said in late 1991, "the integration of Western Europe within the EC and NATO has virtually transcended all the old territorial disputes, irredentist claims, and ethnic grievances among and within their member states. Euro-Atlantic integration has made it literally inconceivable that localized disputes could become a source for serious conflict among these states. The incentives for cooperation within these multi- and supranational frameworks are overwhelmingly high compared with the remaining areas of discord."[3]

Further institution building is under way, although the troubles of the EC during the early 1990s cloud the prospects for genuine integration.[4] The more successful this institution building is, both in the economic and security realm, the more peaceful Europe is likely to be.[5] In the best case, Western Europe will have a common currency, open borders, and an increasing political-military identity by the dawn of the twenty-first century. In the worst case, further integration will continue to be stymied, perhaps with some ground lost from where things were in 1992.[6] But even if this latter scenario comes to pass, Western Europe will still have far stronger institutions than it did during the violent first half of the twentieth century. The EC will still stand, as Richard Rosecrance stresses, as a pioneering model for promoting cooperation between "trading states."[7] Access to the markets of the EC can still be used as a system of carrots and sticks to influence the behavior of Eastern European states. And Germany will be far more entwined with its neighbors than it was in either the 1930s or the early 1900s.

At a societal level, Europe is a fundamentally different place today than it was eighty or fifty years ago. The twin phenomena of militarism and hypernationalism have evaporated from Western European societies. In pre–World War I Europe, militaristic propaganda was widespread; now this is no longer the case. The disenchanting experience of modern warfare, combined with the impact of democratic openness, has broken the hold of militarist mythology.

Hypernationalism has also declined sharply in Europe. In the period between 1871 and 1939, Stephen Van Evera has observed, each state in Europe taught its people—in the schools and through propaganda—a mythical history of its own. "This chauvinist myth making poisoned international relations by convincing each state of the legitimacy of its own claims, the rightness of its own cause, and wrongfulness and maliciousness of the grievances of others."[8] In the post–World War II era, however, nationalist propaganda largely disappeared, especially in the schools. No longer are Europeans taught to distrust each other from a young age. Institution building has played a key role in overcoming historic animosities, particularly between France and Germany.[9] With continuing integration through the EC, the trend away from nationalism in Western Europe should continue.

Van Evera argues that militarism and hypernationalism cannot return in Western Europe because the conditions that created these forces are no longer present. Class stratification is the most important of these conditions. In the past, European elites used militarism and nationalism to maintain their positions of social control. By keeping the lower classes focused on external enemies and military dramas abroad, elites sought to distract attention from inequality at home.

This dynamic no longer occurs in Europe. Democratization and the mobilization of the working classes by organized labor has reduced stratification in Western Europe. Democratically elected leaders gain legitimation from public approval and elections, not from propaganda and manipulation.

The German Transformation

American post–Cold War policymakers have strong apprehensions about growing German power. They do not believe that Germany will again become a predatory state, but they do see its disproportionate power as jeopardizing the equilibrium in Europe and they worry that Germany's neighbors, still harboring memories of World War II, will fear a unified Germany whose security affairs are not closely supervised by the United States.

This outlook is a questionable basis for policy. The Germany of today exemplifies the transformation of Europe in the past fifty years. Once among the most militaristic of European countries, it is now among the most pacifistic; once a breeding ground for hypernationalism, it is now a leading advocate of European intergration. According to realist predictions, Germany should now be maintaining or enhancing its military position in the face of mounting uncertainty in Europe. But the opposite is happening. In the early 1990s the German government showed little interest in bolstering its military position. The German military budget is slated to decrease through the decade. Current plans call for reducing the German army from twelve divisions to eight.[10] In July 1992 Kohl's government announced that Germany would drop out of a four-nation project to build a new European jet fighter, saying that Germany could ease up on the race for ever more sophisticated weapons in a new and less threatening Europe.[11] (This decision contrasts sharply with continued U.S. development of the F-22 warplane.)

Far from perceiving an increased threat in the new Europe, as Mearsheimer's analysis predicted, many German analysts believe a safer security environment has emerged. As Gottfried Linn wrote in 1993, "For the first time in its history, Germany is surrounded only by democracies. We enjoy friendly relations with all of our neighbors. Germany is no longer a front-line state and no longer within strategic range of an offensive superpower. Our people are much more secure than they were ten years ago. . . . Today peace can be guaranteed with fewer and fewer weapons."[12] Germans are deeply unsettled by the turmoil to the East, but the much feared Russo-German rivalry, at the center of Mearsheimer's pessimistic analysis, shows no signs of materializing within the next decade. Instead, a peaceful interdependence is emerging between the two countries. Germany is Russia's largest trading partner and these economic ties have the potential to grow markedly, with Russia exporting energy supplies in exchange for high technology and quality German goods.[13] Germany has also contributed more aid to the states of the former Soviet Union than any other western country.[14] In the long run, U.S. policymakers may well worry less about a Russo-German rivalry than about a mounting closeness between the two nations that reduces American influence in Berlin.[15]

Increasingly, the German public is questioning the need for strong armed forces—or, indeed, for any armed forces at all. According to one 1992 poll, an astonishing 42 percent of Germans surveyed believed that Germany could get along without armed forces and 20 percent voiced opposition to armed forces on principle.[16] The Gulf War showed that the German public is hesitant about any overseas use of military force, even when part of a U.N.-sanctioned multilateral expedition.

Some analysts suggest that Germany has become more inclined to join international policing operations since the Gulf War, and that this trend will continue as it grows ever harder for the country to shirk a role in maintaining world order. This might be especially true if Germany attains a seat on the U.N. Security Council. But progress in this direction will be slow.[17] It is widely believed in Germany that the constitution stipulates that military forces may be used only for the purpose of defense, and Chancellor Helmut Kohl has failed to pass an amendment that would allow German forces to be used outside the NATO area.[18] However, in April 1993, after six months of debate, Germany agreed to send 1,600 troops to Somalia as part of the U.N. peacekeeping force. Also in that month a German high court ruled that German military forces could help enforce the "no-fly" rule over the former Yugoslavia. The compelling case for U.N. action in both these episodes seems to have affected public opinion, with one poll taken in early 1993 showing that 50 percent of Germans surveyed now believe that Germany should be allowed to send its troops on U.N. missions.[19]

During the postwar era, West Germany emerged as one of the least force-oriented of all the NATO nations, and these sentiments endure today. As former NSC aide Robert Blackwill has observed: "Most Germans have instinctively believed that international problems could be resolved without resort to force if only enough patience and good will were applied. 'Negotiate harder' was the constant advice from Bonn whenever an ally, usually the United States, indicated it was about to undertake violent action against an aggressor."[20] With the German public becoming more pacifistic after the Cold War, not less, it is hard to imagine German governments in the near future adopting a cavalier attitude toward international diplomacy and the use of force.[21] More worrisome than the prospect of a Germany that throws its weight around in the political-military arena, alarming its neighbors, is that of an isolationist Germany that fails to fulfill its collective security obligations.

In scenarios for how things might turn sour in the new Europe, the first step on the road to instability is often imagined to be German adoption of a more independent foreign policy. Even if it did not return to its old militaristic ways, a Germany that charted its own political or economic course could create considerable anxieties. Yet these unsettling thoughts ignore Germany's changed approach to international relations. In the last four decades Germany has evolved into a trading state and shows no signs of changing. For Germany, "economic power is a far more attractive and useful means to influence both West and East than weapons," observes European expert Stanley Hoffmann.[22] If Richard Rosecrance's analysis of trading states is correct, German leaders have little faith that military force can be used to safeguard external economic interests and are unlikely to abandon a proven formula for prosperity to adopt an old-style national strategy predicated on power politics.[23] Realists like Kenneth Waltz and Christopher Layne cite the record of history and the dictates of the international system in predicting that Germany, as an economic great power, will inevitably also become a political-military great power.[24] But the current historical period is unprecedented, for the reasons outlined in the last chapter. In Europe especially, there has never before existed such high levels of democracy and institutionalized cooperation.

Germany today is the leading advocate within Western Europe of deepening integration. Originally, a major motive of integration was to contain German power. West Germany never resisted this idea, becoming instead a practitioner of self-containment and a champion of supranationalism in Europe. The new unified Germany is no different. It recognizes that more so than before its size and weight makes other states nervous. Its enthusiasm for integration stems partly out of a desire to head off tensions on the continent.[25] The tighter the European Community is, the less German power will stand out and create anxieties. In recent years, Germany has sought to push the EC concept to its furthest possible end.[26]

In addition to this, Germany is strongly inclined to keep NATO intact and to continue to host allied troops.[27] This, too, is seen as a key part of a self-containment strategy. Christopher Bertram suggests that for Germany, "the alliance has had, and continues to have, a special function, namely that of making German power controllable and hence acceptable to allies and political adversaries alike."[28] Some analysts argue that a failure to create a fully united Europe through the EC would generate fears of German domination and necessitate that America play a continued role in balancing Germany.[29] But this argument underestimates the fashion in which Germany's self-containment ethos has amplified the positive impact of existing levels of supranationalism in Western Europe. Even if further integration stalls, a democratic Germany committed to self-containment is likely to be a far less troubling presence in a multipolar Europe than many pessimistic observers imagine.

The task of reconstructing East Germany has turned out to be far more daunting than first thought. It has been estimated that 80 percent of East Germany's capital stock will have to be replaced to make its firms competitive. In the first two years after unification, the transfer of resources from East to West was between $71 and $112 billion each year.[30] As one team of German analysts has observed, moreover, most of that money has gone for consumption rather than capital investment, suggesting that the real work of reconstructing the east has only just begun.[31] Because it will be many years before a unified Germany realizes its full potential, Europeans will be allowed to get used to greater German power on a gradual basis. Far from worrying about German domination over the next decade, Europeans are more likely to worry about a preoccupied and overburdened Germany not playing a large enough role in international affairs.[32]

The majority of Germans, particularly political elites, still want Germany to be part of NATO and want the United States to keep troops in their country.[33] But the new generation of Germans are also acutely sensitive to being endlessly blamed for their parents' crimes and never fully trusted. Foreign troops on German soil, in the face of no clear threat, could come to be resented as a symbol of the West's enduring distrust of Germany. Moreover, by keeping troops in Europe in the absence of a clear threat and by talking ominously of imbalanced power and of history repeating itself, the United States legitimates unfounded European fears of German power. It lends credence to the notion that the "German problem" remains unresolved. The consequence may be slower progress toward Germany's emergence as a responsible and fully rehabilitated member of the international community.

Resurgent Russia?

Of course, U.S. troops are not in Europe just for the purpose of containing German power and promoting stability generally. They also serve as a toehold that can be expanded in the case of resurgent Russian militarism. How real is this threat?

Because the current period of Russian history is very much a transitional one, it is difficult to predict the future patterns of Russia's relations with the world. As Russian scholar Alexei Arbatov observed in 1993, a new foreign leadership elite has yet to emerge in Russia and several factions are competing for influence.[34] The outcome of this competition will be determined by a variety of developments. Russia is a country struggling through three revolutionary transitions: from totalitarianism to democracy; from a planned to a market economy; from an empire to a nation-state. Traps lurk in each of these challenges. After hundreds of years of tsarist rule, and seventy years of Communist totalitarianism, Russia is a poor breeding ground for democracy. Current conditions for instituting a new political system could hardly be worse, with Russia going through an economic convulsion worse than the U.S. Great Depression of the 1930s. Russian historian Vladislav Zubok has speculated darkly about the possible consequences of such prolonged agony: "As the experience of many developing countries demonstrates, a right-wing populism fueled by people's misery can become a dangerous political force under an anti-Western, xenophobic banner. The IMF could be vilified, the Westernizers discredited and ousted from Russian leadership. The Russian public might support the components of a neoisolationism: aggressive insecurity, rising nationalism, and revived militarism."[35] In early 1993, Russian expert Stephen Cohen warned that an anti-American backlash was already gaining steam in Russia at both the elite and societal level as a result of arrogant U.S. meddling in Russia's economic and political affairs.[36] The success of nationalist politicians during elections in late 1993 was widely viewed in the West as a disturbing indication of what the future might hold.

In the national security realm it is possible to imagine various tensions between Russia and the West. The dynamics of the security dilemma, in which inadvertent military competitions can arise out of legimate searches for security, could prove difficult to suppress. Russia's strong insecurities ensure deployment of sizable military forces.[37] These are now, and will continue to be, a source of anxiety among U.S. planners who have long tended to focus on capabilities over intentions.

In Russia, even if democracy grows stronger, conservative military leaders could begin to complain about their military inferiority vis-à-vis the United States, exploiting the issue to drum up nationalism and xenophobia. As former Reagan official Fred Ikle has observed, "A long list of growing American threats could easily be compiled: continued U.S. nuclear tests, undiminished U.S. naval superiority, expanded deployments of the 'stealth' and precision technologies that won the Gulf War, and the survival of NATO and of most U.S. bases that are 'encircling' Russia even though the Warsaw Pact has been abolished."[38] To this litany could be added the deployment of some kind of U.S. anti-missile system, now planned for the late 1990s, and the continued modernization of certain elements of the U.S. strategic arsenal, even as the overall size of that arsenal declines. Western defense arrangements with Eastern European nations could also generate anxiety among Russian security officials. In late November 1993, for example, a top Russian intelligence official, Yevgeny M. Primakov, warned that if NATO expanded eastward "the need would arise for a fundamental reappraisal of all defense concepts on our side, a redeployment of armed forces and changes in security plans."[39]

Ultimately, however, even under the worst-case scenario of a failure of democracy, a rise in aggressive nationalism, and deteriorating relations with the West, future governments in Moscow will have only limited freedom of action.

Economically, Russia has no choice but to continue integrating itself in the world of markets and financial institutions controlled by the leaders of the G-7. Whoever rules Russia in the future—be they autocrats or democrats—will face the same stark choices as the current government; they will still be dependent on the West for economic assistance and technology, indeed perhaps even for emergency humanitarian relief to stave off civil unrest. Over the next decade Russian leaders contemplating belligerent foreign policy behavior will not be able to ignore the devastating potential of Western economic retaliation. In the more distant future, when the time comes that Russia is no longer so dependent on the West and has achieved a measure of economic well-being, it is likely that democracy, and the peacefulness toward other liberal states that flows from it, will have a good chance of becoming entrenched.

Realists often make the point that prosperity is not all that states care about. Future Russian leaders may go to war for ideological, ethnic, or religious reasons that overpower economic calculation. To be on the safe side, it is said, the United States must base its defense plans on present and future Russian military capabilities.

What are these capabilities? To begin with, they are unlikely to ever be what the Soviet Union deployed, since Russia has only 60 percent of the Soviet Union's population and has been particularly weakened by the loss of the Ukraine, so central to Soviet might in the past. Also, the defense industrial base in Russia is in a state of acute disarray. Future extremist leaders would have to turn this situation around even as they faced cutoffs of Western economic assistance and technology.

An isolated Russia would be incapable of competing with the West militarily. The level of technological prowess that the United States demonstrated in the Gulf War, particularly in the area of battle-field management, which depends on the high-speed processing of data, is beyond the reach of Russia for the simple reason that it has not yet evolved into an information society.[40] Even without such new weapons as the F-22 fighter or the European Fighter, the West will retain a technological military advantage over any possible revived Russian threat through the foreseeable future.

From a geopolitical perspective, a resurgent Russia would face stiff resistance. Unlike the Soviet Union of the Cold War era, the new Russia would have to either co-opt or conquer a number of its neighbors before its forces could directly threaten Western Europe. Co-option would be unlikely. As Stephen Walt has persausively argued, threatened states do not usually strike deals with aggressors, jumping on the "bandwagon." Instead, the more common response is for states to join together and balance against threats. Walt notes that "every attempt to achieve hegemony in Europe since the Thirty Years War has been thwarted by a defensive coalition formed pre-cisely for the purpose of defeating the potential hegemon."[41]

When the Soviet Union was a superpower, deploying vast forces in Eastern Europe, it took the might of another superpower to bal-ance its power. But today Russia is just another great power, weaker in some respects than Germany. Even without the United States, the states of Western and Central Europe constitute an equal or greater counterweight to Russian power.

In the imagination of Pentagon planners and other analysts, an authoritarian Russia would not try to conquer Western Europe, but instead engage in piecemeal aggression against its neighbors. Pentagon planning documents made public in 1992 suggest that a Russian inva-sion of Lithuania is the kind of scenario that the United States must prepare for in the former Communist bloc. Such aggression on the part of a future Russian nationalist leader appears plausible. The Russians are a historically insecure people and their past is filled with examples of outward expansion in the name of national security.[42]

It is highly doubtful, however, that the United States would take action militarily in the face of local aggression by Russia, and preparing for such action is not a coherent rationale for keeping U.S. troops in Europe. Some 25 million Russians live in non-Russian republics and it is likely that any future conflict between Russia and neighbors such as Lithuania or Ukraine would be sparked by controversies involving these population pockets. Instead of appearing as clear-cut aggression by Russia, such situations would likely be murky imbroglios characterized by ethnic violence in which both sides shared some blame. Under such circumstances, the United States and its allies would be hesitant to get involved. Moreover, even in a case of clear-cut aggression, with Russian nationalists seeking to recapture past imperial holdings, the presence of nuclear weapons would have the same chilling effect as during the Cold War, making the risks of a direct confrontation with Moscow in its sphere of influence too high to contemplate.

Instability in the East

The scenario of a resurgent Russia is not the only threat that exists within the former Communist bloc. In fact, there are numerous possibilities for inter- and intra-state conflict among the twenty or so nations to the east of what was once the Iron Curtain.[43] It is argued that American troops in Western Europe help stabilize Eastern Europe by providing general reassurance to the new democratic governments in that region. There is no reason to doubt this assertion, since it has often been made by Eastern European leaders themselves. However, providing such reassurance is an unsettling basis for policy given that the actual use of U.S. troops in Eastern Europe in the foreseeable future is highly unlikely. After decades of disconnection from the countries of the former Communist bloc, the United States does not have the kind of clear-cut vital interests there that would justify large-scale military intervention. An unprovoked attack by Hungary on Romania would be unfortunate, but such an event would probably not galvanize a consensus in the United States for intervention given the negligible impact it would have on America's well-being. The biggest opponents of sending troops in such situations might well prove to be American military leaders, who have been firm in their insistence that large numbers of U.S. ground forces should only be used when vital interests are threatened, when clear and achievable objectives exist, and when an exit strategy is readily discernible. It hard to imagine that many future conflicts in the East, occurring outside the traditional orbit of U.S. strategic concerns and ethnically colored, will meet this criteria.

The war in the former Yugoslavia is instructive in thinking about the prospects for future intervention in Eastern Europe. The conflict showed that the United States will be hard pressed to insulate itself from turmoil in the East, however much it desires to. Massive human rights abuses in conjunction with international aggression generated outrage in the United States and widespread calls for intervention. But while air strikes against the Serbian aggressors were repeatedly considered by NATO, and finally employed in early 1994, there never existed anything approaching a solid consensus behind a large-scale U.S. military peacemaking (as opposed to peacekeeping) intervention on the ground.[44] The U.S. hesitancy to intervene decisively in Bosnia, despite what Secretary Christopher termed the "destruction of a U.N. member state,"[45] suggests that major intervention in other Eastern Euorpean conflicts is also unlikely. Even the limited application of U.S. military force in the region is probably unlikely. There is strong opposition to incremental intervention among U.S. military leaders and, more important, a widespread view among foreign policy elites that prestige considerations demand that any application of U.S. force must yield clear-cut success—a result that can rarely be guaranteed by limited operations.

It has been argued that stopping conflicts in Eastern Europe may be a vital interest for the United States and NATO because such conflicts can have the potential to trigger a European conflagration. But the logic of this argument is flawed. A European conflagration will only arise from a local conflict in Eastern Europe if great powers allow themselves to be drawn into the fighting. The best way to avoid such a scenario is for the Western powers to forsake large-scale intervention in conflicts in the East, especially if Russia is likely to view this as threatening.[46]

None of this is to suggest that the security of Eastern European states can be ignored by the United States. The Eastern states may not be a direct vital interest, but their symbolic status is enormous. These states represent the central front in the global battle for democratization. In addition, stability in the East does affect conditions in the West, particularly since conflicts there can trigger mass migrations. In November 1991, NATO heads of state declared that "our own security is inseparably linked to that of all other states in Europe."[47] As will be discussed shortly, the United States should back collective security measures to increase stability in Eastern Europe. But these measures should not include automatic U.S. commitments to defend Eastern European states from each other, since such commitments may not be honored. The U.N. Charter contains an obligation to defend member states, and this is the best vehicle for any U.S. involvement in safeguarding the security of Eastern states for two reasons. First, the U.S., French, and British vetos in the Security Council will ensure that U.S. and other Western powers will never get dragged into war in Eastern Europe through automatic treaty requirements; and second, Russia's veto ensures that any multilateral intervention in that region will not be seen as threatening by Moscow.

Means of Influence, Bases for Redeployment

American troops in Europe are seen as having other purposes beyond dealing with security threats on the continent. By offering military protection to the European allies, it is widely thought that Washington can gain concessions on issues such as trade and security cooperation in the Third World.[48] American troops in Europe, moreover, are seen as well positioned to be rapidly shifted to the Middle East during times of crisis.[49]

Neither of these arguments is very compelling on close examination. Predicting whether the United States will gain leverage over Europe by perpetuating its security guarantee is difficult since the historic record on the uses of leverage is ambiguous. Even when the Red Army loomed over Western Europe during the Cold War, balanced only by America's extended nuclear deterrence and conventional forces, U.S. allies often did not bend to America's will on economic and security issues.[50] To the degree that the United States did get its way on these issues, it is hard to establish a direct link between this outcome and the U.S. security guarantee. America's economic hegemony over the allies until the late 1960s and early 1970s may better explain high levels of U.S. influence during much of the post-war period than any leverage that stemmed from the U.S. security guarantee can explain it. Successful U.S. leadership on security issues such as military deployments to the Persian Gulf in 1987–1988 and 1990–1991 can also be explained by other factors, such as basic European agreement with U.S. policy goals and persuasive American diplomacy.[51]

By far the most salient example of U.S. efforts to gain leverage from its security guarantee has been in the area of burden sharing. Ever since NATO's creation the United States has always wanted its allies to spend more on defense, and over the decades both Congress and the executive branch have used the implied threat of U.S. troop withdrawals from Europe to achieve this goal. In 1953 and 1954, for example, at the height of American hegemony over the allies, the Eisenhower Administration warned of an "agonizing reappraisal" of America's commitment to protecting Europe in an effort to assure the approval of the European Defense Community. Little came of this threat then, or in the decades that followed, for the simple reason that no amount of disobedience on the part of the allies could move the United States to leave Europe vulnerable.[52]

The redeployment argument is also weak. During the Gulf crisis, with the Pentagon seeking to move as many troops to Saudi Arabia as quickly as possible, the initial wave of U.S. forces came from bases in the United States, not Europe. Within one month, 150,000 U.S. troops arrived in the Middle East.[53] American forces in Europe were deployed only later in the crisis. In a future crisis it is likely that U.S.-based forces would again be the first deployed. A major reason for this is that much of America's air- and sea-lift capabilities are now, and will always be, based in the United States. The Pentagon's eight fast sea-lift ships, for example, are stationed in U.S. ports with nucleus crews.[54] During the initial phase of a crisis it takes less time to load up these ships in the United States and send them to the theater of operations than it does to deploy them to Europe empty, have them load up there, and then proceed to the crisis. The Gulf War showed that retaining American air bases in Europe is crucial for conducting a rapid and large-scale intervention in the Middle East.[55] But it did not prove that this goal also requires having large ground forces in Europe.

Collective Security in Europe

A conflict between the major powers of Europe is unlikely because of the spread of democracy, economic interdependence, and the high costs of war. But beyond this, collective security has a better chance of working in Europe than anywhere else in world. During the first half of the nineteenth century, European politics was characterized by concert diplomacy among the great powers. The Concert of Europe, put in place after the Napoleonic Wars, was based on restraint and collective action. "No one power could attempt to settle a European question by an independent and self-regulated intitiative," observed Richard Elrod. Instead, the "policies of each were subject to the scrutiny and sanction of all."[56] At least for a few decades, the Concert served to institutionalize cooperation among the great powers of Europe and an unprecedented peace prevailed on the continent.[57]

The Europe of today is ripe for a new concert of powers. The conditions that made a concert possible in the nineteenth century are even more abundantly present today. All the major powers of Europe are satisfied with the status quo and agree that the international system should not be fundamentally changed; there exists a common agreement that war between the major powers would be catastrophic; a great deal of reciprocity characterizes relations among the major powers—that is, there exists a readiness to make concessions of self-interest for the broader good; and there is little secrecy in today's Europe. During the Napoleonic Wars, the coalition fighting France freely shared information among themselves, creating a high degree of transparency. That openness facilitated the climate of trust that made the Concert possible. Today, there is even greater transparency in Europe, thanks to instant communications, satellite technology, and information-sharing arrangements.[58]

In addition to the basic consensus that exists among the major powers, Europe has a strong institutional foundation for promoting collective security. NATO has endured into the new era and has begun establishing ties to the countries of the former Warsaw Pact.

Long dormant, the Western European Union (WEU) is now being revived and strengthened, serving as the security arm of the EC under the Maastricht Treaty. The Conference on Security and Cooperation in Europe (CSCE) has played a major role in dealing with political and military issues on the continent since the 1970s. The CSCE includes all the countries of Europe except Albania. Its purpose has been to build trust between states and reduce the level of military competition in Europe.

Since the end of the Cold War there has been intensive discussion over what kind of collective security arrangements can best guarantee the peace in Europe. This discussion is likely to last for many more years, and a decade from now, Europe may have a different security architecture than it does today. The purpose here is not to suggest what that architecture might optimally look like, but rather to argue that even if no changes are made at all, the current arrangements have the potential to keep Europe stable in the absence of a major American military presence on the continent.

An enduring NATO serves four positive functions. First, whether or not U.S. troops are stationed in Europe, the alliance ensures a U.S. balancing role on the continent by guaranteeing that American power would be brought to bear in the case of any aggression against member states. Second, and related to this, NATO would be the best mechanism for containing a resurgent Russian threat. Third, while NATO probably should not extend membership to the Eastern European states, at least not at this time, it can help to stabilize that region. NATO's liaison program with former Warsaw Pact countries, embodied in the North Atlantic Cooperation Council (NACC), has the potential to foster greater security by building trust and reducing misunderstandings, both between East and West and among the Eastern European countries.[59] Also, NATO can be a useful forum for coordinating Western security policy toward Eastern Europe,[60] helping ensure that Western countries don't forge conflicting policies in the region or, in the worst case, end up on opposite sides of local conflicts. Fourth, there may be instances in which the U.N. approves military intervention in Eastern Europe to thwart aggression. NATO provides a proven command structure for coordinating the interventionary efforts of the Western powers. When the United States and its allies decided to use air strikes in Bosnia in early 1994, for example, NATO was the vehicle for this action.

NATO's obituary has been prematurely written by many commentators in recent years. But the multiple functions the alliance serves makes it likely to endure even as the Cold War fades further into the past. There is little plausibility to claims that NATO's survival hinges on the presence of U.S. troops in Europe.

The Western European Union is not a substitute for NATO, but a supplement to it.[61] The WEU, which unlike NATO includes France, can play a key role in assuring continued security cooperation between the Western European nations.[62] By integrating German military power into a multilateral structure, a strengthened WEU serves to counteract fears of Germany pursuing an independent security policy. In this sense, it can perform the containment function that U.S. troops in Germany have played for decades. Since the need to contain Germany is negligible anyway, given its self-containment, setbacks to the WEU's full revival are not likely to be destabilizing.

Like NATO, the WEU can play a constructive role in regard to Eastern Europe by helping the Western nations coordinate their policy toward the region. Perhaps most important, the WEU could be a vehicle for intervening in Eastern Europe in cases where the United States does not want to get involved and therefore where NATO may not be the appropriate instrument. In the wake of the WEU's failure to take action in Bosnia, it is hard to imagine independent Western European leadership of this kind. But this could change in the future, especially if Germany becomes more willing to contribute its forces to multilateral operations outside the NATO area. Stronger American signals that it will reduce its role in managing Europe's security affairs could also be decisive in injecting the WEU with a capacity for action.

The CSCE now stands as the only continent-wide European collective security organization. It is not, however, a true collective security body in that it guarantees the security of its members. Instead, over the past two decades, the CSCE has overseen a host of confidence-building and surveillance measures designed to eliminate the uncertainty surrounding military activities, thus reducing fears of surprise attack or other aggressive uses of force. Also, by sponsoring the Treaty on Conventional Forces in Europe (CFE), the CSCE made possible major force reductions in Europe before the Cold War formally ended.[63] If the CSCE can achieve such gains in a Cold War environment, where suspicion was rampant, its potential for fostering reassurance in the new Europe should be considerable.

Various suggestions have been made for turning the CSCE into a full-fledged collective security organization.[64] But whether such proposals are implemented or not, even a modestly strengthened CSCE can make a major contribution to European security, particularly in the East. As an organization that contains every member of Europe, the CSCE can play a role in mediating conflicts between states and arriving at agreements to isolate or punish those who challenge the established order. As a forum where information on national armed forces is exchanged, the CSCE can help to ameliorate the secrecy and uncertainty that drives arms races. As an institution with a mandate that includes human rights and international legal issues, the CSCE can monitor the treatment of ethnic minorities and seek to defuse nascent ethnic conflicts.

In the future, new efforts to strengthen collective security in Europe could be enormously beneficial, especially in stabilizing the former Communist bloc. But as things now stand, the current security architecture of Europe is capable of promoting America's most important security aims on the continent, with or without the presence of U.S. troops.

The Future of U.S. Troops in Europe

During the 1970s and 1980s there was sporadic debate in Washington about cutting U.S. troop levels in Europe as a way to force Western Europe to take more responsibility for its own defense. Nothing ever came of such talk, in large part because the stakes were too high; conducting burden-sharing experiments was too risky when a powerful Soviet war machine sat in East Germany. Today the situation in Europe is far less urgent. None of the threats to European security are such that they must be countered by continued U.S. troop deployments. It is therefore now possible to envision a policy that gradually withdraws nearly all U.S. grounds forces from Europe. An "over-the-horizon" approach to guaranteeing Europe's security would represent a return to the kind of limited balancing role that Kennan and other U.S. planners imagined in the immediate postwar period.

Removing most U.S. troops from Europe may be the only way to force Germany and the other European states to take full responsibility for their security. To date, America's post–Cold War foreign policy has contained no strategy for eliminating what is, in effect, a self-per-petuating dynamic of dependency.[65] European nations that grew psy-chologically dependent on U.S. leadership during four decades of Cold War will never be able to prove themselves as long as the United States continues to manage their security affairs. Untested, the Euro-peans will continue to be seen by Washington as unreliable security guarantors.

A withdrawal of American troops from Europe will not eliminate America's balancing role in Europe, which will be perpetuated through NATO. But it could be an important step in signaling that Washington will not automatically take the lead whenever security problems arise in Europe. It can help communicate the view that the U.S. will no longer accept a disproportionate burden for the keeping peace in Europe.

Messages such as these could move the EC countries, especially Germany, to accept greater responsibilities in Eastern Europe. One interpretation of inaction in Bosnia is that "buck passing" occurred during the crisis. The United States wanted Europe to take the lead, while Europe, sticking to habits of the past, waited for the United States to solve its problems. Down the line, when the United States has ended its paternalistic policies and a period of psychological rebuilding has occurred among Western European leaders, it is possi-ble to imagine them being capable of far more decisive independent action. If this does not turn out to be the case, the United States can reassess its policy of reducing hegemony and use NATO to reassert more control in European security affairs. Also, by maintaining a basic military infrastructure in Europe, the United States can retain the option of raising force levels in the future.

EAST ASIA: COMPETITION OR COOPERATION?

The prognosis for stability in East Asia is far more murky than in Europe. The spread of democracy remains uneven and the region enters the new era without well-established structures for promoting economic integration and collective security. The dynamism of both China and Japan make their smaller neighbors uneasy, and North Korea, the world's last bastion of Stalinism, is now one of the most heavily armed anti-Western states in existence.

It is no wonder, then, that U.S. foreign policy analysts look across the Pacific with considerable misgivings. While realist scenarios for instability in Europe often seem farfetched, such pessimism is far more plausible when applied to East Asia.

American analysts see three central reasons for why the United States must maintain its Cold War position of primacy in East Asia. First, it is widely argued that in the absence of a visible U.S. balancing role, East Asia could be consumed by new instability as states take unilateral measures to safeguard their security. In particular, it is worried that an end to America's protection of Japan would lead that country to build up military power that is commensurate with its economic strength and that this development would alarm other states in the region. Second, many have predicted that a U.S. pullback from the region could result in a withering of the U.S.-Japan defense alliance, a development that could damage the already strained relationship between the United States and Japan. Finally, U.S. officials cite the enduring threat from North Korea in justifying a position of vigilance in East Asia.

Yet, as with the arguments for primacy in Europe, the threats that drive America's Asian policy have been exaggerated. Japan, like Germany, is guided in its international policy by an ethos of self-containment; the real danger is not an unnerving resurgence of its military power, along with a failure of good ties with the United States, but a continuation of its pacifism and isolationism. Prospects of structural instability have also been overemphasized; new mechanisms for managing economic interdependence and collective security are rapidly emerging. And although North Korea's efforts in the early 1990s at nuclear proliferation have been alarming, the long-term trends point to a declining threat from a nation that is increasingly weak and isolated.

Japan's Self-Containment

Japan is not likely to become a traditional great power—as realists predict—if the American security guarantee is withdrawn from East Asia. Even more so than Germany, Japan is now a vastly different country than it was before World War II. Its people have a powerful allergy to militarism and its leaders are acutely conscious of the anxieties that surround Japanese strength.[66] While Japan's rise on the regional and global scene would be accelerated by an end to paternalistic U.S. policies, this new prominence would probably take a benign form. Like Germany, Japan is likely to be an assertive "civilian power," wielding its influence in a manner appropriate to a trading state.[67]

Japan's defeat and occupation by the United States in the 1940s fundamentally transformed Japanese society. During the 1930s, the nature of Japanese society allowed militarism and hypernationalism to flourish. The main mission of General Douglas MacArthur, head of the U.S. occupation, was to overhaul and level Japanese society. The working classes were empowered through organized labor; women were given a new role in Japanese political life; and military elites were broken down. Indeed, Japan's military, a leading force in Japanese life through the 1930s, was entirely liquidated. These sweeping measures, along with memories of intense suffering during the war, wiped out militarism as a significant force in Japanese life.[68] Today, Japan has "a culture of anti-militarism" and its political system contains powerful checks on the military establishment.[69] "The structure of the Japanese state has made it virtually impossible, short of a domestic political revolution, for an autonomous and powerful military establishment to emerge in Japan," Peter Katzenstein and Nobuo Okawara write. "The civilians' control over the military is firmly entrenched in Japan. The structure of state-society relations in Japan isolates the military from a public which musters at best no more than passive tolerance for the armed forces."[70]

At the insistence of the United States, near-pacifism became the guiding force of Japanese foreign policy after World War II, with Article 9 of the U.S.-imposed Japanese constitution renouncing war and stating that Japan would never again maintain a military establishment. At the later insistence of the United States, Japan did not conform to the disarmament clause of Article 9 and developed powerful military forces. Today, while generally adhering to a vow not to spend more than one percent of its GDP on defense, Japan has the third largest military budget in the world. Its military establishment is considered extremely capable and among the most modern in the world.

But the Japanese still take the rest of Article 9 seriously. What might be called "constitutional pacifism" remains a powerful force in Japanese society.[71] As one Asian analyst observed, Japanese government officials believe that "it is unconstitutional to join a regional security pact with military obligations or dispatch armed forces outside the country without amending the constitution. Amending the constitution, however, would spark bitter controversy since the 'no-war clause' is still supported by the great majority of the Japanese people."[72]

If anything, the Japanese public is more committed than its leaders to Japan's non-belligerent stance in security matters. As Chalmers Johnson has written, "Most Japanese equate Article 9 of the constitution with democracy itself; to alter one is to alter the other."[73] In December 1993 the Japanese defense minister created a scandal and was forced to resign when he suggested that Japan's constitutional limits on the use of force were out of date.[74] Given this kind of atmosphere, any future Japanese government would face significant obstacles to deploying large military forces abroad, even if the security conditions change. And Japan's pacifism goes even deeper than the resistance to sending forces abroad. According to one 1989 poll, only 20 percent of Japanese surveyed supported the use of military force to resist a military invasion from abroad.[75]

Various observers suggest that militaristic forces are lurking just below the surface of Japanese society. Certainly it is true that some influential Japanese believe that Japan must begin to acquire military and political clout commensurate with its economic power.[76] This viewpoint would probably become more widely accepted if the United States ended its military primacy in East Asia. But it is highly doubtful that such thinking could become the mainstream position in Japan in the near future.

As with Germany, Japan's shortcoming in the post–Cold War era is not likely to be its overassertiveness, as many fear. Instead, isolationism and an unwillingness to take on regional or global responsibilities may be more likely.[77] The recent economic slowdown in Japan could strengthen the tendency to look inward. More international responsibilities would mean larger military or foreign aid budgets. This in turn would require higher taxes, never popular in times of economic stagnation. Even in better economic times, the level of tax increases required to build military forces commensurate with Japan's economic might would probably be unacceptable to a public that is deeply skeptical of the usefulness of force in world affairs.[78]

With the ending of the Cold War, public opposition to higher defense spending increased to a record high of 82 percent in 1990.[79] In 1990 and 1991, Japanese leaders announced that they were scaling back defense spending plans.[80] In 1993, Japan's military budget grew at a rate of 3 percent, after years of growth rates of 6 percent.[81] The Gulf War convinced many Japanese that a more proactive foreign policy was warranted, but it is unclear how far-reaching this attitudinal change will be.[82]

A U.S. pullback from East Asia might compel Japan to pursue a more activist role in the region, but this would not necessarily be a dangerous development, as many analysts think. Realists imagine that all states obsess about their physical security and believe in the utility of force. They thus imagine that an unprotected Japan will behave like other vulnerable states have through history, arming itself to cope with a turbulent world and secure its overseas interests. But this analysis cannot be automatically applied to Japan. Even in the face of rising external threats, Japan's new assertiveness would probably not take the form of stepped-up military activities. As a quintessential trading state, Japan does not want to become a military or "territorial" state because its people and leaders believe it would gain little from such a role while risking much.[83] Japan's leaders, argues Reihard Drifte, believe that "Japan's rising investment abroad cannot be protected by military power, but only by participation in the management of international politics and economics."[84] A 1993 poll showed that some 66 percent of Japanese surveyed believe that acquiring greater military power would increase Japan's chances of being caught up in another war.[85]

Particularly on the regional level, Japanese leaders see increased military activism as counterproductive. They know, notes Drifte, that stepped-up defense efforts "could actually mean, in the end, less security if its neighbors were to perceive increased Japanese rearmament as a threat, during a period of weakening U.S. control."[86] A. Hasnan Habib puts this point in delicate terms: "Japan's twentieth-century history in Asia implies that it will be much better accepted as an economic power and cutural force than as a major military power."[87]

Japan is especially sensitive in its relations with Southeast Asia. This bountiful region, conquered and occupied by Japan in World II, would be the natural place for Japan to flex any new politico-military muscle it might develop in the future. Scenarios for instability in Asia often depict Japan's southern neighbors beefing up their military power to offset growing Japanese assertiveness.

This is unlikely to happen. During the 1970s, Japan gained a terrible reputation in Southeast Asia by pursuing heavy-handed trade and aid policies. Such policies, combined with memories of World War II, served to nurture anti-Japanese sentiment among Southeast Asians. Today, these sentiments are much less pronounced. Japanese policy in the region has become much more sensitive, and Japan and the ASEAN states have a mutually beneficial relationship. Japan relies on the region for its wealth of natural resources and large consumer markets. Southeast Asian nations, in turn, look to Japan for economic aid, investment, and as a market for their natural resources. Some in the region also look to Japan for inspiration. There is a sense among Southeast Asians, observes Filipino scholar Khatharaya Um, that "Japan has much to impart to those seeking to follow its path of acheivements."[88] Singaporean politician Lee Kuan Yew, while stressing that fears of Japan linger in Southeast Asia, acknowledges that Japan has become less culturally aloof in recent years, growing more hospitable to foreigners from Southeast Asia and dramatically increasing the number of foreign students studying in Japan.[89]

Other analysts suggest that there is no real fear of Japanese militarism in Southeast Asia, that these countries are ready for a larger Japanese role in the region, and that ties between Japan and Southeast Asia are likely to grow even better.[90] There now exists in Southeast Asia historically unprecedented levels of political stability and economic prosperity, and current trends point to more of the same. As Southeast Asian nations grow economically they will enjoy greater diversification of trade and investment patterns and a lessening dependence on Japan. This will make them more equal and confident partners in an environment of mounting interdependence. Also, as will be discussed shortly, new mechanisms are developing for managing East Asian interdependence.

To the degree that Japan does play a more assertive role in Asia, becoming an active regional leader, this is likely to be a good thing. American officials regularly implied in the early 1990s that Japan would not be acceptable as a regional hegemon. This is true when stated in political-military terms, and Japan's policy of self-containment in the security sphere is a recognition of that fact. But as a powerful trading state in an economically dynamic region, Japan can be an acceptable leader in other ways. It can use investment, trade, and aid to shape the East Asian economic and political environment. It can be a catalyst for regional cooperation, and indeed, already Japan is hosting regional symposia and conferences on a wide range of issues.[91] Tokyo can also use its growing role in international institutions to represent East Asian interests in the global community.

America and Japan: Friendship Without Hegemony

In the last decade, amid recurrent economic tensions, security cooperation between the United States and Japan has rarely faltered. Disagreement over trade and cultural differences often make it easy for Americans and Japanese to view each other as adversaries. Defense ties, it is said, serve to remind leaders in the two countries that they are on the same side. The U.S.-Japan security relationship has been called the "glue" that binds the two states together. It is seen as a failsafe mechanism in that relationship; ties between the United States and Japan can never become truly adversarial as long as the two nations are military allies.[92] America's paternalistic role in the alliance reinforces this point. For U.S.-Japanese relations to deteriorate fully, Japan would have to become an independent power. But the nature of its defense relationship to the United States makes this implausible. For the last forty years, Japan's national security has largely been entrusted to the United States; as long as the alliance continues in its present form Japan will not be a fully mature and autonomous nation. Ties to Japan will thus be more manageable.

Despite the end of the Cold War, there has been little pressure to alter the nature of U.S.-Japan security relations. Japan is by no means chafing under the current arrangement; most Japanese support the security relationship with the United States in its current form. "The dominant view in Japan is that the most rational foreign policy for the nation to pursue is one that seeks to reinforce rather than challenge American hegemony," notes Gerald Curtis.[93] As with Germany, moreover, Japan sees its security relationship with the U.S. as a desirable part of its self-containment strategy. "For Japan to have American forces on its soil is tantamount to possessing an internationally valid certificate of non-expansionist intentions," one analyst has suggested.[94] For the United States, there is also little incentive to change the status quo. The cost of keeping nearly fifty thousand troops in Japan is negligible: Japan pays higher levels of support for the U.S. troops based there than any other host nation.[95] It is cheaper to deploy American troops in Japan than to keep them in the United States.[96] And with U.S. bases in the Philippines now closed, the importance of the U.S. facilities in Japan is seen as increasing.[97]

Still, in the long run, American hegemony is an unnecessary and perhaps undesirable basis for U.S.-Japan ties. American policymakers tend to invest overseas troop deployments with magical properties. Like some sort of catch-all medication, U.S. troops are imagined to allieviate a variety of ailments, most of which are psychosomatic in nature. However, a good future relationship between the two countries is unlikely to hinge on developments in the security arena. Instead, it will depend on managing economic and cultural differences. These differences are well known and include an American belief that Japan practices unfair trade and a Japanese view that the United States has mismanaged its economy and is seeking to blame Japan for problems of its own making. If relations between the United States and Japan are to improve in the 1990s, the United States must get its economic house in order and Japan must become more open to foreign investment and consumer products. Also, as many observers have pointed out, better U.S.-Japan relations depend on more U.S. attention to the relationship, which was often neglected during the Bush years. Secretary of State James Baker, for example, spent only two nights in Japan during four years.[98]

It is hard to see how security issues will affect whether U.S.-Japan relations are improved in the future. Close security cooperation did not stop the U.S.-Japanese relationship from deteriorating badly in the 1980s. Indeed, if ever there were a moment for using the leverage that supposedly stems from America's security guarantees in Europe and Asia, it was in the 1980s when the United States was getting economically trounced by Japan, in part because of unfair trade practices. Washington's failure to wield the leverage weapon suggests that it either doesn't really exist or that it is considered unusable.[99]

The view of defense ties as a failsafe mechanism in a relationship with a high potential for meltdown is exaggerated. Ties between the United States and Japan are actually quite stable. As Joseph Nye has argued, the interdependence between the two countries is more beneficial than the recent acrimony over trade issues would suggest. "While interdependence causes frictions, it also strengthens groups inside each society that define national interests in ways that resist a disruption of relationships," Nye wrote in 1992. "The degree of reciprocity in the relationship makes it difficult for either side to exploit it for political advantage and, if anything, Japan is more dependent on access to the U.S. market than vice versa."[100]

The real failsafe mechanism in U.S-Japanese relations is the chilling specter of a trade war or some other economic disruption between the two nations. That specter, and all the incentives for cooperation that stem from it, would endure in the wake of a U.S. troop withdrawal from Japan.

As with Germany, a failure to change the security arrangement with Japan could hurt relations in the long run. Among Americans there is already an acute sense that Japan is being coddled in the security realm. Continued U.S. troop deployments in Japan might deepen public resentment over the "protection" given to a wealthy ally.[101] More significant, the United States may have a hard time getting Japan to assume a greater leadership role (and accompanying financial burdens) in international affairs, particularly in multilateral institutions, if inequality and dependency persist in the security realm. As with the West Europeans, it may be that Japan's leaders will emerge as capable actors on the world stage only after a reduction of American paternalism.

Among the Japanese, there may now be acceptance of U.S. hegemony, but that could change. With the Communist threat receding into the past, and a new generation of Japanese leaders coming to power, the special respect for the United States that grew up in the early postwar period may begin to evaporate. "As Japan's strength grows, the Japanese will outgrow and come to resent the dependent relationship," predicts Nye.[102] Japanese may begin to wonder why they are still "occupied" by the United States. Even the Philippines, they will notice, kicked U.S. bases out in 1992. The Japanese may perceive, and accurately so, that a main mission of American troops in Japan is to contain Japan's power. Like the Germans, the Japanese might grow to resent the notion that the United States still does not trust them. This resentment could be especially strong if it is coupled with a perception, currently growing in Japan, that the United States pushes Japan around and makes unreasonable demands.[103]

In time, the Japanese public could also become annoyed about paying the costs of stationing U.S. troops in their country, now about $3 billion a year. Irritation on this matter already sporadically surfaces, as when the Japanese government builds new housing for American service personnel. Japanese ask why their government should build housing for foreign troops who guard against a nonexistent threat when Japan suffers from a major housing crisis.

None of the above observations are meant to suggest that the United States should immediately withdraw its troops from Japan or reduce defense cooperation with Tokyo. Such a precipitous move could make too many people nervous. Rather, the point here is that at least part of the case for maintaining U.S. security hegemony over Japan, namely to preserve good ties between the two countries, is weak and the potential drawbacks of this status quo policy are not fully appreciated.

A Region at Peace?

Instability in East Asia is seen as arising along several axes. Leaving aside for a moment the threat from North Korea, Northeast Asia is seen as home to potential rivalries between Japan and China, Taiwan and China, Japan and a united Korea, and Russia and Japan. In Southeast Asia, lingering worries about Japanese militarism are now less salient than fresh fears of rising Chinese power. All of these fault lines generate occasional tremors; a U.S. withdrawal from East Asia, many worry, might result in multiple earthquakes.

The prospect of renewed rivalry between the powerful nations of Northeast Asia has a strong historical basis. In the early twentieth century Japan dominated the Korean peninsula and parts of China. Profound suspicions toward Japan linger among many Koreans and Chinese and might well be amplified by a withdrawal of the U.S. security presence. At the same time, Seoul and Tokyo cannot ignore China's fast-growing economic and military power. The dynamics of the relations among these three countries could become a textbook case of the security dilemma. Attempts by each state to enhance its security could make the other states feel less secure, triggering further arms buildups. Ancient animosities and fierce economic competition could be aggravating factors.

Ultimately the threat posed by structural instability in Northeast Asia is less serious than many U.S. analysts think. Whether U.S. forces remain in the region or not, there will exist numerous incentives for cooperation. It is true that China, for example, has a natural great-power competition with Japan, a rivalry with Korea dating back to the second century B.C., and an enduring rift with Taiwan. But it is also true that during the 1980s and early 1990s, under Deng Xiao-ping's rule, China moved decisively to integrate itself into the global economy. Economic modernization and growth became a top prior-ity, dominating China's foreign policy agenda. China dropped much of its anti-Western rhetoric and joined such institutions as the IMF and World Bank. It sought to improve relations with Taiwan and the nations of Southeast Asia. It made a concerted effort to show that it was ready to play by the rules, as established by the G-7. This trend is not likely to be reversed. "China has gone too far in its interdepen-dence on foreign trade, credits, training, and technology transfer, all essential to modernization, for another Cultural Revolution retreat into xenophobic isolation," argues China scholar Allen S. Whiting.[104]

It is widely suggested that China views itself as the natural hege-monic power in East Asia.[105] Nicholas Kristof has written that the Chinese powerhouse of the future may feel a need to make up for lost time. "China shares with turn-of-the-century Germany the sense of wounded pride, the annoyance of a giant that has been battered and cheated by the rest of the world." Kristof points to new Chinese mili-tary acquisitions and stepped-up territorial claims as evidence that China may use its growing power to pursue a hegemonic agenda that is partly fueled by historical resentments.[106]

But caution must be exercised in predicting either that China will actually make a bid for hegemony or that such an effort would take a destabilizing form. China shows many signs of still being a traditional territorial state, but it also has been heavily influenced by the success of the trading states in its region, particularly Japan. These states have not only shown the wisdom of following a geo-economic path to success, but they have also created an atmosphere in East Asia in which the primacy of geopolitics is declining.[107]

As China's power grows, so too will interactions with the trading world that surrounds China. Good ties with its dynamic neighbors are integral to China's long-term agenda of economic progress.[108] Japan is already a major trading partner of China, accounting for more than a quarter of its trade, and the two countries have a sound basis for positive interdependence. In 1991 Japanese investment in China increased by 66 percent, even as its investment elsewhere in Asia decreased.[109] The "Spring of Sino-Japanese relations has come," said Chinese Foreign Minister Qian Qichen in April of that year. Another top PRC official commented a month later that "China and Japan share geographical proximity, cultural affinity, and economic complementarity."[110] China needs Japanese technology and investment, while Japan needs access to China's vast market and cheap labor. China also has a tremendous stake in good ties with South Korea, a nation it warred against in the early 1950s. For years China's trade with South Korea has been far larger than its trade with North Korea. That trade is now increasing faster than ever. In 1992 China and South Korea finally moved to normalize relations.

China's recent military acquisitions do not necessarily presage a future belligerence, as some analysts have suggested.[111] These acquisitions can be seen as part of a normal process of modernization, since at the beginning of the 1990s most of China's military hardware was obsolete. The bulk of its air force, for example, is composed of upgraded Mig 19s built in the 1950s and 1960s, while most of its tanks are aged T-54s.[112] Kristof acknowledges that there is a strong element of national pride in China's desire to acquire an aircraft carrier; India already has two.[113]

China shows signs of recognizing, as Japan long has, that an overassertive regional posture could trigger countermoves by its neighbors and result in little overall gain. In a January 1992 speech at the United Nations, Chinese Premier Li Peng sought to allay rising fears, saying that China "will never become a threat to any country or any region of the world" and that it does not "seek hegemony now and will not seek hegemony in the future when it grows stronger." In a March 1992 speech, foreign minister Qichen said: "China opposes hegemonism and it will never seek to be a superpower, so there is no such thing as 'filling up the vacuum.'"[114] Some regional and Western analysts accept these claims.[115] "I think the historical record is really not one of great Chinese expansionism," Nicholas Hardy has suggested. "I think most people who have looked at this issue have argued that China's defense posture is more defensive in character than offensive." Hardy also observed that the significance of China's actions in regard to the Spratley Islands and other offshore areas was being exaggerated, since China had shown flexibility about discussing the future of these territories.[116]

The rivalry between South Korea (or a unified Korea) and Japan could well become intense in the absence of American primacy in the region. Since both states are democracies, however, high levels of military tension or war would be extremely unlikely. Also, as will be discussed later in this chapter, new mechanisms for regional security cooperation are evolving in East Asia that can help defuse tensions between states. Even without a military presence in Korea and Japan, the United States would still have close ties with both states and could help arbitrate differences between them. Finally, evidence of a Chinese bid for hegemony would likely have the effect of bringing Korea and Japan closer together to balance their authoritarian neighbor. Indeed, in this respect, the situation in Northeast Asia may be conducive to a natural balance of power.

North Korea's Declining Threat

The high tensions surrounding North Korea's nuclear program in the early 1990s have reminded the world of that country's enduring threat to East Asian security. But the crisis should not obscure the fact that North Korea's power has waned markedly in recent years and that this trend is likely to continue, with the possibility of communism's total collapse.

North Korea has large advantages over South Korea in key elements of military hardware, such as tanks and artillery, but there is reason to believe that this arsenal may not be as fearsome as it seems. "North Korea's large inventory of weapons is becoming obsolete," CIA director Robert Gates said in March 1992. "The North Korean defense industry is based on 1960s technology and beset by quality problems. Pyongyang lacks the hard currency to purchase more advanced technology. We have seen no deliveries of major weapons from the Soviet Union or its successors since 1989. China cannot provide the types of weapons, such as modern aircraft or surface-to-air missiles systems, that the Soviets supplied." As with Iraq, which was considered a stronger military power than North Korea before the Gulf War, the quantity of North Korea's forces says nothing about their quality. "North Korea's armed forces suffer from many deficiencies," Gates said. "Their training and, consequently, combat readiness is questionable. They have weaknesses in air defenses and logistics." Long-term trends are not favorable to North Korea, Gates argued. "We expect that many of the North's military advantages over the South will erode throughout this decade largely because of decreasing support from the North's traditional allies, coupled with continuing economic problems."[117]

Even without such erosion, South Korea cannot be considered a sitting duck. It now has twice the population of North Korea and a GNP five times greater. With defense spending at just 4 percent of its GNP,[118] South Korea easily could achieve military parity with, or superiority over, North Korea if it so chose. Moreover, whether or not U.S. troops are stationed in South Korea, North Korea would face the certain prospect—as it did not in 1950 and as Iraq did not in 1990—that its aggression would produce a war with the United States. At the same time, most analysts, including those at the CIA, believe it would not be able to count on support from China.[119] "Furthermore," observed Gates, "as Desert Storm demonstrated, U.S. air power is highly effective against massed ground forces. The prospect that South Korea would receive extensive combat air support as well as other support from United States forces is a potent deterrent, even to forces as strong as those North Korea has concentrated along the border."[120]

Prior to the crisis over North Korea's nuclear program, it appeared that the political situation on the Korean peninsula was improving in the wake of the Cold War's end. In December 1991, for example, Seoul and Pyongyang signed a nonaggression pact. In addition to committing both sides to abstaining from acts of aggression or subversion against each other, the agreement opened the way for greater exchanges between the two Koreas. Some South Korean observers such as Kim Dae Jung predict that North and South Korea will move steadily toward unification during the 1990s.[121] The United States should do everything it can to encourage trends in this direction. In addition, assuming resolution of the nuclear issue, it appears that U.S. forces in South Korea could safely be reduced to a token force over the next few years, a suggestion that has been made by former defense secretary Harold Brown, among others.[122]

Cooperation and Collective Security in East Asia

The absence of a tradition of multilateral diplomacy and collective security in East Asia at all comparable to that which exists in Europe is often cited as clenching evidence that American primacy is indispensable to order in the region. However, multilateralism is neither entirely absent nor systemically impossible in East Asia. Some multilateral institutions already exist and are being strengthened, while new ones are being founded. The pace of economic interdependence in the area is quickening, with the consequence that cooperation on a range of issues is becoming both more important and feasible.

It is in the economic realm that multilateralism is growing the fastest. For years, the only major multilateral body in the region was the Association of South East Asian Nations (ASEAN). This organization became increasingly important in Southeast Asia during the 1980s, but it excluded the economically dynamic powers of Northeast Asia—and the United States and Canada, both of which consider themselves Pacific powers. Finally, in November 1989, the Asia-Pacific Economic Cooperation (APEC) was founded.[123] APEC now has over fifteen members, including all six ASEAN nations, plus the United States, China, Canada, Japan, Mexico, and South Korea. The potential clout of APEC remains far from clear, but some see it as presaging a major trend toward integration in the region. Secretary Christopher has called APEC "the cornerstone of regional economic cooperation," saying "it can be a focal point for building a New Pacific Community and will provide the framework for expanded trade and investment flows through the Asia-Pacific region."[124] Similar optimistic predictions were made during the November 1993 APEC conference hosted by President Clinton in Seattle. Donald Crone has written that APEC is evidence that the new cohesion of the Asia-Pacific nations "may soon justify the term 'bloc,' in parallel to the European bloc."[125] APEC can also be seen as evidence of an unprecedented and growing regional consciousness in East Asia, a development that one Japanese observer has called the "Asianization of Asia."[126]

Although formal economic cooperation does not make security

problems disappear, it can help ease the frictions and anxieties that often accompany interdependence, especially during times of extremely fast growth. This can improve the overall political climate in a region, injecting new trust and predictability into relations among states. Habits of cooperation developed in the economic realm can be applied to the politico-military arena.

The evolution of East Asian multilateralism is unlikely to follow the European model, given power asymmetries in the region and the ambiguous nature of potential security threats.[127] In the best-case scenario, the security forum established at the ASEAN Post-Ministerial Conference in 1993 may approach the potential of the CSCE, which is the weakest of Europe's security organizations. Obviously it will be a long time before anything amounting to full collective security emerges to supplement U.N. guarantees, with countries in the region committing themselves to each other's defense. Japan's pacifism is a particularly significant obstacle to such a development.[128] But as Secretary Christopher has said, the new Asian security forum should at least have the capacity to "help reduce tensions, enhance openness and transparency, and prevent destabilizing arms races."[129]

This new region-wide security undertaking can be supplemented by more focused measures. Robert Scalapino imagines various such measures evolving gradually in the form of "concentric arcs"—that is, flexible and custom-designed subregional security arrangements aimed at dealing with specific problems or disputes.[130] One such arrangement might deal with the Korean peninsula or Northeast Asia generally; another could focus on Southeast Asia. Over time, the entire Asia-Pacific region could become home to an elaborate web of limited security systems. Various confidence- and security-building measures already exist in the region. These measures, usually bilateral in nature, are aimed at providing information about a state's intentions and capabilities, with the goal of building trust and lowering the likelihood of inadvertent conflict.[131]

The most immediate challenge for multilateralism in East Asia is to constrain new arms races in the region. In 1991 the Asia-Pacific nations accounted for 35 percent of all imports of major weapons, more than any other region of the world.[132] States such as Thailand, Singapore, Taiwan, Malaysia, and Indonesia are the main buyers of these weapons. All plan substantial increases in military spending during the 1990s.[133]

Controlling an escalating arms race in Asia will not be easy, but there are grounds for optimism. Over 80 percent of major weapons are sold by the five major powers that sit as permanent members of the U.N. Security Council.[134] In theory it should be possible to work out restraints on the transfer of conventional arms given the small number of suppliers. But efforts along these lines will not succeed without U.S. backing, which is particularly true in regard to East Asia, where the United States is the biggest supplier of weapons.

The United States must confront a major contradiction in its East Asian policy: on the one hand, officials worry about militarization and instability in the region, citing such concerns to justify continued U.S. primacy. On the other hand, it floods the region with weapons and fails to take a leadership role in promoting arms restraints. The next chapter argues that an attempt to reduce the conventional arms trade should be a key part of an idealist foreign policy agenda.

The Future of U.S. Forces in East Asia

In discussions about the future of U.S. commitments in East Asia, one basic idea always returns to the center of debate: there is no compelling reason to alter the status quo. The cost of keeping nearly 100,000 troops salaried and deployed in Japan and South Korea is a small portion of the overall defense budget, and those nations do not desire a withdrawal of U.S. forces. If there is even a hint that withdrawing troops might be destabilizing, why take the risk?

This line of argument has some appeal, but it is ultimately unsatisfactory. Major foreign commitments should not be maintained out of inertia. To be acceptable to the American public and those elements in host countries that may chafe at the presence of U.S. forces, the case for an indefinite deployment in East Asia must be able to stand on its merits.

The case is stronger in East Asia than it is in Europe, where democracy is more widespread and multilateral institutions are stronger. But it is equally evident that central elements of the case are unconvincing, hinging on a misapplication of realist assumptions about Japan and an underappreciation of trends that are fostering cooperation in East Asia.

It is possible that a quick withdrawal of U.S. troops from East Asia could produce instability there. However, a gradual withdrawal that proceeded alongside efforts to promote cooperation on security and economic issues would be far less of a shock. Arguably this process would produce lower levels of anxiety than that which followed America's ignominious pullout from Southeast Asia in the 1970s. Making withdrawal an explicit goal of U.S. foreign policy, and setting a timetable to achieve this goal, would force the Asian countries to work harder to build multilateral institutions and bilateral understandings that can keep the peace when American primacy finally ends. As with Europe, the maintenance of some elements of the U.S. military infrastructure in East Asia would allow for a rebuilding of force levels if the need arises.

THE DECLINING DANGER FROM THE THIRD WORLD

In contending that the world remains a dangerous place after the Cold War, U.S. policymakers have issued particularly ominous warnings about new threats in the Third World. Four main planning assumptions underlie calls for retaining powerful interventionary forces: that the United States will again face regional challengers as formidable as Saddam Hussein; that the timing and location of new aggression is impossible to predict; that the United States must be able to fight two major regional wars at once; and that U.S. forces must be able to handle future threats by itself if necesssary.

All of these arguments have weaknesses. In retrospect, Iraq appears to be an exceptional rather than typical threat and no similar regional powers now exist. Moreover, far from being unpredictable, large-scale U.S. intervention is only likely to occur in a few spots in the world, and the likelihood of having to undertake two major regional contingencies at once is extremely remote. Finally, the United States is likely to receive substantial assistance in the course of thwarting future clear-cut acts of aggression.

Iraq: An Exceptional Threat

The *Bottom-Up Review* completed under Secretary of Defense Aspin in September 1993 warned in general terms of regional threats the United States may face in the future. While focusing specifically on the threats posed by a revived Iraq or North Korea, it implied that there were a variety of other powerful Third World nations that could threaten regions important to the United States.[135] Such claims to the contrary, it is unclear that the United States will again face an adversary like Iraq in the foreseeable future. No Third World nation possesses forces as great as those Iraq deployed on the eve of the Gulf War, and the Third World nations that do come close to matching both Iraq's power and its anti–Western hostility are balanced by strong neighbors. South Korea is closing the military gap with North Korea; Syria is militarily inferior to its southern neighbor, Israel, and faces Turkey and Iraq on its other borders; Iran remains counterbalanced by Iraq and is technologically inferior to Saudi Arabia and the Gulf states in key areas, particularly air power; and Libya is substantially weaker than Egypt.

With the exception of North Korea, Pentagon leaders have not been able to identify a regional power that comes close to representing the threat that Iraq did in 1990. Paul Wolfowitz, in warning of well-armed Third World adversaries in 1991, acknowledged that "the forces of perhaps the most serious regional threat, Iraq, have been reduced by half and otherwise substantially eliminated as a near-term external threat."[136] Wolfowitz also made the point that after Iraq's devastation, regional powers will think twice before they overrun their neighbors.[137]

Iraq was unique in many ways. Surveying the world, there exists no Third World nation that matches Iraq's 1990 military capabilities, its proximity to vital U.S. interests, its opportunity for successful aggression, and its leader's self-destructive pugnacity. In April 1991, Colin Powell professed himself to be at a loss for comparable threats. "I would be very surprised if another Iraq occurred," Powell said.[138]

In theory, the potential for new threats from the Third World is wide and varied. Nations like Brazil, Argentina, Taiwan, and other newly industrialized states have the population and wealth to deploy large and well-equipped armies. Such states also have the technological know-how to build weapons like ballistic missiles and chemical and nuclear arms. But in practice, many of the countries with the greatest potential to become heavily armed show little evidence of moving in that direction.

Brazil is a typical example. A nation of 153 million people and substantial wealth, Brazil is often cited as a potential regional superpower. It has the technological capability for developing highly sophisticated weapons, including ballistic missiles and nuclear arms. Yet Brazil's overall military power is negligible. Its defense budget in 1991 was an eighth of what Iraq's was in 1990. It has less than 300,000 people under arms and unimpressive ground and air forces.[139] Building armed forces of Iraq's size would require Brazil to drain huge resources from other sectors of society over a period of many years. Such a move would be unpopular both domestically and internationally. It might also not be feasible, given Brazil's financial difficulties and its need to maintain good ties with international lending institutions. In short, despite the fact that Brazil's GDP is nearly seven times that of 1989 Iraq, it would be no easy task for Brazil to field the kind of armed forces that Iraq possessed before Desert Storm. Other potential regional powers face the same situation. In most states, internal and external constraints would prevent a single-minded focus on building military power to the level that Iraq attained in 1990. For pariah states like Iran, massive military buildups are also made difficult by international efforts to prevent new arms purchases.

In any case, it is far from clear that even the most heavily armed Third World states present the dangers that Pentagon officials suggest. Despite a level of strength unlikely to be matched by other Third World powers in the near future, Iraq was defeated in one of the most lopsided battles in military history. Iraq, it was commonly said, had one of the finest integrated air defenses in the Third World. It also had a highly advanced air force, which boasted some of the best French- and Soviet-made fighters available.[140] On the ground, it deployed top-of-the-line T-72 tanks and sophisticated, long-range artillery that was said to be even better than U.S. artillery. When war came, however, this equipment proved nearly worthless. Iraq's air defenses were rapidly rendered inoperable and destroyed. Its much vaunted air force barely came up to intercept coalition attackers, and when it did it was no contest against American planes. On the ground, Iraqi artillery was rendered virtually inoperable because of U.S. systems that can pinpoint the origin of an enemy artillery attack within moments and direct a counterbarrage. Much of Iraq's armor was destroyed by the cheapest combat aircraft in the U.S. Air Force, the A-10 Thunderbolt.[141]

In easily defeating one of the Third World's most advanced military powers, the United States was aided by the use of cruise missiles and the F-117 stealth fighter, but these big ticket weapons were not decisive (although arguably they saved American lives). Far more central to U.S. operations was less glamorous military technology like laser-bomb kits, electronic warfare equipment, night vision devices, and navigation and target pods. Many of these technologies were mounted on planes as old as twenty years, making them extremely effective. Aged FB-111 bombers built in the late 1960s, for example, were made capable of destroying dug-in Iraqi tanks at night through the use of infrared systems and laser-guided bombs.[142]

Following the Gulf War, U.S. officials focused with concern on the North Korean threat. Although North Korea deploys military forces that are as large as Iraq's were in 1990, the quantity of these forces says nothing about their quality. If war came to the Korean peninsula, North Korean commanders might find themselves, like their Iraqi counterparts in January 1991, largely blinded within the first few hours or days of hostilities as U.S. air strikes wipe out key command and control nodes. North Korean forces in the field could find, as the Iraqis did, that turning on mobile air defenses means having them destroyed by radar-seeking HARM missiles. North Korean artillery crews might similarly find that employing their weapons tempts an instant counterstrike. North Korean combat pilots might quickly learn, as the Iraqi pilots did, that taking off in their aircraft is nearly suicidal in the face of U.S. systems that can track them from the moment they left the runway and attack them with air-to-air missiles from outside of visual range. Without air defenses or close air support, North Korean forces might soon conclude, as did tens of thousands of Iraqi soldiers, that flight or surrender is their best option.

None of this means that a new Korean war would be effortlessly won; on the contrary, most analysts agree that it would be far bloodier than the Gulf conflict. But it is clear that North Korea, now the leading "threat state" following Desert Storm, suffers from many of the same weaknesses that assured Iraq's defeat.

Given low rates of literacy and technological competence in the Third World, advanced military equipment can often not be used to its maximum potential.[143] And given the crucial importance of troop morale in even high-tech wars, the conscripted armies of Third World dictatorships will tend to face a basic disadvantage. vis-à-vis highly motivated Western forces.[144] In both the Falklands War and the Gulf War, for example, Western forces were aided by an early collapse of enemy morale.[145] Far from substantiating the Pentagon's case that Third World threats can in some cases be of First World caliber, Desert Storm undermined that case by showing the ease with which even the strongest Third World challenger can be destroyed by a Western military power. (The Israeli–Syrian skirmish of 1982 illustrated the same point. Indeed, it is easy to imagine that if Israel and Iraq were squared off in 1990 with Jordan as the battleground, Israel alone could have won a war against Iraq.)

Predictable Battlefields

The language of Pentagon planning documents suggests that the United States must be ready to intervene in nearly every corner of the globe. The unpredictability of the new security environment is stressed; challenges can come anywhere, with little notice, and require U.S. forces to fight in a variety of terrains. "History shows that we frequently fail to anticipate the location and timing of aggression, even large-scale attacks against our interests," stated the *Bottom-Up Review*.[146]

In actuality the situation is less complicated. In addition to Korea, most analysts agree that there are only a few regions where the United States should ever intervene with ground troops in the Third World: Central America and the Caribbean, and the Persian Gulf. No analysts seriously suggest that the United States should be prepared to intervene on a large scale anywhere in Africa, South Asia, or Southeast Asia. There is also no speculation of ever intervening on the South American continent.

Central America and the Caribbean will continue to be seen as a U.S. sphere of interest. In planning documents leaked to the press in 1992, the Pentagon imagined a replay of the 1989 invasion of Panama, should the canal in that country ever be threatened. But threats of Iraq's scope in this region will never materialize, given the limits of wealth, population, and industrial potential. The invasion of Panama required less than twenty thousand troops, and future

U.S. operations in the area would probably be of a similar scope.

It is the Persian Gulf that looms largest in Pentagon plans for future intervention in the Third World. The Gulf region is probably the only part of the Third World where the United States would deploy large numbers of ground troops in a future crisis. The high stakes involved suggest little room for complacency: no less than 67 percent of the world's proven oil reserves are located in the Gulf, which remains one of the most unstable regions on earth.[147] In the decades ahead, the importance of Gulf oil supplies to developed nations is expected to grow greater as reserves in other regions are depleted.

Pentagon planners still consider Iraq to be the main long-term threat in the Persian Gulf, with worries also expressed about Iran's growing power. Iraq, it is imagined, will eventually be able to rebuild its military power when it again is allowed access to oil revenues. A resurgent Iraq is seen as having a strong motivation to intimidate its neighbors in order to raise oil prices and thus improve its financial position. Many worry that the Iraq of the future will again be an aspiring regional hegemon, especially if the United States allows its position of primacy in the Gulf to wane.[148] A key planning assumption of the *Bottom-Up Review* is that the United States will again be called upon to repulse an Iraqi invasion of Kuwait and Saudi Arabia sometime in the future.

But the threat of a resurgent Iraq is exaggerated. The Gulf War shattered Iraq's ground forces and air defenses. For the foreseeable future Iraq will not be in a position to rebuild fully its military forces to their 1990 levels. The oil embargo against Iraq may well slacken or be lifted, allowing Iraq to rebuild its economy, but there is no reason why the arms embargo would be lifted as well, especially if Saddam Hussein remains in power. Assuming an even modest level of international cooperation against Iraq, it hard to imagine Iraq reequipping its tank divisions and rebuilding its air force over the next decade, as Pentagon documents envision. Following the Gulf War, Iraq's fleet of main battle tanks was reduced to 2,300 from 5,500. To build back up to just 3,500 tanks, Iraq would have to conduct a large-scale arms purchasing effort on the international market, which could be easily detected.

It is difficult to imagine Iraq repeating its attack on Kuwait. In

1990 Baghdad did not think that the United States would come to Kuwait's rescue; now it knows otherwise. It did not think the international community could sustain an embargo; now it knows otherwise. It did not think the United States would actually go to war against Iraq; now it knows otherwise. It clearly didn't realize the vulnerability of its armor in desert terrain to modern air power; now it knows otherwise. Even without an explicit U.S. security commitment in the region, Saddam or a future Iraqi leader would have to believe that any aggressive move on Iraq's part would provoke a U.S. response, and that even if that response was limited to the use of air power, it could be devastating. This knowledge would likely constitute an enormous deterrent.

Another exaggerated threat to Gulf oil supplies is Iran. Given its population and position, Iran is often cited as a natural hegemon in the region. Yet Iran's potential to threaten seriously pro-Western Gulf states is limited. Geographically it is not positioned to mount an overland invasion of Kuwait or Saudi Arabia, and in any case its ground forces are weak, containing only seven hundred main battle tanks.[149] It can threaten the Gulf states with air attack and attempt to interfere with Gulf shipping. But these threats are not of the scope that would require a massive U.S. intervention. The air forces of the Gulf states are superior to Iran's, and the United States demonstrated in 1987–1988 that a modest naval deployment is adequate for handling Iranian attacks on Gulf shipping.

In the early 1990s there was much discussion of Iran's rising military power, but its potential to approach Iraq's 1990 level of power is likely to remain limited through the foreseeable future. Iran's defense budget in 1991 was $3.8 billion.[150] To reach Iraq's 1990 level of defense spending of $8.6 billion, Iran would have to channel significant new resources into defense at the same time it is experiencing economic difficulties.[151] To overcome its weakness in ground forces or its technological inferiority in air power, Iran would have to acquire large quantities of arms on the global market, a goal that may prove difficult to achieve in the face of multilateral restrictions.

The Two-War Illusion

Post–Cold War plans for fighting two regional conflicts at once translate into the need for substantially larger active forces than would be required if the Pentagon planned to fight two wars in quick succession. According to one estimate, as much as $35 billion a year could be saved if the U.S. pursued the "win–hold–win" approach that Aspin originally favored instead of a "win–win" strategy as recommended in the *Bottom-Up Review*.[152] A policy that did not envision two wars occurring at once in the world could save even more money. In releasing the *Bottom-Up Review*, Powell said that if the United States planned to fight only one war at a time, while having enough troops left over for peacekeeping or humanitarian operations similar to the Somalia intervention, it would need eight carriers instead of the planned twelve and eight Army divisions instead of the planned ten.[153]

The two–war assumption, which imagines a conflict in Korea and another in the Persian Gulf, is overly pessimistic. According to a 1992 study by the RAND Corporation, and other analyses, a "win–hold–win" strategy would be a prudent approach to sizing defense forces in the new era. The RAND study simulated a future Iraqi invasion of the Saudi peninsula involving a force that is larger than the one it deployed in 1990 and that thrusts farther south. The study showed that U.S. air power alone would be able to stop the enemy offensive in two weeks and largely destroy the bulk of Iraq's armor in another ten days or less.[154]

This conclusion is consistent with the performance of air power during the Gulf War. Ultimately it was the awesomely destructive application of U.S. air power that won the war against Iraq, not the hundreds of thousands of U.S. ground troops and their armored equipment. As one report stated, noting what was obvious to even a casual viewer of CNN: "The final ground offensive was of secondary importance in accomplishing the key objective of compelling the Iraqis to quit Kuwait. . . . Air power reduced the Iraqi army to an inert mass acutely vulnerable to allied ground fire and maneuver and, for the most part, capable only of flight or surrender. Air power shattered the Iraqi Field Army's morale by severing its command, control, and communication links, interdicting its supplies, and pummeling its positions unopposed for six weeks."[155] The report also argued that the United States could have inflicted this crippling level of damage with much less air power than it deployed in the Gulf.

The ground offensive was deemed politically desirable by the Bush Administration, both to end the war more quickly and to decisively humiliate Saddam. It seems likely, however, that Iraqi forces could have been finished off by the air campaign alone—especially in light of the U.S. success in locating and destroying dug-in armor and artillery from the air. The nearly complete destruction of Iraq's forces in the field was only a matter of time.

The results of the Gulf War suggest that air power can effectively contain a threat to U.S. interests in one part of the world while a fully rounded U.S. force handles a threat elsewhere. Instead of building enough ground forces to sustain two major regional deployments at once, the United States can plan to defeat one enemy and then shift forces to defeat what remains of the other enemy following attacks by U.S. air power.

A strategy that assumes that only one conflict will occur at a time may also be prudent. American officials argue that inadequate U.S. forces may make simultaneous wars more likely by tempting regional powers to move against their neighbors at a time that the United States is bogged down in a war in another part of the world. Yet this seems highly unlikely because it exaggerates the degree to which the strength of American interventionary forces determines the calculations of Third World states. If it is true that the costs of interstate aggression have grown in the post–Cold War era and that states have many incentives to avoid challenging the established order, bold territorial conquests are likely to become more rare regardless of what policy the United States follows. While U.S. planners are most worried about simultaneous aggression by Iraq and North Korea, it seems that those two states—both of which suffered earlier defeats at U.S. hands and lasting punishment by the international community—would be particularly aware of the disincentives of aggression.

Going It Together

A final flawed Pentagon planning assumption is that the United States must be able to thwart future regional aggressors almost entirely by itself. This thinking ignores the growing strength of U.S. allies and experience of the Gulf War, in which numerous countries contributed to the anti-Iraq coalition.

In the Persian Gulf, the military power and competence of Saudi Arabia and the other Gulf states has grown significantly in recent years. Equipped with some of the most advanced defense technology in the world, Saudi Arabia has an advantage in air power over both Iraq and Iran. Its ground forces have also grown more robust since the Gulf War and include many new weapons from the United States, including 150 of the highly capable M-1 tanks. Given its far smaller population, Saudi Arabia will never be able to balance Iraq militarily by itself, but its increasing arsenal of high-tech weapons can both make Iraqi leaders think twice about new aggression and contribute significantly to any U.S. effort to thwart such aggression.

The United States could probably also count on other allied help in another Gulf War. Roughly sixty thousand British and French troops were involved in the fighting against Iraq. There is no reason not to expect similar force commitments in a future conflict.

As already discussed, South Korea is approaching military parity with North Korea. This trend is likely to continue through the decade as North Korea's military forces grow increasingly obsolete. Moreover, with its far greater wealth, South Korea could move faster to close the remaining gap if it so chose. Given this strength, the United States would not have to bear the majority of the burden of defeating a new North Korean invasion.

Beyond the growing strength of U.S. allies, the assumption of near-unilateral action ignores two other important points. First, if other states are not willing to join the United States in a regional conflict, then this should be a warning flag as to the wisdom of U.S. actions. Without international support, the United States could find itself isolated or even in violation of law in mounting an intervention. Second, public support within the United States might be difficult to sustain if U.S. forces were operating alone in a regional conflict. Overall, the assumption that America must be prepared to act nearly alone runs counter to trends of increasing multilateral cooperation on security affairs, especially through the U.N., and counter to growing domestic constraints on intervention abroad.

In arguing that the United States must stay number one, American foreign policy elites have put forth a number of arguments that erode under scrutiny. Not only has the nature of world politics changed for the better, but American military power has become less important for guaranteeing security in key regions of the world, particularly

Europe and East Asia. Military power remains vital for protecting U.S. interests in the Third World, but official assessments of the threats to those interests and the level of force needed to handle them are overly pessimistic.

Members of the American foreign policy establishment tend to think of U.S. primacy as indispensable. That is not surprising, since the United States was the salvation of the Western world during the three great emergencies of the twentieth century. Today, however, this view is hampering fresh thinking about foreign policy in a changed world. In the early 1990s, instead of initiating a fundamental debate about how the United States can best promote stability in the world, U.S. foreign policy elites reflexively sought to modify Cold War policies for the new era. They have claimed that both the record of history and contemporary international realities dictate the need for continued overwhelming primacy in the security arena. This claim, as suggested here, is flawed on a number of counts.

Reconstructing American foreign policy in the post–Cold War era begins with a recognition that the United States can safely move away from the realist assumptions that underpin calls for primacy, but it does not end there. America should not withdraw from a world that it views as no longer dangerous because many perils do still exist and active U.S. global leadership is needed to deal with them. The challenge is to reorient policy so that scarce U.S. national security resources are used to address real threats rather than phantom ones.

8

AN IDEALIST FOREIGN POLICY

For over two centuries idealist goals have been relegated to the sidelines of American foreign policy. The United States has not let its values at home drive its actions abroad, both because of a lack of consensus over this goal through much of U.S. history and, more recently, because the exigencies of the Cold War seemed to dictate the need for policies of geopolitical expediency. To the degree that the United States has sought to promote its values abroad, it has done so in the context of crusades against evil—the two world wars and the Cold War. Never have idealist goals by themselves been the centerpiece of foreign policy.

Idealists recognize the chance that now exists for a new beginning in foreign policy. With America fully engaged in the world, as it was not before World War II, yet facing no mortal foe, as it did in the Cold War, there is now an unprecedented opening for efforts to shape the international environment with a foreign policy that reflects American values. Idealists argue, in fact, that only such a foreign policy can sustain long-term public support for an activist U.S. world role.[1]

Advocates of an idealist foreign policy enter the new era from a position of disadvantage. Those who espouse the primacy of power politics have been so dominant for so long in the foreign policy world that cogent opposing viewpoints have withered. Once there was a tradition of idealism in U.S. foreign policy, but that tradition was discredited by the middle of this century and again rejected when it attempted a modest comeback during the presidency of Jimmy Carter. Today, the tradition remains on the margins of the political system and realists have easily prevailed in debates over the direction of post–Cold War foreign policy. The Democrats, finally back in control of the executive branch after twelve years, have labored hard to shake their idealistic image in national security affairs. They may prove unwilling to risk a revival of that image, despite Clinton's declaration during his campaign that "the cynical calculus of pure power simply does not compute."[2] The Clinton Administration seeks modest changes in foreign and military policy, placing a greater emphasis on the classic idealist goals of promoting democracy and strengthening collective security. These changes are not likely to result in an overhaul of how national security resources are allocated. Many of those who now advise Clinton have voiced support for the key realist assumptions of the Bush Administration's foreign policy, and it is this thinking that remains dominant in Washington.

Idealism as a compass for foreign policy remains discredited in part because it has yet to be reinvented for the new era. Idealists have not adequately risen to the challenge of constructing an alternative foreign policy paradigm, so it is no wonder that policymakers continue to rely on old formulas. Intellectually, challenges to the realist orthodoxy have often been weak or uncomprehensive. On a policy level, there has been no shortage of suggestions for how to reduce U.S. global commitments and defense spending, but these suggestions are often not backed up by persuasive argument. A stronger vision of an idealist foreign policy waits to be articulated.

The challenge of creating an idealist foreign policy paradigm is twofold: the chasm between realist analyses and global realities must be recognized, and it must be shown how an idealist outlook can translate into a policy agenda that at once safeguards U.S. interests and reflects American values.

Up to this point, I have been concerned primarily with the first task, seeking to show how changes in world politics now make it possible for the United States to reduce its emphasis on security matters. I have suggested that the United States now has more freedom of action in foreign policy, given the reduced level of danger in the world, and that it can lower its military forces below levels currently planned.

A strong case can be made that the resources freed up from this process should be spent on pressing domestic needs.[3] This argument cannot be ignored and is, in fact, already shaping policy, but it risks the danger of becoming the basis for a new isolationism. The United States cannot simply place foreign policy on the back burner and turn to domestic matters, as some have suggested. Over the next few years in particular, with historic transitions underway, the United States must stay engaged to shape a more stable and prosperous world or face deleterious consequences later. Cold War–style American leadership on security issues may be no longer indispensable to world order, but American leadership more broadly conceived is as vital as ever.

This leadership must be backed up with resources. A national security budget that is now shaped by dated realist assumptions should not be hastily slashed. Instead, for the time being, it should be largely preserved but reconfigured to implement an idealist agenda that better addresses global problems. Policymakers must understand that some of the money now spent on defense can "buy" more security in the long run if it is spent on other things.

The two traditional idealist goals of promoting democracy and strengthening collective security should lie at the center of a new U.S. foreign policy. In addition, the United States should give greatly increased attention to fostering sustainable development in the Third World and a more equitable distribution of global wealth. All three of these goals are controversial, but a foreign policy consensus over each is within reach. Two of the goals, democracy and development, require large infusions of new financial resources, and these funds can only be found in the defense budget.

In focusing on these three goals, it is not my intention to downplay the importance of economics. Although the possibility of politico-military tensions arising between the industrial democracies is negligible, the emergence of serious economic rifts is entirely possible, if not likely, and the United States must work to sustain an open world-trading order in an era that could become dominated by three regional trading blocs. As C. Fred Bergsten has persuasively argued, maintaining smooth economic relations with Japan and a united

Europe "must replace the Cold War's containment of military risk as a primary purpose of U.S. foreign policy."[4]

Beyond the necessity of limiting the scope of my inquiry, I have chosen not to explore this challenge further because in recent years, especially with Clinton's ascendancy, there has emerged widespread agreement on Bergsten's basic point. In contrast, the foreign policy goals discussed in this chapter remain hotly contested.

CONSOLIDATING AND ENLARGING THE ZONE OF PEACE

There are two separate enterprises that fall under the rubric of promoting democracy: the consolidation of fragile democracies and the creation of democracies where they do not exist. As a candidate for president, Bill Clinton devoted himself to both goals, declaring that "no national security issue is more urgent than securing democracy's triumph around the world," and saying it is "time for America to lead a global alliance for democracy as united and steadfast as the global alliance that defeated communism."[5]

Yet the Clinton Administration, while doing better than its predecessor, has failed to devote the kind of resources to democratization that its urgent rhetoric suggests is warranted. Equally problematic, there still exists no firm consensus about how to make the promotion of democracy a primary goal of foreign policy.

Breaking this impasse hinges on two accomplishments. First, U.S. national security budgetary priorities must be reorganized to free up more funds for helping the former Communist bloc. One part of this task is to reslice the shrinking foreign aid pie so that Russia and other Eastern countries get much bigger pieces. The other part is to shift funds from the defense budget. Currently, the Pentagon spends far more money to prepare for a resurgence of Russian militarism and instability in the East than other agencies spend on trying to consolidate democracy in the former bloc. This approach risks ensuring a self-fulfilling prophecy.

Second, the objections to centering U.S. foreign policy on promoting democracy, voiced on both the left and the right, must be more effectively rebutted. It must be shown why the pursuit of this goal will neither damage U.S. interests by estranging key nondemocratic friends or lead to limitless crusades and overintrusive policies.

Democracy in the East

President Clinton has said that the success of democracy in the former Communist bloc "presents the greatest security challenge for our generation."[6] This is no understatement. If Russia sinks into militarized authoritarianism, the United States would almost certainly assume a more vigilant national security stance than currently envisioned. This would entail spending far more on defense than now planned. If new tensions and conflicts engulf Eastern Europe, the consequences would also be expensive for the United States: a less stable security climate in Europe will make it harder to greatly reduce U.S. troops on the continent. For these reasons, foreign aid to the former Communist bloc must be seen as preventive medicine of the highest priority. But such aid must also be seen in positive terms. American investment in helping the former Soviet Union can pay economic dividends in the future by establishing U.S. trade links with a market that is vast in size.[7]

In 1993 Congress approved $2.5 billion in aid for the former Soviet republics as part of the 1994 foreign operations appropriations.[8] It is widely recognized that this amount is only a drop in the bucket, given that Germany has been spending in the range of $100 billion a year to modernize the economy of its eastern half, with a population of only 17 million. Higher levels of aid for the former Soviet Union will be required from all the Western countries and the United States should not be a laggard in this effort.[9]

Reslicing the Foreign Aid Pie

A first step toward finding new funds for Russia is to shift spending priorities within the foreign aid budget. Not long after the collapse of Communist rule in Eastern Europe, Senator Bob Dole made a modest proposal: Washington should cut aid by 5 percent to the top five recipients—Egypt, Israel, Pakistan, Turkey, and the Philippines—to free up new money to help newly democratic nations. "To me, it boils down to this," said Dole in January 1990. "Are big gains for freedom worth a small cut in a few huge foreign aid programs? I say yes."[10] Dole's colleagues, however, said no. His proposal touched off a firestorm of criticism, and though much aid has now been shifted away from several of the states Dole mentioned, the basic problem he identified remains: the United States must cut existing aid programs if it wants to fund major new initiatives in the East.

The key to reslicing the foreign aid budget so that it can better promote democracy in the former Communist bloc lies in the area of security assistance to Egypt and Israel. More than a third of U.S. foreign aid, or $5.6 billion out of the FY 1994 budget of $13 billion, is spent on security assistance for these two countries, a sum which is more than twice that allocated to the entire former Soviet Union.[11] Maintaining Egypt as a stable and cooperative regional partner is important, but it cannot possibly be as important as the goal of consolidating democracy in the over twenty nations of the former Communist bloc, as the distribution of aid funds would imply. Moreover, while the United States has deep ties to the five million people of Israel, its national interests are more dramatically affected by the fate of the 400 million people who live east of what was once the Iron Curtain.[12]

On Capitol Hill, there has been a growing willingness on the part of key lawmakers to consider shifts of aid away from Egypt and Israel.[13] Other security assistance programs have already been gradually disassembled, with major cutbacks being made in aid to the Philippines, Pakistan, and El Salvador. In 1992, Turkey, Greece, and Portugal were "graduated" to loan programs.[14] The programs for Egypt and Israel, however, have remained untouched. Cuts are unlikely to occur without support from the executive branch. Such leadership is long overdue.

Taking from Defense

If consolidating democracy in the former Communist bloc is a security goal of overriding importance, why should funds for this endeavor have to be carved out of a foreign aid budget that is already small to begin with? The Clinton Administration succeeded in passing higher levels of aid to the former Soviet Union in its first budget, but that victory came at a price. Funding for a range of other important programs was either cut or not increased. The administration's request for the Agency for International Development, for example, was lower than the request of the previous year.[15] And Congress cut spending for multilateral institutions, African development, AIDS prevention, and other programs.[16]

Clearly, significant increases in foreign aid will be needed in the years ahead, and since this money is unlikely to come from either new taxes, cuts in domestic spending, or additional borrowing, the defense budget is the only place to turn for it. That budget is also the most logical place to find new resources, since foreign aid and defense spending are both geared toward the goal of safeguarding America's interests abroad.

The case for some shifting of resources from defense to foreign aid becomes compelling when the security "purchasing power" of programs in the two areas is compared. Take the F-22 as an example. In 1994, the United States will spend roughly $2.2 billion on this advanced warplane, which is still in development. This amount is almost equal to the entire aid package to the former Soviet Union that Congress appropriated for 1994. A central rationale of the F-22, as with many other military programs kept alive after the Cold War, is that the United States may have to face a remilitarized Russia some-day. Leaving aside the point that the F-22 is probably not needed to deal with such a contingency, the logic of U.S. priorities as illustrated here is deeply misguided. Experts on Russia's economic situation, and Russian leaders themselves, persuasively argue that higher levels of Western assistance will translate into enhanced prospects for democracy's consolidation. While there are no guarantees in this area, it is likely that another $2.2 billion in U.S. assistance in 1994 could have made an important, even crucial, difference in contributing toward such goals as stabilizing Russia's monetary system, alleviating immediate social pressures, and beginning the process of industrial restructuring.[17] In contrast to this concrete gain for Russian stability and therefore U.S. security, spending the same money on the F-22 only buys insurance against an eventuality that may or may not come to pass. Worse still, this spending on insurance may have the effect of increasing the chances of a future threat from Russia by diverting funds from measures that can help to consolidate democracy.

Some defense expenditures to prepare for the contigency of a "Weimar Russia" are justified. But these should not continue to far exceed expenditures aimed at consolidating democracy in Russia. In a 1983 essay on the challenge of redefining security, Richard Ullman wrote that expenditures to address nonmilitary security threats are often politically controversial because those threats are less readily apparent.[18] Technically, the prospect of democracy's failure in Russia falls into the category of a nonmilitary security threat, but in practice it would have major security ramifications, as Clinton Administration officials have acknowledged. Among Defense Secretary Aspin's early steps at the Pentagon was to designate explicitly the promotion of democracy as one of the four major goals of U.S. national security policy.

Analyzing the cost effectiveness of expenditures on defense versus foreign aid is also revealing in regard to the issue of troops in Europe. A main argument for this presence is that it promotes stability in Eastern Europe by reassuring democratic leaders there. But it may be that funds spent on keeping 100,000 troops salaried and stationed in Europe into the twenty-first century could buy more stability in the long run if they were used to aid the economies of Eastern Europe. Indeed, given that U.S. forces are unlikely ever to intervene on a major scale in Eastern Europe, for reasons argued earlier, spending money on economic aid rather than maintaing troop deployments would mean replacing a psychological benefit with a material one. And with aid to the states of Eastern Europe virtually frozen in place from 1992 through 1994 because of fiscal constraints, new funding must come from somewhere.

A Dangerous Crusade?

The objective of consolidating democracy in the former Communist bloc raises little controversy in U.S. policy circles, even as the scope and nature of the means to this end are fiercely debated. American missionary efforts in this case carry only a minor risk of cultural or political imperialism, since the people of the Eastern countries themselves have chosen a democratic path. In such circumstances the promotion of democracy boils down to a financial and logistical problem.

Promoting democracy in nondemocratic countries is far more controversial.[19] Consensus on this goal remains elusive in the United States because critics from both the realist and radical traditions have persistently raised objections.

In the 1940s and 1950s early realists such as Morgenthau, Kennan, and Lippmann argued that the promotion of American values abroad was a formula for dangerous excesses. These arguments continue to resonate today. Efforts to promote democracy have no logical end, it is said. If all democrats are equally worthy of support, how can one justify supporting some and not others? In a world with over sixty democratic governments, the chances are high of one or more of those governments finding themselves under internal or external attack at a given time.[20] The United States cannot be committed to defending all democratic governments on principle. Also, in a world where painfully prolonged transitions to democracy are common, and backsliding regularly occurs, the United States may find that the promotion of democracy is an exceptionally frustrating business. An idealistic public could grow weary of a crusading foreign policy that continually produced checkered results. Finally, many doubt that democracy can indeed "triumph" in the world. Some countries with no tradition of liberal government may never be able to achieve it, while deteriorating conditions in selected Third World countries that do have such a tradition might necessitate authoritarian rule. To see democratic government as a global norm is naive, if not condescending, it is said. More important, to insist on democratic governance in all circumstances may be harmful to U.S. interests. Washington would be foolhardy, for example, to so pressure the Arab Gulf states to become democratic that it estranged them, derailing cooperation on security matters. As Bush NSC aide Richard Haass said after the Gulf War, the United States cannot "dictate the social contract for societies and cultures with long and distinct traditions of their own."[21] Certainly it wouldn't want to attempt such a move given the strategic stakes involved in the Persian Gulf.

The final destination of this logic chain is the claim that national interest remains the only sensible foundation for U.S. foreign policy.[22] The United States should remain focused on moves that directly increase its security or prosperity, realists say. When promoting democracy supports this goal, as it did in Western Europe during the Cold War, all the better. When occasional opportunities arise for securing democracy's triumph abroad through modest actions, as in the Philippines in 1986, fine. But democracy's promotion can never be an end in itself, realists insist, and often the United States will find it advantageous to support undemocratic regimes.

Radical observers of American foreign policy come at this issue from a different angle. They believe that the lofty rhetoric of democratization has been all too often misappropriated by a foreign policy elite with quasi-imperialist ambitions. They charge that democracy is a sham in many U.S.-supported Third World countries. Elections are held periodically and U.S. aid dollars keep flowing, but power is never truly contested and mechanisms of repression endure. Radical analysts and many others also ask whether democracy is really a solution in much of the Third World. In countries like the Philippines and Honduras, for example, democratization during the 1980s was widely celebrated, yet its impact on the lives of most citizens in those countries was limited because it did not improve their standard of living. In many Third World countries a tiny fraction of the population controls most of the wealth. If democratization does not lead to a major redistribution of wealth, and usually it does not, then it can be an essentially meaningless development. By this logic, the United States should be more concerned with breaking the power of Third World elites than supporting the perpetuation of that power through nominally democratic governance.

Realists and radicals both raise valid concerns about placing democratization at the forefront of the U.S. foreign policy agenda. There does exist a danger of uncontained missionary ambitions and there is a tendency among U.S. leaders to see democracy as a panacea in the Third World. Also, there are numerous practical problems with promoting democracy, most notably the dilemma of how to influence the internal affairs of a country without infringing on that country's sovereignty.

None of these many objections should be seen as fatal to centering U.S. foreign policy on the promotion of democracy.

Democratization and the National Interest

Whether it is bettering the lot of the poor or cleaning up the environment, government is constantly engaged in endeavors that have no logical cutoff point. Resource constraints, however, usually act to impose limits. In the years ahead U.S. leaders will be acutely aware of the budgetary limitations they face in promoting democracy. They will know that the overall amount of money that can be spent on international affairs will probably keep falling, so they will make new material commitments very cautiously. This alone will put a brake on any tendency that might exist to overexpand U.S. commitments to support democracy anywhere and everywhere. American leaders will be forced to select their targets with care, a point already widely recognized. "I think there is a pretty strong consensus that you want to put your efforts into fertile soil," commented State Department official Jessica Matthews in 1993. "That is, into countries where there already is a commitment to moving in the direction that we would like to see societies moving in. Democracy is not something that you can impose. It is something, however, that you can fertilize where it is growing."[23] One consequence of emphasizing only the most promising investments is that success should be more common than failure, minimizing public disappointment with policies that promote democracy.

It is true that democracy will probably never triumph in the world because the conditions for it do not exist in all countries. The United States could become guilty of cultural and political arrogance if it tried too hard to spread its values. However, even in a region like the Saudi peninsula, the United States cannot use this line of argument to turn its back on democratic aspirations. The United States should not dictate the social contract for states but neither should it give unconditional support to regimes that violate basic human rights. To do so lowers U.S. moral credibility worldwide. How can the United States pretend to stand as a force for global liberalization if it turns a blind eye to abuses by friendly states? If the United States wants to exercise moral leadership, it must be consistent. As Larry Diamond observes, "Symbols matter in a world of intense and rapid communication, ideas diffuse across borders, and double standards can be devastating."[24]

Realists worry that putting democracy first may harm U.S. geopolitical interests, as vital but nondemocratic allies are estranged. This could be a short-term result, but in the long term, U.S. global interests will be aided by a reduced tolerance for authoritarian regimes. If the United States and other Western nations give the cold shoulder to repressive leaders, limiting aid, trade, and arms, such leaders will become more isolated and may feel pressure to institute democratic reforms. The logic here is simple, and hardly fuzzy-headed: America's overriding foreign policy goal is to create a world of democratic states, because such states are inherently less likely to threaten the United States or its allies. Coddling nondemocratic regimes delays the realization of this goal by making it is easier for them to perpetuate themselves.

Realists suggest that an amoral conception of the national interest ensures a foreign policy that best heads off threats to U.S. security. But recent history casts doubt on this assertion. The policy of supporting Saddam Hussein before the Gulf War was a classic realist undertaking aimed at sustaining the balance of power in the Persian Gulf. Saddam was known to be an unusually ruthless tyrant, but Bush Administration officials saw him as a potential friend and counterweight to Iran in a vital region. They ignored the nature of his regime. Instead of isolating Iraq in the late 1980s and through the first half of 1990, the United States aided it.[25]

Under a more idealist foreign policy, such a mistake would never have occurred. Iraq would have been recognized for the pariah state that it was and would have been denied U.S. agricultural credits and high technology. Washington would also have led its Western allies in an effort to curb arms transfers to Iraq and in international forums condemn its treatment of the Kurds. In such an environment, Saddam might not have felt that he could get away with an invasion of Kuwait.[26]

During the Cold War the high stakes of geopolitics made it risky to place values first in the pursuit of foreign policy. A state that Washington didn't maintain as a friend could be cultivated by Moscow, with negative consequences for U.S. security. Today, this zero-sum game is no longer being played. The United States can afford to end its support for nondemocratic regimes without worrying that such regimes will become strategic assets for a mortal enemy. Washington can be consistent in its long-range policy of promoting democracy knowing that the short-term costs will not be catastrophic.

The uneasiness of radical critics with the promotion of democracy is also unfounded. If the United States backs sham democracies and helps to engineer "demonstration elections," as it often did in the Cold War to keep aid flowing to anti-Communist allies, then it is not really promoting democracy. Under a truly idealist foreign policy, such charades would not occur.

The concern about Washington's focus on democracy over equity is more serious, but it too leads nowhere. Given the massive inequity that exists in democratic Third World countries, even those like Brazil that are prosperous, it is valid to observe that democratization is no panacea. The Western development model of economic growth and political democracy has not bettered life for hundreds of millions of the Third World poor. This doesn't mean that democratization is not important. In new democracies old patterns of inequality and repression can often thrive unchallenged. However, in more advanced democracies one can expect to see efforts at redistribution and political empowerment as labor is granted greater rights, grass roots groups become more sophisticated, the central government becomes more able to regulate the private sector, and a welfare state comes into existence. This model of democracy is harder to scoff at, and the sooner a country gets on the path to democratization, the sooner it will have a chance to achieve this model.

The Importance of Human Rights

The United States has never consistently supported democratic activists living under tyranny. A rejection of realist arguments for subordinating American values to geopolitical imperatives is a key first step toward doing so. The next step is to build on the foundation for a strong human rights policy that is already in place. As a nation that sells arms, provides aid, or trades with nearly every country on earth, the United States has a wide range of options for penalizing human rights violators without impinging on their sovereignty. U.S. laws passed in the mid-1970s prohibit military and economic aid to countries engaged in a pattern of "gross violations of internationally recognized human rights."[27] There is also ample precedent for denying repressive countries favored trading status in U.S. markets.

American policymakers will always be tempted to make exceptions to a firm human rights policy. This is shortsighted, even when dealing with strategic allies like the Persian Gulf states. Quite apart from the devastating impact that double standards in foreign policy can have, the United States risks losing its strategic allies if it supports their tyrannical rule unequivocally. In part, this is what happened in Iran. By failing to push the Shah toward more open and responsive government, and by directly aiding his repression, the United States helped Iran to become a revolutionary powder keg. It also assured that when the explosion finally came, the new regime would be anti-American in nature.

Prodding the Gulf states to become more democratic, using penalities if need be, may estrange them from Washington in the short run. This is a tolerable price to pay for a policy that may produce more liberal and stable friends in the long run. The current lack of any pressing threats in the Gulf region gives the United States an unprecedented opportunity to take this gamble.

To be successful, a U.S. human rights policy will have to be coordinated with other democratic states, particularly other suppliers of arms and aid. A dictator will be unfazed by U.S. penalties if he can find more cooperative partners elsewhere. This was always the fear during the Cold War, and today that fear remains, although it is economically rather than geopolitically grounded. The United States worries that if it penalizes a repressive regime by not selling it arms, another country like France or Britain will get the deal—and the jobs that go with it.

The United States government has never harnessed the full potential of its diplomatic effort to the cause of democratization and human rights. By doing so within the G-7 forum it can dramatically increase cooperation among democratic states to deny arms, aid, and other forms of sustenance to regimes that violate liberal norms. Such cooperation has already succeeded in various instances.

A NEW COMMITMENT TO DEVELOPMENT

Pentagon officials and other analysts exaggerate the gravity of direct Third World threats to U.S. interests, but they do not exaggerate the deteriorating conditions in the Third World. Life for many people in the poorer countries is bad and getting worse. Nearly a quarter of the globe's population now live in a state of absolute poverty,[28] while mounting demographic pressures, environmental degradation, ethnic conflict, arms proliferation, AIDS, and other trends have the potential to foster acute disorder in parts of the Third World. Such disorder can jeopardize U.S. export markets and access to raw materials. More broadly, the massive gap in wealth between developed and developing countries has the potential to generate global tension and thwart international cooperation on a host of vital issues, most notably the environment.

The end of the Cold War presented a logical juncture to think anew about the problems of the Third World. But the United States government has yet to do this in a far-reaching fashion. The principal thinkers about the Third World in the U.S. government have been in the Pentagon. Instead of talking about new initiatives for development, official U.S. rhetoric has focused on new military strategies and force configurations to deal with emerging Third World threats. In the early 1990s the U.S. government argued that hundreds of billions of defense dollars would have to be spent in the years ahead to deal with mounting instability in the Third World. Yet no serious suggestion has been made for addressing the causes of this instability through increased aid spending. Instead, the commitment to foreign aid in the United States has collapsed in recent years. Japan has now surpassed the United States as the world's largest supplier of development aid, and the U.S. ranks far behind other industrial countries in the percentage of its GNP devoted to aid.[29]

There is a bitter irony here. Much as the United States is spending far more money to prepare for the failure of democracy in Russia and Eastern Europe than to foster it, the United States is also readying for the worst in the developing world while doing little to better conditions there. The main U.S. agency for promoting development, AID, has a 1994 budget of only $2.9 billion.[30] By contrast, the United States will spend $3.6 billion in the same budget to purchase three new destroyers and an amphibious assault ship, expenditures that represent just a tiny portion of a Navy budget now justified primarily in terms of Third World threats.[31]

Reinventing Foreign Aid

It is easy be cynical about increasing foreign aid to developing countries. Many on both the left and the right have complained that such aid is a waste of money, or worse. Left critics argue that foreign aid is often actually detrimental to recipient countries, since much of it is funneled through elites who have no interest in equitable growth or environmentally sustainable development. Foreign aid can help entrench such elites, making positive change all the more difficult.[32] Critics on the right have criticized foreign aid as a gigantic overseas welfare program that interferes with the free market and creates dependency. Isolationist right-wingers like Pat Buchanan suggest that foreign aid money is better spent at home.[33] In between these two extremes are legions of disillusioned liberals who believe that foreign aid, as currently administered, is unable to effect much change. Finally, the position of the American public on this issue is well known: large portions of Americans have consistently favored cutbacks in foreign aid.[34] Foreign aid, in fact, is probably the least favored of all U.S. government endeavors.

In the face of these sentiments, building a consensus for new foreign aid initiatives in the Third World will be difficult. Yet if presented correctly, the case for a commitment of this kind can be politically viable. At the core of that case is the notion, also true in regard to the former Communist bloc, that America faces a choice: it can pay less now to address nascent problems or it can pay a lot more later when those problems flower. Polls show that the American public is deeply concerned about global trends like environmental degradation and population growth, which are already showing their potential to produce disorder and decline in large parts of the world.[35] A foreign aid program that is focused on such problems would be likely to win much more public support than one that resembles an entitlement program, annually renewing huge bloc grants to a few friendly countries. New development spending may also become easier to sell if funding for this enterprise, like new spending for democratiziation, is taken out of the defense budget. The logic of shifting funds is the same in both cases: military spending in today's world often does not buy as much security over the long run as other sorts of internationalist spending.

Foreign aid must be overhauled and revitalized.[36] To answer criticisms from the left, the United States must finally do what it should have done long ago: restructure its foreign aid program to ensure that benefits do not bypass poor people. Various proposals have been put forth to this end, most important the idea of channeling a far larger portion of aid through indigenous and international non-government organizations (NGOs).[37] This path should be followed, as U.S. officials are beginning to realize,[38] even if it means incurring the ire of recipient governments. U.S. aid policies should reflect the reality that foreign elites are often not agents of change and that growth without equity does little to aid the cause of stability.

American aid dollars should be stretched more widely across the globe, especially to help poorer countries. Today, the most needy countries often get the least foreign aid. As a whole, the industrial democracies give only 40 percent of all aid to poor, low-income countries, such as those in sub-Saharan Africa. The U.S. record on this score is especially bad: only some 24 percent of its aid goes to such countries.[39] Overall, the U.S. foreign aid effort has never been a serious development undertaking and in the next five years, without changes, development spending in the foreign aid budget is expected to decline more rapidly than security assistance.[40] To reverse this situation and maximize both the effectiveness of increased development aid spending and its political viability, the United States should focus on a few carefully chosen priorities in cooperation with other donor nations.

Population

A world of eight to ten billion people is difficult to imagine. The next three to four decades will witness dramatic and disturbing developments. In Egypt, where the falling level of the Nile River is fast decreasing agricultural productivity, population is expected to increase by 40 million. Mexico, already coping with high unemployment, is expected to double in population from its current 91 million. India will also double in population, becoming nearly 40 percent larger than China is today. Impoverished Bangladesh will experience a huge increase and will have some 240 million people living in a flood-plagued country the size of Wisconsin. El Salvador, now the most densely populated country in Central America with 6 million people, may have as many as 15 million by 2030. And the population of Africa as a whole is expected to nearly triple, from 650 million people today to 1.5 billion by the year 2025.[41] These trends should not be surprising given that 60 percent of the Third World's population is under the age of twenty.

Almost every social, economic, and environmental problem that now exists in the Third World is likely to be severely aggravated by demographic pressures, a fact that has become increasingly recognized by U.S. national security officials.[42] Population growth also has ominous long-term implications for North-South relations. At the end of World War II developed countries accounted for roughly 40 percent of world population. Today this percentage has fallen to 20 percent and may fall as low as 12 percent. At the same time, there is no foreseeable shift in what is now a highly inequitable distribution of global wealth. "What are the prospects for long-term stability on a planet where about 10 percent of the people consume more than 90 percent of the resources, a small island of wealth in a sea of great poverty?" asked Under Secretary of State Tim Wirth in 1993.[43]

From the 1960s to the early 1980s the United States was a leading contributor to the cause of population control, helping to fund a wide variety of effective programs aimed at curbing birth rates in high-fertility countries. In the last decade, however, U.S. population aid has been slashed. In 1993 the United States spent less in this area than it did in 1981. The Clinton Administration has begun to reverse this pattern of neglect with changes in policy toward international family planning organizations and new funding for population programs.[44] But these efforts are only the first steps in restoring the United States to a position of leadership on this issue. Stopping population growth at 9 billion people by the middle of the twenty-first century will require major increases in spending on population programs over the next ten years. In 1990 developing countries spent an estimated $4.6 billion on such programs. By the year 2000 these expenditures would need to rise to $10.5 billion. More than half of these new expenditures will have to come from foreign donors. To meet its share of this burden, the U.S. budget for population will need to roughly double from its 1994 level of $663 billion by the end of the decade.[45] In 1993 Under Secretary Wirth suggested that spending on population is "the most important investment" that the national security establishment can make.[46] Like aid to the former Soviet Union, population spending addresses a nonmilitary security threat that is indisputably real.

Agriculture

As population skyrockets over the next few decades, global agricultural productivity is likely to fall. Lester Brown of the Worldwatch

Institute has noted that 24 billion tons of topsoil is being lost each year, and that between 1970 and 1990, the world's farmers lost 480 billion tons of topsoil, roughly equivalent to the amount of all the crop land of India. During the same period, deserts expanded at a rapid rate, claiming an area of land greater than that farmed in China. The implications of these trends cannot be underestimated at a time when world population is increasing by 90 to 100 million people a year.[47] While there are now 2,800 square meters of arable land for each person on earth, world population growth will reduce this average to 1,700 meters a person by 2025.[48] Global food production continues to increase, but at a slower rate than in previous years.[49] In sub-Saharan Africa, food production is growing at 2 percent while population is growing at 3 percent.[50]

There are clear security reasons for the United States to take a leadership role in confronting Third World agriculture problems. Today, an ever growing number of the Third World's poorest people are jammed into massive cities such as Jakarta, Cairo, Bangkok, Lagos, and Mexico City, and this trend will get far worse. In 1993 there were roughly 1.5 billion people living in the urban areas of the Third World; by 2025 that number may rise to over 4 billion.[51] Many of the cities that are likely to grow fastest in the developing world are seats of national government, home to diplomatic branches, international NGOs, and much foreign investment. If global food production fails to keep up with population growth, prices for food will climb and shortages will occur. The consequence could be urban disorder on a large scale in pivotal Third World countries that threatens the stability of friendly governments and the welfare of Americans who are diplomatic personnel, NGO employees, and business representatives.

Over recent years, efforts to increase agricultural productivity have become a less central priority of the U.S. aid program. AID spends hundreds of millions of dollars annually to fund programs in this area, but its main focus lies elsewhere. In 1993, for example, AID Administrator Brian Atwood did not once mention the subject of agriculture in either his opening statement at his confirmation hearing or in his first budget request to the House Foreign Affairs Committee.[52]

There does not exist a satisfactory solution to the world's growing global agricultural problems. Advances in biotechnology hold some promise for alleviating future pressures on food supplies, but the potential impact of such breakthroughs for developing countries remains unclear.[53] With no new green revolution in sight, the gap between population growth and food production will continue to grow.[54] To slow this trend a greater international effort is required to protect soil, conserve water, and restore the productivity of degraded land.[55] If the United States wants to provide leadership in this effort it must be prepared to spend considerably more money on agricultural programs than it now does.

Environment

Environmental degradation increasingly threatens the stability of Third World regions and therefore affects the national security of the United States, as U.S. officials now acknowledge. Within Third World countries, ethnic and regional competition for dwindling natural resources will likely become more common and more violent. Pollution and sanitation problems in huge urban centers, already worse than any ever seen before, can aggravate social tensions. Between Third World countries there is the potential for conflicts centering around shared water supplies. On a global level, the depletion of rain forests and new economic activity in the Third World may contribute to global warming, plunging biodiversity, and ozone layer depletion.

The world faces a difficult dilemma. To close the yawning chasm between the haves of the North and the have-nots of the South—an inequity that could become the source of serious global tensions in the future—there must be new economic growth in the Third World. Yet the planet is already reaching the ecological limits of the economic activity that it can sustain. Two developments are required to escape from this trap: the industrial world, particularly its most wasteful member, the United States, must consume less and pollute less. At the same time, the Third World must adapt a path of sustainable development that allows it to grow without hastening the earth's environmental decline.

The first of these challenges will involve significant changes in domestic policy, and is thus beyond the scope of this inquiry. But the second challenge is clearly a foreign policy issue. The developing countries cannot engineer sustainable growth policies on their own. They need major assistance from the North. Take the issue of energy use as an example. Today, the four billion people in the 130-plus developing countries, representing 77 percent of the earth's population, account for 25 percent of global energy use. By the year 2020 that portion is expected to climb to 50 percent.[56] If investment is not made now in sustainable and clean energy, the consequences in terms of air pollution and global warming could be devastating. Only with funding from the North will such investment occur on a large scale.

The central purpose of the Earth Summit in Rio de Janeiro in June 1992 was to institutionalize a sense of shared fate between North and South. The South committed itself to the goal of environmentally sound development, while the North agreed to assist that endeavor through new aid. A core achievement of the summit was the signing of Agenda 21 by 178 countries, a detailed policy manifesto that embodied this compact.[57] However, for all its success, the Rio summit stands as only a modest first step. It is estimated that the poorer nations will require roughly $125 billion a year in foreign aid to implement Agenda 21, some $70 billion more than the $55 billion they now receive in assistance from the northern countries.[58] To meet its share of this increase, the United States will need at least to double its development assistance.

EMBRACING MULTILATERALISM

The United States remains a natural leader in world affairs. Despite economic problems at home, it has an array of power resources unlikely to be matched by any other country through the foreseeable future.[59] But to maximize the influence that comes from this position the United States must reconceptualize its global role. A United States that devotes the bulk of a shrinking international budget to defense, as is now the case, will not be achieving its full leadership potential. It will have less a positive impact on world affairs than it might otherwise have, finding itself without adequate means for shaping the international environment and, in particular, doing far less than it can to further the all-important goals of democratization and development.

Reallocating national security dollars on a large scale is a crucial step toward reinventing American global leadership. At the same time, the United States must work harder to promote cooperative solutions to world problems. Like democratization and development, multilateralism is a traditional idealist goal that now stands as indispensable for advancing U.S. interests in the new era. It is also a goal that can inspire the American public and help sustain support for an internationalist foreign policy.

A United States willing to spend more money on democratization and development should be able to forge creative new partnerships with other donor nations and with international institutions. After World War II, the United States had to rebuild Western Europe alone, spending as much as 3 percent of its GNP annually on foreign assistance to achieve this goal. In the 1990s the United States is positioned to lead the community of wealthy nations in rebuilding the former Communist bloc and in revitalizing development efforts in the Third World. The leverage for this leadership must come from increasing foreign assistance above the current abysmal level of 0.3 percent of the GNP and focusing new diplomatic energies on democratization and development.

This is the easy kind of multilateralism. The hard kind will come in the security field. It is here where the United States is most accustomed to pursuing policy unilaterally. And it is here where old habits will be the hardest to kick.

Two vital multilateral enterprises illustrate the challenge that lies ahead: reducing the global trade in conventional arms and empowering the United Nations. In the past the United States has been indifferent or hostile to both these goals. Today, while these aims are more widely embraced by U.S. officials, Washington has taken few real steps toward achieving them. Closing this gap between the real and the ideal will be a crucial test of the U.S. commitment to multilateralism.

Arms Out of Control

In a world awash with advanced weaponry, and with Third World nations importing tens of billions in arms each year,[60] it is not surprising that Pentagon planners imagine a future of proliferating threats. An unfortunate irony is that the United States may be helping to make this future come true through its own arms exports, which accounted for 57 percent of total sales to the Third World in 1991.[61]

Although the United States is now pursuing a vigorous new policy aimed at curbing the proliferation of chemical, biological, and nuclear weapons, along with ballistic missile technology, the end of the Cold War did not bring about a reassessment of U.S. conventional arms transfers and security assistance. These remain a cornerstone of American national security policy, with many U.S. security officials believing that arms sales promote global security by strengthening responsible states. In recent years almost no friend of the United States has been denied weapons to defend themselves or to police their region.

But it is far from clear that greater stability is the overall consequence of U.S. policies. In much of the Third World, where traditions of cooperative diplomacy are scarce, the influx of arms can heighten existing rivalries or create new instabilities. Even states with no natural reason to fear each other can be caught up in spiraling military competitions. Selling arms to the most responsible U.S. ally can backfire if such sales alarm that state's neighbors, provoking them to beef up their own arsenals. And one lesson of recent history is that friendly governments can become renegade regimes virtually overnight. The large U.S. arsenal sold to the Shah in the 1970s fell into the hands of Islamic extremists in 1979. And three members of the U.N. Security Council—the Soviet Union, France, and China—supplied Iraq with over 80 percent of its military hardware.[62]

While the United States may not sell arms to rogue regimes, other countries invariably will. In the current arms marketplace nearly any dictator can amply equip himself with the latest tools of war for use against weaker neighbors or internal enemies. Saddam Hussein proved how threatening a wealthy shopper for arms can become. By legitimizing this marketplace, and acting as the biggest merchant within it, the United States is working at odds with its stated goal of reducing tensions in the Third World. It is also undermining the cause of development, since paying for arms imports can be a major drain on impoverished Third World countries. In the 1980s Third World nations spent nearly half a trillion dollars on arms imports.[63] While much of this hardware was imported by wealthy oil-producing states, other big buyers included some of the poorest countries in the world.

Current U.S. policy makes a major distinction between conventional arms and weapons of mass destruction, doing little to stem proliferation of the former while sparing no effort to curb the latter.[64] This double standard is unsatisfactory. In many ways the spread of conventional weapons is more serious than other kinds of proliferation because it is more pervasive, more economically burdensome, and often more damaging to regional stability, since conventional arms are more likely to be used for aggression. In 1990 it was not Iraq's ballistic missiles and chemical weapons that were most threatening to its neighbors, but rather its 5,500 tanks, hundreds of combat aircraft, and masses of sophisticated artillery.

A comparison of ballistic missiles and combat aircraft illustrates the misplaced distinction between conventional and unconventional weapons. In recent years the United States has led an international effort to put in place and enforce the Missile Technology Control Regime (MTCR), while making no efforts to regulate combat aircraft. Yet for many kinds of offensive operations combat aircraft are more effective than ballistic missiles. In many regions, the proliferation of these systems poses an equal if not greater threat to stability than the proliferation of ballistic missiles. Clearly anti-proliferation efforts must address both problems.[65]

In the past, the Cold War often made the goal of limiting arms exports to the Third World seem naive. Today, there is a historic opportunity to pursue such limits. This is an example of idealist policy that is also smart policy. What might a workable conventional arms control plan look like? In May 1977 a newly inaugurated Jimmy Carter announced a comprehensive approach to arms transfers. It involved both unilateral restraints and multilateral diplomacy; key elements of this approach remain attractive over fifteen years later. The United States, said Carter, should not introduce new and sophisticated weapons to Third World regions of potential conflict; it should not export the technological know-how for building weapons to developing countries; it should link arms sales to human rights performance; and it should observe an overall dollar ceiling on its arms exports.[66] Most important, Carter initiated talks with the Soviet Union on arms export restraints, the Conventional Arms Transfer Talks (CATT). The talks failed amid rising Cold War tensions in the late 1970s, and during the following decade, the Reagan Administration abandoned Carter's unilateral restraints, which were often ignored in any case, and made no effort to revive CATT. The global arms trade boomed through the 1980s, leaving Third World nations better armed than ever by the early 1990s.

Carter's vision is more viable today than it was in the 1970s. The end of the Cold War has both removed a major obstacle to cooperation on Third World issues between the two largest arms suppliers, Russia and the United States, and reduced the pressures for the advanced nations to arm allies in the Third World. Partly as a consequence of the Cold War's end and partly because of new economic constraints, arms imports in much of the Third World have been declining since the late 1980s. This decline makes control efforts more feasible.[67] At the same time, America's overwhelming dominance of the arms market has increased the potential impact of its leadership in seeking controls. Russia has huge arms surpluses that could flood the international market, but its growing dependence on foreign aid gives the West leverage over Moscow's export policies. Finally, despite the diffusion of arms-making technology to the Third World, the five permanent members of the U.N. Security Council still account for nearly 90 percent of the global arms trade.[68]

Following the Gulf War there was widespread agreement that a major new effort was needed to curb the arms trade.[69] The Bush administration showed leadership in suggesting that representatives of the five permanent members of the Security Council should meet to work out guidelines for the control of arms exports. In October 1991 a meeting in London among these powers produced a commitment to refrain from arms transfers that would aggravate an existing armed conflict, contribute to regional tensions, introduce destabilizing military capabilities in a region, contravene embargoes or other internationally agreed upon restraints, or be used other than for the legitimate defense and security needs of the recipient state.[70]

These guidelines, if truly followed, contained the potential to curb the worst aspects of the international arms trade. But little ever became of the so-called P-5 talks. Through a flurry of new sales around the world, the United States immediately distinguished itself as one of the least committed parties to post–Gulf War efforts to control conventional arms. Perhaps most notable was the U.S. decision in September 1992 to sell 150 F-16 fighters to Taiwan, a move that sent the wrong signal in a region where new efforts to restrain conventional arms imports is growing ever more apparent.

The Clinton Administration proposed no new initiatives for restraining the conventional arms trade in 1993. Top administration officials like Under Secretary of State Lynn Davis entered office opposed to broad guidelines of the kind sought by the Carter Administration. During the Carter years, commented Davis, who worked in the Pentagon for Harold Brown, "we discovered that overall guidelines don't work and that these issues had to be approached regionally." What happened under Carter is that "we often made policy by exception to the general guidelines. So I take from that experience the view that that's the way we ought to focus on the future of arms control with respect to arms and technologies. We should look at regional insecurities and U.S. interests in friends and allies in the region and define arms sales policies consistent with those. . . . Sales for defense purposes or to keep a balance of power can make a good deal of sense from an American point of view."[71] But this approach is tantamount to having no control policy at all. As long as the United States claims the right to supply any friend it wants with sophisticated arms, other states will claim the same right and make sales that strengthen dangerous Third World powers.

It is not my intention to suggest specific unilateral and multilateral steps that the United States can take to restrain the conventional arms trade. The problem in this area is not a shortage of sound proposals along these lines; it is a lack of desire on the part of U.S. officials to implement any serious measures at all. As with the issue of development, a change in U.S. policy regarding arms sales to the Third World must be part of a broader shift in the way national security threats are addressed. The United States must replace a militarized focus on the symptoms of instability in the Third World with long-range plans for dealing with its multiple causes.

Like the United States, the other top arms exporting nations are hurting economically and badly need the revenue that comes from arms sales. Getting them to subordinate financial gain to the goal of global stability will be no easy task. The United States will have to cajole and persuade other states in a process that may take years. However, if America wants to be a leader in the new era, this is precisely the sort of painstaking multilateral enterprise to which it must become accustomed.

Empowering the United Nations

On the last day of January 1992, leaders of the fifteen nations represented on the United Nations Security Council gathered in New
York for an unprecedented summit meeting. Their purpose was to
chart a path for the United Nations in the post–Cold War era. After
over a year of loose talk about a "new world order," wide agreement
existed that concrete efforts were needed to resuscitate the collective
security powers of the Security Council. The New York summit was
intended to get this process going.

As it turned out, the meeting was something of a flop. None of
the leaders from the five permanent members of the Security Council
addressed, in any substantive way, the three issues which are most
central to the Security Council's future: the reconstitution of the
Council to reflect changed geopolitical realities, the need for some
kind of U.N. rapid deployment force, and the fiscal constraints that
hobble U.N. operations around the world. More than two years later,
these challenges remain.

Although the international climate is now more conducive to
collective security than ever before, the extent to which this promise
is realized, and in particular the prospects for empowering the U.N.,
ultimately hinge in large measure on Washington's attitude toward
collective security. This attitude remains one of ambivalence, and it is
here where the clash between the idealist and realist approaches to
foreign policy is likely to be most intense in the years ahead.

In formulating post–Cold War foreign policy, Bush Administration officials favored a strengthening of the U.N. but did not envision
a dominant role for it in maintaining international security. The Gulf
War was considered a showcase for the helpful but limited manner in
which the United Nations would function in the new era. "The
coalition effort established a model for the collective settlement of
disputes," Bush said after Iraq's defeat.[72] Global order, it was imagined, would be more a product of undisputed U.S. political-military
strength than the bolstered capacity of international organizations.
Today, as indicated by the Clinton Administration's retreat from its
early hopeful rhetoric on the U.N., this realist-based vision exerts a
tremendous hold on U.S. foreign policy.

A Flawed Ad Hoc System

Empowering the United Nations might be a more urgent priority of U.S. officials if it were seen as either the only or the most desirable way of managing global security operations. But this is not the case. Many analysts argue that major collective security undertakings of the future can and should be ad hoc affairs similar to Operation Desert Shield/Desert Storm. Under this model, the United States persuades the international community to follow its lead in security emergencies and gets the best of both worlds: Washington calls the shots and retains military control of the operation while its junior partners pick up much of the financial burden. By not getting the U.N. too heavily involved, the United States avoids the possibility of deadlock in the Security Council over how security enterprises should be managed. At the same time, U.N. blessing gives U.S.-led coalitions greater moral authority, thus bolstering both domestic and international support for intervention.

This model has multiple appeals, and even strong advocates of revitalizing the U.N.'s enforcement powers acknowledge that U.S. leadership becomes more crucial as the size and complexity of a security action grows. However, the ad hoc model also contains significant weaknesses that make it unreliable.

In the future, developed states in Europe and Asia may prove ready to confront security threats in their own region. Yet these same states could be unenthusiastic about dealing with more distant threats. Take the NATO countries as an example. During and after the Gulf crisis, the Bush Administration pushed the long-standing American case that NATO should be used to coordinate for "out-of-area" operations in the Third World.[73] In a speech to NATO officials in Brussels on December 17, 1990, Baker said: "Iraq's aggression in the tinderbox of the Middle East certainly poses a danger to Western Europe that could be as important as any direct threat to NATO territory. If we let formalistic logic paralyze our efforts to adapt this alliance to meet these kinds of dangers, we will simply repeat the deadly errors of earlier generations."[74] President Bush made similar remarks in April 1991, saying that "we look to Europe to act as a force for stability outside its own borders."[75] However, over the next two years, the United States met substantial resistance when it pushed for a greater NATO commitment to tackling regional security problems. Such resistance is likely to endure. As an independent report on NATO's future stated: "When it comes to Third World regions, there are substantial differences of perspective, and of interests, between the United States and most West European countries, as well as among West European states themselves. Any attempts to coordinate military actions out-of-area can only emphasize these differences and possibly mar cooperation within Europe as well."[76]

In the past, the United States has worked with mixed success outside of formal alliance arrangements to convince select NATO members to join in Third World operations. Absent a new consensus in NATO on out-of-area undertakings, this ad hoc system or "shadow alliance"[77] would remain the primary means for securing European cooperation in regard to Third World threats.[78]

Such a mechanism suffers from three deficiencies. First, it has rarely yielded a fair sharing of the military burden. It didn't in Operation Desert Shield/Desert Storm and it didn't in 1987–1988 when the United States and its allies intervened in the Gulf to stop Iranian shipping attacks. Second, while Britain and France have proven comfortable working in these ad hoc arrangements, this approach holds less promise of consistently winning the cooperation of other Western nations. In particular, to the degree that Germany overcomes its pacifist isolationism, this development is most likely to take place through the United Nations. Finally, an ad hoc system carries no guarantee of functioning in every crisis; allies may opt out of security operations for a variety of reasons, especially if they believe that the United States will protect their interests whether they help or not.

A collective security model that hinges on active U.S. leadership has other limitations. The United States is willing to lead cooperative efforts against aggression when it perceives U.S. vital interests to be threatened; it is far less likely to do so when no such interests are at stake. In Bosnia, for example, an international community accustomed to taking its cues from Washington found itself virtually immobilized when the United States failed to take the lead in repulsing Serbian aggression.

Beyond these basic problems, there lies the danger that if the United States plays an overly dominant role in global policing, international enforcement operations can get mired in controversy about American power. In both the Korean and Gulf wars, international outlaws sought to portray themselves, albeit with little success, as fighting the United States rather than the world community. In future U.S.-led operations this charge might have a better chance of sticking.

To have maximum legitimacy, collective security efforts must appear to reflect the will of the international community, not any single country or particular bloc of nations. To be fair, such efforts cannot be chiefly the burden of the United States, especially given its growing resource constraints. To be reliable, a collective security system must be able to function when U.S. vital interests are not at stake. Whether a nation exports oil to the West or bananas to India, it should be assured of at least some assistance in the face of unprovoked aggression. The Gulf operation is a flawed model for future collective security operations because its success hinged entirely on American initiative and power. "Collective security cannot be dependent upon a U.S. secretary of state flying 100,000 miles over many long months to build the necessary coalition for an enforcement action," observed David Scheffer.[79]

The weaknesses of an ad hoc collective security system underscore the need for a more serious U.S. commitment to reviving the United Nations. American efforts should be focused on reconstituting the Security Council and bolstering U.N. peacemaking capabilities.

Reconstituting the Security Council

The U.N. Security Council faces a crisis of legitimacy. "The idea that the five great powers of the world of 1945 should forever retain the leading role in the maintenance of international peace and security simply doesn't play well anymore with the rest of the planet," Tad Daley has commented.[80] Challenges to the Security Council are heard in both the developed and developing worlds. Japan and Germany are now the second and third largest contributors to the United Nations. Japan alone contributes more to the U.N. than Britain and France combined. In both countries, there are increasing complaints about "taxation without representation."[81] The Japanese government has said that Tokyo expects a seat on the Security Council by 1995. Germany has also requested a seat. The United States has backed both requests.

The grumbling on the part of Third World nations is even louder. Charges that the United Nations is not a representative institution have been made for decades and are now intensifying. "Poorer countries have never had much power at the U.N.," commented one Third World critic in September 1992. "Since 1946, Third World nationals have held fewer than a third of top posts at U.N. agencies. The organization has been marching to the West's tune for years."[82] Growing U.S. domination of the Security Council is cited to confirm this charge, and it raises the specter among some observers that the U.N. is becoming a tool used by the North to suppress the South.

Amid such suspicions it will be difficult for the Security Council to sustain its legitimacy without becoming more representative of Third World peoples. In early 1992 Nigeria President Ibrahim Babangida said that "to retain the structure of the Security Council in its present form is to run the risk of perpetuating what is at best a feudal anachronism."[83] Suggestions have been made for granting a seat on the Council to one or more of the large Third World countries like India, Brazil, or Nigeria. Demands of this kind are sure to increase if the U.N.'s Charter is amended to include Japan and Germany.

Broadening the Security Council's membership is probably unavoidable. But this move, many worry, could weaken the Council's role in safeguarding global security. More members would increase the possibility of disagreement and deadlock; the use of the veto might become more common. The Security Council could again find itself frequently paralyzed.

But this is not the only possible scenario. A broadening of the Security Council could be positive in the long run. The inclusion of Germany and Japan, even without veto power, could help both countries overcome their resistance to sending forces abroad as part of U.N. operations, resulting in each playing a greater role in dealing with international emergencies. This would go a long way toward lightening the global policing role that is now largely carried by just three powers: the United States, France, and Britain. Membership in the Security Council would also further bind emerging German and Japanese power into multilateral institutions. As for Japan and Germany blocking decisive U.N. action, this seems unlikely. Both countries are industrial democracies with global interests very similar to those of the United States.

Granting permanent Security Council membership to one or two Third World nations could also turn out to have positive effects. Such representation would greatly increase the Security Council's moral authority in the Third World, which is crucial since this is where most U.N. policing operations are likely to take place in the future. The prospect of paralysis from this broadening of membership is also unlikely. During the Persian Gulf crisis, for example, nearly all major Third World countries backed action against Iraq. In considering the prospects of greater democratization at the U.N., Tad Daley makes an important point: "The various democratic decision-making structures around the world today are rarely paralyzed into complete inaction. Though often contentious in their procedures, they usually manage to produce some kind of public policy, however imperfect."[84] Why is global decision-making so different?

Peacemaking That Works

The Cold War's end has greatly enhanced the prognosis for an empowered United Nations, but it has not eliminated the most serious obstacle to global collective security: the resistance of nations to sending troops to faraway battlegrounds to uphold the principles of international law. Serious logistical and management problems also surround the United Nations, and with even medium-size peacekeeping operations often going awry, many doubt that the U.N. is ready for bigger things. In part, this skepticism explains the Clinton Administration's cautious approach to empowering the U.N., as codified in Presidential Review Directive 13. "We thought at this point that it was better to get the U.N.'s structure for managing peacekeeping in good shape," commented Assistant Secretary Douglas Bennet in explaining why the directive did not advocate new enforcement capabilities for the Security Council.[85]

Since the end of the Gulf War a host of suggestions have been put forth for reviving the U.N.'s collective security apparatus, the most notable being the July 1992 report by U.N. Secretary General Boutros Boutros-Ghali, *Agenda for Peace.* These proposals generally revolve around U.N. members earmarking in advance large contingents of national troops for participation in U.N. operations under the command of the Military Staff Committee of the Security Council, guaranteeing the availability of those forces through formal treaty commitments with the U.N., and ensuring their inter-operability through regular joint training exercises.[86] Advocates of such steps acknowledge that a U.N. force would be inadequate, at least at first, for handling large conflicts like the war with Iraq, but they observe that even in the biggest of emergencies, where Washington takes the lead, pre-earmarked troops would speed response time, lighten the burden on the United States, and give the operation a stronger multilateral character.

It is not my aim to analyze in depth the various proposals for reviving U.N. enforcement powers and to suggest which are most workable. As with conventional arms restraints the problem is not a paucity of plausible proposals but rather an absence of U.S. enthusiasm for experimenting with those that have been put forth. This will only change when there is a better understanding of the advantages of building a U.N. enforcement system that can supplement a U.S.-led ad hoc system in the short run and perhaps replace it in the long run.

The attraction of a U.N. force is that, at least in theory, it would be a more reliable mechanism for dealing with aggression than anything that now exists. "The barbarism in Bosnia instructs us," commented Senator Joseph Biden in 1992. "For months now, the world has debated: Should NATO act? Should the CSCE take charge? Is there a role for the West European Union or the European Community? But little has been done. We have institutional gridlock. . . . Were the U.N. Security Council adequately equipped with the ready availability of military forces, the question of intervention could at least now be addressed on its merits, without the impediment of massive institutional complexity."[87] Perhaps more important, international responses to aggression would be far less contingent on an assessment by U.S. political leaders that there existed a pressing threat to vital American interests. And, while U.S. leaders would probably insist on a high degree of operational control over any U.S. troops deployed as part of a U.N. force, such enterprises as a whole, especially those smaller in scope, would not be U.S.-led operations, inextricably linked in both international and domestic opinion with the United States. This could have the effect of reducing the enormous anxieties on the part of U.S. leaders about a loss of prestige that now accompanies even the most limited use of force.

In justifying their budgets, Pentagon officials talk often of the mounting threat to international security posed by ethnic conflict and other kinds of internal warfare. Yet in practice, U.S. forces are not likely to be used often in such conflicts in the future. The hands-off approach to Bosnia in 1992 and 1993 was grounded in a deep reluctance among military officers to enter less than clear-cut combat situations. The U.S. experiences in Lebanon in 1983 and Somalia a decade later are searing memories for many in the military.

Given this, U.N. forces may be the only viable mechanism for dealing militarily with future internal wars. If the United Nations had a very small, highly trained, ready-reaction force made up of professional volunteers, as has been suggested in several proposals, it could engage in military actions that did not put at risk either the prestige or national soldiers of the United States or another U.N. member state.[88] A few thousand battle-hardened U.N. troops could have made a crucial contribution to the defense of Bosnia in 1992 and 1993, and even high casualties among this force would not have triggered political outcry in Western capitals. In Somalia the deaths of eighteen U.S. Army Rangers in October 1993 was widely considered a humiliation for the United States. But if the U.N. had had its own high-quality combat forces, it is these forces, rather than U.S. troops, which could have led the treacherous hunt for Somali warlord General Mohammed Farah Aidid.

Beyond a ready-reaction force of ground troops, other standing U.N. forces might be desirable. During the Bosnian crisis, a major objection in Washington to the limited use of air power to attack Serbian artillery and other targets was that anything less than clear-cut success would tarnish American prestige, and that the capture of downed U.S. pilots could draw the United States more deeply into the war. However, if the United Nations had possessed its own small aircraft carrier, manned by professional volunteers and deployed in the Adriatic Sea, the air strike option could have been discussed without these considerations of national prestige and perhaps used earlier in the conflict.

Under a U.S.-led ad hoc system, aggressors know that the likelihood of an international response will be governed by the level of threat posed to U.S. interests. Strengthening the U.N.'s enforcement capability would create a higher degree of deterrence to aggression in areas that do not directly affect U.S. interests.

The resuscitation of Article 43 will be a long and fitful process. Nations might balk at formal commitments to place large numbers of troops at the Security Council's disposal. In the United States there is already clear opposition to any such an arrangement.[89] American political leaders have a long-standing uneasiness about international covenants that appear to impinge on national sovereignty. (It took nearly forty years to ratify the 1949 convention on genocide.) Also, though Americans are more positively disposed toward military action abroad that reflects the will of the international community, this does not mean that the public would support the deployment of large American troop contingents when no U.S. vital interests are at stake. "It is difficult to imagine Congress agreeing to this police role for the United States, or the American public marching off to wherever the United Nations has voted it should go," argued Robert Art.[90] Beyond these political problems, a large U.N. army would face substantial difficulties in the area of command and logistics.

But these obstacles are not insurmountable. During the years immediately after World War II, the United States overcame a tradition of isolationism to forge the NATO alliance and other security pacts around the world. These ties compromised the freedom of action that comes with isolation by linking America's destiny to the fate of other nations. A commitment to a stronger U.N. collective security system would not be a radical extension of this compromise. Indeed, whereas the United States now has virtually inescapable treaty obligations to defend allies ranging from South Korea to Turkey to Norway, it has far more flexibility about using force to uphold its commitments under the U.N. Charter. Contrary to Art's statement, the United States would not have to comply blindly with misguided U.N. decisions because, like each permanent member of the Security Council, it has a veto over U.N. military operations. Thus there is no danger that American forces could be used in a way that the United States opposed. (Richard Gardner has suggested that contributing nations without a veto might be given the right to opt out of U.N. operations.)[91] Moreover, there are many ways that the United States can be assured of a large measure of operational control over the troops it contributes to U.N. operations. As for the problem of coordinating multilateral operations, four decades of NATO history and the lessons of Desert Shield/Storm suggest that such coordination is possible. Admiral Leon Edney, former chief of the U.S.

Atlantic Command, has commented that the experience of NATO is highly applicable to the challenge of forming a U.N. enforcement capability. In particular, Edney suggests continuous multinational training and a strengthened and permanent Military Staff Committee at the U.N. with a chairman who serves two- or three-year stints in the fashion of NATO's supreme allied commander.[92]

Furthering international cooperation has never been easy, and the ultimate feasibility of empowering the Security Council remains far from clear. Some nations might renege on commitments to provide forces or not provide them expediently enough. Even after military action is successfully intiated, there could be fierce disagreements about the strategic goals of U.N. forces. Waging war by committee could prove difficult, to say the least. But the goal of empowering the United Nations stands as a logical next step in the evolution of the international security system.

No agenda along these lines will get anywhere in the absence of successful efforts to put the United Nations on a stronger financial footing. "It is a great irony that the United Nations is on the brink of insolvency at the very time the world community has entrusted the organization with new and unprecedented responsibilities," commented Javier Perez de Cuellar, before stepping down as Secretary General in late 1991.[93] Between 1988 and 1992, the U.N. began eight new peacekeeping operations, compared with fourteen during its previous forty-three years of existence. In 1993 the cost of running thirteen peacekeeping missions that included over 75,000 troops had risen to over $3 billion.[94] Outstanding dues to the United Nations as of 1992 were heading toward the $2 billion mark with the United States some $600 million in arrears.[95] This is a poor foundation on which to build an enforcement capability, an undertaking that will entail substantial new expenditures.

The United States bears a disproportionate share of the U.N.'s costs: 25 percent of the general U.N. budget and 30 percent of the peacekeeping budget. Optimally, in the years ahead, this share can be reduced as U.N. contributions grow from the new industrial states of East Asia and the oil-rich Gulf states. Nevertheless, the United States will probably still have to pay more money overall than it now does if the U.N. is both to adequately finance new peacekeeping operations and establish an enforcement capability.

In thinking about its future contributions to the United Nations and other international organizations, U.S. policymakers should employ the same logic behind new spending on democratization and development. It must recognize that money spent to bolster the infrastructure of multilateralism can often be a wiser investment than money devoted to military forces.

The necessity for greatly increased spending on democratization, development, and international institutions requires the U.S. government to take a new approach to national security budgeting. Currently there exists no effective mechanism to force hard choices among national security priorities. Every year the Defense Department must defend its budget, arguing first to the White House Office of Management and Budget (OMB) and then to Congress that its needs are more important than those of other government agencies. The State Department mounts it own annual campaign to defend the foreign aid budget. However, these two budgets never have to compete directly against each other, or against the budgets of the intelligence agencies, even though they are all aimed at achieving the same goal of safeguarding America's position in the world. Defense competes against State in the same fashion that it competes with the Department of Agriculture or Health and Human Services. Instead of there existing a single national security budgetary pie, there are several separate pies.

Within the Pentagon competition between the various services ensures serious debate over what sort of forces provide the most security at the lowest cost. Yet within the executive branch as a whole no such focused debate is guaranteed over whether America's national security dollars, broadly defined, are well spent. Thus, while the government has an effective mechanism for choosing between the C-17 transport plane and other Pentagon programs, it has a far less effective mechanism for choosing between the C-17 and programs geared toward democratization or development.

In addition, the current budgeting system for foreign and military policy is not user-friendly. The American public is not provided with a single figure on how much money the United States spends each year promoting its interests abroad. Instead, interested citizens must tally up the Pentagon budget, the State Department budget, the portion of the Energy Department budget devoted to nuclear weapons, and estimates of the intelligence agencies budgets.

It is time to put all national security spending into a single annual budget. In 1992 Senator Joseph Biden proposed, without success, a National Security Budget Act that would achieve this goal. A combined budget, he observed, would break down the artificial barriers that divide defense spending from other programs that make an equal or greater contribution to U.S. national security.[96] A major advantage of this move is that it could make foreign aid more politically viable. Typically, the foreign operations appropriations bill is one of the most difficult to get members of Congress to vote for because of its unpopularity with the public. By embedding foreign aid within a single national security budget, members of Congress would be spared the need to cast a highly visible vote on the issue. This move, along with a clear targeting of foreign aid on global issues that Americans are concerned about, can help ensure the political success of substantially higher foreign aid appropriations.

Within the executive branch, the national security advisor should be given a central role in developing each year's combined budget. Currently, the national security advisor is an integrator of policy and an advisor to the president. The position does not have an explicit budgetary responsibility. This could be changed by upgrading the security advisor to Director of National Security Affairs, a post similar to that of Director of the Office of Management and Budget.[97] Much as the OMB head is charged with integrating the entire U.S. budget, often through much bitter cutting and pasting, and then explaining that budget to Congress, the new national security director could perform the same function for the combined national security budget. This would assure first a serious annual debate in the executive branch over internationalist spending priorities, and second a clear presentation every year to Congress and the American people of exactly what the international budget is and how spending on defense, foreign aid, and intelligence all fits together into a balanced approach to furthering U.S. interests abroad.

CONCLUSION

In his influential 1979 treatise on international politics, Kenneth Waltz summed up the realist outlook: "Because some states may at any time use force, all states must be prepared to do so—or live at the mercy of their militarily more vigorous neighbors."[1] A central argument of this book has been that ever larger parts of the world are escaping from the dilemma that Waltz described. Among well-established democratic nations the use of force to settle disputes has become virtually unimaginable, making a revival of historic military rivalries unlikely. In the former Communist bloc, nationalist and ethnic passions coexist with widespread insecurities and territorial disputes, yet the fragile democracies of this region, dependent on aid from the West and trade with one another, have enormous incentives to practice the politics of cooperation. Even in the Third World, where dictators still often rule, the allure of territorial conquest is declining, both because of the staggering economic penalties that can be imposed upon aggressors in a single-system world and the dubious benefit of occupying new lands.

A U.S. foreign policy based on realist assumptions courts irrelevancy by underappreciating the changing nature of world politics, and it reduces America's global leadership potential by misappropriating scarce national security resources. Realists have been able to seize the upper hand in post–Cold War policy debates in part because they have monopolized the rhetoric of geopolitical urgency. They have also succeeded because the idealist tradition in U.S. foreign policy remains weak and idealist arguments have been poorly articulated. While misguided realist policies tend to be quickly forgotten, mistaken idealist policies are repeatedly seized upon as evidence that success in the rough business of world politics is often incompatible with the promotion of American values. Idealists must thus labor twice as hard to gain credibility in debates over foreign policy.

Today, however, it is realists who have a credibility problem. Exaggerating the threats that can be addressed through the familiar instruments of reassurance, coercion, and intervention, realists show little capacity for inventing policies to cope with a range of less traditional threats to America's national security. Consequently, the realist approach to world affairs translates into policies of complacency.

An idealist foreign policy would not assume that the end of the Cold War allows the United States to now return home, having vanquished the last of the free world's great foes. While embracing the optimistic worldview of liberal theorists, such a foreign policy would not take for granted those trends creating a safer world. It would shift attention away from the dangers that now structure American national security efforts, but would, at the same time, highlight other dangers. It would seek to address the causes of new threats emerging in the world, rather than simply invoking those threats to justify American primacy and continued high defense spending.

Crucial efforts to consolidate democracy and market economies in the former Soviet Union, now underfunded by the United States, would take priority over Pentagon programs justified in part by the specter of resurgent Russian militarism. Development efforts in poorer countries, now neglected while vast resources are poured into interventionary forces, would be reinvented to make them both effective and politically viable. Collective security and other multilateral endeavors, now untrusted to keep the peace, would be given a new salience in national security planning, with bolder experimentation in this area laying the groundwork for reducing the disproportionate security burdens carried by the United States.

American leaders today cannot afford to emphasize foreign policy at the expense of domestic policy. President Bush was rightly criticized for wielding the power of his office more enthusiastically on the world stage than within the United States. Yet President Clinton and future leaders must be wary of making the opposite mistake, especially during the current period of transition. With his priorities elsewhere, the president could opt not to fight the big battles and expend the political capital necessary to reinvent foreign policy and redistribute the national security budget. Worrying about any perception of weakness in the realm of defense, he could prove unwilling to gamble on policy shifts that play down traditional threats and seek to redefine security. Hoping to avoid political missteps and foreign distractions, he could rely on cautious national security advisors charged not with imagining a new kind of American leadership but simply with keeping foreign policy off the front page.

The consequence of such neglect would prove debilitating. Trapped between the two worlds of realism and idealism, embracing the latter rhetorically while following the former in practice, the United States would become less and less effective in shaping a world where its interests are secure. In the absence of a foreign policy revolution, it is likely that five years hence the United States will still have substantial forces in Europe and Asia to curb instability, and will still spend vast sums of money to hedge against the emergence of a new global enemy, but that the former Communist world, never adequately aided in its difficult transition, may be in even worse shape than it is now. Down the road, if current plans are followed, hundreds of billions of dollars will have gone into fielding forces that can thwart interstate aggression anywhere in the Third World at a moment's notice but will be unusable in the face of the internal violence that is likely to be so common. In the meantime, during the same five years, spending to curb the causes of such violence—spending that is already pathetically low—is likely to fall even further in real terms.

American foreign policy could become a self-fulfilling prophecy. Left unassisted on a massive scale, Russia and some of the other former Communist states could slip back to tyranny, as imagined in Pentagon worst-case scenarios. The poorer regions of the world, if allowed to continue on their downward spiral, could increasingly be a source of threats to American security. The United Nations, never adequately funded and never given an enforcement capability, would remain an ineffective institution for curbing global instability and reversing aggression.

A policy agenda that seeks to avoid this self-fulfilling prophecy would be rooted in America's idealist tradition of foreign policy. But it would be neither idealistic nor naive. And therein lies the beauty of it: two hundred years after the founding of the United States, the values Americans embrace at home now have become the best foundation for the foreign policy their government conducts abroad.

NOTES

1: BECOMING NUMBER ONE

1. The term *primacy* is defined here as a position of clear political leadership and unquestioned military superiority among non-Communist states during the Cold War, and all states in the post–Cold War era. Primacy entails having a far greater ability and willingness than any other state to establish and enforce the rules of the political-military order. Throughout this work I will use the terms *primacy, leadership,* and *preeminence* interchangeably. Occasionally I will use the term *hegemony,* although I generally seek to avoid this term because it implies economic as well as political-military dominance and has negative connotations. For recent attempts to define and assess the importance of primacy, see: Samuel P. Huntington, "Why International Primacy Matters," *International Security,* vol. 17, no. 4 (Spring 1993), pp. 68–83; and Robert Jervis, "International Primacy: Is the Game Worth the Candle?" *International Security,* vol. 17, no. 4 (Spring 1993), pp. 52–67.

2. Foster Rhea Dulles, *America's Rise to World Power: 1898–1954* (New York: Harper and Brothers, 1954), p. 2.

3. *Ibid.,* p. 3.

4. The full text of Washington's Farewell Address is found in Felix Gilbert, *To the Farewell Address: Ideas of Early American Foreign Policy* (Princeton: Princeton University Press, 1961), pp. 144–47.

5. A succinct overview of how America's early leaders viewed Europe's balance of power can be found in Gordon A. Craig, "The United States and the European Balance," in William P. Bundy, ed., *Two Hundred Years of American Foreign Policy* (New York: New York University Press, 1977), pp. 67–73.

6. Lawrence S. Kaplan, *Entangling Alliances with None: American Foreign Policy in the Age of Jefferson* (Kent, Ohio: Kent State University Press, 1987), p. 112.

7. *Ibid.*, p. 112.

8. *Ibid.*, p. 11.

9. Walter Lippmann, *U.S. Foreign Policy: Shield of the Republic* (Boston: Little, Brown and Company, 1943), p. 162.

10. Gilbert, *To the Farewell Address,* p. 89.

11. Walter Lippmann, *Isolation and Alliances* (Boston: Little, Brown and Company, 1952), p. 19.

12. Dulles, *America's Rise to World Power,* p. 5. As Samuel Flagg Bemis points out, the turmoil in Latin America in the early nineteenth century showed that John Quincy Adams's fervent neutrality extended to wars in the New World, as well as the Old World. Samuel Flagg Bemis, *John Quincy Adams and the Foundations of American Foreign Policy* (New York: Knopf, 1965), pp. 342–43.

13. I do not mean to imply here that the nineteenth century was a period of no significant diplomatic events but simply that concerns about balanced power in Europe and Asia were not central to U.S. diplomacy during this period. For a discussion of nineteenth-century U.S. foreign policy, see: Eugene V. Rostow, *Toward Managed Peace: The National Security Interests of the United States, 1759 to the Present* (New Haven: Yale University Press, 1993), pp. 121–70; and Charles S. Campbell, *The Transformation of American Foreign Relations, 1865–1900* (New York: Harper and Row, 1976).

14. Brooks Adams, *America's Economic Supremacy* (New York: Macmillan Company, 1900), pp. 190, vi.

15. *Ibid.*, p. 192.

16. Robert Dallek, *The American Style of Foreign Policy: Cultural Politics and Foreign Affairs* (New York: Knopf, 1983), p. 35.

17. Dulles, *America's Rise to World Power,* p. 68.

18. *Ibid.*, p. 62.

19. Alfred T. Mahan, *The Interest of America in International Conditions* (New York, 1910).

20. Robert E. Osgood, *Ideals and Self-Interest in America's Foreign Relations: The Great Transformation of the Twentieth Century* (Chicago: University of Chicago Press, 1953), p. 136.

21. Foster Rhea Dulles argues in his 1937 study of American-Japanese relations that in fact U.S. leaders did worry about power politics in the Pacific long before the acquisition of the Philippines or the announcement of the Open Door policy. He writes that "the idea that no other power should be allowed to establish dominion in the Pacific or exclusive control of its commerce may be traced back" to the mid-nineteenth century. Foster Rhea Dulles, *Forty Years of American-Japanese Relations* (New York: D. Appleton-Century Company, 1937), p. 3. This view, though, is not shared by Albert Hart, a historian closer to the period. See Albert B. Hart, *The Foundations of American Foreign Policy* (New York: Macmillan Company, 1905), pp. 37–40.

22. T. A. Bisson, *America's Far Eastern Policy* (New York: Macmillan Company, 1945), p. 12.

23. Adams, *America's Economic Supremacy,* p. 197.

24. Bernard K. Gordon, *Toward Disengagement in Asia: A Strategy for American Foreign Policy* (Englewood Cliffs, N.J.: Prentice-Hall, 1969), p. 54. In raising the specter of

Russian domination of China, Brooks Adams had also stressed the absence of any power besides the United States that could play a balancing role in the Far East. Adams, *America's Economic Supremacy*, p. 197.

25. Nicholas J. Spykman, *America's Strategy in World Politics: The United States and the Balance of Power* (New York: Harcourt, Brace and Company, 1942), p. 155.

26. Dallek, *The American Style of Foreign Policy*, p. 45.

27. Dulles, *Forty Years of American-Japanese Relations*, p. 62.

28. *Ibid.*, p. 79

29. *Ibid.*, p. 104.

30. Bruce Klunk, *Consensus and the American Mission* (New York: University Press of America, 1986), p. 7.

31. Lippmann, *U.S. Foreign Policy*, p. 33.

32. Osgood, *Ideals and Self-Interest in America's Foreign Relations*, p. 112. Foster Rhea Dulles emphasizes this point in regard to the mass of ordinary citizenry, writing of Lippmann's thesis in 1954 that the U.S. public "hardly understood the implications of an overturn in the existing European balance of power. They wanted the Allies to win because of their feeling that England and France stood for things in which they themselves believed, rather than because of fear for their own security." Dulles, *America's Rise to World Power*, p. 98.

33. Osgood, *Ideals and Self-Interest in America's Foreign Relations*, p. 117.

34. H. H. Powers, *America Among the Nations* (New York: Macmillan Company, 1917), p. 273. For more on Powers's views, see also his *The Things Men Fight For* (Boston: The University Prints, 1916).

35. Osgood, *Ideals and Self-Interest in America's Foreign Relations*, p. 161.

36. *Ibid.*, p. 162. House wrote Wilson in 1916: "It is impossible for any unprejudiced person to believe that it would be wise for Americans to take part in this war unless it comes about by intervention based upon the highest motives."

37. Lippmann, *Shield of the Republic*, pp. 36–37. See also Robert W. Tucker and David C. Hendrickson, *The Imperial Temptation: The New World Order and America's Purpose* (New York: Council on Foreign Relations, 1992), pp. 178–79.

38. Osgood, *Ideals and Self-Interest in America's Foreign Relations*, p. 411

39. Franklin D. Roosevelt, *The Public Papers of and Addresses of Franklin D. Roosevelt, 1937* (New York, 1941–1950), p. 408.

40. For an interesting attempt to show that warnings of American vulnerability during this period were highly exaggerated and must be seen as part of a broader pattern of overestimating national security threats to the United States, see John A. Thompson, "The Exaggeration of American Vulnerability: Anatomy of a Tradition," *Diplomatic History*, vol. 16, no. 1 (Winter 1992), pp. 23–43.

41. Livingston Hartley, *Is America Afraid?* (New York: Prentice Hall, 1937), pp. 74–75.

42. *Ibid.*, pp. 113–25.

43. Livingston Hartley, *Our Maginot Line* (New York: Carrick and Evans, Inc., 1939).

44. Edward Meade Earle, *Against This Torrent* (Princeton: Princeton University Press, 1941), p. 39.

45. Edward Meade Earle's main works of this period, include "American Military Policy and National Security," *Political Science Quarterly*, vol. 53 (March 1938), pp. 1–13; "National Defense and Political Science," *Political Science Quarterly*, vol. 55 (December 1940), pp. 481–95; "The Future of Foreign Policy," *The New Republic*, vol. 8 (November 1939), pp. 86–94.

46. The document is found in Robert Sherwood, *Roosevelt and Hopkins* (New York: 1948), pp. 410–18.

47. Lippmann, *U.S. Foreign Policy*, p. 164.

48. For a discussion of Spykman's book that shows its place within the literature of geopolitical approaches to world politics and particularly the work of British geopolitical theorist Sir Halford Mackinder, with whom he disagreed, see: G. R. Sloan, *Geopolitics in United States Strategic Policy, 1890–1987* (Sussex, England: Wheatsheaf Books, 1988), pp. 62–64. While Mackinder argued that whoever controlled the heartland, or Eurasian landmass, controlled the world, Spykman's emphasis was more on control of key maritime routes.

49. Spykman, *America's Strategy in World Politics*, pp. 448, 20–21.

50. *Ibid.*, pp. 124, 89.

51. John Lewis Gaddis, *The Long Peace: Inquiries into the History of the Cold War* (New York: Oxford University Press, 1987), p. 49.

52. John C. Campbell and Research Staff of the Council on Foreign Relations, *The United States in World Affairs: 1945–1947* (New York: Harper and Brothers, 1947), p. 25.

53. *Ibid.*, p. 26.

54. One of the authors of the speech was Walter Lippmann. Richard Barnet, *The Alliance: America, German, Japan: Postwar Makers of the Modern World* (New York; Simon and Schuster, 1983), p. 105.

55. Roland N. Stromberg, *Collective Security and American Foreign Policy: From the League of Nations to NATO* (New York: Praeger, 1963), p. 158.

56. Gregory F. Treverton, *America, Germany, and the Future of Europe* (Princeton: Princeton University Press, 1992), p. 20.

57. Cordell Hull, *The Memoirs of Cordell Hull* (New York: Macmillan, 1948), p. 1607.

58. Henry L. Stimson and McGeorge Bundy, *On Active Service in Peace and War* (New York: Harper and Brothers, 1947), p. 577.

59. Barnet, *The Alliance*, p. 34.

60. Hull, *Memoirs of Cordell Hull*, p. 1617.

61. Barnet, *The Alliance*, p. 33.

62. Melvyn P. Leffler, *The Elusive Quest: America's Pursuit of European Stability and French Security, 1919–1933* (Chapel Hill, N.C.: University of North Carolina Press, 1979), p. 363.

63. Stromberg, *Collective Security and American Foreign Policy*, p. 164.

64. Treverton, *America, Germany, and the Future of Europe*, p. 38.

65. Campbell, *The United States in World Affairs*, pp. 43–45.

66. On American postwar planning that took place during World War II, see Michael S. Sherry, *Preparing for the Next War: American Plans for Postwar Defense, 1941–1945* (New Haven: Yale University Press, 1977).

67. SWNCC 282, "Basis for the Formulation of a U.S. Military Policy," 19 September 1945. Reprinted in Thomas H. Etzold and John Lewis Gaddis, eds., *Containment: Documents on American Policy and Strategy, 1945–1950* (New York: Columbia University Press, 1978), p. 42.

68. For secondary accounts of national security thinking during this period, see James F. Schnabel, *The History of the Joint Chiefs of Staff: The Joint Chiefs of Staff and National Policy,* vol. 1, 1945–1947 (Wilmington: Michael Glazier, 1979); and Melvyn P. Leffler, "The American Conception of National Security and the Beginning of the Cold War, 1945–1948," *American Historical Review,* vol. 89, no. 2 (April 1984), pp. 346–81.

69. United States Strategic Bombing Survey, *Summary Report* (Pacific War) (Washington, D.C.: GPO, 1946), p. 30.

70. *Ibid.,* p. 31.

71. Of course, this avowed optimism may be seen as disingenuous. Paul Nitze had been deeply alarmed after reading a speech that Stalin gave in February 1946 and which his long-time friend and Navy Secretary James Forrestal had been citing as evidence of a coming clash with Moscow. David Callahan, *Dangerous Capabilities: Paul Nitze and the Cold War* (New York: HarperCollins, 1990), p. 52. Also, military planning envisioning war with the Soviet Union was already under way elsewhere in the government by late 1945 and early 1946. Steven T. Ross, *American War Plans, 1945–1950* (New York: Garland, 1988).

72. PPS 13, "Resume of the World Situation," 6 November 1947. Reprinted in *Ibid.,* p. 91.

73. John Lewis Gaddis, *Strategies of Containment: A Critical Appraisal of Postwar American National Security Policy* (New York: Oxford University Press, 1982), p. 57.

74. Sloan, *Geopolitics in United States Strategic Policy,* p. 139.

75. NSC 48/1, "The Position of the United States with Respect to Asia," 23 December 1949. Reprinted in Etzold and Gaddis, *Containment,* p. 252.

76. Gaddis, *Strategies of Containment,* p. 38.

77. PPS 23, "Review of Current Trends: U.S. Foreign Policy," 24 February 1948. Reprinted in Etzold and Gaddis, *Containment,* pp. 118–19. See also PPS 37, "Policy Questions Concerning a German Settlement," 12 August 1948. Reprinted in *Ibid.,* p. 141.

78. For example, at an August 1953 NSC meeting, both Secretary of Defense Charles Wilson and Secretary of State John Foster Dulles agreed that they were concerned about the possibility of resurgent German militarism and believed that plans to rearm Germany needed safeguards to prevent that eventuality. See Memorandum of Discussion at the 159th Meeting of the National Security Council, 13 August 1953, U.S. Department of State, *Foreign Relations of the United States, 1952–1954,* vol. 7, pt. 1 (Washington, D.C.: GPO, 1986), p. 503. James Conant, Eisenhower's choice to become U.S. High Commissioner to Germany, also was intensely apprehensive about the dangers of German rearmament. For a description of his fears, see James G. Hershberg, "'Explosion in the Offing': German Rearmament and American Diplomacy, 1953–1955," *Diplomatic History,* vol. 16, no. 4 (Fall 1992), pp. 513–19.

79. For background on this issue, see *Ibid.,* pp. 511–49; and Robert McGeehan, *The German Rearmament Question: American Diplomacy and European Defense After World War II* (Urbana, Ill.: University of Illinois Press, 1971).

80. Memorandum by the Secretary of State, 6 July 1951. *Foreign Relations of the United States,* vol. 3, 1951 (Washington, D.C.: GPO, 1981), pp. 813–14.

81. For a description of the important discussions held in late 1950 among the allies about the German defense contribution to NATO, and alternatives, see Paper Prepared by the Department of State, Integrated Forces and European Army, 26 January 1951, *Ibid.*, p. 755–59.

82. Thomas Alan Schwartz, *America's Germany: John J. McCloy and the Federal Republic of Germany* (Cambridge, Mass.: Harvard University Press, 1991), pp. 210–34. For the diplomatic record surrounding the negotations of the EDC, see FRUS, vol. 3, 1951, pp. 765–1047. For more general background, see Edward Fursdon, *The European Defense Community: A History* (New York: St. Martin's Press, 1980).

83. On Eisenhower's personal support for the EDC and EC, see Memorandum by the Special Assistant to the President, 13 August 1953, FRUS, 1952–1954, vol. 7, p. 509. For a detailed account of Dulles's advocacy of the EDC and EC, see Rolf Steininger, "John Foster Dulles, the European Defense Community, and the German Question," in Richard H. Immerman, ed., *John Foster Dulles and the Diplomacy of the Cold War* (Princeton: Princeton University Press, 1990), pp. 79–108. For an analysis that emphasizes the high hopes that Dulles and Eisenhower had that the EDC could carry much of the burden of Western Europe's defense, see Brian R. Duchin, "The 'Agonizing Reappraisal': Eisenhower, Dulles, and the European Defense Community," *Diplomatic History*, vol. 16, no. 2 (Spring 1992), pp. 201–21.

84. NSC 160/1, United States Position with Respect to Germany, FRUS, 1952–1954, vol. 7, p. 514.

85. For a clear and brief overview of the complicated events of this period, see William C. Cromwell, *The United States and the European Pillar: The Strained Alliance* (New York: Macmillan, 1992), pp. 1–15. For a detailed discussion of the negotiations over Germany's entry in NATO, see Duchin, "The 'Agonizing Reappraisal,'" pp. 215–21.

86. JCS Paper, Guidance for the Peacetime Conduct of Military Activities in Support of U.S. National Strategy with Respect to Germany, FRUS, 1952–1954, vol. 7, p. 522. Gregory Treverton likewise argues that France accepted Germany's rearmament and its 1954 entry into NATO because the United States—and Britain—were "finally prepared to offer concrete assurance against the revival of German power that France most feared." Treverton, *America, Germany, and the Future of Europe,* p. 89

87. Thomas J. McCormick, *America's Half Century: United States Foreign Policy in the Cold War* (Baltimore: Johns Hopkins Press, 1989), p. 107.

88. Robert A. Scalapino, "The Foreign Policy of Japan," in Roy C. Macridis, ed., *Foreign Policy in World Politics: States and Regions,* 7th ed. (Englewood Cliffs, N.J.: Prentice-Hall, 1989), p. 315.

89. Richard B. Stebbins and the Council on Foreign Relations, *The United States in World Affairs: 1951* (New York: Harper and Brothers, 1952), pp. 197–99.

90. Memorandum by the Joint Chiefs of Staff to the Secretary of Defense, 9 April 1954, U.S. Department of State, *Foreign Relations of the United States, 1952–1954,* vol. 12, pt. 1 (Washington, D.C.: GPO, 1954), p. 417.

91. Memorandum of Conversation by the Assistant Secretary of State for Far Eastern Affairs, 21 August 1952, *Ibid.*, p. 212.

92. NSC 5429/5, Current U.S. Policy Toward the Far East, December 22, 1954, *Ibid.*, p. 1064.

93. The Acting Director of the Office of Northeast Asian Affairs to the Ambassador in Japan, 16 September 1954, *Ibid.*, p. 912.

94. Essentially, there was little left to drive the debate over the potential threat posed by Germany and Japan once the security arrangements involving those two countries were settled. However, in the case of Germany, the question of its destabilizing impact on the continent would continue to be debated whenever the issue of unification was raised. Thus, according to the minutes of an NSC meeting in February 1958, Dulles had the following to say when the topic of unification was broached: "With respect to Germany the policies of the United States and of the Soviet Union have something in common—namely, that it was not safe to have a unified Germany in the heart of Europe unless there were some measure of external control which could prevent the Germans from doing a third time what they had done in 1914 and in 1939." The United States could not "accept a unified Germany except as part of an integrated Western European community. We simply could not contemplate re-unifying Germany and then turning it loose to exercise its tremendous potentialities in Central Europe." Discussion at the 354th Meeting of the National Security Council, 6 February 1958. Eisenhower Papers, 1953–1961, Ann Whitman File, Dwight D. Eisenhower Library, pp. 7–8. Similar thoughts would be expressed by foreign policy analysts in 1990 and 1991.

2: REALISM, IDEALISM, AND AMERICA'S RISE TO PRIMACY

1. Paul Varg, *Foreign Policies of the Founding Fathers* (East Lansing: Michigan State University Press, 1963), p. 146.

2. Robert Osgood, *Ideals and Self-Interest in America's Foreign Relations: The Great Transformation of the Twentieth Century* (Chicago: University of Chicago Press, 1953), p. 29.

3. For an extensive analysis of Mahan's influence, see G. R. Sloan, *Geopolitics in United States Strategic Policy, 1890–1987* (Sussex, England: Wheatsheaf Books, 1988), pp. 80–126.

4. Charles A. Beard, *The Idea of National Interest: An Analytical Study in American Foreign Policy* (Westport, Conn: Greenwood Press, 1934), pp. 1–2.

5. Foster Rhea Dulles, *America's Rise to World Power: 1898–1954* (New York: Harper and Brothers, 1954), p. 33.

6. *Ibid.*

7. Walter Lippmann, *The Stakes of Diplomacy* (New York: Henry Holt, 1915), pp. 212–15.

8. Walter Lippmann, *Isolation and Alliances* (Boston: Little, Brown and Company, 1952), p. 23.

9. Walter Lippmann, *U.S. Foreign Policy: Shield of the Republic* (Boston: Little, Brown and Company, 1943) p. 71.

10. *Ibid.*, p. 72.

11. *Ibid.*, p. 55.

12. Walter R. Sharp and Grayson Kirk, *Contemporary International Politics* (New York: Farrar and Rinehart, Inc., 1940), p. 7.

13. Nicholas J. Spykman, *America's Strategy in World Politics: The United States and the Balance of Power* (New York: Harcourt, Brace and Company, 1942), p. 448.

14. *Ibid.*

15. Roland N. Stromberg, *Collective Security and American Foreign Policy: From the League of Nations to NATO* (New York: Praeger, 1963), pp. 157–58.

16. *Ibid.*, p. 157.

17. Henry L. Stimson and McGeorge Bundy, *On Active Service in Peace and War* (New York: Harper and Brothers, 1947), p. 603.

18. Cordell Hull, *Memoirs of Cordell Hull* (New York: Macmillan, 1948), p. 1651.

19. Stromberg, *Collective Security and American Foreign Policy*, p. 181.

20. George Kennan, *American Diplomacy: 1900–1950* (Chicago: University of Chicago Press, 1951), p. 95.

21. Hans J. Morgenthau, *Politics Among Nations: The Struggle for Power and Peace*, 4th ed. (New York: Knopf, 1967), pp. 29–35.

22. Hans J. Morgenthau, *In Defense of the National Interest: A Critical Examination of American Foreign Policy* (Washington, D.C.: University Press of America, 1982), pp. 96–100.

23. *Ibid.*, pp. 102–3.

24. Kennan, *American Diplomacy*, p. 101.

25. Lippmann, *Isolation and Alliances*, p. 23.

26. Joel Rosenthal, *Righteous Realists: Political Realism, Responsible Power, and American Culture in the Nuclear Age* (Baton Rouge: Louisiana State University Press, 1991), p. 33.

27. George Kennan, *The Realities of American Foreign Policy* (Princeton: Princeton University. Press, 1954), p. 47.

28. For a succinct summary of realism's rise, see Ray Maghoori, "Major Debates in International Relations," in Ray Maghoori and Bennett Ramberg, eds., *Globalism Versus Realism: International Relations' Third Debate* (Boulder, Colo.: Westview Press, 1982), pp. 9–20.

29. Robert Keohane and Joseph Nye, *Power and Interdependence* (Boston: Little, Brown and Company, 1977).

30. See, for example, Robert Hunter, "Power and Peace," *Foreign Policy*, no. 9 (Winter 1972/73).

31. Zbigniew Brzezinski, *Between Two Ages: America's Role in the Technotronic Era* (New York: Viking Press, 1970).

32. Bruce Klunk, *Consensus and the American Mission* (New York: University Press of America, 1986), p. 130.

33. Robert Gilpin, "The Politics of Transnational Economic Relations," in Maghoori and Ramberg, *Globalism Versus Realism,* p. 191.

34. Kenneth Waltz, "The Myth of National Interdependence," in *Ibid.*, p. 82.

35. Kenneth Waltz, *Theory of International Politics* (Reading, Mass.: Addison-Wesley Publishing Company, 1979).

36. Norman Graebner, *Ideas and Diplomacy: Readings in the Intellectual Tradition of American Foreign Policy* (New York: Oxford University Press, 1964), p. ix.

37. Paul Kennedy, *The Rise and Fall of the Great Powers: Economic Change and Military Conflict from 1500 to 2000* (New York: Random House, 1987), pp. 199–202.

38. Rosenthal, *Righteous Realists,* p. 34.

39. Franklin said in 1777: "Tyranny is so generally established in the rest of the world, that the prospect of an asylum in America for those who love liberty, gives general joy, and our cause is esteemed the cause of all mankind. . . . " Varg, *Foreign Policies of the Founding Fathers,* p. 3.

40. Felix Gilbert, *To the Farewell Address: Ideas of Early American Foreign Policy* (Princeton: Princeton University Press, 1961), pp. 55–56.

41. *Ibid.,* pp. 60–61. See also Varg, *Foreign Policies of the Founding Fathers,* p. 2.

42. Varg, *Foreign Policies of the Founding Fathers,* p. 147.

43. Gilbert, *To the Farewell Address,* pp. 72–73.

44. Beard, *The Idea of National Interest,* pp. 358–59.

45. *Ibid.,* p. 365.

46. *Ibid.,* p. 368.

47. *Ibid.,* pp. 374, 385.

48. Robert Bacon and James Brown Scott, eds., *Men and Policies: Addresses by Elihu Root* (Cambridge, Mass.: Harvard University Press, 1924), p. 180.

49. For a discussion of efforts in the United States to promote international legal solutions to conflict during the nineteenth century, see Merle Eugene Curti, *The American Peace Crusade, 1815–1860* (New York: Octagon Books, 1965).

50. Dulles, *America's Rise to World Power,* p. 106.

51. Morgenthau, *In Defense of the National Interest,* p. 27.

52. For more on Woodrow Wilson's foreign policy thinking, see N. Gordon Levin, Jr., *Woodrow Wilson and World Politics: America's Response to War and Revolution* (New York: Oxford University Press, 1968); Arthur S. Link, *Wilson the Diplomatist* (Baltimore: Johns Hopkins University Press, 1957); and Harley C. Notter, *Origins of the Foreign Policy of Woodrow Wilson* (Baltimore: Johns Hopkins University Press, 1937).

53. For more on Wilson's Fourteen Points, the League of Nations, and U.S. foreign policy, see T. J. Knock, *To End All Wars: Woodrow Wilson and the Quest for a New World Order* (New York: Oxford University Press, 1992); Robert Lansing, *The Peace Negotiations, A Personal Narrative* (Boston: Houghton-Mifflin Co., 1921); Gilbert Murray, *From the League of Nations to the U.N.* (London: Oxford University Press, 1947); Osgood, *Ideals and Self-Interest in America's Foreign Relations;* Stromberg, *Collective Security and American Foreign Policy;* and Charles Webster, *The League of Nations in Theory and Practice* (Boston: Houghton-Mifflin, 1933).

54. Stromberg, *Collective Security and American Foreign Policy,* pp. 46–65. In his discussion of interwar U.S. collective security efforts, Stromberg argues that "The 'isolationism' of the 1920s has been exaggerated . . . " but suggests that this term can be more accurately applied to the 1930s (pp. 64–65).

55. Hull, *Memoirs of Cordell Hull,* p. 1625.

56. *Ibid.,* p. 1648.

57. For a good discussion of the founding of the U.N., see Robert C. Hilderbrand, *Dumbarton Oaks: The Origins of the United Nations and the Search for Postwar Security* (Chapel Hill, N.C.: University of North Carolina Press, 1990).

58. The Military Staff Committee of the U.N. Security Council is a body considered crucial to the U.N.'s enforcement procedures. For an interesting look at how efforts

to empower it in the immediate postwar period were derailed by Soviet instransigence, see Eric Grove, "UN Armed Forces and the Military Staff Committee: A Look Back," *International Security*, vol. 17, no. 3 (Spring 1993), pp. 172–82.

59. The interagency debate over the proposal showcased arguments over the U.N. that would be made more than three decades later after the Cold War ended. A top state official argued for a permanent U.N. force on pragmatic grounds, citing the success of the United Nations Emergency Force (UNEF) that had been deployed in the Middle East after the 1956 Arab-Israeli War: "The existence of various situations where United Nations observation or patrol might either deter the outbreak of hostility or facilitate the cessation of hostilities after they have broken out, suggests that the UNEF experience might now constructively be built upon to augment the available tools for dealing with international disputes, particularly those in the non-Communist world." Such a force would be modest in scope. "A proposal for a U.N. corps should be considered as an adjunct to U.N. procedures for the pacific settlement of disputes, rather than as a collective security-type fight force designed to repel military aggression." Memorandum from the Assistant Secretary of State for International Organization Affairs to the Secretary of State, *Foreign Relations of the United States, 1955–1957,* vol. 11 (Washington, D.C.: GPO, 1988), p. 173. The U.S. military responded negatively even to this modest proposal, arguing that there was no "assurance that the employment of this force would be in the interest of the United States and it could possibly result in its use to the contrary"; that many countries would probably resist contributing forces to the U.N. if it meant reducing their national defenses; that the problems of logistics, standardization, and command and control would be formidable, if not irresolvable; and that financing such an enterprise would be difficult. The military memo concluded: "Proposals for an internationally recruited force owing allegiance to the United Nations under direct control of a United Nations agency are not technically feasible or politically acceptable." Memorandum from the Chairman of the Military Staff Committee to the Mission at the United Nations to the Chairman of the Joint Chiefs of Staff, *Ibid.*, pp. 177–85.

60. Memorandum by the Secretary of State, 28 August 1957, *Ibid.*, pp. 248–50.

61. See Robert Kuttner, *The End of Laissez-Faire: National Purpose and the Global Economy After the Cold War* (New York: Knopf, 1991).

62. Joshua Muravchik, *Exporting Democracy: Fulfilling America's Destiny* (Washington, D.C.: American Enterprise Institute Press, 1991), p. 82.

63. *Ibid.*, pp. 91–112.

64. For a lively discussion of the occupation and transformation of these two countries, see Richard Barnet, *The Alliance: America, Europe, Japan: Makers of the Postwar World* (New York: Simon and Schuster, 1983). On the transformation of Japanese society, see Robert E. Ward and Sakamoto Yoshikazu, eds., *Democratizing Japan: The Allied Occupation* (Honolulu: University of Hawaii Press, 1987). On how Japanese foreign policy was affected, see Robert A. Scalapino, "The Foreign Policy of Japan," in Roy C. Macridis, ed., *Foreign Policy in World Politics: States and Regions,* 7th ed. (Englewood Cliffs, N.J.: Prentice-Hall, 1989), pp. 298–344. For a discussion of the occupation of Germany, see Thomas Alan Schwartz, *America's Germany: John J. McCloy and the Federal Republic of Germany* (Cambridge, Mass.: Harvard University Press, 1991).

65. Charles W. Kegley, "The Neoidealist Moment in International Studies? Realist

Myths and New International Realities," *International Studies Quarterly*, no. 37 (1993), pp. 131–46; Stanley Kober, "Idealpolitik," *Foreign Policy*, no. 79 (Summer 1990), pp. 3–24.

3: PRIMACY REAFFIRMED: STAYING NUMBER ONE AFTER THE COLD WAR

1. The phrase "mainstream foreign policy establishment" is not meant to be a rigorous one that conjures up the image of a clearly delineated group of people or a select fraternity of "wise men" but rather to describe the world of analysts and commentators who generally operate within the confines of existing policy debates and precedents. Members may include individuals who have previously served in government; whose views are not so extreme that they would likely be excluded from government service in an admininstration of either party; who are regularly asked to testify before congressional committees; who are occasionally appointed to semi-official blue ribbon commissions; who work at such organizations as the Council on Foreign Relations, Center for Strategic and International Studies, Carnegie Endowment for International Peace, and Johns Hopkins Foreign Policy Institute; whose articles are published in journals such as *Foreign Affairs, The Washington Quarterly,* and *Foreign Policy.*

2. Address by Paul Wolfowitz, "North American, European, and Japanese Security: An American Perspective," Knokke-Heist, Belgium, 18 June 1990, p. 8.

3. James A. Baker III, "America in Asia," *Foreign Affairs*, vol. 70, no. 5 (1991), p. 11.

4. Joseph S. Nye, Jr., *Bound to Lead: The Changing Nature of American Power* (New York: Basic Books, 1990), p. 239; Nye, "American Power and a Post–Cold War World," in Aspen Strategy Group, *Facing the Future: American Strategy in the 1990s* (Lanham, Md.: University Press of America, 1991), p. 52.

5. For one of the best accounts of Bush foreign policy, emphasizing the competence of the Bush national security teams but their frequent failures of vision, see Terry L. Deibel, "Bush's Foreign Policy: Mastery and Inaction," *Foreign Policy*, no. 84 (Fall 1991), pp. 3–23.

6. Address by James Baker, "Power for Good: American Foreign Policy in a New Era," *Department of State Bulletin*, June 1989, p. 9.

7. Secretary Baker, "U.S. Foreign Policy Priorities and FY 1991 Budget Request," *U.S. Department of State Dispatch*, 3 September 1990, p. 1.

8. Address by Robert Gates, "Change, Hope and Uncertainty," Washington, D.C., 4 June 1990, p. 19.

9. The White House, *National Security Strategy of the United States*, August 1991, p. 2.

10. President-elect Clinton, "A New Era of Peril and Promise," *U.S. Department of State Dispatch*, vol. 4, no. 5 (1 February 1993), p. 57.

11. U.S. Congress, 102d Cong., 1st sess., House Foreign Affairs Committee, Hearings: *U.S. Post–Cold War Foreign Policy* (Washington, D.C.: GPO, 1993), p. 219.

12. Jack Snyder, "Averting Anarchy in Europe," *International Security*, vol. 14, no. 4 (Spring 1990), p. 10. See also Lawrence S. Eagleburger, "The 21st Century: American

Foreign Policy Challenges," in Edward K. Hamilton, ed., *America's Global Interests* (New York: W. W. Norton, 1989), p. 249.

13. Henry A. Kissinger, "Balance of Power Sustained," in Graham T. Allison and Gregory Treverton, eds., *Rethinking American Security: Beyond Cold War to New World Order* (New York: W. W. Norton, 1992), p. 239.

14. U.S. Congress, 101st Cong., 2d sess., House Armed Services Committee, Hearings: *Building a Defense That Works for the Post–Cold War World* (Washington, D.C.: GPO, 1991), p. 62.

15. *The New York Times,* 2 October 1992.

16. Address by President Bush, "Future of Europe," *Current Policy,* no. 1177. Not long after the collapse of Eastern European communism in late 1989, National Security Advisor Brent Scowcroft promised during a speech in Munich that "the United States intends to remain engaged in Europe with a substantial military and political presence. We are a European power, with an abiding and permanent interest in European security." Scowcroft suggested that the United States would continue to feel this responsibility no matter what became of Soviet power. Address by Brent Scowcroft, Munich, Germany, 3 February 1990, p. 1.

17. Interview with Brent Scowcroft, "America Can't Afford to Turn Inward," *NPQ* (Summer 1992), p. 8.

18. John Mearsheimer, "Back to the Future: Instability in Europe After the Cold War," *International Security*, vol. 15, no. 1 (Summer 1990), p. 55.

19. U.S. Congress, 101st Cong., 2d sess., Senate Foreign Relations Committee. *Relations in a Multipolar World* (Washington, D.C.: GPO, 1991), pp. 267–71. For more on Mandlebaum's views, see Michael Mandlebaum, "The Bush Foreign Policy," *Foreign Affairs,* vol. 70, no. 1 (Winter 1990/91), pp. 3–22.

20. The Soviet Union maintained for some time after the fall of the Berlin Wall that maintaining two separate German states was crucial to the security and stability in Europe and that unification could only be considered if the new German state were demilitarized. For a discussion of this position and the deep-seated fears of Germany that drove it, see Russian scholar Aleksandr Kokeev's "Moscow and Bonn: From Confrontation to Partnership," in Vladimir Baranovsky and Hans-Joachim Spanger, eds., *In from the Cold: Germany, Russia, and the Future of Europe* (Boulder, Colo.: Westview Press, 1992), pp. 211–36. See also W. R. Smyser, "U.S.S.R.–Germany: A Link Restored," *Foreign Policy*, no. 84 (Fall 1991), pp. 125–41.

21. Michael R. Beschloss and Strobe Talbott, *At the Highest Levels: The Inside Story of the End of the Cold War* (Boston: Little Brown, 1993), pp. 185–86; and Don Oberdorfer, *The Turn: From Cold War to a New Era, the United States and the Soviet Union, 1983–1990* (New York: Poseidon Press, 1991), pp. 391–97.

22. Working Group on Changing Roles and Shifting Burdens in the Atlantic Alliance, *The United States and NATO in an Undivided Europe* (Washington, D.C.: Johns Hopkins Foreign Policy Institute, 1991), p. 6. Those who endorsed the conclusions of this report included David Abshire, Bill Bradley, Harold Brown, Zbigniew Brzezinski, Lee Hamilton, Edward Meyer, Sam Nunn, and Patrica Shroeder.

23. U.S. Congress, 102nd Cong., 2d sess., Senate Armed Services Committee. *Defense Planning Guidance and Security Issues* (Washington, D.C.: GPO, 1992), p. 52.

24. House Foreign Affairs Committee, *U.S. Post–Cold War Foreign Policy,* p. 93. It must be stressed that Brown's comments and the conclusion of the Johns Hopkins report are entirely unexceptional in both their tone and substance. A variety of former national security officials echoed these sentiments during the early 1990s. See, for example, retired JCS chairman David Meyer's comment in June 1992 that "we want to prevent a leadership vacuum from developing that might pressure Germany to assume a leadership role with the concomitant unease that it would create on the part of its partners." Senate Armed Services Committee, Defense Planning Guidance and Security Issues, p. 417. See also a 1992 RAND report that stated that American withdrawal from Europe could result in Germany moving in the "direction of militarization, nuclearization, and chronically insecure policies." Richard L. Kugler, *The Future U.S. Military Presence in Europe: Forces and Requirements for the Post–Cold War Era,* R-4194-EUCOM/NA (Santa Monica, Calif.: RAND, 1992).

25. Beschloss and Talbott, *At the Highest Levels,* p. 192.

26. In an essay on U.S.-German relations, Robert Blackwill, Scowcroft's top European expert at the NSC, stated after leaving office that "Europeans want U.S. troops in Europe because they believe an American military presence reduces the likelihood that historical patterns of intra-European rivalry and conflict that produced war will again resurface." See Robert D. Blackwill, "Patterns of Partnership: The U.S.-German Security Relationship in the 1990s," in Steven Miller and Gebhard Schweigler, eds., *From Occupation to Cooperation: The United States and Germany in a Changing World Order* (New York: W. W. Norton and Company, 1992), pp. 114–47. In the same volume, Christoph Bertram points out that the Germans themselves, in a kind of "self-containment," are among the greatest supporters of NATO. "For Germany, the alliance has had, and continues to have, a special function, namely that of making German power controllable and hence acceptable to allies and political adversaries alike." Christoph Bertram, "Visions of Leadership: Germany," in *Ibid.,* p. 61. For more on Germany in post–Cold War Europe, see Gregory Treverton, *America, Germany, and the Future of Europe* (Princeton: Princeton University Press, 1992); Stephen Van Evera, "Primed for Peace: Europe After the Cold War," *International Security,* vol. 15, no. 3 (Winter 1990/91), pp. 7–53; Robert Gerad Livingston, "United Germany: Bigger and Better," *Foreign Policy,* no. 87 (Summer 1992), pp. 157–74; Thomas Kielinger and Max Otte, "Germany: The Pressured Power," *Foreign Policy,* no. 91 (Summer 1993), pp. 44–62; David Calleo, "American National Interest and the New Europe: The Millennium Has Not Yet Arrived," in Charles W. Kegley, Jr., and Eugene R. Wittkopf, eds., *The Future of American Foreign Policy* (New York: St. Martin's Press, 1992); Elizabeth Pond, "Germany in the New Europe," *Foreign Affairs,* vol. 71, no. 4 (Summer 1992).

27. U.S. Congress, 102nd Cong., 2d sess., Senate Armed Services Committee, *Threat Assessment, Military Strategy and Defense Planning* (Washington, D.C.: GPO, 1992), p. 422.

28. House Foreign Affairs Committee, *U.S. Post–Cold War Foreign Policy,* p. 221.

29. Mearsheimer, "Back to the Future: Instability in Europe After the Cold War," p. 47.

30. Owen Harries, "The Collapse of the West," *Foreign Affairs,* vol. 72, no. 4 (September/October 1993), pp. 41–53. Christopher Layne, "The Unipolar Illusion:

Why New Great Powers Will Rise," *International Security*, vol. 17, no. 4 (Spring 1993), pp. 5–51. Layne uses neo-realist theory to argue that balancing by European powers against the U.S. is inevitable. "Proponents of America's preponderance have missed a fundamental point: other states react to the threat of hegemony, not the hegemon's identity. American leaders may regard the United States as a benevolent hegemon, but others cannot afford to take such a relaxed view"(p. 35). For a more conventional and sanguine view on transatlantic relations after the Cold War, see David Owen, "Atlantic Partnership or Rivalry?" in Henry Brandon, ed., *In Search of a New World Order: The Future of U.S.-European Relations* (Washington, D.C.: The Brookings Institution, 1992), pp. 13–32.

31. Department of Defense, *The National Military Strategy of the United States* (Washington, D.C.: GPO, January 1992), p. 3. For a similar example, see Baker's December 1989 comment that "a Europe undivided may not necessarily be a Europe peaceful and prosperous. . . . Some of the divisive issues that once brought conflict to Europe are reemerging." Secretary Baker, "A New Europe, A New Atlanticism: Architecture for a New Era," 12 December 1989. *Current Policy,* no. 1233.

32. Mearsheimer, "Back to the Future," pp. 5–56.

33. For more on multipolarity, see Karl W. Deutsch and J. David Singer, "Multipolar Power Systems and International Stability," *World Politics*, vol. 16, no. 3 (April 1964), pp. 390–406; and Thomas J. Christensen and Jack Snyder, "Chain Gangs and Passed Bucks: Predicting Alliance Patterns in Multipolarity," *International Organization*, vol. 44, no. 2 (Spring 1990), pp. 137–68.

34. Waltz, *Theory of International Politics,* p. 165. Waltz first outlined his basic views on the desirability of a bipolar system in 1964, predicting that the bipolar world would last into the twenty-first century. See Kenneth N. Waltz, "The Stability of a Bipolar World," *Daedalus*, vol. 93, no. 3 (Summer 1964), pp. 881–909.

35. Mearsheimer, "Back to the Future," p. 34.

36. Working Group on Changing Roles and Shifting Burdens in the Atlantic Alliance, *The United States and NATO in an Undivided Europe*, p. 6.

37. This was seen as particularly true in the Balkans, even before the carnage in Yugoslavia was under way. See F. Stephen Larrabee, "Long Memories and Short Fuses: Change and Instability in the Balkans," *International Security*, vol. 13, no. 3 (Winter 1990/91), pp. 58–91.

38. Senate Foreign Relations Committee, *Relations in a Multipolar World,* p. 271.

39. Writing in 1992, David Albright commented that "even CIS leaders with a pro-Western orientation might feel compelled to embark on, or could get drawn into, conventional military actions that could damage United States security interests." Albright cited as an example the possibility of a military move against one or more of the Baltic states in response to their expulsion of Russian minorities. Other analysts speculated about efforts by a future reactionary government in Russia to recapture portions of its lost empire or to menace democracies in Eastern Europe. In light of these considerations, Albright spoke for many in arguing that it would be "folly to rely solely on the discernible intentions of existing CIS leaders to gauge the potential threat to the United States from the conventional military forces of the CIS or its individual members over the next decade or so." David E. Albright, "Threats to United States Security in a Post-Containment World: Implications for United States Military Strategy and

Force Structure, Part II," *In Depth*, vol. 2, no. 3 (Fall 1992), pp. 153–54.

40. U.S. Congress, 102nd Cong., 1st sess., Senate Armed Services Committee, *Department of Defense Authorization for Appropriations for Fiscal Years 1992 and 1993* (Washington, D.C.: GPO, 1991), p. 557.

41. Senate Armed Services Committee, *Threat Assessment, Military Strategy and Defense Planning*, p. 422, 430. See also Department of Defense, *The National Military Strategy of the United States*, p. 2.

42. *Ibid.*, p. 509.

43. For a sampling of this debate, see Stephen J. Flanagan, "NATO and Central and Eastern Europe: From Liaison to Security Partnership," *The Washington Quarterly*, vol. 15, no. 2 (Spring 1992), pp. 141–51; Ronald D. Asmus, Richard L. Kugler, and F. Stephen Larrabee, "Building a New NATO," *Foreign Affairs*, vol. 72, no. 4 (September/October 1993), pp. 28–40; Adrian A. Basora, "Central and Eastern Europe: Imperative for Active U.S. Engagement," *The Washington Quarterly*, vol. 16, no. 1 (Winter 1993), pp. 67–78; Jenonne Walker, "Avoiding Risk and Responsibility," *Current History* (November 1992), pp. 364–68; Ian William Honig, *NATO: An Institution Under Threat* (New York: Institute for East-West Security Studies, 1991).

44. For a statement of administrative thinking on NACC, see "Secretary Baker, NACC Intervention," U.S. Department of State, Bureau of Public Affairs. For an excellent discussion of the liaison program by a member of the State Department's Policy Planning Staff under Baker, see Flanagan, "NATO and Central Europe: From Liaison to Security Partnership," pp. 141–51.

45. U.S. Congress, 102nd Cong., 1st sess., House Foreign Affairs Committee, Hearings: *Developments in Europe, October 1991* (Washington, D.C.: GPO, 1992), p. 52. For military views, see 1992 testimony by General Galvin. U.S. Congress, 102nd Cong., 2d sess., House Committee on Appropriations, Hearings: *Department of Defense Appropriations for 1993* (Washington, D.C.: GPO, 1992), p. 541. Colin Powell also made this point. U.S. Congress, 102nd Cong., 2d sess., House Foreign Affairs Committee, Hearings: *The Future of U.S. Foreign Policy in the Post–Cold War Era* (Washington, D.C.: GPO, 1992), p. 355.

46. U.S. Congress, 102nd Cong., 2d sess., House Foreign Affairs Committee, Hearings: *U.S.-European Relations* (Washington, D.C.: GPO, 1992), p. 11.

47. *The New York Times*, 29 July 1993.

48. For an excellent critical examination of the political-military dynamics within NATO, see David Calleo, *Beyond Hegemony: The Future of the Western Alliance* (New York: Basic Books, 1987). For a more theoretical perspective that examines the way that a hegemonic power wields influence by shaping the views within subordinate states, see G. John Ikenberry and Charles A. Kupchan, "Socialization and Hegemonic Power," *International Organization*, vol. 44, no. 3 (Summer 1990), pp. 283–315.

49. U.S. officials saw the U.S. troop presence in Europe and influence in NATO as intricately linked. General Galvin, in arguing in 1992 against cutting troops below 150,000, said that this number was "the minimum level which will allow us to continue to have a seat at the table and, therefore, a strong influence on the shaping of security of Western Europe in the future, a security that is so vital to us." House Committee on Appropriations, Department of Defense Appropriations for 1993, p. 500.

50. For an exploration of this issue in regard to the Gulf Conflict, see Andrew Fen-

ton Cooper, Richard A. Higgott, Kim Richard Nossal, "Bound to Follow? Leadership and Followership in the Gulf Conflict," *Political Science Quarterly*, vol. 106, no. 3 (Fall 1991), pp. 391–410.

51. Baker called for new efforts along these lines in a speech to NATO leaders during the Gulf crisis. Secretary Baker, "Challenges Facing the Atlantic Alliance," U.S. Department Dispatch, 24 December 1990, p. 353. Bush echoed the point in April 1991. President Bush, "The New World Order: Relations with Europe and the Soviet Union," *Foreign Policy Bulletin* (May/June 1991), p. 33. For background on the long-standing debate over out-of-area operations, see Elizabeth Sherwood, *Allies in Crisis: Meeting Global Challenges to Western Security* (New Haven: Yale University Press, 1990); and Richard J. Payne, *The West European Allies, the Third World, and U.S. Foreign Policy: Post–Cold War Challenges* (Westport, Conn.: Greenwood Press, 1991).

52. Layne cites a belief in this idea among U.S. policymakers as one factor that will eventually cause Europeans to resist a unipolar world and balance against American power. Christopher Layne, "The Unipolar Illusion," pp. 34–35. For further, but ultimately unsatisfactory, discussion on the uses and limitations of primacy, see Samuel P. Huntington, "Why International Primacy Matters," *International Security*, vol. 17, no. 4 (Spring 1993), pp. 68–83; and Robert Jervis, "International Primacy: Is the Game Worth the Candle?" *International Security*, vol. 17, no. 4 (Spring 1993), pp. 52–67.

53. Ronald Steel, "Europe After the Superpowers," in Kegley and Wittkopf, *The Future of American Foreign Policy,* p. 170.

54. Most proposals imagined a transition period during which NATO would continue to exist for some time side-by-side with a new organization. See, for example: Richard Ullman, *Securing Europe* (Princeton: Princeton University Press, 1991); and Charles A. Kupchan and Clifford Kupchan, "Concerts, Collective Security, and the Future of Europe," *International Security*, vol. 16, no. (Summer 1991), pp. 114–61.

55. Address by Robert Zoellick, "The New Europe in a New Age: Insular, Itinerant, or International? Prospects for an Alliance of Values," *Current Policy,* no. 1300, U.S. Department of State, p. 2.

56. "America Can't Afford to Turn Inward," *NPQ* (Summer 1992), p. 8. Assistant Secretary of State Niles told Congress on several occasions that the Administration would not oppose the so-called Franco-German Corps, or Eurocorps, if it did not detract from or undermine NATO. Niles even said that there were potential benefits in the proposal in that it might bring French military forces closer to NATO. See House Foreign Affairs Committee, Developments in Europe, October 1991, p. 32; and U.S. Congress, 102nd Cong., 2d sess., House Foreign Affairs Committee, Hearings: *Developments in Europe, June 1992* (Washington, D.C.: GPO, 1993), p. 29.

57. *The New York Times,* 13 May 1993.

58. Secretary Christopher, "NATO and US Foreign Policy," *U.S. Department of State Dispatch*, vol. 4, no. 9 (March 1, 1993) p. 120.

59. In fact, Congress had earlier set a ceiling on U.S. troops in Europe of 100,000 by FY 1996. On the *Bottom-Up Review,* see Les Aspin, Secretary of Defense, *Force Structure Excerpts: Bottom-Up Review,* 1 September 1993, p. 14. Clinton and Christopher also stressed this number. See President Clinton, German Chancellor Kohl, "U.S.-German

Relations," *U.S. Department of State Dispatch*, vol. 4, no. 14 (April 5, 1993), p. 203; and Secretary Christopher, "U.S. Leadership After the Cold War: NATO and Transatlantic Security," *U.S. Department of State Dispatch*, vol. 4, no. 25 (June 21, 1993), p. 448.

60. Secretary Christopher, "U.S. Leadership After the Cold War," p. 450.

61. Secretary Christopher, "NACC's Essential Role," *U.S. Department of State Dispatch*, vol. 4, no. 25 (June 21, 1993), p. 454, and "NATO and U.S. Foreign Policy," p. 120. At his confirmation hearing, Christopher said that "the promise of Article 43 can be fulfilled in a number of different ways. One of the most interesting options is to use organizations like NATO to fulfill it. NATO is really in search of a role." U.S. Congress, 103rd Cong., 1st sess., Senate Foreign Relations Committee, Hearings: *Nomination of Warren M. Christopher to Be Secretary of State* (Washington, D.C.: GPO, 1993), p. 113.

62. William Drozdiak, "Rewriting the Lyrics to 'Over There,'" *Washington Post National Weekly Edition*, 17–23 January 1994, p. 19.

63. Secretary Christopher, "New Steps Toward Conflict Resolution in the Former Yugoslavia," *U.S. Department of State Dispatch*, vol. 4, no. 7 (February 15, 1993), pp. 81–82.

64. Senate Foreign Relations Committee, *Relations in a Multipolar World*, p. 271.

65. I. M. Destler and Michael Nacht, "Beyond Mutual Recrimination," in Kegley and Wittkopf, *The Future of American Foreign Policy*, pp. 214–16.

66. Lee Kuan Yew, "Japan: From Economic Clout to Political Influence," *Global Affairs*, vol. 8, no. 1 (Winter 1993), p. 18.

67. R. Jeffrey Smith, "Fire Sale on Weapons," *Washington Post National Weekly Edition*, 16–22 March 1992, p. 16.

68. According to some estimates, China now has the third largest economy in the world and is fast headed for second place. A CIA report presented to Congress in late July 1993 said that China had a GDP of $2.35 trillion, matching Japan's and growing at 13 percent a year. *The New York Times*, 1 August 1993.

69. Gerald Segal, "The Coming Confrontation Between China and Japan?" *World Policy Journal*, vol. 10, no. 2 (Summer 1993), p. 28. See also Zakaria Haji Ahmad, "Japan and China in Pacific Asia's Evolving Security Environment," *Global Affairs*, vol. 7, no. 1 (Winter 1993), pp. 26–35.

70. Tatsumi Okabe, "A Proposal for Lasting Security in East Asia," *Japan Review of International Affairs*, vol. 6, no. 2 (Fall 1992), p. 226.

71. Reihard Drifte, *Japan's Foreign Policy* (London: Routledge, 1990), p. 53. For a much more optimistic view of Japanese-ASEAN relations (to be presented in greater depth in later chapters), see Harry H. Kendall and Clara Jeowono, eds., *Japan, ASEAN, and the United States* (Berkeley, Calif.: Institute of East Asian Studies, 1991).

72. For an excellent review of the literature on Southeast Asian security issues, see Jason D. Lewis, "Southeast Asia—Preparing for a New World Order," *The Washington Quarterly*, vol. 16, no. 1 (Winter 1993), pp. 187–200.

73. The literature analyzing U.S.-Japan relations has proliferated rapidly in recent years. For a small sampling, see Michael Mastanduno, "Do Relative Gains Matter? America's Response to Japanese Industrial Policy," *International Security*, vol. 16, no. 1 (Summer 1991), pp. 73–113; Yoichi Funabashi, "Japan and America: Global Partners,"

Foreign Policy, no. 86 (Spring 1992), pp. 24–39; Howard H. Baker, Jr., and Ellen L. Frost, "Rescuing the U.S.-Japan Alliance," *Foreign Affairs*, vol. 71, no. 2 (Spring 1992), pp. 97–113; Ernst-Otto Czempiel, "U.S.-Japan Relations in a Post–Cold War Context," *Japan Review of International Affairs*, vol. 6, no. 3 (Fall 1992), pp. 300–321; Joseph S. Nye, Jr., "Coping With Japan," *Foreign Policy*, no. 89 (Winter 1992/93), pp. 96–115; Selig Harrison and Clyde V. Prestowitz, Jr., "Pacific Agenda: Defense or Economics?" *Foreign Policy*, no. 79 (Summer 1990), pp. 77–93.

74. Alan D. Romberg, "U.S.-Japan Relations in a Changing Strategic Environment," in Allison and Treverton, *Rethinking American Security*, p. 371.

75. I. M. Destler and Michael Nacht, "Beyond Mutual Recrimination," pp. 214–16. For an extreme version of this scenario, see George Friedman and Meredith LeBard, *The Coming War with Japan* (New York: St. Martin's Press, 1990).

76. U.S. Congress, 102nd Cong., 2d sess., House Armed Services Committee, Hearings: *Regional Threats and Defense Options for the 1990s* (Washington, D.C.: GPO, 1993), p. 285.

77. In 1992, the PRC's National People's Congress passed legislation officially declaring all disputed territories in the East and South China seas "inalienable Chinese territory." James B. Linder, "Chinese Military Strategy," *Global Affairs*, vol. 8, no. 1 (Winter 1993), p. 69. In an assessment of the dispute over the Spratleys, one Singaporean analyst wrote: "The islands have great political symbolism, particularly in China: by controlling the islands, China could spread its wings to cover, in a geographical sense, almost half of Southeast Asia. This geographical reach is intended to match Beijing's political power. . . . The unequivocal political message is that China should be recognized as the most powerful force in the region. . . . The 'Chinese threat' has come alive again in Southeast Asia." Ton That Tien, "Southeast Asia's Post–Cold War Geopolitics," *Global Affairs*, vol. 7, no. 1 (Winter 1993), pp. 44–45.

78. For an interesting analysis of the Kurile issue (especially its significance in Russian domestic politics) and Russia policy toward Japan and East Asia more generally, see Leszek Buszynski, "Russia and the Asia-Pacific Region," *Pacific Affairs*, vol. 65, no. 2 (Summer 1992), pp. 486–509.

79. Douglas M. Johnston, "Anticipating Instability in the Asia-Pacific Region," *The Washington Quarterly*, vol. 15, no. 3 (Summer 1992), pp. 104–5.

80. Harry Harding, "American Security in the Pacific Rim," in John Weltman et al., eds., *Challenges to American National Security* (New York: Plenum Press, 1991), p. 142.

81. Okabe, "A Proposal for Lasting Security in East Asia," p. 226.

82. For specific figures on increases, see Michael T. Klare, "The Next Great Arms Race," *Foreign Affairs*, vol. 72, no. 3 (Summer 1993), p. 139.

83. Gerald Segal, "Managing New Arms Races in the Asia/Pacific," *The Washington Quarterly*, vol. 15, no. 3 (Summer 1992), p. 83.

84. For a good analysis of the nature of these purchases, see *Ibid.*, pp. 83–10; and Klare, "The Next Great Arms Race," pp. 138–45.

85. Mark Kramer has argued that Chinese arms can be directly linked to its regional ambitions: "It seems clear that one of the specific motivations all along for the Chinese arms buying spree was Beijing's desire to stake out as formidable a position as

possible for a future confrontation over the Spratleys. Were that not the case, it would be hard to explain why the Chinese authorities purchased amphibious assault ships, why they brought supply vessels to sustain far-flung operations in the South China Sea, why China was intent on developing an in-flight refueling capability . . . and why the PRC sought to acquire 18 TU–160 Blackjack heavy bombers from Ukraine." Mark Kramer, "The Global Arms Trade After the Persian Gulf War," *Security Studies*, vol. 2, no. 2 (Winter 1992/93), p. 265. Admiral Linder, the former commander of U.S. forces in Taiwan, argues similarly that "Beijing's current military strategy of small wars is calculated to make the PRC a dominant regional power," and that "given its declared policies, its military doctrine, and the calculated emergence of its special forces, the Beijing regime has evolved into a serious security threat to the region." Linder, "Chinese Military Strategy," pp. 69–70.

86. Klare, "The Next Great Arms Race," p. 144.

87. Johnston, "Anticipating Instability in the Asia-Pacific Region," p. 106.

88. For details on APEC, see Donald Crone, "The Politics of Emerging Pacific Cooperation," *Pacific Affairs*, vol. 65, no. 1 (Spring 1992), pp. 68–83.

89. U.S. Congress, 102nd Cong., 1st sess., Senate Foreign Relations Committee, Hearings: *Overview of Foreign Assistance* (Washington, D.C.: GPO, 1991), p. 21.

90. House Committee on Appropriations, *Department of Defense Appropriations for 1993*, p. 679.

91. Statement of the Director of Central Intelligence before the Senate Armed Services Committee, 22 January 1992, p. 13.

92. U.S. Congress, 101st Cong., 2d sess., Senate Armed Services Committee, Hearings: *The President's Report on the U.S. Military Presence in East Asia* (Washington, D.C.: GPO, 1990). The views of the report would be regularly echoed in the early 1990s, at times almost verbatim, by U.S. military officials in explaining the need for continued presence in East Asia. For example, in early 1991, Admiral Charles Larson, head of the U.S. Pacific Command, commented on America as balancer: "No other power is currently able or acceptable to play such a role. The great majority of Pacific nations openly welcome the stabilizing U.S. forward presence, and any U.S. reluctance to continue in this role would be inherently destabilizing. . . . A security vacuum could develop which other nations might be tempted or compelled to fill." U.S. Congress, 102nd Cong., 1st sess., House Committee on Appropriations, Hearings: *Department of Defense Appropriations for 1992* (Washington, D.C.: GPO, 1992), p. 71.

93. Winston Lord, "Statement Before the Senate Foreign Relations Committee," Washington, D.C., 31 March 1993," U.S. Department of State Dispatch, vol. 4, no. 14 (April 5, 1993), p. 220. See also: Winston Lord, "East Asia and the Pacific: U.S. Policy and Assistance," *U.S. Department of State Dispatch,* vol. 4, no. 21 (May 24, 1993), p. 380; and Secretary Christopher, "The United States: A Full Partner in a New Pacific Community," *U.S. Department of State Dispatch,* vol. 4, no. 31 (August 2, 1993), pp. 449–50.

94. Aspin, *Force Structure Excerpts,* p.14.

95. Clinton gave an extensive statement of U.S. economic policy toward East Asia in an address to a university in Tokyo on July 7, 1993. President Clinton, "Building a New Pacific Community," *U.S. Department of State Dispatch,* vol. 4, no. 28 (July 12, 1993), pp. 485–88.

96. Lord, "Statement Before the Senate Foreign Relations Committee," pp. 220–21.

97. *The New York Times,* 27 July 1993. For Christopher's statement in Singapore, see Christopher, "The United States: A Full Partner in a New Pacific Community," pp. 549–51. See also Winston Lord, "Vision for a New Pacific Community," *U.S. Department of State Dispatch*, vol. 4, no. 36 (September 6, 1993), p. 613.

98. *The New York Times,* 27 July 1993.

99. *The New York Times,* 8 March 1992. For more on the history and significance of this document, see the June 1992 testimony of I. Lewis Libby, Deputy Under Secretary of Defense for Policy, in Senate Armed Services Committee, Defense Planning Guidance and Security Issues.

100. *The New York Times,* 24 May 1992. In his testimony, Libby echoed the central thrust of the original document: "It is not in our interests or those of the other democracies to stand back and leave a vacuum in regions critical to our interests and thereby increase the chances of returning to earlier periods when multiple military powers balanced one against another in what passed for security structures while regional or even global peace hung in the balance." *Ibid.*, p. 6.

101. For a good analysis of the second draft of this document, see Francis Fukuyama, "The Beginning of Foreign Policy," *The New Republic,* 17 and 24 August 1992, pp. 30–32.

102. The 1991 Summer Study was organized by the Director of the Office of Net Assessment. Layne, "The Unipolar Illusion," p. 6.

103. Dick Cheney, "Active Leadership? You Better Believe It," *The New York Times,* 15 March 1992, p. E-17.

104. See Statement of the Secretary of Defense Dick Cheney Before the Senate Armed Services Committee in Connection with the FY 1993 Budget for the Department of Defense, 31 January 1992, pp. 4–5.

105. House Foreign Affairs Committee, *The Future of U.S. Foreign Policy in the Post–Cold War Era,* p. 424.

106. As Charles William Maynes wrote in early 1990: "For most of the postwar period the majority of Third World countries were of immediate interest to the United States only because of Cold War considerations. . . . American involvement in such different and insignificant states as Chad, Grenada, and Laos can only be explained by reference to the larger global struggle. . . . If the Cold War ends, therefore, it seems to follow that most of America's security concerns in the Third World will disappear." Charles William Maynes, "America Without the Cold War," *Foreign Policy*, no. 78, (Spring 1990), p. 10.

107. Robert Kimmitt, "Impact of Recent World Changes on U.S. Defense and Foreign Policies," *Current Policy*, no. 1260, p. 3.

108. For scholarly arguments to this effect, see Robert Jervis, "The Future of World Politics: Will It Resemble the Past?" *International Security*, vol. 16, no. 3 (Winter 1991/92), pp. 59–61, and Stephen David, "Why the Third World Still Matters," *International Security*, vol. 17, no. 3 (Winter 1992/93), pp. 142–48.

109. Zoellick, "The New Europe in a New Age," p. 2. Wolfowitz made the same

point in April 1991 testimony to Congress, and elsewhere. Statement of the Under Secretary of Defense Paul Wolfowitz before the Senate Committee on Armed Services, 11 April 1991, p. 8.

110. Alberto R. Coll, "American as the Grand Facilitator," *Foreign Policy*, no. 87 (Summer 1992), p. 49. At the time of the writing, Coll served in the Pentagon as principal deputy assistant secretary of defense for special operations and low-intensity conflict.

111. For analyses of the connection between environmental degradation, economic stagnation, and political instability in the Third World, see Thomas F. Homer-Dixon, "On the Threshold: Environmental Changes as Causes of Acute Conflict," *International Security*, vol. 16, no. 2 (Fall 1991), pp. 76–116; Robert Myers, "Environment and Security," *Foreign Policy*, no. 74 (Spring 1989), pp. 23–41; and Jessica Tuchman Matthews, "Redefining Security," *Foreign Affairs*, vol. 68, no. 2 (Spring 1989). In outlining future security threats, annual posture statements by the U.S. Army began mentioning "competition for scarce resources," "environmental degradation," and "uneven economic development" in the early 1990s. See, for example, the FY 1993 statement in House Committee on Appropriations, Department of Defense Appropriations for 1993, p. 161.

112. For a comprehensive look at this argument, see Stephen R. David, "Why the Third World Matters," in John J. Weltman et al., eds., *Challenges to American National Security in the 1990s* (New York: Plenum, 1991), pp. 179–203.

113. Robert Gates, "Change, Hope and Uncertainty," p. 15.

114. Secretary Baker, "After the NATO Summit: Challenges for the West in a Changing World," *Current Policy*, no. 1181, p. 3.

115. Paul Wolfowitz, "Strategic Planning in Today's Dynamic Times," *Defense 90* (January/February 1990), pp. 8–11.

116. For a good overview of this topic, see Lewis A. Dunn, "New Weapons and Old Enmities: Proliferation, Regional Conflict, and Implications for U.S. Strategy in the 1990s," in Weltman et al., eds., *Challenges to American National Security in the 1990s*, pp. 179–203. For a specific analysis of nuclear proliferation, see Leonard Spector, *Nuclear Ambitions* (Boulder, Colo.: Westview Press, 1990).

117. Stephen David argues this point in some depth. David, "Why the Third World Still Matters," pp. 151–55.

118. Kimmitt, "Impact of Recent World Changes on U.S. Defense and Foreign Policies," p. 3.

119. Remarks by Anthony Lake, "From Containment to Enlargement," Washington, D.C., 21 September 1993, p. 9.

120. Aspin, *Force Excerpts: Bottom-Up Review,* p. 10.

121. Aspin said in March, for example, that the United States doesn't want to "only be able to fight in those situations where allies help." Speech by Secretary of Defense Aspin at the National Defense University, Washington, D.C., 25 March 1993, p. 3. Lake said in September that the United States must be prepared to strike at 'backlash' states "decisively and unilaterally." Lake, "From Containment to Enlargement," p. 9.

4: REALISM VS. IDEALISM IN POST–COLD WAR
FOREIGN POLICY

1. Morgenthau, *Politics Among Nations: The Struggle for Power and Peace*, 4th ed. (New York: Knopf, 1967), p. 29.

2. Bush quoted in address by Robert Gates, "The Future of American Intelligence," Langley, Virginia, 4 December 1991, p. 1.

3. Address by Paul Wolfowitz, "North American, European, and Japanese Security: An American Perspective," 18 June 1990, p. 14.

4. Francis Fukuyama, *The End of History and the Last Man* (New York: The Free Press, 1992), p. 246.

5. Robert Jervis, "Cooperation Under the Security Dilemma," *World Politics*, vol. 30, no. 2 (January 1978), pp. 167–214. For a broader and richly textured discussion on how tensions can spiral out of control, see Robert Jervis, *Perception and Misperception in International Politics* (Princeton: Princeton University Press, 1976).

6. U.S. Congress, 102nd Cong., 1st sess., House Armed Services Committee, Hearings: *Potential Threats to American Security in the Post–Cold War Era* (Washington, D.C.: GPO, 1992), p. 8.

7. Statement of Robert Gates before the Senate Armed Services Committee, 22 January 1992, pp. 2, 5–6.

8. John Mearsheimer, "Back to the Future: Instability in Europe After the Cold War," *International Security*, vol. 15, no. 1 (Summer 1990), pp. 33–34.

9. U.S. Congress, 102nd Cong., 2d sess., House Committee on Appropriations, Hearings: *Department of Defense Appropriations for 1993* (Washington, D.C.: GPO, 1992), pp. 544–45.

10. *The New York Times,* 8 March 1992.

11. Kenneth N. Waltz, "The Emerging Structure of International Politics," *International Security*, vol. 18, no. 2 (Fall 1993), p. 66.

12. Christopher Layne, "The Unipolar Illusion: Why New Great Powers Will Rise," *International Security*, vol. 17, no. 4 (Spring 1993), pp. 5–51.

13. Mearsheimer, "Back to the Future," pp. 46–47.

14. Waltz stresses that these concerns will be intense even if the use of military force in the future is not seen as likely. Waltz, "The Emerging Structure of International Politics," p. 60.

15. Francis Fukuyama, "The End of History," *The National Interest,* no. 16 (Summer 1989), pp. 3–18.

16. Michael Doyle, "Kant, Liberal Legacies, and Foreign Affairs," Part 1, *Philosophy and Public Affairs*, vol. 12, no. 3 (Summer 1983), pp. 205–35; Part 2, *Philosophy and Public Affairs*, vol. 12, no. 4 (Fall 1983), pp. 323–53; and "Liberalism and World Politics," *American Political Science Review*, vol. 89, no. 4 (December 1986), pp. 1151–69.

17. Samuel Huntington, "No Exit: The Errors of Endism," *The National Interest,* no. 17 (Fall 1989), pp. 6–7. See also Waltz, "The Emerging Structure of International Politics," p. 78.

18. U.S. Congress, 101st Cong., 2nd sess., Senate Foreign Relations Commit-

tee, Hearings: *Relations in a Multipolar World* (Washington, D.C.: GPO, 1991), pp. 185–87.

19. Mearsheimer, "Back to the Future," p. 50.

20. Secretary Baker, "Democracy and American Diplomacy," *Current Policy*, no. 1266, p. 2.

21. For statements to this effect by each individual, see President Clinton, "A Strategic Alliance with Russian Reform," *U.S. Department of State Dispatch*, vol. 4, no. 14 (April 5, 1993), pp. 190–91; Secretary Christopher, "Support for Global Human Rights Strengthens Democracy at Home," *U.S. Department of State Dispatch*, vol. 4, no. 18 (May 3, 1993), p. 312; Statement of Secretary of Defense Les Aspin Before the House Armed Services Committee in Connection with the Clinton Defense Plan, 30 March 1993, p. 4; remarks by Anthony Lake, "From Containment to Enlargement," 21 September 1993.

22. Joseph M. Grieco, "Anarchy and the Limits of Cooperation: A Realist Critique of the Newest Liberal Institutionalism," *International Organization*, vol. 42, no. 3 (Summer 1988), p. 487.

23. Senate Foreign Relations Committee, *Relations in a Multipolar World*, p. 187.

24. Michael Mastanduno, "Do Relative Gains Matter? America's Response to Japanese Industrial Policy," *International Security*, vol. 16, no. 1 (Summer 1991), pp. 73–113. Another poll, taken in 1990, revealed that 60 percent of Americans believed that Japanese economic power threatened U.S. vital interests while only 33 percent said the same thing about Soviet military power. John E. Reilly, ed., *American Public Opinion and U.S. Foreign Policy 1991* (Chicago: Chicago Council on Foreign Relations, 1991), p. 20. A July 1993 poll revealed that 64 percent of Japanese describe U.S.-Japan relations as unfriendly, up from 55 percent in May 1987. The poll also found that 45 percent of Americans think Japanese companies are competing unfairly, while 85 percent of Japanese think Japan is being blamed for America's own economic problems. *The New York Times,* 6 July 1993.

25. Waltz, *Theory of International Politics,* pp. 151–57.

26. Although Samuel Huntington's argument about the clash of civilizations doesn't explicitly express pessimism regarding relations among democracies, he does suggest that this clash can be so primal as to overwhelm ideological or economic solidarity. Samuel P. Huntington, "If Not Civilizations, What? Paradigms of the Post–Cold War World," *Foreign Affairs*, vol. 72, no. 5 (November/December 1993), pp. 186. See also Samuel P. Huntington, "The Clash of Civilizations?" *Foreign Affairs*, vol. 72, no. 3 (Summer 1993), pp. 22–49.

27. *The New York Times,* 4 February 1992; *The New York Times,* 4 March 1992.

28. Waltz, "The Emerging Structure of International Politics," pp. 55–71.

29. Layne, "The Unipolar Illusion," p. 39.

30. Fukuyama, *The End of History and the Last Man,* p. 276

31. James M. Goldgeier and Michael McFaul, "A Tale of Two Worlds: Core and Periphery in the Post–Cold War Era," *International Organization*, vol. 46, no. 2 (Spring 1992), p. 470.

32. This term is used here, and will be used throughout, to include all spending on defense, foreign aid, and intelligence.

33. Secretary Baker, "Power for Good," *Department of State Bulletin*, June 1989, p. 9.

34. Secretary Baker, "U.S. Foreign Policy Priorities and FY 1991 Budget Request," *U.S. Department of State Dispatch*, 3 September 1990, p. 1.

35. Secretary Baker, "Democracy and American Diplomacy," *Current Policy*, no. 1266, pp. 2–3.

36. Roger W. Sullivan, "Discarding the China Card," *Foreign Policy*, no. 86 (Spring 1992), pp. 3–23.

37. See, for example, Kenneth R. Timmerman, *The Death Lobby: How the West Armed Iraq* (Boston: Houghton-Mifflin, 1991).

38. U.S. Congress, 103rd Cong., 1st sess., House Foreign Affairs Committee, Hearings: *The Future of U.S. Foreign Policy (Part II): Functional Issues* (Washington, D.C.: GPO, 1993), pp. 450–51. Of course, putting an exact figure on money spent on democracy promotion is difficult, since definitions can vary. One could argue, for example, that the over $2 billion in annual aid to Egypt is promoting democracy since any chance of this country advancing further toward stable democratic governance hinges on economic stability, which in turn depends on U.S. support. Or it can be said that the aid given to Nicaragua after the Sandinistas lost power in an election was aimed at promoting democracy by helping to bolster the position of the new government. It is also widely argued by U.S. military officials that money spent on military training and education programs helps promote democracy by teaching foreign military officers to accept civilian leadership of the armed forces.

39. International Affairs Budget Request, FY 1993, Department of State, Bureau of Public Affairs, 29 January 1992.

40. Theodore Sorenson, "Rethinking National Security," *Foreign Affairs*, vol. 69, no. 3 (Summer 1990), pp. 1–18.

41. Joshua Muravchik, *Exporting Democracy: Fulfilling America's Destiny* (Washington, D.C.: American Enterprise Institute Press, 1991).

42. Larry Diamond, "Promoting Democracy," *Foreign Policy*, no. 87 (Summer 1992), p. 37.

43. For a good overview of this issue, see Graham T. Allison, Jr., and Robert P. Beshel, Jr., "Can the United States Promote Democracy?" *Political Science Quarterly*, vol. 107, no. 1 (1992), pp. 81–98.

44. *The New York Times,* 2 October 1992.

45. Secretary Christopher, "Democracy and Human Rights: Where America Stands," *U.S. Department of State Dispatch*, vol. 4, no. 25 (June 21, 1993), p. 441.

46. President Clinton, "A Strategic Alliance with Russian Reform," *U.S. Department of State Dispatch*, vol. 4, No. 14 (April 5, 1993), p. 190.

47. Interview with author. The final results of this undertaking were not known as of this writing. But Matthews indicated that the focus of U.S. policy would be on aiding existing democracies. "I think there is a pretty strong consensus that you want to put your efforts into fertile soil. That is, into countries where there already is a commitment to moving in the direction that we would like to see

societies moving in. Democracy is not something that you can impose. It is something, however, that you can fertilize where it is growing."

48. Statement of Secretary of Defense Les Aspin before the Senate Armed Services Committee in connection with the Clinton Defense Plan, 1 April 1993, p. 4.

49. Les Aspin, Commencement Address at Beloit College, 16 May 1993, p. 2.

50. Carroll J. Doherty, "House Forgoes Usual Reluctance on Foreign Aid to Pass Bill," *Congressional Quarterly,* 19 June 1993, p. 1583.

51. DOD requested $2.2 billion for the F-22 fighter in FY 1994. Statement of Secretary of Defense Les Aspin before the House Armed Services Committee, p. 24.

52. The State Department explicitly said as much later in a press release: "President Bush, a former ambassador to the U.N., signaled our commitment by inviting the U.N. Secretary General to the White House before any other world leader." Rochelle Stanfield, "Back in Fashion," *National Journal,* 4 October 1989, p. 2688.

53. U.S. Congress, 101st Cong., 2nd sess., Senate Foreign Relations Committee, Hearings: *Supplemental State Department Authorization, S. 2296* (Washington, D.C.: GPO, 1990), pp. 14–15.

54. Rochelle Stanfield, "Back in Fashion," p. 2688.

55. For an argument to this effect, see David J. Scheffer, "Use of Force After the Cold War: Panama, Iraq, and the New World Order," in Council on Foreign Relations, *Right v. Might: International Law and the Use of Force,* 2d ed. (New York: Council on Foreign Relations Press, 1991), pp. 111–24.

56. Soviet Foreign Minister Eduard Shevardnadze reiterated Soviet proposals in a September 1990 speech to the General Assembly once the Gulf crisis began. Eduard Shevardnadze, "The Rebirth of the U.N.," *Vital Speeches,* vol. 17, no. 1 (October 15, 1990), pp. 8–12. See also John Mackinlay and Jarat Chopra, "Second Generation Multinational Options," *The Washington Quarterly,* vol. 15, no. 3 (Summer 1992), pp. 115–16

57. For a discussion of how the Military Staff Committee is supposed to function see Edward C. Luck and Toby Trister Gati, "Whose Collective Security?" *The Washington Quarterly,* vol. 15, no. 2 (Spring 1992), p. 50.

58. President Bush, "Toward a New World Order," address before a joint session of Congress, 11 September 1990. *U.S. Department of State Dispatch,* vol. 1, no. 3 (September 17, 1990), p. 92. For a more in-depth early definition of the New World Order, see the 4 September 1990, testimony by Secretary Baker before the House Foreign Affairs Committtee. U.S. Congress, 101st Cong., 2nd sess., House Committee on Foreign Affairs, Hearings and Markup: *Crisis in the Persian Gulf* (Washington, D.C.: GPO, 1990), pp. 6–12. For an analysis that relates the New World Order concept to Bush's background and personality, see Burt Solomon, "Bush's Beloved New World Order May Entail Some Policing," *National Journal,* 9 March 1991, pp. 594–95.

59. Peacemaking is the use of force to intervene in, and try to affect the outcome of, an ongoing conflict. Peacekeeping is the use of force in the wake of conflicts to help separate belligerents or uphold peace agreements.

60. I do not mean to imply here that the Bush Administration did not see

U.N. political and economic actions against Iraq as central to its strategy for dealing with the crisis. The administration moved deftly from the first hours of the crisis to utilize the Security Council to condemn and punish Iraq. Bob Woodward, *The Commanders* (New York: Simon and Schuster, 1991), pp. 225–26. For concise description of early U.N. actions, see Lawrence Freedman and Efraim Karsh, *The Gulf Conflict 1990–1991: Diplomacy and War in the New World Order* (Princeton: Princeton University Press, 1993), pp. 80–84.

61. For a description of U.S. military attitudes toward the command structure set up in the Gulf, see John D. Morrocco, "U.S. Opposes Formal U.N. Command Role in Middle East," *Aviation Week and Space Technology,* 29 October 1990, p. 23. Secretary General Javier Perez de Cuellar later said that the three permanent Security Council members waging the war-Britain, France, and the United States—did not actively consult him about their military activities but instead provided him only with after-action reports every two or three days. David Morrison, "Beyond NATO," *National Journal,* 23 February 1991, p. 452. For more analysis of the U.N.'s role in managing the Gulf conflict, see Bruce Russett and James S. Sutterlin "The U.N. in a New World Order," *Foreign Affairs,* vol. 70, no. 2 (Spring 1991); and Robert Johansen, "Lessons for Collective Security," *World Policy Journal,* vol. 8, no. 3 (Summer 1991), pp. 561–73.

62. As Secretary Baker told a Congressional Committee on September 8, 1990: "In this effort America must lead, and our people must understand that. We remain the one nation that has the necessary political, military, and economic instruments at our disposal to catalyze a successful collective response by the international community." U.S. Congress, 101st Cong., 2nd sess., Senate Committee on Foreign Relations, Hearings: *U.S. Policy in the Persian Gulf* (Washington, D.C.: GPO, 1990), pp. 10–11.

63. "President's Address Before Joint Session of Congress on the State of the Union, January 29, 1991," *Foreign Policy Bulletin,* January–April 1991, pp. 57–59. Brent Scrowcroft echoed this point in May 1991 speech on the New World Order: "The task cannot be done without us. . . . No one else is in a position to mobilize the world community in such a manner." Address by Brent Scowcroft to the Graduating Class of the Citadel, Charleston, South Carolina, 11 May 1991, p. 8. Other administration officials sounded the theme in speeches around the same time. Address by Robert Gates, "American Leadership in a New World," Vancouver, British Columbia, 7 May 1991; address by Richard Haass, "Beyond the Gulf War: the United States, the Middle East and the Gulf," Washington, D.C., 9 May 1991.

64. Weekly Compilation of Presidential Documents, April 22, 1991, p. 432. For a sampling of the many critical examinations of the New World Order, see Robert W. Tucker and David C. Hendrickson, *The Imperial Temptation: The New World Order and America's Purpose* (New York: Council on Foreign Relations Press, 1992); Ted Galen Carpenter, "New World Disorder," *Foreign Policy,* no. 84 (Fall 1991), pp. 24–39; and Jerry Sanders, "Retreat from World Order: The Perils of Triumphalism," *World Policy Journal,* vol. 8, no 2 (Spring 1991).

65. A leading academic proponent of reviving Article 43 was Richard Gardner, who advocated that the U.N. establish a multinational Rapid Deployment Force of

up to 30,000 troops to move preemptively into zones of likely conflict or deal with small-scale aggression once it occurred. He acknowledged that U.S.-led ad hoc forces would continue to be necessary for dealing with major aggression, such as Iraq's invasion of Kuwait. See Richard Gardner, "Practical Internationalism," in Graham Allison and Gregory F. Treverton, eds., *Rethinking America's Security: Beyond Cold War to New World Order* (New York: W. W. Norton and Company, 1992), pp. 273–75. In 1992, a study sponsored by the United Nations Association and chaired by R. James Woolsey recommended two tiers of U.N. forces: a) a small permanent ready reaction force, under Security Council Command, that is highly trained and motivated and made up of largely homogeneous troops; b) tens of thousands of forces earmarked for rapid transfer to U.N. command from a handful of national armies. These forces would train together occasionally. For larger crises, the Woolsey panel recommended that ad hoc coalitions, ideally made up mostly of pre-earmarked troops, should operate under U.N. authorization but not necessarily U.N. command. Senators David Boren and Joseph Biden, Jr., two leading advocates of reviving Article 43 on Capitol Hill, backed legislation in Congress in 1992 aimed at furthering U.S. cooperation on this goal. For details of the Woolsey Panel and the legislation, see U.S. Congress, 102nd Cong., 2, Senate Foreign Relations Committee, Hearings: *Arming the United Nations Security Council—The Collective Security Participation Resolution, S.J. Res. 325* (Washington, D.C.: GPO, 1992). For other calls to implement Article 43, see Luck and Gati, "Whose Collective Security?"; Mackinlay and Chopra, "Second Generation Multinational Options"; Russett and Sutterlin, "The U.N. in a New World Order"; Johansen, "Lessons for Collective Security."

66. Joseph R. Biden, Jr., *On the Threshold of the New World Order: The Wilsonian Vision and American Foreign Policy in the 1990s and Beyond. Addresses in the United States Senate* (Washington, D.C.: 1992), pp. 45–46.

67. For details on the summit, see Tad Daley, "Can the U.N. Stretch to Fit Its Future?" *Bulletin of Atomic Scientists* (April 1992), pp. 38–42.

68. Luck and Gati, "Whose Collective Security?" p. 53.

69. International Affairs Budget Request, FY 1993, p. 9; Statement of Secretary of Defense Dick Cheney before the Senate Armed Services Committee in Connection with the FY 1993 Budget for the Department of Defense, p. 50.

70. U.S. Congress, 103rd Cong., 1st sess., Senate Foreign Relations Committee, Hearings: *Nomination of Warren M. Christopher to Be Secretary of State* (Washington, D.C.: GPO, 1993), pp. 23–24.

71. Madeline K. Albright, "Building a Collective Security System," *U.S. Department of State Dispatch*, vol. 4, no. 19 (May 10, 1993), pp. 333–34.

72. Madeline K. Albright, "Myths of Peace-Keeping," *U.S. Department of State Dispatch*, vol. 4, no. 26 (June 28, 1993), p. 464.

73. *Ibid.*, p. 466. For more on the issue of management at the U.N., see U.S. Congress, 103rd Cong., 1st sess., House Committee on Foreign Affairs, Hearings: *Management and Mismanagement at the United Nations* (Washington, D.C.: GPO, 1993). The full text of Dick Thornburgh's report to the Secretary General on improving management is reprinted on pp. 71–105.

74. U.S. Congress, 103rd Cong., 1st sess., Senate Foreign Relations Committee, Hearings: *Nomination of Madeline K. Albright to Be United States Ambassador to the United Nations* (Washington, D.C.: GPO, 1993), p. 19.

75. U.S. Congress, 103rd Cong., 1st sess., House Foreign Affairs Committee, Hearings: *Collective Security in the Post–Cold War World* (Washington, D.C.: GPO, 1993), p. 165.

76. *The New York Times,* 28 September 1993.

77. House Foreign Affairs Committee, *Collective Security in the Post–Cold War World,* p. 165.

78. *The New York Times,* 28 September 1993.

79. Bob Dole, "Peacekeeping and Politics," *The New York Times,* 24 January 1994, p. A15.

80. *The New York Times,* 29 January 1994. As codified in PRD-13 and later Presidential Decision Directive 24, approved in April 1994, the Clinton Administration's U.N. policy has four central components. First, and most broadly, U.S. forces will not join a U.N. peacekeeping operation unless the administration believes that international security is threatened, that a major disaster requires outside intervention or that gross violations of human rights need to be addressed. Second, as National Security Advisor Anthony Lake explained in February, the administration will ask a number of hard questions: "Is there a clearly defined mission? A distinct end point? How much will it cost? Are the resources available? What is the likelihood of success?" Third, PDD-25 provides guidance for the command and control of U.S. troops in U.N. operations. American forces could still be placed under foreign U.N. commanders, but this arrangement would be avoided in operations that are considered complex and dangerous. Fourth, the new U.N. policy calls for a more equitable sharing of the financial costs for peacekeeping operations. Under a formula set up in 1973, the United States pays 30 percent of the cost of peacekeeping operations; the Clinton Administration wants to reduce that to 25 percent. Finally, PDD-25 calls for reform efforts to improve the management and efficiency of peacekeeping operations. See Anthony Lake, "The Limits of Peacekeeping," *The New York Times,* 6 February 1994, p. A17.

81. *The New York Times,* 13 September 1993.

82. Robert Gilpin, *War and Change in World Politics* (Cambridge: Cambridge University Press, 1981), p. 34.

83. *Ibid.,* p. 31.

84. David Callahan, *Dangerous Capabilities: Paul Nitze and the Cold War* (New York: HarperCollins, 1990), pp. 92–123.

85. Michael Klare, *Beyond the Vietnam Syndrome: U.S. Interventionism in the 1980s* (Washington, D.C.: Institute for Policy Studies, 1983). Klare argues that, in fact, the divisions separating Democrats and Republicans on the issue of intervention were never very deep and were fading even by the late 1970s.

86. For the views of some Congressional leaders, see "Members Speak Out on Panama," *Congressional Quarterly,* 23 December 1989, p. 3535.

87. It must be noted, however, that world order justifications were not cited as part of the U.S. justification for the Panama invasion. See text of Bush's address to

nation on Panama invasion, *Congressional Quarterly,* 23 December 1989, p. 2534; and Ambassador Thomas Pickering's address to the U.N., "Panama: A Just Cause," *Current Policy,* no. 1240.

88. Bob Woodward, "The Conversion of General Powell," *Washington Post National Weekly Edition,* 25–31 December 1989, p. 16.

89. Baker made reference to this argument in his September 4, 1990, testimony to Congress. U.S. Congress, 101st Cong., 2nd sess., House Foreign Affairs Committee, Hearings: *Crisis in the Persian Gulf* (Washington, D.C.: GPO, 1990), p. 8. Cheney cited commitments to Saudi security by U.S. presidents stretching back to Franklin Roosevelt on December 3, 1990. U.S. Congress, 101st Cong., 2nd sess., Senate Armed Services Committee, Hearings: *Crisis in the Persian Gulf Region: U.S. Policy Options and Implications* (Washington, D.C.: GPO, 1991), pp. 641–43.

90. *Ibid.,* p. 120.

91. *Ibid.,* pp. 115–16.

92. *Ibid.,* p. 329. Perle was known as something of an extremist while in government. But in this instance his views were much in the mainstream. In December 1990, he was involved with a group formed to urge a military solution in the Gulf. Called the Committee for Peace and Security in the Gulf, the group spanned the ideological spectrum of American politics, including prominent liberals like Ann Lewis and Tony Coelho, conservatives like Perle and Jeane Kirkpatrick. The group urged the Bush Administration to resist any diplomatic agreement in the Gulf and to destroy Iraq's power.

93. Bush and his top aides argued that, in Bush's words, "There's nothing to negotiate, other than the acceptance of the United Nations–mandated resolutions." *Weekly Compilation of Presidential Statements,* vol. 26, no. 48, p. 1949. But others suggested that there was plenty of room for discussion with Iraq that would not mean backing away from the U.N. positions. See, for example, the testimony to Congress of Harvard negotiating expert Roger Fisher. U.S. Congress, 101st Cong., 1st sess., Senate Foreign Relations Committee, Hearings: *U.S. Policy in the Persian Gulf* (Washington, D.C.: GPO, 1991), pp. 14–27. Bob Woodward reports that Bush had basically made up his mind to abandon serious efforts at negotiation by mid-December. Woodward, *The Commanders,* p. 345.

94. Since no administration officials have publicly acknowledged the punishment rationale, this point must remain speculative. Clearly, though, the administration did come to see the destruction of Iraq's military capabilities as a goal in itself, unrelated to the goal of compelling a withdrawal from Kuwait. As Cheney said in December 3, 1990 testimony to the Senate Armed Services Committee: "My own personal view is that it is far better for us to deal with him now, while the coalition is intact, while we have the United Nations behind us, while we have some 26 other nations assembled with military forces in the Gulf, than it will be for us to deal with him five or 10 years from now, when the members of the coalition have gone their disparate ways and when Saddam has become an even better armed and more threatening regional super power than he is at present." Senate Armed Services Committee, *Crisis in the Persian Gulf,* p. 650.

95. See, for example, comments by Under Secretary of Defense Paul Wol-

fowitz. U.S. Congress, 102nd Cong., 1st sess., Senate Armed Services Committee, Hearings: *Department of Defense Authorization for Appropriations for Fiscal Years 1992 and 1993* (Washington, D.C.: GPO, 1991), p. 556.

96. U.S. Congress, 102nd Cong., 2d sess., Senate Armed Services Committee, Hearings: *Situation in Bosnia and Appropriate U.S. and Western Responses* (Washington, D.C.: GPO, 1992), p. 70.

97. *Ibid.*, p. 16.

98. Secetary Christopher, "New Steps Toward Conflict Resolution in the Former Yugoslavia," *U.S. Department of State Dispatch*, vol. 4, no. 7 (February 15, 1993), p. 81. President Clinton made a similar point early in his presidency: "I think we have an interest in standing up against the principle of ethnic cleansing. . . . If you look at the turmoil all through the Balkans, if you look at the other places where this could play itself out in other parts of the world, this is not just about Bosnia." Quoted in U.S. Congress, 103rd Cong., 1st sess., Senate Foreign Relations Committee, Report: *To Stand Against Aggression: Milosevic, The Bosnian Republic, and the Conscience of the West* (Washington, D.C.: GPO, 1993), p. vi.

99. Clinton later defended himself from this criticism, saying that critics "who wanted us to do more acted as if there were something I could do to force the British and French to change their positions. . . . But they had all the leverage." Clinton said that British Prime Minister John Major told him his government might fall if he backed intervention in Bosnia. "No government is going to risk falling, even to the most intense pressure by the United States," Clinton said. Ann Devroy and R. Jeffrey Smith, "Bosnia: The Echo of Reversal," *Washington Post National Weekly Edition,* 25–31 October 1993, p. 9.

100. Senate Armed Services Committee, *Situation in Bosnia and Appropriate U.S. and Western Responses,* p. 18. This outlook was central to the thinking about the use of force by JCS Chairman Colin Powell, who was serving as Defense Secretary Caspar Weinberger's military aide in 1983 when 241 Marines were killed in Lebanon. On June 10, 1993, Powell commented: "Before committing our armed forces, we have to be clear about what we want them to achieve. We must always define our political goals. We must be sure that military force is the appropriate way to achieve those goals. Sometimes the issue is straightforward, such as in Kuwait and Somalia. At other times it is far, far more difficult, as in Bosnia." Sidney Blumenthal, "Why Are We In Somalia?" *The New Yorker,* 25 October 1993, p. 58.

101. *Ibid.*, p. 51

102. *The New York Times,* 31 October 1993. Another former Bush Defense Department official, Zalmay M. Khalilzad, made a similar point in November, saying that "Recent events in Somalia and Haiti may have emboldened the North Koreans. . . . " Zalmay M. Khalilzad, "A Deadline on Diplomacy," *The New York Times,* 8 November 1993, p. A19.

5: ARMED FOR PRIMACY

1. For a good overview of the Bush Administration's plans, see Defense Budget Project, *Responding to Changing Threats: A Report of the Defense Budget Project's Task*

Force on the FY 1992–FY 1997 Defense Plan (Washington, D.C.: Defense Budget Project, June 1991). See also Statement of the Secretary of Defense Dick Cheney Before the Senate Armed Services Committee in Connection with the FY 1992–1993 Budget for the Department of Defense, 21 February 1991, pp. 1–22.

2. Remarks by the President at the Aspen Institute Symposium, 2 August 1990, pp. 2–3.

3. Transcript, "The MacNeil/Lehrer NewsHour," 17 January 1992, p. 4.

4. U.S. Congress, 102nd Cong., 2nd sess., Senate Armed Services Committee, Hearings: *Department of Defense Authorization for Appropriation for Fiscal Year 1993 and the Future Years Defense Program, Part 1* (Washington, D.C.: GPO, 1992), p. 93.

5. William W. Kaufmann and John D. Steinbruner, *Decisions for Defense: Prospects for a New Order* (Washington, D.C.: Brookings Institution, 1991), p. 47.

6. Address by General Colin L. Powell to the City Club of San Diego, San Diego, 16 September 1991, p. 15.

7. Statement of General Colin L. Powell before the Senate Armed Services Committee, 20 March 1992, pp. 10–11.

8. Statement of Secretary of Defense Dick Cheney, p. 4.

9. Mentioning the *Bottom-Up Review* in a May 1993 speech, Aspin said: "I have long felt that if we merely cut our Cold War forces from the top, we'd simply wind up with smaller Cold War forces. This review is looking at the threats we face; it's looking at what we need to meet those threats, and it's examining how our existing forces can change to fit those needs." Les Aspin, address to Beloit College, 14 May 1993, p. 3.

10. Les Aspin, *Force Structure Excerpts: Bottom-Up Review*, 1 September 1993; Secretary of Defense Les Aspin, General Colin Powell, *Bottom-Up Review* news briefing, 1 September 1993.

11. Aspin stated on March 25, 1993: "Clearly, when we design the defense budget of the United States now, we've got to be in a position to handle those kinds of regional threats. And frankly, handle them by ourselves, if we must." Aspin said it was better to fight with allies, but the U.S. doesn't want to "only be able to fight in those situations where allies help." Speech by Secretary of Defense Les Aspin at the National Defense University, Washington, D.C., 25 March 1993, p. 3.

12. *The New York Times*, 24 May 1992.

13. Statement by Army Chief of Staff Gordon R. Sullivan before the House Armed Services Committee, 26 February 1992, p. 31.

14. Statement of Colin L. Powell before the Senate Armed Services Committee, 31 January 1992, p. 4. For more on Powell's lessons of World War II see Colin L. Powell, "U.S. Military Doctrine: The Way We Were and Are," *Defense 89* (March/April 1990), pp. 16–20.

15. Remarks by Paul Wolfowitz to the American Bar Association Breakfast, 21 November 1991, pp. 5, 2.

16. In the early 1990s, Powell used the "hollow army" concept to describe U.S. military forces not just after Vietnam but also during previous periods. There were few issues he was more passionate about. As he said shortly before leaving office, in August 1993: "There have been times in our history when we let our

strength go to flab, when we neglected our men and women in uniform, when we tried to take fashionable shortcuts around our basic values of service and honor and discipline. We turned our fleets and armies and squadrons into hollow shells that lacked weapons, that didn't have the parts and the training necessary to put together first class fighting forces. And every time we did that, every time we made that mistake, we ended up paying a price later on, a price that was paid with blood of American youngsters. We paid at Pearl Harbor. We paid at the Pusan Perimeter in Korea. We are not going to pay that price again." Remarks by General Colin L. Powell to the International Platform Association, Washington, D.C., 9 August 1993, p. 3.

17. Statement of Secretary of Defense Dick Cheney, p. 4.

18. For an overview of the issue of overseas bases that focuses on the Third World but also provides some analysis of bases in Europe and Asia, see Michael C. Desch, "Bases for the Future: U.S. Military Interest in the Post–Cold War Third World," *Security Studies*, vol. 2, no. 2 (Winter 1992), pp. 201–24.

19. Joint Military Net Assessment, 1991 (Washington, D.C.: Department of Defense, March 1991), pp. 2-4, 4-2.

20. Statement of Secretary of Defense Dick Cheney, p. 3.

21. Statement of Lt. Gen. James R. Clapper, Jr., USAF, Director, Defense Intelligence Agency, to the Senate Armed Services Committee, 22 January 1992, pp. 11, 3.

22. U.S. Congress, 102nd Cong., 2d sess., House Appropriations Committee, Hearings: *Department of Defense Appropriations for 1993* (Washington, D.C.: GPO, 1992), p. 544.

23. Speech by Secretary of Defense Les Aspin at the National Defense University, Washington, D.C., 25 March 1993, p. 2.

24. Aspin and Powell, *Bottom-Up Review* news briefing, 1 September 1993, p. 22.

25. *The New York Times,* 15 March 1994.

26. Leaked documents about these scenarios were summarized in *The New York Times,* 17 February 1992. This scenario should not necessarily be seen as representing government-wide views since it was later revealed that neither CIA Director Robert Gates nor the State Department's European Bureau were consulted by the Pentagon when it was devising its Lithuania scenario. Instead, the scenarios were based on background information provided by the Defense Intelligence Agency. For Gates's comments on this, see U.S. Congress, 102nd Cong., 2d sess., House Foreign Affairs Committee, Hearings: *The Future of U.S. Foreign Policy in the Post–Cold War Era* (Washington, D.C.: GPO, 1992), p. 216. For the comments of Assistant Secretary of State Thomas M. T. Niles, see U.S. Congress, 102nd Cong., 2d sess., House Foreign Affairs Committee, Hearings: *Developments in Europe,* February 1992 (Washington, D.C.: GPO, 1992), p. 31. Niles dismissed the scenario: "We have no security guarantee extended to Lithuania. I would also say that I don't consider that to be a very likely scenario."

27. James Sherr, "Russian Orthodoxies: Little Change in Military Thinking," *The National Interest*, no. 30 (Winter 1992/93), pp. 41–49. For more sanguine anal-

ysis, see Vladislav Zubok, "Tyranny of the Weak: Russia's New Foreign Policy, *World Policy Journal*, vol. 9, no. 2 (Spring 1992), pp. 191–215. Zubok writes: "Despite the fears of the international community, Russia is simply too weak to hazard expansion or attempt isolation. It is constrained by its own dependency. Whether enthusiastically or involuntarily, then, the Russian knight will choose the path of cooperation and learn to accept the values of openness, integration, and compromise"(p. 191). This issue will be treated in a later chapter.

28. At a November 4, 1993, hearing Secretary Christopher was closely questioned about the doctrine by members of the Senate Foreign Relations Committee. Christopher professed himself unconcerned: "What we're seeing here is Russian military doctrine trying to catch up with the new reality in Russia," he said. Christopher said he saw no evidence that the Russian military was preparing to violate international norms. *The New York Times,* 5 November 1993. In September 1993, Aspin announced that U.S. and Russian forces would conduct joint training operations and begin to exchange officers in military training schools.

29. House Foreign Affairs Committee, Hearings: *The Future of U.S. Foreign Policy in the Post–Cold War Era,* pp. 291–292.

30. Aspin, *Force Structure Excerpts: Bottom-Up Review,* p. 10.

31. Remarks by the President at the Aspen Institute Symposium, 2 August 1990, pp. 4.

32. *Ibid.,* p. 16.

33. U.S. Congress, 102nd Cong., 1st sess., Senate Armed Services Committee, Hearings: *Department of Defense Authorization for Fiscal Years 1992 and 1993* (Washington, D.C.: GPO, 1991), pp. 949–54. For more on this complex issue, see Theodore H. Moran, "The Globalization of America's Defense Industries," *International Security,* vol. 15, no. 1 (Summer 1990), pp. 57–99; and Aaron L. Friedberg, "The End of Autonomy," *Daedalus,* vol. 120, no. 4 (Fall 1991), pp. 69–90.

34. Joint Military Assessment, 1991, pp. 5-2.

35. Senate Armed Services Committee, *Department of Defense Authorization for Fiscal Years 1992 and 1993,* p. 949. For scholarly views, see Ethan B. Kapstein, "Losing Control: National Security and the Global Economy, *The National Interest,* no. 18 (Winter 1989–1990), pp. 85–90, and Moran, "The Globalization of American Defense Industries," pp. 57–99.

36. Samuel Huntington expressed this point in a 1993 article on the virtues of America maintaining a position of primacy. "American national security obviously is weakened to the extent to which the United States becomes dependent upon Japanese technology for its sophisticated weapons," Huntington wrote, citing U.S. reliance on Japan for certain electronic parts during the Gulf War. "In a future war where the United States was not so clearly fighting in Japan's interests, the willingness to supply those parts could easily evaporate." Samuel Huntington, "Why Primacy Matters," *International Security,* vol. 17, no. 4 (Spring 1993), p. 77.

37. U.S. Congress, 102nd Cong., 1st sess., House Committee on Appropriations, Defense Subcommittee, Hearings: *Department of Defense Appropriations for 1992, Part 1* (Washington, D.C.: GPO, 1991), p. 666. Barton Gellman, "A Coming Revolution in Fighter Aircraft," *Washington Post National Weekly Edition,* 29 April–5

May 1991, p. 10. David Callahan, "The F-22: An Exercise in Overkill," *Technology Review* (August/September 1992), pp. 42–49.

38. U.S. Congress, 101st Cong., 2nd sess., House Armed Services Committee, Hearings: *National Defense Authorization Act for FY 1991* (Washington, D.C.: GPO, 1990), p. 332.

39. U.S. Congress, 102nd Cong., 2d sess., Senate Armed Services Committee, Hearings: *Department of Defense Authorization for Appropriation for Fiscal Year 1993 and the Future Years Defense Program, Part 4* (Washington, D.C.: GPO, 1992), p. 26. In an amusing exchange with Senator Carl Levin, Welch denied that the sole original mission of the F-22 had been to counter new Soviet fighters (p. 43).

40. For example, Senator Levin pointed out in early 1992 that the once powerful Soviet Mikoyan aircraft design bureau had shut down. *Ibid.*, p. 53.

41. Joint Military Net Assessment, 1991, p. 5-5.

42. In 1992 testimony to Congress, Powell said that only a few segments of the defense industry deserved such special treatment: "We are going to have to find selected technologies and selected production capability that truly is so unique and so different that you could not reconstitute it over a 2- or 3-year period of warning that a new crisis is emerging. And I think there are probably relatively few of these." U.S. Congress, 102nd Cong., 2d sess., Senate Armed Services Committee, Hearings: *Threat Assessment, Military Strategy and Defense Planning* (Washington, D.C.: GPO, 1992), p. 509.

43. Aspin, *Bottom-Up Review* news briefing, p. 18

44. In a February 1992 paper, Aspin wrote: "In the highly specialized area of naval nuclear propulsion, for example, our production base has already contracted to sole suppliers for key components. For these remaining suppliers there is a minimum level of orders without which they cannot stay in business. . . . If we want to use nuclear propulsion in future ships, we have to ensure that these suppliers remain viable. That may mean sustaining a rate of procurement even if it exceeds our short-term needs." Les Aspin, *Tomorrow's Defense from Today's Industrial Base: Finding the Right Resource Strategy for a New Era,* 12 February 1992, p. 6. Certainly the Navy had not changed its arguments along these lines. A March 1993 Navy document stated: "Nuclear propulsion technology is one area that has been identified as an essential, unique capability which will be difficult to maintain if there were a period in which there is a gap in the production of submarines. Naturally, the best way to retain the nuclear submarine industrial base is to build nuclear submarines." Department of the Navy, 1993 Posture Statement, March 1993, p. 46.

45. Statement of Defense Secretary Cheney, p. 17.

46. For an examination of why there may also be constant tensions between military leaders and civilian officials in a democracy, see Samuel Huntington, *The Soldier and the State: The Theory and Politics of Civil-Military Relations* (Cambridge, Mass.: Harvard University Press, 1964). Huntington argues that much of the tension can be traced to the military's inherently realist view of international politics, an outlook that civilian leaders do not always share.

47. Senate Armed Services Committee, *Department of Defense Authorization for Appropriations for Fiscal Years 1992 and 1993,* p. 12.

48. Statement of Colin Powell, 20 March 1992, p. 11.

49. Address by Colin Powell, Washington, D.C., 21 January 1992, pp. 14–17.

50. Barton Gellman, "This Time the Pentagon Tries a Different Way," *Washington Post National Weekly Edition,* 30 December 1991–5 January 1992, p. 8.

51. *Ibid.*

52. Quoted in Statement of Secretary of Defense Les Aspin before the House Armed Services Committee in Connection with the Clinton Defense Plan, 30 March 1993, p. 28. More concretely, Clinton's first defense budget plan included no cuts for training, maintenance, and other readiness-related activities. "This contrasts sharply with a 17 percent real decline in procurement," noted Aspin. "This illustrates that the end of the Cold War justifies some reductions in procurement, but not in readiness" (p. 6).

53. Department of Defense Appropriations for FY 1991, p. 148.

54. Statement of Colin Powell, 20 March 1992, p. 1.

55. Congressman Les Aspin, *An Approach to Sizing American Conventional Forces for the Post-Soviet Era,* 25 February 1992. See also Morton Kondracke, "The Aspin Papers," *The New Republic,* 27 April 1992, p. 11.

56. Robert J. Lieber, "Oil and Power After the Gulf War," *International Security,* vol. 17, no. 1 (Summer 1992), pp. 154–76.

57. Michael Klare, *Beyond the Vietnam Syndrome: U.S. Interventionism in the 1980s* (Washington, D.C.: Institute for Policy Studies, 1983), pp. 22–23.

58. Gernot Kohler, "Global Apartheid," *Alternatives: A Journal of World Policy,* vol. 4, no. 2 (1978).

59. Klare, *Beyond the Vietnam Syndrome,* p. 17.

60. *Ibid.,* p. 42.

61. See, for example, Robert W. Tucker, "Oil: The Issue of American Intervention," *Commentary* (January 1975), pp. 21–31, and Miles Ignotus, "Seizing Arab Oil," *Harper's* (March 1975), pp. 45–62.

62. For background on the RDF, see David Eshel, *The U.S. Rapid Deployment Force* (New York: Arco Publishing, 1985); Thomas McNaugher, *Arms and Oil: U.S. Military Strategy and the Persian Gulf* (Washington, D.C.: Brookings, 1985); and Jeffrey Record, *The Rapid Deployment Force and U.S. Intervention in the Persian Gulf* (Cambridge, Mass.: Institute for Foreign Policy Analysis, 1983).

63. CIA Director Robert Gates was one of the first Bush Administration officials to cite population growth as a national security threat. See U.S. Congress, House Foreign Affairs Committee, Hearings: *The Future of U.S. Foreign Policy in the Post–Cold War Era* (Washington, D.C.: GPO, 1992), p. 212. For a sweeping analysis of the future of global politics with a Malthusian argument as its centerpiece, see Paul Kennedy, *Preparing for the Twentieth Century* (New York: Random House, 1993). For a more specific argument of this point by an environmental expert who went on to become a top State Department official, see the March 1993 testimony of Jessica Tuchman Matthews, U.S. Congress, 103rd Cong., 1st sess., House Foreign Affairs Committee, Hearings: *The Future of U.S. Foreign Policy (Part II): Functional Issues* (Washington, D.C.: GPO, 1993), pp. 122–23. See also Lester R. Brown, "The New World Order," in Worldwatch Institute, *The State of the World 1991* (W.

W. Norton and Company, 1991), pp. 3–20. See 1991 figures on global poverty from the Overseas Development Council in U.S. Congress, 102nd Cong., 1st sess., Senate Foreign Relations Committee, Hearings: *Overview of Foreign Assistance* (Washington, D.C.: GPO, 1991), p. 55. On the issue of Third World urbanization, development expert John W. Sewell writes: "By the turn of the century, half of the world's population will be urban, and eighteen of the world's twenty-one largest cities will be located in the developing world. Third World cities are growing very fast, but squatter settlements, shantytowns, and low-income neighborhoods within cities are growing about twice as fast." John W. Sewell, "The Metamorphosis of the Third World: U.S. Interests in the 1990s," in Charles W. Kegley, Jr., and Eugene R. Wittkopf, eds., *The Future of U.S. Foreign Policy* (New York: St. Martin's Press, 1992), p. 229.

64. Testimony by General Carl Stiner, Commander in Chief, Special Operations Command. Senate Armed Services Committee, Hearings: *Department of Defense Authorization for Appropriations for Fiscal Years 1992 and 1993,* p. 134. During testimony before the House Armed Services Committee in 1992, Stiner was more specific about how threats to U.S. interests would arise, saying that population growth, gaps between rich and poor, and social upheaval "could lead to the establishment of repressive regimes that may threaten the very security interests the United States is trying to nurture and preserve." U.S. Congress, 102nd Cong., 2d sess., House Armed Services Committee, Hearings: *Regional Threats and Defense Options for the 1990s* (Washington, D.C.: GPO, 1993), pp. 185–86. Army documents from the early 1990s expressed similar concerns. See, for example, the U.S. Army Posture Statement for FY 1992–1993 in U.S. Congress, 102nd Cong., 1st sess., House Armed Services Committee, Hearings: *National Defense Authorization Act for Fiscal Years 1992 and 1993, H.R. 2100* (Washington, D.C.: GPO, 1991), p. 201.

65. *Department of Defense Authorization for Appropriations for Fiscal Years 1992 and 1993,* p. 134.

66. *Discriminate Deterrence: Report of the Commission on Integrated Long-Term Strategy,* January 1988. See also *Supporting U.S. Strategy for Third World Conflict,* June 1988, by the Commission's Working Group on Regional Conflict, pp. 11–13.

67. U.S. Congress, 101st Cong., 1st sess., Senate Armed Services Committee, Hearings: *Nominations Before the Senate Armed Services Committee* (Washington, D.C.: GPO, 1990), p. 178.

68. Paul Wolfowitz, "Strategic Planning in Today's Dynamic Times," *Defense 90* (January/February 1990), pp. 8–11.

69. Senate Armed Services Committee, *Deparment of Defense Authorizations for Fiscal Years 1992 and 1993,* p. 182.

70. Remarks by the President at the Aspen Institute Symposium, 2 August 1990, p. 3–4.

71. Senate Armed Services Committee, *Threat Assessment, Military Strategy and Defense Planning,* p. 509.

72. Statement of Colin Powell, 31 January 1992, p. 8. See also Paul Wolfowitz, "The New Defense Strategy," in Graham Allison and Gregory F. Treverton,

Rethinking America's Security: Beyond Cold War to New World Order (New York: W. W. Norton and Company, 1992), p. 180.

73. Former Defense Department officials also attacked the idea. See, for example, "A New Name for Winning: Losing," Dov S. Zakheim, *The New York Times,* 19 June 1993, p. 21.

74. Aspin, Powell, *Bottom-Up Review* news briefing, p. 6. The *Review* also gave another reason for the policy: "Fielding forces sufficient to win two wars nearly simultaneously provides a hedge against the possibility that a future adversary—or coalition of adversaries—might one day confront us with a larger-than-expected threat." *Force Structure Excerpts: Bottom-Up Review,* p. 10.

75. *The New York Times,* 30 May 1993. For more on this issue, see Dov S. Zakheim and Jeffrey M. Ranney, "Matching Defense Strategies to Resources: Challenges for the Clinton Administration," *International Security*, vol. 18, no. 1 (Summer 1993), pp. 70–78.

76. Aspin, Powell, *Bottom-Up Review* news briefing, p. 8; *The New York Times,* 30 May 1993. Powell explained at the news briefing that war gaming had been used to establish that eight Army divisions (with six reserve divisions), eight carrier battle groups, a much smaller Air Force, and a robust Marine Corps "would give us one major regional conflict capability with some left over. . . . We didn't find this to be an adequate force" (p. 10). He did not specify what degree of allied cooperation Pentagon analysts assumed, although he had previously stated on a number of occasions that the United States had to be prepared to handle major regional contingencies without allied assistance. For more analysis on the specific issue of carriers and naval deployment requirements under a two-war strategy, see the 1991 congressional testimony of Admiral Frank B. Kelso II, Chief of Naval Operations. *Department of Defense Authorizations for Fiscal Years 1992 and 1993,* p. 294. See also "Secretary of the Navy's Posture Statement for 1992–1993," reprinted in *Department of Defense Appropriations for 1992,* pp. 857–82.

77. Statement by Paul Wolfowitz, 11 April 1991, p. 8.

78. Statement by Army Chief of Staff Gordon R. Sullivan, p. 13.

79. On the cost of the C-17 and other lift issues, see the testimony of General Hansford T. Johnson, head of the U.S. Transportation Command. U.S. Congress, 102nd Cong., 2d sess., House Appropriations Committee, Hearings: *Department of Defense Appropriations for 1993* (Washington, D.C.: GPO, 1992), pp. 738–63.

80. Aspin, Powell, *Bottom-Up Review* news briefing, p. 16. For a discussion of the important issue of crew rotation, and explanation for why carriers can only be forward deployed for six months at a time, see the May 1992 testimony of Chief of Naval Operations Admiral Frank Kelso. U.S. Congress, 102nd Cong., 2d sess., Senate Armed Services Committee, *Department of Defense Authorization for Appropriation for Fiscal Year 1993 and the Future Years Defense Program, Part 1,* p. 50. For a discussion of carrier deployment plans envisioned during the 1990s, see Aspin, *Force Excerpts: Bottom-Up Review,* pp. 15–16. It should be noted that the costs of these plans include not just that of keeping twelve carriers on duty, but also that of replacing aging carriers. Navy plans as of 1993 envision adding two new nuclear carriers now under construction to the force in the 1990s, and beginning construc-

tion on two additional ones beyond that, to be commissioned in the early twenty-first century. For details on these plans, see Department of the Navy, *1993 Posture Statement*, p. 25.

81. Senate Armed Services Committee, *Threat Assessment, Military Strategy and Defense Planning*, p. 509.

82. Statement by General Gordon R. Sullivan, Chief of Staff United States Army, before the Senate Armed Services Committee, 19 May 1993, p. 22.

83. House Appropriations Committee, *Department of Defense Appropriations for FY 1991*, pp. 303–6.

84. Aspin, *Force Excerpts: Bottom-Up Review,* p. 17.

85. Senate Armed Services Committee, *Department of Defense Authorizations for Fiscal Years 1992 and 1993*, p. 292.

86. House Armed Services Committee, *Department of Defense Appropriations for 1993*, p. 261.

87. Senate Armed Services Committee, *Department of Defense Authorizations for Fiscal Years 1992 and 1993*, p. 102.

88. "My projection is that within 5 or 10 years, the ocean's surface in the approaches to hostile shores will become a very dangerous place," commented former Chief of Naval Operations Admiral C. A. H. Trost, in 1992. Senate Armed Services Committee, *Department of Defense Authorization for Appropriations for Fiscal Year 1993 and the Future Years Defense Program, Part 1,* p. 443. Navy officials argued that new research and development programs, along with the acquisition of different submarines, would be needed to counter sub threats in shallow water areas. Department of the Navy, *1993 Posture Statement*, p. 25.

89. Senate Armed Services Committee, *Department of Defense Authorization for Appropriations for Fiscal Year 1991*, p. 80.

90. Statement of Donald B. Rice, Secretary of the Air Force, to the House Armed Services Committee, 20 February 1992, p. 16.

91. Statement of the Secretary of Defense Dick Cheney, p. 17. Also on this point, see Dick Cheney, "Persian Gulf Conflict: Lessons Learned," *Defense Issues*, vol. 6, no. 32, p. 5.

92. Aspin, *Force Excerpts: Bottom-Up Review,* p. 4. In his first budget statement to Congress, Aspin implied that America's technological superiority was a central reason for its victory in the Gulf. Statement by Les Aspin, p. 7.

93. U.S. Department of the Air Force, *Reaching Globally, Reaching Powerfully: The United States Air Force in the Gulf War,* September 1991, p. 55.

94. Statement of the Secretary of Defense Dick Cheney, p. 28.

95. Statement of Donald B. Rice, p. 14.

96. General Merrill A. McPeak, Chief of Staff, United States Air Force, Statement Before the Senate Armed Services Committee, 19 May 1993, p. 5.

97. Aspin, *Force Excerpts: Bottom-Up Review,* p. 12.

98. Aspin, Powell, *Bottom-Up Review* news briefing, pp. 13–14. This decision had been made well before the *Bottom-Up Review* was completed. For an explanation of how the change in orientation is reflected in the FY 1994 budget, compared to the FY 1993 budget, see U.S. Congress, 103rd Cong., 1st sess., Senate Appropri-

ations Committee, Hearings: *Department of Defense Appropriations, Fiscal Year 1994* (Washington, D.C.: GPO, 1993), p. 19

99. Statement of the Secretary of Defense Dick Cheney, p. 22.

100. However, Aspin has pressed a plan to provide Japan with the technology needed to build a theater anti-missile system to protect it against a growing North Korean missile threat. Defense officials have also extended similar offers to NATO allies. These steps do appear to lead in the direction of making other Western countries dependent on American protection. Not only would the United States provide the anti-missile technology, but it might also have a large measure of control over the use of such systems because of its unique capabilities in the area of satellite detection systems. Japan, for example, has no military spy satellites of its own because of a ban on using space for military purposes. *The New York Times,* 18 September and 4 November 1993.

101. Statement by Paul Wolfowitz, p. 16.

102. Aspin, *Force Structure Excerpts: Bottom-Up Review,* p. 5.

103. Aspin, Powell, *Bottom-Up Review* news briefing, p. 7.

104. "International Security Relationships," *Defense 89* (September/October 1989), pp. 44–46.

105. Large percentages of the American public have always opposed military aid and arms sales to foreign countries. According to one 1990 poll, public support for such activities dropped between 1986 and 1990. John E. Reilly, ed., *American Public Opinion and U.S. Foreign Policy 1991* (Chicago: Chicago Council on Foreign Relations, 1991), p. 30.

106. For background on the history and political motives behind U.S. arms sales and military assistance, see Michael T. Klare, *American Arms Supermarket* (Austin, Tex.: University of Texas Press, 1984), p. 29–33.

107. See, for example, the June 1990 testimony of State Department officials defending new arms sales to Saudi Arabia. U.S. Congress, 101st Cong., 2nd sess., House Committee on Foreign Affairs, Hearings: *Proposed Sales and Upgrades of Major Defense Equipment to Saudi Arabia* (Washington: GPO, 1991). For an interesting personal account that illuminates how arms sales to Saudi Arabia were seen within the U.S. government during the Carter and Reagean years, see Howard Teicher and Gayle Radly Teicher, *Twin Pillars to Desert Storm: America's Flawed Vision in the Middle East from Nixon to Bush* (New York: William Morrow and Company, 1993). For general background on the U.S.-Saudi defense relationship, see Nadav Safran, *Saudi Arabia: The Ceaseless Quest for Security* (Ithaca, N.Y.: Cornell University Press, 1988).

108. For an articulation of the arguments regarding both Turkey and Egypt's importance after the cold war, see the March 1991 congressional testimony of Lt. Gen. Teddy Allen, Director of the Defense Security Assistance Agency. U.S. Congress, 102nd Cong., 1st sess., Senate Foreign Affairs Committee, Hearings: *Overview of Foreign Assistance* (Washington, D.C.: GPO, 1991), pp. 29–30.

109. Statement of Reginald Bartholomew, 11 June 1991.

110. U.S. Congress, 101st Cong., 2nd sess., Senate Armed Services Committee, Hearings: *Threat Assessment, Military Strategy and Operational Requirements* (Washington, D.C.: GPO, 1990), p. 589.

111. House Committee on Appropriations, *Department of Defense Appropriations for 1993*, p. 581.

112. Testimony of Under Secretary of State Lynn E. Davis before the Senate Appropriations Committee, Subcommittee on Foreign Operations, 12 May 1993, p. 4. See also 1991 testimony by Colin Powell. U.S. Congress, 102nd Cong., 1st sess., House Armed Services Committee, *National Defense Authorization Act for Fiscal Years 1992 and 1993—H.R. 2100*, p. 44.

113. H. Allen Holmes, "FY 1990 Security Assistance Program," *Current Policy*, no. 1159, p. 2.

114. Robert Litwik et al., *Detente and the Nixon Doctrine: American Foreign Policy and the Pursuit of Stability, 1969–1976* (New York: Cambridge University Press, 1984).

115. Testimony of Under Secretary of State Lynn E. Davis before the Senate Appropriations Committee, Subcommittee on Foreign Operations, p. 5.

116. Security assistance is seen as curbing proliferation tendencies in three ways: reassuring potential proliferant states that America is committed to their security and therefore decreasing the fears that drive nations to acquire weapons of mass destruction; inculcating military leaders, through training programs and other contacts with U.S. military officials, in the virtues of cooperation with international regimes; and providing U.S. officials with both carrots and sticks for dealing with proliferators—the carrots being further assistance or access to military technology, the sticks being a cutoff of these things. In 1993, the Clinton Administration sought to use security assistance to more directly curb proliferation by reprogramming $50 million in assistance funds to a new fund that would, among its other goals, seek to educate and train foreign government officials about nonproliferation issues. Testimony of Under Secretary Lynn E. Davis before the Senate Foreign Relations Committee, Subcommittee on International Economic Policy, Trade, Oceans and Environment, 16 June 1993, p. 7.

117. On this point regarding Saudi Arabia, see Under Secretary Bartholomew's October 1990 testimony, in U.S. Congress, 101st Cong., 2nd sess., House Committee on Foreign Affairs, Hearings: *Proposed Sales to Saudi Arabia in Association with the Conduct of Operation Desert Storm* (Washington: GPO, 1991), pp. 50–51.

118. For an example of this kind of reasoning in the Bush Administration, see address by Henry Rowen, Assistant Secretary of Defense for International Security Affairs, "Outlook for Security Assistance and Its Relationship to National Security," MacDill AFB, Florida, 22 May 1990, p. 6. Rowen states that security assistance serves as "a kind of military diplomacy, a process which introduces military personnel from other nations to the professionalism and democratic ethos of our own military. These ties help promote cooperation between the civil and military sectors of society in countries which may not have such a tradition." Under Secretary of State Davis made a similar point in 1993 in defending spending on the International Military Education and Training (IMET) program: "The proposed funding for IMET will help inculcate their militaries in the importance of law, civilian control of the military, legislative oversight, and transparency in defense programs and budgets." Testimony of Under Secretary of State Lynn E. Davis

before the Senate Appropriations Committee, Subcommittee on Foreign Operations, p. 6.

119. U.S. Congress, 101st Cong., 2nd sess., House Committee on Armed Services, *Study by the Congressional Research Service: U.S. Low-Intensity Conflicts, 1899–1990* (Washington, D.C.: GPO, 1990). For a study that focuses on low-intensity conflict in the 1980s, see Michael T. Klare and Peter T. Kornbluh, eds., *Low-Intensity Warfare: Counterinsurgency, Proinsurgency, and Anti-Terrorism in the Eighties* (New York: Pantheon Books, 1988).

120. House Armed Services Committee, *National Defense Authorization Act for Fiscal Years 1992 and 1993—H.R. 2100,* p. 131.

6: A SAFER WORLD: INTERNATIONAL RELATIONS AFTER THE COLD WAR

1. For a good overview of the mounting assault on realism, see Charles W. Kegley, Jr., "The Neoidealist Moment in International Studies? Realist Myths and New International Realities," *International Studies Quarterly*, vol. 37 (1993), pp. 131–46.

2. For three examples of uneven efforts that have been made at blending the liberal critiques of realism, see Robert Jervis, "The Future of World Politics: Will It Resemble the Past?" *International Security*, vol. 16, no. 3 (Winter 1991/92), pp. 46–58; James M. Goldgeier and Michael McFaul, "A Tale of Two Worlds: Core and Periphery in the Post–Cold War Era," *International Organization*, vol. 46, no. 2 (Spring 1992), pp. 467–91; and Fareed Zakaria, "Is Realism Finished?" *The National Interest*, no. 30 (Winter 1992/93), pp. 21–32.

3. For a critique of the concept of anarchy, as it is widely used by realists and others, see Helen Milner, "The Assumption of Anarchy in International Relations Theory: A Critique," *Review of International Studies*, vol. 17, no. 1 (January 1991), pp. 67–85.

4. For a full discussion of Waltz's neorealism that includes excerpts from *Theory of International Politics* and critiques and commentaries on that work, see Robert O. Keohane, *Neorealism and its Critics* (New York: Columbia University Press, 1986). For a work that analyzes Waltz's contribution and then seeks to extend and strengthen structural realism as a coherent theory of the international system, see Barry Buzan, Charles Jones, and Richard Little, *The Logic of Anarchy: Neorealism to Structural Realism* (New York: Columbia University Press, 1993). For a volume in which neorealist views are directly juxtaposed with neoliberalism, see David Baldwin, ed., *Neorealism and Neoliberalism: The Contemporary Debate* (New York: Columbia University Press, 1993).

5. Kenneth Waltz, *Theory of International Politics* (Reading, Mass.: Addison-Wesley, 1979), pp. 161–93.

6. Interestingly, John Mearsheimer and others have argued this point in recent years much more vigorously than Waltz himself. See John Mearsheimer, "Back to the Future," *International Security*, vol. 15, no. 1 (Summer 1990), pp. 5–56. Waltz hardly emphasizes this point at all in a 1993 article—indeed he says that "bipolarity

endures, but in an altered state. Bipolarity continues because militarily Russia can take care of itself and because no other great powers have yet emerged." Kenneth Waltz, "The Emerging Structure of International Politics," *Interational Security*, vol. 18, no. 2 (Fall 1993), p. 52.

7. Robert Gilpin, *War and Change in World Politics* (New York: Cambridge University Press, 1981).

8. *Ibid.*, pp. 231–44.

9. Christopher Layne, "The Unipolar Illusion: Why New Great Power Will Rise," *International Security*, vol. 17, no. 4 (Spring 1993), p. 42.

10. Joseph S. Nye, Jr., "Neorealism and Neoliberalism," *World Politics*, vol. 55, no. 2 (January 1988), p. 235.

11. Thomas J. Christensen and Jack Snyder, "Chain Gangs and Passed Bucks: Predicting Alliance Patterns in Multipolarity," *International Organization*, vol. 44, no. 2 (Spring 1990), pp. 137–68.

12. Layne, "The Unipolar Illusion," p. 35.

13. Layne fails to cite compelling evidence of German and Japanese unhappiness with America's security hegemony. He appears more comfortable with the clear lessons produced by abbreviated historical accounts than the muddy, or contradicting, reality of the contemporary situation that he seeks to explain. His discussion of how the United States uses its hegemony to gain leverage on other issues is extremely brief and hardly proves that the leverage strategy is a central characteristic of U.S. relations with its allies. Nor does he show that these allies are so threatened by that leverage that they seek to mitigate it. Layne suggests that Japan is likely to view its dependence on America's defense of Persian Gulf oil as more threatening in a unipolar world than in a bipolar one. But he cites no evidence that Japan is seriously considering ways to remedy this situation. Overall, Layne's discussion of new Japanese and German geopolitical assertiveness—which he exaggerates—is an unconvincing effort to substantiate his argument because he muddles the basic terms of the debate. Those experts, including U.S. officials, who fear new German and Japanese assertiveness believe that it is likely to stem from a withdrawal of America's security hegemony in Europe and East Asia, not from a deliberate effort to challenge that hegemony. *Ibid.*, pp. 33–39.

14. Robert Jervis, "The Future of World Politics: Will It Resemble the Past?" *International Security*, vol. 16, no. 3 (Winter 1991/92), p. 40.

15. For a good overview of why domestic factors matter in international relations, see Richard Rosecrance and Arthur A. Stein, "Beyond Realism: The Study of Grand Strategy," in Richard Rosecrance and Arthur A. Stein, *The Domestic Bases of Grand Strategy* (Ithaca, N.Y.: Cornell University Press, 1993), pp. 3–21. For a detailed model of how domestic and international policy interacts, see Robert Putnam, "Diplomacy and Domestic Politics," *International Organization*, vol. 42, no. 3 (Summer 1988).

16. For a look at how U.S. executive branch advisory structures, which often reflect presidential personality, can influence foreign policy decisions, see Fred Greenstein and John Burke, *How Presidents Test Reality: Decisions on Vietnam, 1954 and 1965* (New York: Russell Sage Foundation, 1989). On the ways that personal-

ity factors shaped policy during one of the most dangerous periods of the Cold War, the early 1960s, see Michael R. Beschloss, *The Crisis Years: Kennedy and Khrushchev, 1960–1963* (New York: HarperCollins, 1991). On the influence of Nancy Reagan in the area of U.S.-Soviet relations, see Don Oberdorfer, *The Turn: From the Cold War to a New Era, The United States and the Soviet Union, 1983–1990* (New York: Poseidon Press, 1991), p. 91. This type of analysis can also apply to those who advise leaders. America's actions in the immediate postwar era, for example, were profoundly affected by a core group of elite policy advisors who shared a strong internationalist outlook and a commitment to public service. see Walter Isaacson and Evan Thomas, *The Wise Men: Six Friends and the World They Made* (New York: Simon and Schuster, 1986); and Richard Barnet, *Roots of War* (New York: Atheneum Publishers, 1972).

17. This issue has received increasing attention from scholars in recent years, mostly within the context of the Cold War. See George W. Breslauer and Philip E. Tetlock, eds., *Learning in U.S. and Soviet Foreign Policy* (Boulder, Colo.: Westview Press, 1991); Richard E. Neustadt and Ernest R. May, *Thinking in Time: The Uses of History for Decision Makers* (New York: The Free Press, 1986).

18. U.S. Congress, 101st Cong., 2nd sess., Senate Foreign Relations Committee, Hearings: *Relations in a Multipolar World* (Washington, D.C.: GPO, 1991), p. 181.

19. David Abshire, "Strategic Challenge: Contingencies, Force Structures, Deterrence," *The Washington Quarterly*, vol. 15, no. 2 (Spring 1992), pp. 33–34.

20. Michael Doyle, "Kant, Liberal Legacies, and Foreign Affairs," Part 1, *Philosophy and Public Affairs*, vol. 12, no. 3 (Summer 1983), pp. 205–35; Part 2, *Philosophy and Public Affairs*, vol. 12, no. 4 (Fall 1983), pp. 323–53. For Doyle's updated versions of this argument, see "Liberalism and World Politics," *American Political Science Review*, vol. 89, no. 4 (December 1986), pp. 1151–69; and "An International Liberal Community," in Graham Allison and Gregory Treverton, eds., *Rethinking America's Security: From Cold War to New World Order* (W. W. Norton and Company, 1992), pp. 307–33.

21. For an analysis of the competing explanations of what it is about democracies that ensures their peacefulness toward each another—one line of thought emphasizes political culture and liberal solidarity, the other emphasizes domestic constraints on war initiation—see T. Clifton Morgan and Valerie L. Schwebach, "Take Two Democracies and Call Me in the Morning: A Prescription for Peace?" *International Interactions*, vol. 17, no. 4 (1992), pp. 305–20. For a cross-cultural approach using anthropological methods that argues that participatory systems of a variety of types—not just formal democracies—are more peaceful toward one another, see Carol R. Ember, Melvin Ember, and Bruce Russett, "Peace Between Participatory Polities: A Cross-Cultural Test of the 'Democracies Rarely Fight Each Other' Hypothesis," *World Politics*, vol. 44, no. 4 (July 1992), pp. 573–99. For an argument focusing on specific phenomena of preventive war, and which concludes that "Only nondemocratic regimes wage preventive war against rising opponents," see Randall L. Schweller, "Domestic Structures and Preventive War," *World Politics*, vol. 44, no. 2 (January 1992), pp. 235–69.

22. Jack S. Levy, "The Causes of War: A Review of Theories and Evidence," in Robert Jervis et al., eds., *Behavior, Society, and Nuclear War* (New York: Oxford University Press, 1989), p. 270.

23. Francis Fukuyama, "The End of History," *The National Interest,* no. 16 (Summer 1989), p. 4.

24. See Fukuyama's 1990 testimony before Congress. Senate Foreign Relations Committee, *Relations in a Multipolar World,* p. 175.

25. On this point, see Francis Fukuyama, *The End of History and the Last Man* (New York: The Free Press, 1992), p. 276.

26. Layne's argument about the possibility of such conflict is not contingent on backsliding into authoritarianism on the part of Germany and Japan, as is sometimes suggested by other observers. Layne, "The Unipolar Illusion," pp. 42–43.

27. John Mearsheimer, "Back to the Future," p. 49.

28. Samuel P. Huntington, "If Not Civilizations, What? Paradigms of the Post–Cold War World," *Foreign Affairs,* vol. 72, no. 5 (November/December 1993), p. 194. For Huntington's original statement of his argument, see "The Clash of Civilizations?" *Foreign Affairs,* vol. 72, no. 3 (Summer 1993), pp. 22–49.

29. Waltz, "The Emerging Structure of International Politics," p. 78.

30. Samuel Huntington, "No Exit: The Errors of Endism," *The National Interest,* no. 17 (Fall 1989), pp. 3–11.

31. Stephen Van Evera, "Primed for Peace: Europe After the Cold War," *International Security*, vol. 15, no. 3 (Winter 1990/91), p. 26.

32. *Ibid.*, pp. 27–28

33. Mearsheimer, "Back to the Future," p. 50.

34. Robert O. Keohane and Joseph S. Nye, *Power and Interdependence,* 2d ed. (New York: Harper and Row, 1989), p. 3.

35. Charles Lipson, "International Cooperation in Economic and Security Affairs," *World Politics*, vol. 37, no. 1 (October 1984), pp. 1–23; Stephen D. Krasner, ed., *International Regimes* (Ithaca, N.Y.: Cornell University Press, 1983). For a reflection by Keohane and Nye on the arguments of their influential 1977 book a decade later, see Robert O. Keohane and Joseph S. Nye, Jr., "Power and Interdependence Revisited," *International Organization*, vol. 41, no. 2 (Autumn 1987), pp. 725–53. For a succinct contrasting of the new liberal thinking with neorealism, see Nye, "Neorealism and Neoliberalism," *World Politics*, vol. 40, no. 2 (Jaunary 1988), pp. 235–51.

36. Regimes are distinct from institutions and agreements in that they are not necessarily formal arrangements, although they can be. Narrow definitions of regimes see them as multilateral agreements among states that seek to regulate interactions in a given area. A broader definition treats regimes as any kind of patterned behavior governed by norms or rules. For a useful overview on this topic, see Stephen Haggard and Beth A. Simmons, "Theories of International Regimes," *International Organization*, vol. 41, no. 3 (Summer 1987), pp. 491–517.

37. Robert O. Keohane, *After Hegemony: Cooperation and Discord in the World Political Economy* (Princeton, N.J.: Princeton University Press, 1984), pp. 5, 242.

38. Richard Rosecrance, "Force or Trade: The Costs and Benefits of Two

Paths to Global Influence," in Charles W. Kegley, Jr., and Eugene R. Wittkopf, eds., *The Global Agenda: Issues and Perspectives,* 2d ed. (New York: McGraw-Hill Publishing Company, 1988), p. 22; Richard Rosecrance, *The Rise of the Trading State: Commerce and Conquest in the Modern World* (New York: Basic Books, 1986).

39. Keohane and Nye, *Power and Interdependence,* pp. 24–25.

40. *Ibid.,* p. 26. For Kissinger's views on how the energy crisis raised basic questions about international cooperation, see his essay "The Energy Crisis and World Order," in Henry Kissinger, *For the Record: Selected Statements, 1977–1980* (Boston: Little, Brown and Company, 1981), pp. 47–68.

41. For a succinct statement of this view, see Joseph Grieco, "Anarchy and the Limits of Cooperation: A Realist Critique of the Newest Liberal Institutionalism," *International Organization,* vol. 42, no. 3 (Summer 1988), pp. 485–507. Grieco writes: "Driven by interest in survival, states are acutely sensitive to any erosion of their relative capabilities, which are the ultimate basis for their security and independence in an anarchical, self-help international context. . . . States fear that their partners will achieve relatively greater gains; that, as a result, the partners will surge ahead of them in relative capabilities; and, finally, that their increasingly powerful partners in the present could become all the more formidable foes at some point in the future." For another argument on this topic, see Robert Powell, "Absolute and Relative Gains in International Relations Theory," *American Political Science Review,* vol. 85, no. 4 (December 1991), pp. 1303–20.

42. Waltz, *Theory of International Politics,* p. 105.

43. *Ibid.,* pp. 106–7; and John Mearsheimer, "Back to the Future," pp. 44–45.

44. Waltz, "The Emerging Structure of International Politics," p. 60.

45. Huntington, "The Clash of Civilizations," p. 25.

46. Huntington, "If Not Civilizations, What?" p. 192.

47. Mearsheimer, "Back to the Future," p. 47.

48. Jervis, "The Future of World Politics," p. 51.

49. *Ibid.*

50. The decreasing size of states can be measured by the number of states in the world. Since the 1930s, the number of states in the world has almost tripled. On how the size of states affects economic interdependence, see Rosecrance, *The Rise of the Trading State,* p. 176.

51. On the decreasing sacrosanctity of state sovereignty in the post–Cold War era, see Terry L. Deibel, "Internal Affairs and International Relations in the Post–Cold War World," *The Washington Quarterly,* vol. 16, no. 3 (Summer 1993), pp. 13–33. James M. Goldgeiger and Michael McFaul make the additional point that nations with state-centered or protectionist economies can face devastating exclusion from key institutions. Goldgeiger and McFaul, "A Tale of Two Worlds: Core and Periphery in the Post–Cold War Era," p. 476.

52. For a brief overview of these trends, see Walter B. Wriston, *The Twilight of Sovereignty: How the Information Revolution Is Transforming Our World* (New York: Scribner's, 1992).

53. Lester Brown, "The New World Order," in Worldwatch Institute, *State of the World, 1991* (New York: W. W. Norton and Company, 1991), pp. 3, 19.

54. James Gustave Speth, "A Post-Rio Compact," *Foreign Policy*, no. 88 (Fall 1992), pp. 145–51.

55. K. J. Holsti, "International Theory and War in the Third World," in Brian Job, ed., *The Insecurity Dilemma: National Security of Third World States* (Boulder, Colo.: Lynne Rienner Publishers, Inc., 1992), p. 37.

56. For an analysis of war's permanence from a social theory perspective, see Robin Fox, "Fatal Attraction: War and Human Nature," *The National Interest,* no. 30 (Winter 1992/93), pp. 11–20.

57. John Mueller, *Retreat from Doomsday: The Obsolescence of Major War* (New York: Basic Books, 1988).

58. Peter Liberman, "The Spoils of Conquest," *International Security*, vol. 18, no. 2 (Fall 1993), pp. 139–42.

59. *Ibid.*, pp. 125–53.

60. *Ibid.*, pp. 139–40.

61. For a succinct statement of the argument about the declining profitability of war, see Carl Kaysen, "Is War Obsolete?" *International Security*, vol. 14, no. 4 (Spring 1990), pp. 42–64. See also: Rosecrance, *The Rise of the Trading State,* pp. 31–38.

62. On the ever rising costs of weaponry, see Rosecrance, *The Rise of the Trading State,* p. 33.

63. Aaron Friedberg, "The Changing Relationship Between Economics and National Security," *Political Science Quarterly*, vol. 106, no. 2 (Summer 1991), p. 271.

64. Richard Rosecrance, *The Rise of the Trading State*, pp. 36–37.

65. Mueller, *Retreat from Doomsday,* pp. 240–44.

66. Rosecrance and other liberals acknowledge that ideological factors can override the calculus of prosperity. Rosecrance, *The Rise of the Trading State,* p. 38.

67. A revived Russian hegemonic effort is considered more likely by U.S. planners than any other new great power threat, as discussed in previous chapters. But as Fukuyama cautions, an enduring Russian imperial instinct should by no means be taken for granted: "There are many precedents for countries with very long histories of imperialism giving up their empires. . . . And all them did so in the twentieth century, which places the burden of proof on those who suggest that Russia will prove the exception to the general modern pattern of imperial divestment." Francis Fukuyama, "The Beginning of Foreign Policy," *The New Republic,* 17 and 24 August 1992, p. 25.

68. Rosecrance, *The Rise of the Trading State,* p. 59.

69. Keohane, *After Hegemony*, pp. 50, 183.

70. Flora Lewis, "The 'G-7½' Directorate," *Foreign Policy,* no. 85 (Winter 1991/92), pp. 25–40.

71. For a succinct history of the G-7 and an analysis of some of the challenges it faces in the future, see W. R. Smyser, "Goodbye, G-7," *The Washington Quarterly*, vol. 16, no. 1 (Winter 1993), pp. 15–28.

72. For an argument along these lines, see Richard Rosecrance, "A New Concert of Power," *Foreign Affairs*, vol. 71, no. 2 (Spring 1992), pp. 64–82.

73. For the classic statement of this dynamic, see Robert Jervis, "Cooperation

Under the Security Dilemma," *World Politics*, vol. 30, no. 2 (January 1978), pp. 167–214.

74. The literature advocating new efforts at collective security has expanded rapidly in recent years. For a sampling, see Charles A. Kupchan and Clifford A. Kupchan, "Concerts, Collective Security, and the Future of Europe," *International Security*, vol. 16, no. 1 (Summer 1991), pp. 114–61; Gregory Flynn and David J. Scheffer, "Limited Collective Security," *Foreign Policy*, no. 80 (Fall 1990), pp. 77–101; Andrew Bennett and Joseph Lepgold, "Reinventing Collective Security After the Cold War and Gulf Conflict," *Political Science Quarterly*, vol. 108, no. 2 (Summer 1993), pp. 213–37; Edward C. Luck and Toby Trister Gati, "Whose Collective Security?" *The Washington Quarterly*, vol. 15, no. (Spring 1992), pp. 43–56; John Mackinlay, "Second Generation Multinational Options," *The Washington Quarterly*, vol. 15, no. 2 (Summer 1992), pp. 113–31; Thomas G. Weiss, "New Challenges for U.N. Military Operations: Implementing an Agenda for Peace," *The Washington Quarterly*, vol. 16, no. 1 (Winter 1993), pp. 51–66.

75. Kupchan and Kupchan, "Concerts, Collective Security, and the Future of Europe," p. 126.

76. Grieco, "Anarchy and the Limits of Cooperation," p. 499.

77. For skeptical looks at collective security in Europe after the Cold War, see Richard Betts, "Systems for Peace or Causes of War? Collective Security, Arms Control, and the New Europe," *International Security*, vol. 17, no. 1 (Summer 1992), pp. 5–43; Charles L. Glaser, "Why NATO is Still Best," *International Security*, vol. 18, no. 1 (Summer 1993), pp. 26–33; Eugene V. Rostow, "Should U.N. Charter Article 43 Be Raised from the Dead?" *Global Affairs*, vol. 8, no. 1 (Winter 1993), pp. 109–24.

78. Kupchan and Kupchan, "Concerts, Collective Security, and the Future of Europe," p. 124.

79. *Ibid.*, p. 144.

80. Holsti, "International Theory and War in the Third World," p. 43.

81. The concept of weak state used here differs from what is used to describe states that are small in size and lacking in power resources. For a comprehensive discussion of these kinds of weak states, see Michael I. Handel, *Weak States in the International System* (London: Frank Cass, 1990).

82. *Ibid.*, p. 55.

83. Brian L. Job, "The Insecurity Dilemma: National, Regime, and State Security in the Third World," in Job, *The Insecurity Dilemma*, p. 17. For one of the best overviews of ethnic conflict, see Donald L. Horowitz, *Ethnic Groups in Conflict* (Berkeley, Calif.: University of California Press, 1985).

84. For an interesting discussion of why survival-minded Third World leaders may purposely take measures that result in a weak state apparatus and continued societal fragmentation, see John S. Migdal, "Strong States, Weak States: Power and Accommodation," in Myron Weiner and Samuel P. Huntington, eds., *Understanding Political Development* (Boston: Little, Brown and Company, 1987), pp. 391–436.

85. Stephen R. David, *Choosing Sides: Alignment and Realignment in the Third World* (Baltimore: Johns Hopkins University Press, 1991).

86. Holsti, "International Theory and War in the Third World," pp. 45–46.

87. Stephen R. David, "Why the Third World Still Matters," *International Security*, vol. 17, no. 3 (Winter 1992/93), pp. 134–44.

88. Moises Naim, "Latin America: Post-Adjustment Blues," *Foreign Policy,* no. 92 (Fall 1993), p. 134; Samuel P. Huntington, *The Third Wave: Democratization in the Late Twentieth Century* (Norman, Okla.: University of Oklahoma Press, 1991), p. 25.

89. Carol Lancaster, "Democracy in Africa," *Foreign Policy,* no. 85 (Winter 1991/92), p. 148.

90. Huntington, *The Third Wave,* pp. 312–15. For a classic examination of the conditions that promote democracy, see Robert Dahl, *Polyarchy: Participation and Opposition* (New Haven: Yale University Press, 1971).

91. Robert Rothstein has cautioned against extending the peacefulness-of-democracy thesis to Third World states, noting that the weakness of many of these democracies makes them function differently from more stable democracies in the developed world. Robert L. Rothstein, "Democracy, Conflict, and Development in the Third World," *The Washington Quarterly*, vol. 14, no. 2 (Spring 1991), pp. 43–63. However, it is important to reiterate that even modest steps toward a more participatory political system that do not result in full-scale, stable democracy can have the effect of promoting peacefulness toward other participatory polities. Ember, Ember, and Russett, "Peace Between Participatory Polities," pp. 573–99.

92. Huntington, *The Third Wave.* Huntington counts 59 states in the world as democratic in 1990, representing 45 percent of states in the world, as opposed to 36 democracies in 1962, or 32 percent of states in the world (p. 26). He cautions that "formidable obstacles to the expansion of democracy exist in many societies. The third wave, the 'global democratic revolution' of the late twentieth century, will not last forever. It may be followed by a new surge of authoritarianism constituting a third reverse wave. That, however, would not preclude a fourth wave of democratization development some time in the twenty-first century" (p. 315).

93. Mark J. Gasiorowski, "The Structure of Third World Interdependence," *International Organization*, vol. 39, no. 2 (Spring 1985), pp. 331–42.

94. Stephen Krasner, *Structural Conflict: The Third World Against Global Liberalism* (Berkeley, Calif.: University of California Press, 1985).

95. Holsti, "International Theory and War in the Third World," p. 56.

96. Keith Krause, "Arms Imports, Arms Production, and the Quest for Security in the Third World," in Job, *The Insecurity Dilemma,* pp. 121–42. See also Michael T. Klare, "Wars in the 1990s: Growing Firepower in the Third World," *The Bulletin of Atomic Scientists* (May 1990), pp. 9–14.

97. For an overview of the problem, see Steven Fetter, "Ballistic Missiles and Weapons of Mass Destruction: What Is the Threat? What Should Be Done?" *International Security*, vol. 16, no. 1 (Summer 1991), pp. 5–42.

98. For an argument that the impact of proliferation on stability is "ambiguous" and "generally a function of political context," see Brad Roberts, "From Nonproliferation to Antiproliferation," *International Security*, vol. 18, no. 1 (Summer 1993), pp. 157–60. For an argument that the acquisition of nuclear weapons leads to cautious security policy, and nuclear proliferation in the Third World states

might actually lead to less war, see Kenneth Waltz, *The Spread of Nuclear Weapons: More May Be Better, Adelphi Paper No. 171* (London: International Institute of Strategic Studies, 1981).

99. David, "Why the Third World Still Matters," p. 152.

100. For a discussion of some these risks and costs, see Roberts, "From Non-proliferation to Antiproliferation," pp. 150–51.

101. For a persuasive argument about the weakness of regional organizations such as the Organization of African Unity and the Organization of American states, see S. Neil McFarlane and Thomas G. Weiss, "Regional Organizations and Regional Security," *Security Studies*, vol. 2, no. 1 (Autumn 1992), pp. 6–37. The authors argue that the institutional capacities of regional organizations are weak and, more important, that the "so-called comparative superiority of organizations in the actual region of conflict—familiarity with the issues, insulation from outside powers, need to deal with acute crises—are more than offset by such practical disadvantages as partisanship, local rivalries, and lack of resources"(p. 11).

102. For an interesting analysis of how Third World states have reacted to the Gulf War, and the heightened threat of U.S. intervention under the aegis of the U.N., see Patrick J. Garrity, "Implications of the Perian Gulf War for Regional Powers," *The Washington Quarterly*, vol. 16, no. 3 (Summer 1993), pp. 153–70.

103. For a succinct overview of the options for increasing the U.N.'s power, see John Mackinlay and Jarat Chopra, "Second Generation Multinational Operations," *The Washington Quarterly*, vol. 15, no. 3 (Summer 1992), pp. 113–31.

104. For an explanation and critique of the preventive diplomacy suggestions contained in an Agenda for Peace, see Thomas G. Weiss, "New Challenges for U.N. Military Operations: Implementing an Agenda for Peace," *The Washington Quarterly*, vol. 16, no. 1 (Winter 1993), pp. 58–59.

105. Johansen, Robert, "Lessons for Collective Security," *World Policy Journal*, vol. 8, no. 3 (Summer 1991), pp. 561–73.

106. For a good overview of how U.N. peacemaking could work, see Bruce Russett, "The U.N. in a New World Order," *Foreign Affairs*, vol. 70, no. 2 (Spring 1992), pp. 64–83. For more on the U.N. after the Cold War, see Erskine B. Childers, "The Future of the United Nations: The Challenges of the 1990s," *Bulletin of Peace Proposals*, vol. 21, no. 2 (1990), pp. 143–52; and Ted Daley, "Can the U.N. Stretch to Fit Its Future?" *The Bulletin of Atomic Scientists*, vol. 48, no. 3 (Spring 1992), pp. 38–43.

107. *The New York Times,* 20 June 1992.

108. U.S. Congress, 102nd Cong., 2d sess., Senate Foreign Relations Committee, Hearings: *Arming the United Nations Security Council—The Collective Security Participation Resolution, S.J. 325* (Washington, D.C.: GPO, 1992), p. 13. Woolsey testified as chairman of a panel sponsored by the United Nations Association.

7: RECONSIDERING AMERICAN PRIMACY

1. Richard H. Ullman, *Securing Europe* (Princeton, N.J.: Princeton University Press, 1991), chapter two.

2. This is a key point, since realists suggest that concerns about relative gains serve as an ultimate check on cooperation among states. Robert Keohane emphasizes the contribution of institutions when he notes that: "Insofar as they reassure states about their security, institutions allow governments to emphasize absolute rather than relative gains and therefore maintain the conditions for their own existence." Robert O. Keohane, "The Diplomacy of Structural Change: Multilateral Institutions and State Strategies," in Helga Haftendorn and Christian Tuschhoff, eds., *America and Europe in an Era of Change* (Boulder, Colo.: Westview Press 1993), p. 53.

3. U.S. Congress, 102nd Cong., 1st sess., Senate Foreign Relations Committee, Hearings: *Consolidating Free-Market Democracy in the Former Soviet Union* (Washington, D.C.: GPO, 1992), p. 131.

4. Those troubles included a rejection of the Maastricht Treaty in 1992 by Denmark and near rejection by the French, as well as major monetary instability in 1993. Failure to stem fighting in the former Yugoslavia was another major blow to the EC's credibility. For an analysis that suggests that European integration will continue to crawl forward amid various setbacks and backlashes, see Stanley Hoffmann, "Goodbye to a United Europe?" *New York Review of Books,* 27 May 1993, pp. 27–31. For a more pessimistic but inconclusive analysis that highlights the negative consequences of not resolving the Yugoslavia situation, see Michael J. Brenner, "EC: Confidence Lost," *Foreign Policy*, no. 91 (Summer 1993), pp. 24 –43. In the security arena, despite discussion of new collective security mechanisms (which will be discussed later), prospects for further institution building were clouded by a weakening of military integration among Western European nations in the late 1980s and early 1990s. See Jan Willem Honig, "The 'Renationalization' of Western European Defense," *Security Studies*, vol. 2, no. 1 (Autumn 1992), pp. 122–38.

5. For a good argument along these lines, see Jack Snyder, "Averting Anarchy in the New Europe," *International Security*, vol. 14, no. 4 (Spring 1990), pp. 5–41. Like Keohane, Snyder argues that institutions can successfully mitigate the negative effects of anarchy.

6. For an overview of the promise and problems associated with further integration of the EC, and also of the consequences this may have for dealing with transnational problems like global warming, see Paul Kennedy, *Preparing for the Twenty-first Century* (New York: Random House, 1993), pp. 255–89.

7. Richard Rosecrance, "Trading States in a New Concert of Europe," in Haftendorn and Tuschhoff, *America and Europe in an Era of Change,* p. 128.

8. Stephen Van Evera, "Primed for Peace: Europe After the Cold War," *International Security*, vol. 15, no. 3 (Winter 1990/91), p. 24.

9. For an account of the rapprochement between France and Germany during the 1950s and 1960s and role that such institutions as the European Coal and Steel Community played in that process, see Edwina S. Campbell, *Germany's Past and Europe's Future: The Challenges of West German Foreign Policy* (New York: Pergamon-Brassey's, 1989), pp. 73–94.

10. Honig, "The 'Renationalization' of Western European Defense," p. 135.

11. *The New York Times,* 2 July 1992.

12. Gottfried Linn, "New Tasks for the Bundeswehr," *German Comments,* no. 30 (April 1993), p. 5.

13. W. R. Smyser, "U.S.S.R.–Germany: A Link Restored," *Foreign Policy,* no. 84 (Fall 1991), p. 132.

14. Thomas Kielinger and Max Otte, "Germany: The Pressured Power," *Foreign Policy,* no. 91 (Summer 1993), p. 52; Aleksandr Kokeev, "Moscow and Bonn: From Confrontation to Partnership," in Vladimir Baranovsky and Hans-Joachim Spanger, eds., *In from the Cold: Germany, Russia, and the Future of Europe* (Boulder, Colo.: Westview Press, 1992), pp. 227–30.

15. Smyser suggests that U.S. policymakers are already thinking in these terms and he notes the long history of Western fears that Germany will turn East, forging a deadly pact with Russia. Smyser, "U.S.S.R.–Germany," pp. 136–37.

16. *The New York Times,* 20 June 1992.

17. German scholar Gebhard Schweigler observes: "There is little inclination in Germany to join the ranks of an international police force. German history, now internalized in German attitudes and politics as constraints on any forceful German role abroad, allegedly argues against it, though it may be increasingly difficult for Germans to convince others of the moral rectitude of such reticence in cases where forceful intervention could prevent much human suffering." Gebhard Schweigler, "Problems and Prospects for Partners in Leadership," in Steven Miller and Gebhard Schweigler, eds., *From Occupation to Cooperation: The United States and Germany in a Changing World Order* (New York: W. W. Norton and Company, 1992), p. 243.

18. Robert Gerald Livingston, "United Germany: Bigger and Better," *Foreign Policy,* no. 87 (Summer 1992), p. 172. For more discussion of the issue of Germany's constitution and the use of force, see Lother Ruehl, "Limits of Leadership: Germany," in Miller and Schweigler, *From Occupation to Cooperation,* pp. 89–113. Ruehl argues that Germany's constitution does not bar the use of force outside of the NATO area and would not have to be amended to allow for such operations. For another argument along these lines, see Hans-Joachim Falenski, "Peacekeeping Missions with the German Armed Forces," *German Comments,* no. 30 (April 1993), pp. 10–24. Falenski notes that the "overwhelming majority of German experts on constitutional law are of the opinion that the Basic Law does not limit the deployment of the Bundeswehr (Federal Armed Forces) to the defense of the country and to the fulfillment of alliance obligations arising from Article 5 of the NATO Treaty" (p. 10). He argues instead that this is a political self-restraint German leaders have imposed on themselves.

19. *The New York Times,* 21 April 1993.

20. Robert D. Blackwill, "Patterns of Partnership: The U.S.-German Security Relationship in the 1990s," in Miller and Schweigler, *From Occupation to Cooperation,* p. 144.

21. Christopher Layne argues that Germany has already begun to become more assertive in geopolitical affairs, in large measure as a response to American unipolarity. But his only evidence in this regard is insignificant: Germany's lead in securing EC recognition of Croatia and Slovenia; talk by German defense minister of acquiring large transport aircraft; German insistence that its diplomats speak only

German at international conferences; and Germany's quest for a seat on the U.N. Security Council. Layne fails to address the more important fact of Germany's declining defense budget or the inward turn that has been brought about by the need to focus on unification issues. Christopher Layne, "The Unipolar Illusion," *International Security*, vol. 17, no. 4 (Spring 1993), pp. 37–38.

22. Stanley Hoffmann, Letter to the Editors, *International Security*, vol. 15, no. 2 (Fall 1990), p. 192.

23. Richard Rosecrance, *The Rise of the Trading State: Commerce and Conquest in the Modern World* (New York: Basic Books, 1986).

24. Kenneth Waltz, "The Emerging Structure of International Politics," *International Security*, vol. 18, no. 2 (Fall 1993), p. 66; Layne, "The Unipolar Illusion," p. 37.

25. Michael Brenner emphasizes also the recognition by German leaders that their people could conceivably once again give in to the temptation of nationalism and that a "European Germany" is the best way to foreclose this possibility. Brenner, "EC: Confidence Lost," p. 35.

26. Christopher Bertram, "Visions of Leadership: Germany," in Miller and Schweigler, *From Occupation to Cooperation,* p. 57; Elizabeth Pond, "Germany in the New Europe," *Foreign Affairs*, vol. 70, no. 4 (Summer 1992), p. 115.

27. David G. Haglund and Olaf Mager, "Homeward Bound?" in David G. Haglund and Olaf Mager, eds., *Homeward Bound: Allied Forces in the New Germany* (Boulder, Colo.: Westview Press, 1992), pp. 274–85. The authors argue that while a consensus now exists in Germany favoring participation in NATO and the hosting of allied troops, this consensus could deteriorate over time as no new external threat emerges.

28. Bertram, "Visions of Leadership: Germany," p. 61.

29. Stephen D. Krasner, "Power Polarity, and the Challenge of Disintegration," in Haftendorn and Tuschhoff, *America and Europe in an Era of Change,* p. 38.

30. For figures on the higher side, $98 billion to $112 billion, see Livingston, "United Germany: Bigger and Better," pp. 160–61; on the lower side, $71 billion to $91 billion, see Thomas Kielinger and Max Otte, "Germany: The Pressured Power," *Foreign Policy,* no. 91 (Summer 1993), p. 46.

31. Kielinger and Otte, "Germany: The Pressured Power," p. 46.

32. On the potential for German isolationism, see Schweigler, "Problems and Prospects for Partners in Leadership," p. 245. For a broad argument highlighting Germany's weakness and its consequences on development in the former Communist bloc and other issues, see Kielinger and Otte, "Germany: The Pressured Power," pp. 44–62.

33. Pond, "Germany in the New Europe," p. 128; Karl Kaiser, "Patterns of Partnership," in Muller and Schweigler, *From Occupation to Cooperation,* p. 168. Kaiser notes, however, that polls have begun to show a decline in public support for U.S. troops.

34. Alexei G. Arbatov, "Russia's Foreign Policy Alternatives," *International Security*, vol. 18, no. 2 (Fall 1993), p. 7.

35. Vladislav Zubok, "Tyranny of the Weak: Russia's New Foreign Policy," *World Policy Journal*, vol. 9, no. 2 (Spring 1992), p. 213.

36. U.S. Congress, 103rd Cong., 1st sess., House Foreign Affairs Committee, Hearings: *The Future of U.S. Foreign Policy: Regional Issues (Part I)* (Washington, D.C.: GPO, 1993), pp. 457–61.

37. Vladimir Lukin provides a sample of how some Russian analysts view the emerging security environment. Lukin writes that threats to Russia have "actually multiplied to the point at which it should be recognized, frankly, that Russia increasingly faces a new encirclement. Although there are no hostile alliances around Russia, it faces serious or potentially serious problems with almost all of the large countries on its new periphery." Vladimir P. Lukin, "Our Security Predicament," *Foreign Policy*, no. 88 (Fall 1992), p. 61.

38. Fred C. Ikle, "Comrades in Arms: The Case for a Russian-American Defense Community," *The National Interest*, no. 26 (Winter 1991/92), p. 26.

39. *The New York Times*, 26 November 1993.

40. For a good overview of Russia's state of technological and economic development as it compares with other countries, see Kennedy, *Preparing for the Twenty-first Century*, pp. 228–49.

41. Stephen Walt, "Alliances: Balancing and Bandwagoning," in Robert J. Art and Robert Jervis, eds., *International Politics: Enduring Concepts and Contemporary Issues* (New York: HarperCollins, 1992), p. 74.

42. For a discussion of the kinds of conflicts that could arise on Russia's periphery, see Paul Goble, "Russia and Its Neighbors," *Foreign Policy*, no. 90 (Spring 1993), pp. 79–88; Arbatov, "Russia's Foreign Policy Alternatives," pp. 34–36.

43. Adrian A. Basora, "Central and Eastern Europe: Imperative for Active U.S. Engagement," *The Washington Quarterly*, vol. 16, no. 1 (Winter 1993), pp. 69–70; Ronald D. Asmus, Richard L. Kugler, and F. Stephen Larrabee, "Buiding a New NATO," *Foreign Affairs*, vol. 72, no. 4 (September/October 1993), p. 30.

44. Even Senator Joseph Biden, one of the leading congressional advocates of intervention, never suggested such a level of intervention. For his recommendations for handling the conflict, see U.S. Congress, 103rd Cong., 1st sess., Senate Foreign Relations Committee, Report: *To Stand Against Aggression: Milosevic, the Bosnian Republic, and the Conscience of the West* (Washington, D.C.: GPO, 1993). For an example of some of the military arguments against intervention, see U.S. Congress, 102nd Cong., 2d sess., Senate Armed Services Committee, Hearings: *Situation in Bosnia and Appropriate U.S. and Western Responses* (Washington, D.C.: GPO, 1992).

45. Secretary Christopher, "New Steps Toward Conflict Resolution in the Former Yugoslavia," *U.S. Department of State Dispatch*, vol. 4, no. 7 (February 15, 1993), p. 81.

46. Charles L. Glaser, "Why NATO Is Still Best: Future Security Arrangements for Europe," *International Security*, vol. 18, no. 1 (Summer 1993), pp. 12–13.

47. Stephen J. Flanagan, "NATO and Central and Eastern Europe: From Liaison to Security Partnership," *The Washington Quarterly*, vol. 15, no. 2 (Spring 1992), p. 143.

48. For an example of this rationale for keeping troops in Europe, see Johns Hopkins Foreign Policy Institute, "The Franco-German Corps and the Future of European Security: Implications for U.S. Policy," p. 2. This report was endorsed by

a large bipartisan group of foreign policy experts and is reprinted in U.S. Congress, 102nd Cong., 2d sess., Senate Armed Services Committee, Hearings: *Defense Planning Guidance and Security Issues* (Washington, D.C.: GPO, 1992).

49. See 1992 testimony by General John Galvin to U.S. Congress, 102nd Cong., 2d sess., House Appropriations Committee, Hearings: *Department of Defense Appropriations for 1993* (Washington, D.C.: GPO, 1992), pp. 515, 540–41. It should be stressed that this rationale does not appear to be central to U.S. reasoning for keeping troops in Europe. It was not even mentioned, for example, in a January 1992 statement of U.S. military strategy. See Department of Defense, *National Military Strategy of the United States* (Washington, D.C.: Department of Defense, 1992), pp. 20–22. For an independent view that U.S. troops should be kept in Europe for deployment to the Middle East, see David Abshire, "Strategic Challenge: Contingencies, Force Structures, Deterrence," *The Washington Quarterly*, vol. 15, no. 2 (Spring 1992), p. 36. Abshire writes that such forward deployed forces provide a more credible deterrent to would-be aggressors in the Middle East than forces in the United States. For an interesting exploration of U.S. influence in NATO, written from a European's perspective, see Dan Smith, *Pressure: How America Runs NATO* (London: Bloomsbury Publishing, 1989).

50. For example, neither of two recent studies on U.S. relations with its allies regarding Third World issues establish any link between the U.S. security guarantee in Europe and allied cooperation with Washington in the Third World. On the contrary, both studies document numerous instances where Washington failed to win backing for its Third World policies. See Elizabeth D. Sherwood, *Allies in Crisis: Meeting Global Challenges to Western Security* (New Haven: Yale University Press, 1990); Richard J. Payne, *The West European Allies, the Third World, and U.S. Foreign Policy* (Westport, Conn.: Greenwood Press, 1991).

51. Sherwood argues that during the first Gulf crisis Britain and France "continued to spurn Washington's requests for greater assistance until the threat to their own shipping had grown demonstrably." *Ibid.*, p. 180. Payne echoes this conclusion, emphasizing Europe's own massive interests in the Gulf rather than U.S. coercion. *Ibid.*, p. 129. For an analysis that takes issue with the interpretation of the 1990–1991 Gulf War as an example of how U.S. hegemony can still be used to compel allies to comply with U.S. policy goals, see Andrew Fenton Cooper, Richard A. Higgoot, and Kim Richard Nossal, "Bound to Follow? Leadership and Followership in the Gulf Conflict," *Political Science Quarterly*, vol. 106, no. 3 (1991), pp. 391–410.

52. Brian R. Durchin, "The 'Agonizing Reappraisal': Eisenhower, Dulles, and the European Defense Community," *Diplomatic History*, vol. 16, no. 2 (Spring 1992), pp. 201–21. Hints of troop withdrawals in the late 1960s and 1970s were somewhat more effective, but not so much so that this did not remain a major irritant in transatlantic relations right up until the Cold War's end. William C. Cromwell, *The United States and the European Pillar: The Strained Alliance* (New York: Macmillan, 1992), pp. 43–55, 82–83.

53. Lawrence Freedman and Efraim Karsh, *The Gulf Conflict, 1990–1991: Diplomacy and War in the New World Order* (Princeton, N.J.: Princeton University Press, 1993), p. 203.

54. House Appropriations Committee, *Department of Defense Appropriations for 1993*, p. 724; Norman Friedman, *Desert Victory: The War for Kuwait* (Annapolis, Md.: The Naval Institute Press, 1991), p. 101.

55. U.S. Congress, 102nd Cong., 2d sess., House Armed Services Committee, Hearings: *Regional Threats and Defense Options for the 1990s* (Washington, D.C.: GPO, 1993), p. 13.

56. Richard B. Elrod, "The Concert of Europe: A Fresh Look at an International System," in Robert O. Matthews et al., eds., *International Conflict and Conflict Management* (Scarborough, Ontario: Prentice-Hall of Canada, Inc.), p. 413.

57. For more on the Concert, see Edward Vose Gullick, *Europe's Classic Balance of Power* (Ithaca, N.Y.: Cornell University Press, 1955).

58. Charles A. Kupchan and Clifford A. Kupchan, "Concerts, Collective Security, and the Future of Europe," *International Security*, vol. 16, no. 1 (Summer 1991), pp. 144–48; Richard H. Ullman, *Securing Europe*, p. 41; Richard Rosecrance, "A New Concert of Powers," *Foreign Affairs*, vol. 71, no. 2 (Spring 1992), pp. 64–82.

59. For a description of the liaison program, see Flanagan, "NATO and Central and Eastern Europe," pp. 144–45.

60. Glaser, "Why NATO Is Best," p. 48.

61. For discussion on the background and potential of the WEU, see Cromwell, *The United States and the European Pillar;* Ullman, *Securing Europe*, pp. 64–65.

62. For an argument by a German analyst that the WEU can more effectively achieve this goal than NATO, see Karl-Heinz Hornhues, "European Security Structure a Must," *German Comments*, no. 30 (April 1993), pp. 21–23.

63. Johnathan Dean and Randall Watson Forsberg, "CFE and Beyond: The Future of Conventional Arms Control," *International Security*, vol. 17, no. 1 (Summer 1992), pp. 76–109.

64. See in particular, Kupchan and Kupchan, "Concerts, Collective Security, and Europe," pp. 151–61.

65. On this dependency, see Mark M. Nelson, "Transatlantic Travails," *Foreign Policy*, no. 92 (Fall 1993), p. 79, and congressional testimony of William Hyland. House Foreign Affairs Committee, *The Future of U.S. Foreign Policy (Part I)*, p. 236.

66. The following analysis of Japan draws heavily on two articles: Thomas U. Berger, "From Sword to Chrysanthemum: Japan's Culture of Anti-Militarism," *International Security*, vol. 17, no. 4 (Spring 1993), pp. 119–50; Peter J. Katzenstein and Nobuo Okawara, "Japan's National Security: Structures, Norms and Policies," *International Security*, vol. 17, no. 4 (Spring 1993), pp. 84–118.

67. Hanns W. Maull, "Germany and Japan: New Civilian Powers," *Foreign Affairs*, vol. 69, no. 5 (1990). Maull's definition of a civilian power is useful to bear in mind. A civilian power accepts the necessity of cooperation with others in the pursuit of international objectives, concentrates on nonmilitary, primarily economic, means to secure national goals, with military power left as a residual instrument to safeguard other means of international interaction, and supports the development of supranational structures to address critical issues of international management (pp. 92–93).

68. Robert A. Scalapino, "The Foreign Policy of Japan," in Roy C. Marcridis, ed., *Foreign Policy in World Politics: States and Regions,* 7th ed. (Englewood Cliffs, N.J.: Prentice-Hall, 1989), pp. 314–17.

69. Berger, "From Sword to Chrysanthemum," pp. 119–50.

70. Katzenstein and Okawara, "Japan's National Security," p. 86.

71. For statements of this view by Prime Minister Noboru Takeshita in May 1989, see A. Hasnan Habib, "Japan's Role in the Asia-Pacific Region: An ASEAN Perception," in Harry H. Kendall and Clara Joewono, eds., *Japan, ASEAN, and the United States* (Berkeley, Calif.: Institute of East Asian Studies, 1991), p. 261. See also remarks by Japanese Foreign Minister Taro Nakayama, *Foreign Policy Bulletin* (September/October 1990), p. 44.

72. Habib, "Japan's Role in the Asia-Pacific Region," p. 254.

73. Chalmers Johnson, *Japan in Search of a "Normal" Role* (University of California: Institute on Global Conflict and Cooperation, July 1992), p. 24.

74. *The New York Times,* 3 December 1993.

75. David B. Bobrow, "Japan in the World: Opinion from Defeat to Success," *Journal of Conflict Resolution,* vol. 33, no. 4 (December 1989), p. 597.

76. I. M. Destler and Michael Nacht, "Beyond Mutual Recrimination: Building a Security Relationship in the 1990s," in Charles W. Kegley, Jr. and Eugene R. Wittkopf, eds., *The Future of American Foreign Policy* (New York: St. Martin's Press, 1992), p. 219.

77. Scalapino, "The Foreign Policy of Japan," p. 338.

78. Tatsumi Okabe, "A Proposal for Lasting Peace in East Asia," *Japan Review of International Affairs,* vol. 6, no. 3 (Fall 1992), p. 227; Katzenstein and Okawara, "Japan's National Security," p. 116.

79. Taifu Yu, "The Impact of the Cold War's End on Japan's Defense Policy," *Global Affairs,* vol. 8, no. 1 (Winter 1993), p. 89.

80. *Ibid.,* pp. 103–106

81. Berger, "From Sword to Chrysanthemum," p. 127.

82. Courtney Purrington, "Tokyo's Policy Responses During the Gulf War and the Impact of the 'Iraqi Shock' on Japan," *Pacific Affairs,* vol. 65, no. 2 (Summer 1992), pp. 161–78.

83. Rosecrance, *The Rise of the Trading State,* p. 16; Katzenstein and Okawara, "Japan's National Security Policy," p. 116.

84. Reihard Drifte, *Japan's Foreign Policy* (London: Routledge, 1990), p. 109.

85. *The New York Times,* 6 July 1993.

86. Drifte, *Japan's Foreign Policy,* p. 104.

87. Habid, "Japan's Role in the Asia-Pacific Region," p. 255.

88. Khatharaya Um, "Southeast Asia and Japan: Political, Economic, and Security Implications for the 1990s," in Kendall and Joewono, *Japan, ASEAN, and the United States,* p. 210.

89. Lee Kuan Yew, "Japan: From Economic Clout to Political Influence," *Global Affairs,* vol. 8, no. 1 (Winter 1993), p. 15; Ernst-Otto Czempiel, "U.S.-Japan Relations in a Post–Cold War Context," *Japan Review of International Relations,* vol. 6, no. 3 (Fall 1992), p. 317.

90. Hisahiko Okazaki, "Political Stability and Asia's New Security Picture," *Global Affairs*, vol. 8, no. 1 (Winter 1993), pp. 36–39.

91. David Arase, "U.S. and ASEAN Perceptions of Japan's Role in the Asian Pacific Region," in Kendall and Joewono, *Japan, ASEAN, and the United States,* p. 268.

92. For an example of this kind of thinking, see Destler and Nacht, "Beyond Mutual Recrimination," p. 215.

93. Gerald L. Curtis, "America's Evolving Relationship with Japan and Its Implications for ASEAN," in Kendall and Joewono, *Japan, ASEAN, and the United States,* p. 146. A more subtle version of this point is echoed by the Japanese scholar Takashi Inoguchi, who writes, "Any drastic restructuring of Japan's foreign relations away from the ties with the United States seems virtually impossible to the majority of Japanese." See Takashi Inoguchi, "Four Japanese Scenarios for the Future," in Jeffrey Frieden and David A. Lakes, eds., *International Political Economy* (New York: St. Martin's Press, 1987).

94. Czempiel, "U.S.-Japan Relations in a Post–Cold War Context," p. 310.

95. Howard Baker, Jr. and Ellen L. Frost, "Rescuing the U.S.-Japan Alliance," *Foreign Affairs*, vol. 71, no. 2 (Spring 1992), p. 99. U.S. officials have predicted that Japan will be paying 73 percent of all nonsalary costs of keeping U.S. forces in Japan by 1995. See U.S. Congress, 102nd Cong., 1st sess., House Foreign Affairs Committee, Hearings and Markup: *Assistance Legislation for Fiscal Years 1992–1993, Part 5* (Washington, D.C.: GPO, 1991), pp. 17–18.

96. Czempiel, "U.S.-Japan Relations in a Post–Cold War Context," p. 310.

97. For a discussion of U.S. basing options in East Asia, see Michael C. Desch, "Bases for the Future: U.S. Military Interests in the Post–Cold War Third World," *Security Studies*, vol. 2, no. 2 (Winter 1992), pp. 211 13.

98. House Foreign Affairs Committee, *The Future of U.S. Foreign Policy, Part 1,* p. 119.

99. It has been argued that in recent years the United States has effectively used its military protection of South Korea for economic leverage. According to one observer, the U.S. ambassador to Seoul under the Bush Administration, Donald Gregg, was considered to be one of the most powerful people in the country because of the U.S. strategic presence. Due to this position, Gregg is alleged to have had some success in the early 1990s in convincing Korean businesses to do more business with Americans. See March 1993 congressional testimony of Donald Zagoria, *Ibid.*, p. 121. This example, however, seems isolated when compared to broader patterns. For an argument that the United States has consistently subordinated economic objectives to security goals in its East Asian relationships and that with the end of the Cold War it can and should reverse that pattern, see Selig S. Harrison and Clyde V. Prestowitz, Jr., "Pacific Agenda: Defense or Economics?" *Foreign Policy,* no. 79 (Summer 1990), pp. 56–76. This theme also runs through Robert Kuttner's analysis of America's geo-economic dilemma after the Cold War. Kuttner argues that in its desire to not alienate key geopolitical allies, the United States has ignored the fact that many nations, especially in Asia, are not playing by the same international economic rules as the United States. Robert Kuttner, *The*

End of Laissez-Faire: National Purpose and the Global Economy After the Cold War (New York: Knopf, 1991).

100. Joseph S. Nye, Jr., "Coping with Japan," *Foreign Policy,* no. 89 (Winter 1992–93), p. 99.

101. According to a November 1990 poll, two thirds of Americans surveyed— including both ordinary citizens and people in leadership positions—opposed both Japan and Germany playing a larger military role in world affairs. At the same time, the Gulf conflict showed—as the long-standing burden-sharing issue had revealed in the Cold War—that Americans were annoyed by allied free-riding. Some 90 percent of respondents to the 1990 poll said both countries should pay more of the cost of sending U.S. forces to the Gulf. John E. Reilly, ed., *American Public Opinion and U.S. Foreign Policy, 1991* (Chicago: Chicago Council on Foreign Relations, 1991), p. 35.

102. Nye, "Coping with Japan," p. 113.

103. Richard Rosecrance, "A New Concert of Powers," p. 78. See also: Baker and Frost, "Rescuing the U.S.-Japan Alliance," p. 98.

104. Allen S. Whiting, "Foreign Policy of China," in Macridis, *Foreign Policy in World Politics,* p. 289.

105. Richard J. Ellings and Edward A. Olsen, "A New Pacific Profile," *Foreign Policy,* no. 89 (Winter 1992/93), p. 122; Gerald Segal, "The Coming Confrontation Between China and Japan?" *World Policy Journal,* vol. 10, no. 2 (Summer 1993), p. 28.

106. Nicholas D. Kristof, "The Rise of China," *Foreign Affairs,* vol. 72, no. 5 (November/December 1993), pp. 59–74. Gerald Segal ominously suggests that this might be particularly true in its policy toward Japan. Segal, "The Coming Confrontation Between China and Japan?" p. 28.

107. This point is stressed by Edward Luttwak in 1993 congressional testimony. House Foreign Affairs Committee, *The Future of U.S. Foreign Policy, Part 1,* p. 115.

108. Okabe, "A Proposal for Lasting Security in East Asia," p. 233.

109. Yew, "Japan: From Economic Clout to Political Influence," p. 22.

110. *Ibid.,* pp. 22–23.

111. Mark Kramer, "The Global Arms Trade After the Persian Gulf War," *Security Studies,* vol. 2, no. 2 (Winter 1992), p. 265; Tadashi Tajiri, "Korea in Japan's Arc of Crisis," *Global Affairs,* vol. 8, no. 3 (Summer 1993), p. 81.

112. International Institute for Strategic Studies, *The Military Balance, 1991–1992* (London: Brassey's, 1991), pp. 150–53; James B. Linder, "Chinese Military Strategy," *Global Affairs,* vol. 8, no. 1 (Winter 1993), pp. 67–68.

113. Kristof, "The Rise of China," p. 70.

114. Ton That Tien, "Southeast Asia's Post–Cold War Geopolitics," *Global Affairs,* vol. 8, no. 1 (Winter 1993), p. 41.

115. Zakaria Haji Ahmad, "Japan and China in Pacific Asia's Evolving Security Environment," *Global Affairs,* vol. 8, no. 1 (Winter 1993), p. 30.

116. Senate Armed Services Committee, *Defense Planning and Guidance and Security Issues,* p. 207.

117. House Armed Services Committee, *Regional Threats and Defense Options for the 1990s,* p. 321.

118. Figures are taken from 1992 testimony of General Robert Riscassi, commander of U.S. forces in Korea. House Committee on Appropriations, *Department of Defense Appropriations for 1993*, p. 679.

119. In addition to Gates's testimony on this point, see Tajiri, "Korea in Japan's Arc of Crisis," p. 83.

120. House Armed Services Committee, *Regional Threats and Defense Options for the 1990s*, p. 320.

121. Kim Dae Jung, "The Once and Future Korea," *Foreign Policy*, no. 86 (Spring 1992), p. 43.

122. See May 1992 congressional testimony by Brown. U.S. Congress, 102nd Cong., 2d sess., House Foreign Affairs Committee, Hearings: *U.S. Post Cold War Foreign Policy* (Washington, D.C.: GPO, 1993), p. 90.

123. For the initial U.S. vision of APEC, see Secretary Baker, "Address at the Asia-Pacific Economic Cooperation, Opening Session, Singapore," *Foreign Policy Bulletin* (September/October 1990), pp. 48–49.

124. Secretary Christopher, "The United States: A Full Partner in a New Pacific Community," *U.S. Department of State Dispatch*, vol. 4, no. 31 (August 2, 1993), p. 550.

125. Donald Crone, "The Politics of Emerging Pacific Cooperation," *Pacific Affairs*, vol. 65, no. 1 (Spring 1992), p. 68

126. Yoichi Funabashi, "The Asianization of Asia," *Foreign Affairs*, vol. 72, no. 5 (November/December 1993), pp. 75–85.

127. Douglas M. Johnston, "Anticipating Instability in the Asia-Pacific Region," *The Washington Quarterly*, vol. 15, no. 3 (Summer 1992), p. 106.

128. As Katzenstein and Okawara have written, "As long as Japan has not been the target of direct aggression, public opinion appears to support the domestic laws that make it unconstitutional for Japan to come to the assistance of an allied country that has been attacked by a hostile third country. . . . The domestic norms that circumscribe Japan's security policy make formal collective defense arrangements a highly implausible policy option for Japan's political leaders." Katzenstein and Okawara, "Japan's National Security," p. 111.

129. Secretary Christopher, "The United States: A Full Partner in a New Pacific Community," p. 550.

130. Robert A. Scalapino, "The United States and Asia," *Foreign Affairs*, vol. 71, no. 1 (Winter 1991/92), pp. 38–39. This idea is elaborated upon in congressional testimony by Donald Zagoria. House Foreign Affairs Committee, *The Future of U.S. Foreign Policy (Part 1)*, pp. 111–12.

131. Johnston, "Anticipating Instability in the Asia-Pacific Region," pp. 108–9.

132. Gerald Segal, "Managing New Arms Races in the Asia/Pacific," *The Washington Quarterly*, vol. 15, no. 3 (Summer 1992), p. 83.

133. Michael T. Klare, "The Next Great Arms Race," *Foreign Affairs*, vol. 72, no. 3 (Summer 1993), pp. 136–52. Johnston, "Anticipating Instability in the Asia-Pacific Region," p. 103.

134. Segal, "Managing New Arms Races in the Asia/Pacific," p. 88.

135. Les Aspin, *Force Structure Excerpts: Bottom-Up Review,* 1 September 1993, p. 5.

136. Statement of Paul Wolfowitz before the Senate Armed Services Committee, 11 April 1991, p. 8.

137. For a further discussion of the lessons that regional powers may have learned from the Gulf War, see Thomas G. Mahnken, "America's Next War," *The Washington Quarterly,* vol. 16, no. 3 (Summer 1993), pp. 171–84; Patrick J. Garrity, "Implications of the Persian Gulf War for Regional Powers," *Ibid.,* pp. 153–70.

138. Jim Wolfe, "Cuba and North Korea Top the Chairman of the Joint Chiefs' List of World Villains," *Army Times,* 15 April 1991, p. 4.

139. *The Military Balance 1991–1992,* pp. 189–90.

140. For a comprehensive account of the air war, see Richard P. Hallion, *Storm over Iraq: Air Power and the Gulf War* (Washington, D.C.: Smithsonian Institution Press, 1993).

141. Kevin Page, Greg Williams, and Charles Broll, Jr., *High Tech Weapons in Desert Storm: Hype or Reality?* (Washington, D.C.: The Project on Government Procurement, 1991), p. 4.

142. Colin Powell mentioned the F-111 success in his remarks to the National Strategy Forum, Chicago, 9 May 1991, p. 16. For a study of high-technology weapons in the Gulf War, see Kevin Page et al., *High-Tech Weapons in Desert Storm: Hype or Reality?*; and Carl Conetta and Charles King, *After Desert Storm,* p. 15–21.

143. Brad Roberts notes, for example, that both China and Libya are unable to operate portions of their submarine force. Roberts, "From Nonproliferation to Antiproliferation," p. 152.

144. In testimony to Congress, Gulf War commander General Norman Schwarzkopf cited the quality of personnel, the rigor of U.S. training, and the effectiveness of U.S. logistics as reasons for success that were more important than the sophistication of U.S. weapons. See U.S. Congress, 102nd Cong., 1st sess., House Committee on Appropriations, Hearings: Defense Subcommittee, *Department of Defense Appropriations for 1992, Part 2* (Washington, D.C.: GPO, 1991) pp. 260–61.

145. Significantly, Iraqi desertions had become substantial well before coalition air attacks on Iraqi forces had begun. James F. Dunnigan and Austin Bay, *From Shield to Storm: High-Tech Weapons, Military Strategy, and Coalition Warfare in the Persian Gulf* (New York: William Morrow and Company, 1992), p. 292.

146. Aspin, *Force Structure Excerpts: Bottom-Up Review,* p. 6.

147. Robert J. Lieber, "Oil and Power After the Gulf War," *International Security,* vol. 17, no. 1 (Summer 1992), p. 158.

148. *Ibid.,* p. 169.

149. International Institute for Strategic Studies, *The Military Balance 1991–1992,* p. 106.

150. *Ibid.*

151. Amin Saikal, "The United States and Persian Gulf Security," *World Policy Journal,* vol. 9, no. 3 (Summer 1992), p. 523.

152. Carl Conetta, Charles Knight, Rob Leavitt, Project on Defense Alterna-

tives, "Free Reign for the Sole Superpower? The Pentagon Confronts the New Era," unpublished manuscript, p. 5.

153. Aspin, Powell, *Bottom-Up Review news briefing,* p. 10.

154. Christopher Bowie et al., *New Calculus: Analyzing Airpower's Changing Role in Joint Theater Campaigns* (Santa Monica, Calif.: RAND, 1993). For a critical assessment of the RAND report, see Carl Conetta and Charles Knight, *Rand's New Calculus and the Impasse of U.S. Defense Restructuring* (Cambridge, Mass.: Commonwealth Institute, August 1993).

155. Carl Conetta and Charles King, *After Desert Storm: Rethinking U.S. Defense Requirements* (Cambridge, Mass.: Project on Defense Alternatives, Commonwealth Institute, 1990), p. 3.

8: AN IDEALIST FOREIGN POLICY

1. This idea was a running theme, for example, in a series of foreign policy speeches that Senator Joseph Biden gave on the Senate floor in 1992. See the published collection of the speeches: Joseph R. Biden, Jr., *On the Threshold of the New World: The Wilsonian Vision and American Foreign Policy in the 1990s and Beyond* (Washington, D.C.: 1992).

2. *The New York Times,* 2 October 1992.

3. The debate about whether the U.S. defense budget should be cut with the specific intention of transferring resources to the domestic sector crescendoed in the late 1980s and has been a key element in the argument about U.S. decline. Advocates of the decline thesis argued that the United States had to reduce its defense spending if it hoped to address domestic problems. Critics of this view persuasively argued that defense spending was not the main cause of U.S. economic decline and said that if the U.S. economy were well managed the United States could afford a defense burden of between 5 to 7 percent of the GNP. My own view is that while the latter point may be correct in principle, the reality is that the U.S. economy will not be well managed any time soon and hence the U.S. government will face direct tradeoffs every year between spending for defense and spending for domestic programs. See Paul Kennedy, *The Rise and Fall of the Great Powers: Economic Change and Military Conflict from 1500 to 2000* (New York: Random House, 1987); David P. Calleo, "Can the United States Afford the New World Order?" *SAIS Review,* vol. 12, no. 2 (Summer/Fall 1992), pp. 23–33; David Calleo, *Beyond Hegemony: The Future of the Western Alliance* (New York: Basic Books, 1987); Aaron Friedberg, "The Political Economy of American Strategy," *World Politics,* vol. 41, no. 3 (April 1989), pp. 381–406; Aaron L. Friedberg, "The Strategic Implications of Relative Economic Decline," *Political Science Quarterly,* vol. 104, no. 3 (Fall 1989), pp. 401–31; Edward N. Luttwak, "From Geopolitics to Geo-Economics: Logic of Conflict, Grammar of Commerce," *The National Interest,* no. 15 (Spring 1989), pp. 17–23; Joseph S. Nye, *Bound To Lead: The Changing Nature of American Power* (New York: Basic Books, 1990); Richard Rosecrance, *America's Economic Resurgence: A Bold New Strategy* (New York: Harper and Row, 1990).

4. C. Fred Bersten, "The Primacy of Economics," *Foreign Policy,* no. 87 (Summer 1992), p. 11.

5. Francis Fukuyama, "The Beginning of Foreign Policy," *New Republic,* 17 and 24 August 1992, p. 28.

6. President Clinton, "A Strategic Alliance with Russian Reform," *U.S. Department of State Dispatch*, vol. 4, no. 14 (April 5, 1993), p. 190.

7. U.S. officials have emphasized this point. See, for example, testimony of Ambassador Strobe Talbott before the House of Representatives, Foreign Operations Appropriations Subcommittee, 19 April 1993, p. 3.

8. Carroll J. Doherty, "House Forgoes Usual Reluctance on Foreign Aid to Pass Bill," *Congressional Quarterly,* 19 June 1993, pp. 1583–85.

9. For an analysis of Russia's financial needs, see 1993 congressional testimony by Jeffrey Sachs. U.S. Congress, 103rd Congr., 1st sess., Senate Armed Services Committee, Hearings: *Current Developments in the Former Sovet Union* (Washington, D.C.: GPO, 1993), pp. 79–89.

10. Bob Dole, "To Help New Democracies, Cut Aid to Israel, 4 Others," *The New York Times,* 16 January 1990.

11. Doherty, "House Forgoes Usual Reluctance on Foreign Aid to Pass Bill," pp. 1583–85. See also "FY 1994 International Affairs Budget Request," *U.S. Department of State Dispatch*, vol. 4, supplement no. 1 (April 1993), pp. 14–15.

12. For an official statement of the arguments for aid to Egypt and Israel, see the April 1993 congressional testimony of Assisant Secretary of State Edward P. Djerejian. U.S. Congress, 103rd Cong., 1st sess., House Committee on Foreign Affairs, Hearings: *Foreign Assistance Legislation for Fiscal Year 1994 (Part 2)* (Washington, D.C.: GPO, 1993), pp. 110–16.

13. Dick Kirschten, "Overhaul Overdue," *National Journal,* 15 May 1993, p. 1166.

14. *Ibid.*, p. 1584.

15. "FY 1994 International Affairs Budget Request," p. 13

16. Doherty, "House Forgoes Usual Reluctance on Foreign Aid to Pass Bill," p. 1585.

17. On the need for greater funding in each of these areas, see Jeffrey Sachs' February 1993 testimony. Senate Armed Services Committee, *Current Developments in the Former Soviet Union,* pp. 78–89.

18. Richard H. Ullman, "Redefining Security," in G. John Ikenberry, ed., *American Foreign Policy: Theoretical Essays* (Boston: Scott, Foresman and Company, 1989), p. 649.

19. For a balanced discussion of this issue, see Graham T. Allison, Jr. and Robert P. Beschel, Jr., "Can the United States Promote Democracy?" *Political Science Quarterly*, vol. 107, no. 1 (Spring 1992), pp. 81–98.

20. Samuel Huntington, *The Third Wave: Democratization in the Late Twentieth Century* (Norman, Okla.: University of Oklahoma Press, 1991), p. 26.

21. Address by Richard Haass to the Overseas Writers Club, 9 May 1991, "Beyond the Gulf War: The United States, the Middle East and the Gulf," p. 6.

22. For a good exposition of this argument, see Alan Tonelson, "What Is the National Interest?" *The Atlantic Monthly,* July 1991, pp. 35–52.

23. Interview with author.

24. Larry Diamond, "Promoting Democracy," *Foreign Policy,* no. 87 (Summer 1992), p. 43.

25. Kenneth R. Timmerman, *The Death Lobby: How the West Armed Iraq* (Boston: Houghton Mifflin, 1991).

26. For an application of the same line of argument to Hitler in the 1930s, see Stanley Kober, "Idealpolitik," *Foreign Policy,* no. 79 (Summer 1990), pp. 10–12.

27. Holly Burkhalter, "Moving Human Rights to Center Stage," *World Policy Journal,* vol. 9, no. 3 (Summer 1992), p. 421.

28. Robert McNamara coined the term absolute poverty while president of the World Bank. In his words it refers to "a condition of life so characterized by malnutrition, illiteracy, and disease as to be beneath any reasonable definition of human decency." See Robert S. McNamara, "Time Bomb or Myth? The Global Population Problem," in Charles W. Kegley, Jr., and Eugene R. Wittkopf, eds., *The Global Agenda: Issues and Perspectives,* 2d. ed. (New York: McGraw-Hill Publishing Company, 1988), p. 388. For statistics on the prevalence of absolute poverty, see Alan B. Durning, "Ending Poverty," in Worldwatch Institute, *State of the World, 1990* (New York: W. W. Norton and Company, 1990), pp. 136.

29. James Gustave Speth, "A Post-Rio Compact," *Foreign Policy,* no. 88 (Fall 1992), p. 148.

30. "FY 1994 International Affairs Budget," p. 12.

31. Statement of Secretary of Defense Les Aspin before the Senate Armed Services Committee in Connection with the Clinton Defense Plan, 1 April 1993, p. 23.

32. Francis Moore Lappe, Rachel Schurman, Kevin Danaher, and Joseph Collins, *Betraying the National Interest* (New York: Grove Press, 1987); Herman E. Daly and John B. Cobb, Jr., *For the Common Good: Redirecting the Economy Toward Community, the Environment and a Sustainable Future* (Boston: Beacon Press, 1989), pp. 289–90.

33. Patrick J. Buchanan, "America First—and Second, and Third," *The National Interest,* no. 19 (Spring 1990), pp. 77–82.

34. John Reilly, ed., *American Public Opinion and U.S. Foreign Policy, 1991* (Chicago: Chicago Council on Foreign Relations, 1991), p. 37.

35. On support for protecting the global environment, see *Ibid.* p., 15. On public support for curbing population growth, see Sharon Camp, "Population: The Critical Decade," *Foreign Policy,* no. 90 (Spring 1993), p. 142.

36. For a comprehensive program for reforming foreign aid after the Cold War, see John W. Sewell, "Foreign Aid for a New World Order," *The Washington Quarterly,* vol. 14, no. 3 (Summer 1991), p. 35. See also Speth, "A Post-Rio Compact," pp. 145–61.

37. For a discussion of NGOs and aid policy reforms that could channel more funds to them, see Alan B. Durning, "People Power and Development," *Foreign Policy,* no. 76 (Fall 1989), pp. 66–82.

38. In his April 1993 confirmation hearing, AID Administrator Brian Atwood stressed the need to channel more aid through participatory programs at the community level and nongovernmental organizations based both in recipient countries

and in the United States. "USAID Administrator Confirmation Hearing," *U.S. Department of State Dispatch*, vol. 4, no. 19 (May 10, 1993), p. 339. See also Secretary Christopher, "Foreign Assistance Priorities After the Cold War," U.S. Department of State Dispatch, vol. 4, no. 22 (May 22, 1993), p. 394. In a 1993 interview with the author, Tim Wirth, Under Secretary of State for Global Affairs, emphasized that foreign aid funds should be spent differently to better reach and empower poor people: "First, instead of building massive projects we ought to focus on smaller, grassroots operations. Second, we ought to increasingly work with nongovernmental organizations. Third, AID ought to take a lot more chances in terms of making small grants and taking a grassroots focus."

39. John W. Sewell, "The Metamorphosis of the Third World: U.S. Interests in the 1990s," in Charles W. Kegley, Jr., and Eugene R. Wittkopf, eds., *The Future of U.S. Foreign Policy* (New York: St. Martin's Press, 1992), p. 235.

40. Dick Kirschten, "Overhaul Overdue," *National Journal,* 15 May 1993, p. 1168.

41. Paul Kennedy, *Preparing for the Twenty-first Century* (New York: Random House, 1993); McNamara, "Time Bomb or Myth," pp. 382–93.

42. See, for example, the 1992 testimony of CIA Director Robert Gates. U.S. Congress, 102nd Cong., 2d sess., House Foreign Affairs Committee, Hearings: *The Future of U.S. Foreign Policy in the Post–Cold War Era* (Washington, D.C.: GPO, 1992), p. 212.

43. Testimony of Timothy E. Wirth before the Subcommittee on Foreign Operations, Committee on Appropriations, United States Senate, 11 June 1993, p. 23.

44. Statement by Timothy E. Wirth to the Second Preparatory Committee for the International Conference on Population and Development, 11 May 1993. Dick Kirschten, "About Face," *National Journal,* 3 July 1993, pp. 1692–95. The administration requested an additional $100 million for population in its first foreign aid budget. "FY 1994 International Affairs Budget Request," pp. 14–15.

45. Camp, "Population: The Critical Decade," p. 139.

46. Interview with author.

47. Lester Brown, "The New World Order," in Worldwatch Institute, *State of the World, 1991* (New York: W. W. Norton and Company, 1991), p. 3.

48. Kennedy, *Preparing for the Twenty-first Century,* p. 69.

49. *Ibid.,* 67. Lester R. Brown, "A New Era Unfolds," in Worldwatch Institute, *State of the World, 1993* (New York: W. W. Norton and Company, 1993), pp. 11–14; Brown and Young, "Feeding the World in the Nineties," pp. 59–78.

50. Camp, "Population: The Critical Decade," p. 129.

51. Kennedy, *Preparing for the Twenty-first Century,* p. 26.

52. "USAID Administrator Confirmation Hearing," pp. 337–40; U.S. Congress, 103rd Cong., 1st sess., House Foreign Affairs Committee, *Foreign Assistance Legislation for Fiscal Year 1994, Part 1* (Washington, D.C.: GPO, 1993), pp. 217–25.

53. Kennedy, *Preparing for the Twenty-first Century,* pp. 78–81, 222–23.

54. Brown and Young, "Feeding the World in the Nineties," p. 77.

55. For more on this topic, see Patrick M. O'Brien, "Agricultural Productivity and the Global Food Market," in Kegley and Wittkopf, *The Global Agenda,* pp. 394–408.

56. Speth, "A Post-Rio Compact," p. 151; Nicholas Lenssen, "Providing Energy in Developing Countries," in Worldwatch Institute, *State of the World, 1993,* pp. 101–19.

57. Speth, "A Post-Rio Compact," pp. 145–47.

58. *The New York Times,* 5 April 1992.

59. This argument is made in detail in Joseph S. Nye, Jr., *Bound to Lead: The Changing Nature of American Power* (New York: Basic Books, 1990).

60. Military sales agreements with Third World nations in 1991 were $24.7 billion, down from $41.1 billion in 1990. Mark Kramer, "The Global Arms Trade After the Cold War," *Security Studies*, vol. 2, no. 2 (Winter 1992), p. 263.

61. *Ibid.*

62. Michael T. Klare, "Fueling the Fire: How We Armed the Middle East," *The Bulletin of Atomic Scientists* (January/February 1991), pp. 19–26.

63. Stockholm International Peace Research Institute, *SIPRI Yearbook 1989* (Oxford and New York: Oxford University Press, 1989), pp. 226–27. Richard F. Grimmet, *Trends in Conventional Arms Transfers to the Third World by Major Suppliers, 1981–1988* (Washington, D.C.: Congressional Research Service, Library of Congress, 1989).

64. For a good overview of this subject, see Brad Roberts, "From Nonproliferation to Antiproliferation," *International Security*, vol. 18, no. 1 (Summer 1993), pp. 139–73.

65. John R. Harvey, "Regional Ballistic Missiles and Advanced Strike Aircraft: Comparing Military Effectiveness," *International Security*, vol. 17, no. 2 (Fall 1992), pp. 41–83.

66. William D. Hartung, "Why Sell Arms? Lessons from the Carter Years," *World Policy Journal*, vol. 10, no. 1 (Spring 1993), p. 59.

67. Stephanie G. Neuman, "Controlling the Arms Trade: Idealistic Dream or Realpolitik?" *The Washington Quarterly*, vol. 16, no. 3 (Summer 1993), pp. 56–61.

68. For an excellent in-depth look at the prospects for controlling arms transfers, see Michael T. Klare, "Gaining Control: Building a Comprehensive Arms Restraint System," *Arms Control Today* (June 1991), pp. 9–13.

69. Tom Pfeiffer, "After the War: Challenges to Middle Eastern Arms Control," *Arms Control Today* (March 1991), p. 21; James E. Goodby, "Transparency in the Middle East," *Arms Control Today* (May 1991), pp. 8–11; Carroll J. Doherty, "Baker Provides First Glimpse of Postwar Mideast Goals," *Congressional Quarterly*, 9 February 1991, pp. 380–81.

70. Michael T. Klare, "Business as Usual," *The Nation,* 3 February 1992, p. 120

71. Interview with author.

72. *The New York Times,* 24 September 1991.

73. For the definitive study of how NATO has handled "out-of-area" crises see Elizabeth D. Sherwood, *Allies in Crisis: Meeting Global Challenges to Western Security* (New Haven: Yale University Press, 1990).

74. Secretary Baker, "Challenges Facing the Atlantic Alliance," *U.S. Department Dispatch,* 24 December 1990, p. 353.

75. President Bush, "New World Order: Relations with Europe and the Soviet Union," *Foreign Policy Bulletin* (May/June 1991), p. 33.

76. The Working Group on Changing Roles and Shifting Burdens in the Atlantic Alliance, *The United States and NATO in an Undivided Europe* (Washington, D.C.: The Johns Hopkins Foreign Policy Institute, 1991), p. 6. For a study that explores in depth the different views that European nations and the United States have often taken on Third World issues, see Richard J. Payne, *The West European Allies, the Third World, and U.S. Foreign Policy* (Westport, Conn.: Greenwood Press, 1991).

77. Sherwood, *Allies in Crisis,* p. 1.

78. In a speech in September 1990, State Department official Robert Zoellick spoke hopefully about the future success of such an ad hoc system, saying that "NATO discussions leading to cooperative operations among the United States and other member states with the Western European Union (WEU) could supply a valuable mechanism for tackling regional security problems. We used this combination in the Persian Gulf in 1987 and are employing it with Iraq today." Beyond these generalities, however, neither Zoellick nor other analysts have outlined how this system can be be expected to perform reliably. See Robert Zoellick, "New Europe in a New Age: Insular, Itinerant, or International? Prospects for an Alliance of Values," *Current Policy* no. 1300, U.S. Department of State, p. 3.

79. David Scheffer, "Use of Force After the Cold War: Panama, Iraq, and the New World Order," in Council on Foreign Relations, *Right vs. Might: International Law and the Use of Force* (New York: Council on Foreign Relations Press, 1991), pp. 155–56.

80. Tad Daley, "Can the U.N. Stretch to Fit Its Future," *The Bulletin of Atomic Scientists* (April 1992), p. 38.

81. *Ibid,* p. 41. See also Edward C. Luck and Toby Trister Gati, "Whose Collective Security," *The Washington Quarterly,* vol. 15, no. 2 (Spring 1992), pp. 46–47.

82. *The New York Times,* 28 September 1992.

83. Daley, "Can the U.N. Stretch to Fit Its Future?" p. 41.

84. *Ibid.,* p. 42.

85. Interview with author.

86. The 1992 proposals made by a committee established by the United Nations Association and chaired by R. James Woolsey, along with the proposals of Richard Gardner, are discussed in: U.S. Congress 102nd Cong., 2d sess., Senate Foreign Relations Committee, Hearings: *Arming the United Nations Security Council—The Collective Security Participation Resolution, S.J. Res. 325* (Washington, D.C.: GPO, 1992).

87. *Ibid.,* p. 13.

88. Woolsey's committee suggested that such a force should be relatively homogenous, and recommended making use of British troops and Nepalese Gurkhas. *Ibid.,* p. 38.

89. Senator Bob Dole, for example, introduced legislation in Congress in Jan-

uary 1994 that would bar U.S. forces from any kind of standing U.N. army. Bob Dole, "Peacekeeping and Politics," *The New York Times,* 24 January 1994, p. A15. In the view of some legal experts, however, this view has a poor constitutional foundation. As Columbia law professor Louis Henkin has argued: "Article 43 is mandatory. It creates a legal obligation for all member states to make available to the Security Council forces, et cetera, and to do so in accordance with a special agreement or agreements. Article 43 creates a legal obligation to negotiate such agreements on the initiative of the Security Council as soon as possible." *Ibid.,* p. 21.

90. Robert J. Art, "A Defensible Defense: America's Grand Strategy After the Cold War," *International Security,* vol. 15, no. 4 (Spring 1991), p. 45.

91. Richard Gardner, "Practical Internationalism," in Allison and Treverton, *Rethinking America's Security,* p. 275.

92. Senate Foreign Relations Committee, *Arming the United Nations Security Council,* p. 39.

93. *The New York Times,* 27 January 1991.

94. Madeline K. Albright, "A Strong United Nations Serves U.S. Security Interests," *U.S. Department of State Dispatch,* vol. 4, no. 26 (June 28, 1993), p. 462.

95. *The New York Times,* 6 September 1992. For more details on the U.N. financing system, see U.S. Congress, 103rd Cong., 1st sess., Senate Foreign Relations Committee, Report: *Reform of the United Nations Peacekeeping Operations: A Mandate for Change* (Washington, D.C.: GPO, August 1993), pp. 46–50.

96. Biden, *On the Threshold of the New World Order,* p. 66.

97. Zbigniew Brzezinski put forth this concept in 1983. See U.S. Congress, 98th Cong., 1st sess., Senate Armed Services Committee, Hearings: *Organization Structure, and Decision-making Procedures of the Department of Defense* (Washington, D.C.: GPO, 1984), p. 492.

CONCLUSION

1. Kenneth Waltz, *Theory of International Politics* (Reading, Mass.: Addison-Wesley, 1979), p. 102.

INDEX